Biological Economies

Recent agri-food studies, including commodity systems, the political economy of agriculture, regional development, and wider examinations of the rural dimension in economic geography and rural sociology have been confronted by three challenges. These can be summarized as: 'more than human' approaches to economic life; a 'post-structural political economy' of food and agriculture; and calls for more 'enactive', performative research approaches.

This volume describes the genealogy of such approaches, drawing on the reflective insights of more than five years of international engagement and research. It demonstrates the kinds of new work being generated under these approaches and provides a means for exploring how they should be all understood as part of the same broader need to review theory and methods in the study of food, agriculture, rural development, and economic geography. This radical collective approach is elaborated as the biological economies approach. The authors break out from traditional categories of analysis, reconceptualising materialities, and reframing economic assemblages as biological economies, based on the notion of all research being enactive or performative.

Richard Le Heron is Professor of Geography, School of Environment, The University of Auckland, New Zealand.

Hugh Campbell is Chair of Sociology, Department of Sociology, Gender and Social Work, University of Otago, New Zealand.

Nick Lewis is Associate Professor in Geography, School of Environment, The University of Auckland, New Zealand.

Michael Carolan is Chair of Sociology, Department of Sociology, Colorado State University, USA.

Routledge Studies in Food, Society and the Environment

Street Food
Culture, economy, health and governance
Edited by Ryzia de Cassia Vieira Cardoso, Michèle Companion and Stefano Roberto Marras

Savoring Alternative Food
School gardens, healthy eating and visceral difference
Jessica Hayes-Conroy

Human Rights and the Food Sovereignty Movement
Reclaiming control
Priscilla Claeys

Food Utopias
Reimagining citizenship, ethics and community
Edited by Paul Stock, Michael Carolan and Christopher Rosin

Food Sovereignty in International Context
Discourse, politics and practice of place
Edited by Amy Trauger

Global Food Security Governance
Civil society engagement in the reformed Committee on World Food Security
Jessica Duncan

Civic Engagement in Food System Governance
A comparative perspective of American and British local food movements
Alan R. Hunt

Biological Economies
Experimentation and the politics of agri-food frontiers
Edited by Richard Le Heron, Hugh Campbell, Nick Lewis and Michael Carolan

For further details please visit the series page on the Routledge website:
http://www.routledge.com/books/series/RSFSE/

'In *Biological Economies*, Le Heron and colleagues offer up a path-breaking analysis at the nexus of key agri-food studies issues and propel the reader through existing contradictions and tensions to help us imagine how agri-food systems can be transformed. In defining key international strands, this book enables the reader to both understand the state of the art in food studies and to reconstitute the pieces we have on hand into a more productive whole.' – *Alison Blay-Palmer, Centre for International Governance Innovation Chair in Sustainable Food Systems, Waterloo, Canada.*

'If we are what we eat, then who do we become when we choose to eat differently? This brilliant book offers inspiring answers to this important question. It ranges far beyond the familiar criticisms of processed food, fast food and chemical-intensive farming. It presents arguments for, and examples of, new and better ways to embed food in our material and moral lives.' – *Noel Castree, University Manchester, UK, and University of Wollongong, Australia.*

'An important and timely intervention in agri-food studies, *Biological Economies* has "mind-melting" ambitions – disrupting orthodox categories and fostering a new research agenda. Radically relational, the book's transformative potential is illustrated via a series of provocative case studies.' – *Peter Jackson, University of Sheffield, UK.*

'If you like your agrifoodstudies savvy, layered, decentred, well-storied and lively, this is your book! The cases are varied, the curiosity and dedication run all the way through.' – *Annemarie Mol, University of Amsterdam, the Netherlands.*

'*Biological Economies* is a fascinating collection that breaks new ground in agri-food research. Conceptually and methodologically innovative and supported by rich and diverse case studies, this is a must-read for anyone interested in the political-economies of food in the twenty-first century.' – *Michael Woods, Aberystwyth University, UK.*

Biological Economies
Experimentation and the politics of agri-food frontiers

Edited by Richard Le Heron, Hugh Campbell, Nick Lewis and Michael Carolan

First published 2016 by Routledge

2 Park Square, Milton Park, Abingdon, Oxfordshire OX14 4RN
711 Third Avenue, New York, NY 10017

Routledge is an imprint of the Taylor & Francis Group, an informa business

First issued in paperback 2018

© 2016 Richard Le Heron, Hugh Campbell, Nick Lewis and Michael Carolan, selection and editorial material; individual chapters, the contributors

The right of the editors to be identified as the authors of the editorial material, and of the authors for their individual chapters, has been asserted in accordance with sections 77 and 78 of the Copyright, Designs and Patents Act 1988.

All rights reserved. No part of this book may be reprinted or reproduced or utilised in any form or by any electronic, mechanical, or other means, now known or hereafter invented, including photocopying and recording, or in any information storage or retrieval system, without permission in writing from the publishers.

Trademark notice: Product or corporate names may be trademarks or registered trademarks, and are used only for identification and explanation without intent to infringe.

British Library Cataloguing-in-Publication Data
A catalogue record for this book is available from the British Library

Library of Congress Cataloging in Publication Data
Names: Le Heron, Richard B., editor.
Title: Biological economies : experimentation and the politics of agri-food frontiers / edited by Richard Le Heron, Hugh Campbell, Nick Lewis and Michael Carolan.
Description: London ; New York : Routledge, 2016. | Series: Routledge studies in food, society and environment | Includes bibliographical references and index.
Identifiers: LCCN 2015030225 | ISBN 9781138843011 (hbk) | ISBN 9781315731124 (ebk)
Subjects: LCSH: Agriculture—Economic aspects. | Agriculture—Social aspects. | Agriculture and state. | Agricultural industries. | Rural development.
Classification: LCC HD1415 .B525 2016 | DDC 338.1/9—dc23
LC record available at http://lccn.loc.gov/2015030225

ISBN: 978-1-138-84301-1 (hbk)
ISBN: 978-1-138-58893-6 (pbk)

Typeset in Bembo
by Swales & Willis Ltd, Exeter, Devon, UK

Contents

List of contributors x

1 Assembling generative approaches in agri-food research 1
NICK LEWIS, RICHARD LE HERON, MICHAEL CAROLAN,
HUGH CAMPBELL AND TERRY MARSDEN

PART 1
Re-making knowledges of agri-food 21

2 Biological economies and processes of consumption:
practices, qualities and the vital materialism of food 23
DAVID EVANS

3 The borderlands of animal disease: knowing and
governing animal disease in biological economies 37
GARETH ENTICOTT

4 Re-shaping 'soft gold': fungal agency and the bioeconomy
in the caterpillar fungus market assemblage 51
JANKA LINKE

5 Enacting Swiss cheese: about the multiple ontologies
of local food 67
JÉRÉMIE FORNEY

6 Understanding agri-food systems as assemblages:
worlds of rice in Indonesia 82
ANGGA DWIARTAMA, CHRISTOPHER ROSIN AND
HUGH CAMPBELL

7 Materialising taste: fatty lambs to eating quality – taste projects in New Zealand's red meat industry 95
MATTHEW HENRY AND MICHAEL ROCHE

8 Enactive encounters with the Langstroth hive: post-human framing of the work of bees in the Bay of Plenty 109
ROSEANNA M. SPIERS AND NICK LEWIS

9 Ever-redder apples: how aesthetics shape the biology of markets 127
KATHARINE LEGUN

10 Value and values in the making of merino 141
HARVEY C. PERKINS AND ERIC PAWSON

11 Eating the unthinkable: the case of ENTO, eating insects and bioeconomic experimentation 157
PAUL V. STOCK, CATHERINE PHILLIPS, HUGH CAMPBELL AND ANNE MURCOTT

12 Enacting BAdairying as a system of farm practices in New Zealand: towards an emergent politics of new soil resourcefulness? 170
RICHARD LE HERON, GEOFF SMITH, ERENA LE HERON AND MICHAEL ROCHE

PART 2
Enacting new politics of knowledge 187

13 In your face: why food is politics and why we are finally starting to admit it 189
MICHAEL M. BELL

14 Geographers at work in disruptive human–biophysical projects: methodology as ontology in reconstituting nature–society knowledge 196
ERENA LE HERON, NICK LEWIS AND RICHARD LE HERON

15 Food utopias: performing emergent scholarship and agri-food futures 212
PAUL V. STOCK, CHRISTOPHER ROSIN AND MICHAEL CAROLAN

16 The very public nature of agri-food scholarship, and its problems and possibilities 225
MICHAEL CAROLAN

17 Eating bioeconomies 240
MICHAEL K. GOODMAN

18 Conclusion: biological economies as an academic and political project 256
HUGH CAMPBELL, RICHARD LE HERON, NICK LEWIS AND MICHAEL CAROLAN

Index 271

Contributors

Professor Michael M. Bell, Department of Community and Environmental Sociology, and Center for Integrated Agricultural Systems, University of Wisconsin-Madison, 1535 Observatory Drive, Madison, WI 53706, USA. michaelbell@wisc.edu

Professor Hugh Campbell, Department of Sociology, Gender and Social Work, University of Otago, PO Box 56, Dunedin, New Zealand. hugh.campbell@otago.ac.nz

Professor Michael Carolan, Department of Sociology, Colorado State University, Fort Collins, CO 80523-1784, USA. michael.carolan@colostate.edu

Dr Angga Dwiartama, School of Life Sciences and Technology, Institut Teknologi Bandung (ITB), Jl. Ganesha No.10, Bandung 40132, Indonesia. dwiartama@sith.itb.ac.id

Dr Gareth Enticott, School of Planning and Geography, Cardiff University, Cardiff, CF10 3WA, UK. enticottg@cardiff.ac.uk

Dr David Evans, School of Social Sciences, University of Manchester, Manchester M13 9PL, UK. david.evans-2@manchester.ac.uk

Assistant Professor Jérémie Forney, Anthropology Institute, University of Neuchâtel, Pierre-à-Mazel 7, CH 2000 Neuchâtel, Switzerland. jeremie.forney@unine.ch

Professor Michael K. Goodman, Geography and Environmental Science, University of Reading, Whiteknights, PO Box 227, Reading, RG6 6AB, UK. m.k.goodman@reading.ac.uk

Dr Matthew Henry, School of People, Environment and Planning, Massey University, Private Bag 11 222, Palmerston North 444, New Zealand. m.g.henry@massey.ac.nz

Dr Katharine Legun, Department of Sociology, Gender and Social Work, University of Otago, PO Box 56, Dunedin, New Zealand. katharine.legun@otago.ac.nz

Dr Erena Le Heron, School of Environment, University of Auckland, Private Bag 92019, Auckland, New Zealand. e.leheron@auckland.ac.nz

Professor Richard Le Heron, School of Environment, University of Auckland, Private Bag 92019, Auckland, New Zealand. r.leheron@auckland.ac.nz

Associate Professor Nick Lewis, School of Environment, University of Auckland, Private Bag 92019, Auckland, New Zealand. n.lewis@auckland.ac.nz

Janka Linke, University of Leipzig, Institute for Geography, Johannisallee 19a, D-04103 Leipzig, Germany. jlinke@rz.uni-leipzig.de

Professor Terry Marsden, School of Planning and Geography, Cardiff University, Cardiff, CF10 3WA, UK. marsdentk@cardiff.ac.uk

Professor Anne Murcott, School of Sociology and Social Policy, University of Nottingham, Nottingham, NG7 2RD, UK. anne.murcott@nottingham.ac.uk

Professor Eric Pawson, Department of Geography, University of Canterbury, Christchurch, New Zealand. eric.pawson@canterbury.ac.nz

Professor Harvey C. Perkins, Department of Geography, University of Canterbury, Private Bag 4800, Christchurch 8140, New Zealand. h.perkins@auckland.ac.nz

Dr Catherine Phillips, Institute for Culture and Society, University of Western Sydney, Locked Bag 1797, Penrith NSW 2751, Australia. catherine.phillips@uws.edu.au

Professor Michael Roche, School of People, Environment and Planning, Massey University, Private Bag 11 222, Palmerston North 444, New Zealand. m.m.roche@massey.ac.nz

Dr Christopher Rosin, Centre for Sustainability, University of Otago, Dunedin, New Zealand. chris.rosin@otago.ac.nz

Geoff Smith, Regenerative Farming, Auckland, New Zealand. geof.smith@gmail.com

Roseanna M. Spiers, School of Environment, University of Auckland, Private Bag 92019, Auckland, New Zealand. roseanna.spiers@auckland.ac.nz

Assistant Professor Paul V. Stock, Sociology and the Environmental Studies Program, University of Kansas, Lawrence, KS 66045-7540, USA. paul.stock@ku.edu

1 Assembling generative approaches in agri-food research

Nick Lewis, Richard Le Heron, Michael Carolan, Hugh Campbell and Terry Marsden

The recent study of agri-food economy and its different social worlds has been confronted by multiple material, political, and conceptual challenges that together have disturbed the very foundations of existing research and scholarship. This volume assembles the insights from multiple scholars who have engaged with these challenges by experimenting with uncertain but exciting new ideas. Each contribution disturbs the orthodox categories by which we know and act upon agri-food economy, and each promotes more open and disruptive ways of knowing and doing economy. In this introduction, we trace the lines of emergence of three 'disruptive' intellectual trajectories that run through the different chapters: post-structural political economy (PSPE); the 'more than human' turn in interrogations of economic life; and calls for more performative and 'enactive' research. Individually, each trajectory highlights different questions, seeks to explain different phenomena, and emphasises different ways of working with that knowledge to change agri-food worlds. The book considers the shared concerns and transformative potential of these different trajectories, assembles them into a generative dialogue, and asks how they might be aligned into a collective political project of knowledge making.

At the heart of the volume lie insights generated by more than five years of engagement between the New Zealand-based Biological Economies (BE) research group and its international collaborators. The label 'biological economies' is borrowed from the title of a public-good funded research project which sought to explore possibilities for creating new values (economic and otherwise) in New Zealand's rural economies. Funded to engage widely with thinkers across the world and freed from the constraints of orthodox thinking (applied and critical) by the blue skies nature of the funding programme, the BE group turned for inspiration to scholars. The idea for the book first took shape in a conversation between the BE group and Michael Carolan about the generative potential of such collisions and alignments, in a room in Dunedin, New Zealand. The conversation sought to articulate possible 'contours of coherence' in the emerging global landscape of disruptive agri-food research. Faced with such a task, Michael challenged the BE group to assemble a 'mind-melting' book that would try to bring a coherent narrative to the emerging sense of a pivotal moment of experimentation, transition, and new possibility in agri-food research. This book confirms that we are indeed in such a moment, but that the innovative strands of international scholarship remain to date relatively independent.

Individually, the chapters explore new practices and categories of knowledge making and new possibilities for transformative scholarship. While they draw on multiple lines of scholarship, they also reveal a nascent coherence around the shared political and moral commitments, the theoretical sensitivities of PSPE and more than human thinking, and a methodological politics of enactive research. The book as a whole asks how this research might be understood collectively and mobilised to revive, re-purpose, and re-direct scholarship. There is an urgency for posing this question at a time when a new politics and ethics are required for a world perched across a set of agri-food precipices increasingly shaped by the macro imperatives of the Anthropocene. The challenge is to recompose enduring questions of who is involved in agri-food, why, how, where, when, and in whose interests. This implies a difficult politics of knowledge production and regular efforts to bring disparate threads of new thinking and practice into generative alignment.

This book then is an exercise in assembling potentially co-productive lines of thinking that might foster a new moral economy of agri-food and build a platform for a new generation of more disruptively productive agri-food scholarship. Our opening and closing chapters draw out the ways in which the knowledge assemblage that we generate is more than the sum of its parts. Rather, it is a political project of knowledge production, which we label 'biological economies'. However, consistent with the notion of assemblage and the theoretical spirit of each of the contributions, we represent this political project as a 'platform for' a moral politics of continuous and constructive disturbance rather than a definitively new analytical category. Significantly, we offer it as more than theoretical deconstruction, but less than a definitively new category of thinking that reassembles a new interface of the categories of the biological and the economic. We do not see 'biological economies' as proposing to take us *beyond* anything – post-structuralism, political economy, humanism, and so on – by offering yet another set of analytic and ontological categories. We prefer instead to think of it as taking us *through* already existing concepts and frameworks in a way that allows us to see them anew, and in ways, importantly, that breed hopefulness and difference. We see it as both a historical marker of a series of discussions, dialogues, and translations that have taken place among a globally dispersed group of scholars and a political intervention of assemblage.

Assemblage thinking

Assemblage thinking has been an important conceptual and empirical tool for us, particularly for its ability to destabilise the orthodox categories, techniques, and methodologies with which we all work, whether in the field, in the classroom, at scholarly conferences, or while engaging politicians and policy makers (recognising, however, as Carolan highlights in Chapter 16, that everything we do is public, as it enacts and enlivens publics). To operate from the position that to think and feel is to think and feel as an assemblage allows us to experiment with new ways of grasping what it means to do agri-food scholarship. For instance, our collaborations have helped highlight that we reside in existing categories, their deconstructed elements, and new elements of proto-categories which are partially brought forth *because of* our research. This inhabiting of sameness and otherness is an emergent feature of the approaches with which we are working. The new experiences and expertise that spring from the re-formed (more than human) collaborations and capabilities open new imaginaries and strategies for making previously unthought-of food futures thinkable and doable.

We also believe in experimenting with assemblage thinking. Certain stylings of assemblage thought – actor–network theory (ANT) comes immediately to mind (Elder-Vass 2015) – are uncomfortable talking about the interrelationship between interiority and exteriority, giving rise to assemblages that fail to feel: that are, in other words, dead. We need to work *through* assemblages and come up with ways to understand how these previously disparate realms become together and what they can bring into being (Deleuze and Guattari 1988: 4). Assemblages also have politics, in the sense of having and enacting ethics, notions of the good and just, and feelings for how the world ought to be (Carolan 2015). In this spirit, we acknowledge that this volume is a *living* document – less something to be reflected upon than some-Thing (an assemblage that resists stability, permanence, and representation) that is diffractive, enactive, and multiplying. We admit that this is not unique to scholarship: that all scholarship is a thoroughly collective experiment. Remaining open to this, however, has made us more attuned to how we are not just writing about assemblages but living them. This point comes out more in our conclusion (Chapter 18): how, over the course of labouring through this book, our thinking (and undoubtedly our doing) of biological economies was continually re-examined as we came into contact with collaborators.

Consistent with Deleuze and Guattari (1988), then, we approach assemblage thinking less from the angle of *what* – such as 'What are the things that make *it* up?' – and more from that of *how* – namely, '*How* do coming-togethers happen?' and '*How* do those generative publics get expressed, such as through the affective and effective politics they enact?' Doing this is not always easy. You might even say it can make for rather uncomfortable scholarship. As the gravitational pull of convention weakens our lines of flight we take to spaces that are in some ways unsettling. But is that not the point of scholarship, if not indeed life itself – to be unsettled and surprised?

A situated initiative

Engagements with PSPE, the more than human, and enactive research are recent and particular to discipline and place. Our assemblage of them here is a loose and contestable bundling of diverse intellectual, normative, and political trajectories within and beyond the academy in many parts of the world. These trajectories are entangled in different ways with orthodox theorising of the political economy of food and agriculture, as well as with the different investment trajectories and differently institutionalised policy traditions that have long been entangled with different agri-food research traditions. Situatedness is an important theme taken up by the authors in the volume and is a key theme shared by emergent PSPE, enactive, and more than human trajectories of thought. The chapters will speak to their own situatedness, but here we need to highlight two foundational dimensions of the situatedness of the volume as a whole: BE and the global network of scholars configured around contacts with it; and the Anthropocene, which gives much of the thinking in the book its urgency, its frustration with existing politics, and its more than human emphasis.

We have introduced BE in brief above, and will return to it in more detail in the next section, but it is important to emphasise here that it sits at the core of this book. This is not because it is a book about the project or composed of research funded by it. In fact, the book encompasses much wider material and a wider range of contributions. Rather it is because the conceptual and material struggles that underpin the book are crystallised in a particular way by the BE experience. It was the movements, initiatives, and international connections established under its auspices that made possible the other contributions of the book, and the readings of global agri-food through BE that shaped their assemblage into this book. We imagine the book as an assemblage configured around a network (and networked) architecture of intellectual and interpersonal connectivity best grasped as a hub and spoke model. The hub, BE, is centrally important, but is constituted by, and exists only in relation to, the lines of connection with scholars and groups of scholars elsewhere, who themselves exist in other and wider networks, such as the Australasian Agri-Food Research Network (AFRN).

BE was launched at a moment when nature–culture scholarship first began to be framed by notions of the Anthropocene. Much disruptive contemporary thinking about the global and local challenges facing humankind now takes the Anthropocene as its starting point (Castree et al. 2014). In this volume, the authors do not make this association ritually or presume a stable, singular meaning for the Anthropocene. Rather, as reference to a new geological timescale in which humankind is the most significant force in shaping earth and environmental processes and into which we have been propelled by resource-hungry global social processes, it is a defining context for agri-food futures. The Anthropocene is a discourse that aligns multiple more than human crises looming at local and global scales, and ties them to myriad localised causes and effects (Crist 2013). Individually and collectively crises, causes, and effects demand a far richer enactive and post-human agri-food knowledge making. While the Anthropocene therefore sets a scene of crisis and urgency it also configures a radical new potentiality for knowing and doing differently in the world, should we learn to be affected (Gibson-Graham and Roelvink 2010).

Biological economies in New Zealand

The BE project was a five-year investigation of the creation of values from biological economies at what the group termed the 'nexus' of global economic connectivities and place-based activities and resources that constitute such economies. It involved a team of eight core researchers across five universities, extended engagements with three other New Zealand academics, and funded engagements with multiple postgraduate students. The BE research team can make no special claim to coining the term 'biological economies'. Rather, it owes much to a formative conversation with Morgan Williams, the retiring New Zealand Parliamentary Commissioner for the Environment, at the Dunedin Agri-Food XV meeting in 2006. He was advocating an approach to agriculture and food in New Zealand that transcended the usual and the acceptable. His emphasis on 'biological' was an attempt to trigger a wider conversation, one that would engender a broadening and deepening of how ecological and economic relations were understood and pursued. At the same Agrifood meeting, the keynote speaker – Kathie Gibson – had challenged the assembled leaders of a generation of critical political economy-informed scholarship in Australasia to loosen up their rigid and beloved categories of capitalism, food regimes, and so on, and reflect on what it meant to be captured by them. These discussions immediately resonated with our desire to create and assemble new categories, while the linking of 'biological' with 'economies' suggested a bridge between research on New Zealand's agricultural economy and the nascent more than (or non-) human and community economies turns in agri-food. We saw a metaphor with expressive, affective, and generative potential and implied prospects of new objects of science and potentially of policy.

Specifically, the genealogy of the 'biological economies' metaphor goes back to three moments of anti-contextual declaration in 2009. These moments of intervention sought to shed the intellectual, normative, and political strictures and orthodoxies that framed debates about agriculture and food in New Zealand. The first, a paper in the *New Zealand Journal of Agricultural Research*, was explicitly normative and 'big' political economy in its attachment to environmental sustainability, whole system redesign, and critique of neoliberalism. It was a spirited rejection of current productivist thinking in New Zealand agriculture directed at the authors of this thinking among the readership of the journal (Campbell et al. 2009), and suggested other ways of approaching agriculture and food. The second was a situated critique of food regimes theory in the global literature (Le Heron and Lewis 2009). Published in a special issue of *Agriculture and Human Values* dedicated to rethinking 'food regimes' for a new era, the paper questioned the political potential of a totalising overview of the organisation of globalising agriculture, especially with respect to New Zealand's experience. Significantly, neither of these declarations contained an explicit intellectual project designed and articulated as a new knowledge intervention.

6 *Nick Lewis et al.*

The third intervention was the preparation of an application to the New Zealand Marsden Fund that required a clearly outlined knowledge project. 'Biological Economies: Knowing and Making New Rural Value Relations', as the project was known, sketched the rudiments of an intellectual project that would eventually travel down theoretical and methodological paths far beyond the original intent of the bid's authors. What was to become the BE team deployed the term 'biological economies' to describe the way that value is generated within relations among products, people, places, animals, and plants. This conceptualisation highlighted sites of inquiry and materialities that cross the disciplinary boundaries that have traditionally marked out agricultural scientific knowledge production. While disarmingly simple, this reframing of knowledge production disturbs existing power–knowledge–expertise relations and performs a frighteningly political ontological flattening.

In working with these ideas in the New Zealand science policy context, for example, the BE group glimpsed for the first time the enactive potency of putting different conceptualisations into circulation. In 2009, the group was invited to present its project to the Ministry of Research Science and Technology. Gripped by waves of restructuring, the Ministry latched on to the label 'biological economies' and had within months used it to rebadge its agricultural and horticultural industries funding pool. While within a short period 'economies' had been replaced by 'industry' in official discourse, the renaming had papered a new frame over research investment processes. The metaphor reappeared in 2014 in a visioning statement for the 'Our Land and Water' National Science Challenge (see Chapter 14). In this latest incarnation, the term was defined as an economy largely dependent on its natural resources and biological heritage. While again not fully embracing the BE group's conceptualisation, our point here is three-fold: the language and underpinning understandings used to frame the interactions among political actors and shape investment decision making are open to reworking; metaphors can be changed by serendipitous enactive research interventions; and, even if not picked up in full or in a generative spirit, these metaphors can shift future investment streams. Thus, not only is there a sharp dissonance between this book's chapters and the content of conventional agri-food thinking, but the tensions generated by this dissonance may be richly political with strong moral overtones.

Biological economies in networked association

In developing BE in New Zealand, the team discovered that it was not alone in seeking to frame research that was disruptive, distinctively experimental, and enactive (see Chapter 14). The potential of reconfiguring the discursive elements of 'biological' and 'economy' was being picked up in the fashioning of similar metaphors in the UK, where Terry Marsden and others were adopting the terms 'bio-economy' and 'eco-economy' to describe and juxtapose potentially contrasting agri-food assemblages (Marsden 2010). In Australia, Kathie Gibson and colleagues had launched the post-capitalist challenge to established agri-food practices by promoting diverse and community economies (Gibson-Graham et al. 2013). Elsewhere, interest in alternative food economies was filling the political and moral vacuum left open by a singular diet of political economy critique (Maye et al. 2007), and the more than human challenge was gaining momentum (Whatmore 2006).

The BE team drew on the work of a wide range of agri-food thinkers to identify new methodological and conceptual tools for framing research questions; the very idea of 'biological economies' quickly became an assemblage. In today's hypermobile worlds of scholarship, the team encountered similar trajectories in key sites of scholarship and research practice, and established relationships with the scholars who have contributed chapters to this book. Meetings at international conferences and visits by scholars to New Zealand gave it momentum. In the course of the project, BE ran special sessions at six international conferences: the AFRN, New Zealand Geographical Society, Australian Institute of Geographers, Association of American Geographers (AAG) in Seattle, International Rural Sociological Association (IRSA) in Lisbon, and European Society for Rural Sociology (ESRS) in Florence. These special sessions deliberately positioned BE alongside other groups working on the reconfiguration of agri-food economies to encourage both shared thought and generative intellectual dissonance.

The book is therefore animated by not only multiple voices from many places, but voices that have been engaged in an increasingly collective interrogation of the three intellectual challenges that have been brought together by 'biological economies'. Two features of this collective interrogation are particularly striking. First, while it has a particular geographical starting point, it is, in its completed form, a post-national initiative. Each of the chapters questions established categories of knowledge and action and/or rejects prior scalar or human/non-human hierarchies, eschewing the methodological nationalisms or localisms of more traditional forms of comparative analysis for more complex analyses of relationality. Second, taken-for-granted changes to how we now do scholarship (international conferences, email, Skype, and Google Docs) have enabled us not only to capture the simultaneous emergence of multiple or dispersed sites of challenge and critique, but also to make a once unthought-of collective enterprise thinkable and doable. The book enrols many of those with whom BE had encounters into a shared commitment to rethink agri-food futures, and one that demonstrates the political potential of the PSPE insight that thinking, doing, and feeling inhabit the same ontological space.

Among those enrolled into the project, a number have been particularly significant, albeit differently visible. Michael Carolan visited the Biological Economies group and became a regular participant in discussions at the annual AFRN conferences. He participated in the production of a special issue of the *New Zealand Geographer* in which the BE group published a first tranche of its work (Carolan 2013a), and has continued his connections with the group as BE morphs into a new phase of disparate projects. Michael's own problematisation of the ontological status of scientific knowledge production, his focus on the micro-politics and ethics of practice, and his public sociology gave originating impetus and shape to BE's structuring around the tri-partite intellectual trajectories of PSPE, enactive research, and the more than human. By bringing science and technology studies (STS) to engaged political economy and insisting on a certain wildness of scholarship, he proved a crucial interlocutor. Crucially also, Michael embodies the intergenerationality of agri-food scholarship that is a feature of this book – Michael Bell was Michael Carolan's supervisor, and Paul Stock his Ph.D. student.

Terry Marsden and a Cardiff-based group of interdisciplinary scholars became important interlocutors for BE and partners in the discussions in this book. Terry's long-term work on agri-food governance, his work with Jonathan Murdoch and Kevin Morgan that brought ANT into an uneasy conversation with political economy (see below), and his turn to an enactive, post-political economy engagement with policy and industry actors through the millennial UK-based Food Futures programme, associated with his advocacy for the 'eco-economy', were all significant moments of, and stimuli for, BE's intellectual trajectory. Terry became an important figure in BE's research workshops, and his part in the UK Food Futures project a direct inspiration (see Ambler-Edwards et al. 2009). The work of the wider group, including Lawrence Kitchen, Mara Miele, Ina Horlings, Gillian Bristow, and Gareth Enticott, offers diverse insights into disruptive forms of spatial and economic governance (Lee 2014), 'bio-economy' (see Marsden and Morley 2014), animal welfare (Miele and Evans 2010), bio-security (Enticott 2012), and more than human agency (Latimer and Miele 2013). Individually and as a collective body of work, it has tight parallels with BE in its attempts to bring post-structuralist and 'more than human' perspectives to modified political economy and political ecology approaches. These parallels animated jointly organised BE–Cardiff special sessions at the IRSA in Lisbon and ESRS in Florence, and underpinned a strong resolve to consolidate the exchanges into this edited volume.

The different strands to this work are aligned into a normative project that counterposes the more neoliberalised bio-economy with a more place-based ecological or eco-economy (see Marsden 2013; Marsden and Farioli 2015). The project asks what levels of intentionality, spatial governance, and power relations are implied if we accept the inherent hybridity of human–nature relations, and by whom and for whom. Concern is extended to animals and plants as well as humans, and to how these assemblages operate through and help to create bio-physical and relational spaces. The questions are answered differently in bio-economy or eco-economy framings, the underlying assumptions of which are deeply infused in policy, technological, and scientific debates. The knowledge regimes and investment trajectories associated with each establish a complex and contested political terrain upon which wider post-carbon transition debates around food, energy, and related resources are being mobilised. The Cardiff group call into question the same knowledge formations as those challenged by BE, and have begun to advocate a co-produced and 'post-normal' science that has strong overlaps with enactive research and BE's interest in the moral economy of sustainable place-making and co-designing with others a more normative role for researchers.

Mara Miele, also of the Cardiff group, was one of a group of more shadowed interlocutors. Mara's work helped open for us the more than human in agri-food scholarship, a moral, political, and empirical intellectual domain shadowed by the term 'biological' in the BE project title. Her later theoretical work on naturecultures with Joanna Latimer (Latimer and Miele 2013) provided a vital link back to crucial theorising around agri-food questions at the frontiers of geography by Sarah Whatmore, which provided much inspiration for BE early on, whilst her location among the Cardiff group helped us to see the connections between this work and enactive trajectories. Similarly, the always confronting and constructively disruptive scholarship of Melanie DuPuis (2015) and Mike Goodman (Goodman, M. and Sage 2014) helped us recognise, delineate, and then re-entangle the three intellectual trajectories that underlie this book.

Finally, the figures of prominent geographers Peter Jackson and Kathie Gibson have shaped the project in both embodied and text-based forms. Like Carolan and Marsden, both visited New Zealand at formative moments of BE. Kathie presented the 2006 AFRN keynote address. The intervention which followed immediately after the publication of Gibson-Graham's (2006) own PSPE in *A Postcapitalist Politics* was deeply confronting for many traditional political economists. This confrontation has echoed strongly over the intervening decade as Kathie has led the diverse and community economies challenge to the politics of knowledge production in agri-food and BE researchers and their graduate students have connected repeatedly in conference sessions and writing projects with her challenge to researchers to learn to be affected (Gibson-Graham and Roelvink 2010) and to practise an enactive and affective scholarship in coming to re-know not just agri-food but the way they do knowing. Peter Jackson also gave a keynote address to the AFRN, which provided a platform for BE to co-organise with his Sheffield-based CONANX project, a special session at the 2011 AAG Seattle, examining provenance as an idea around which to disrupt consumption–production relations. Jackson's interest with moral economy (Jackson et al. 2009) in relation to human–non-human relations, 'following' and 'making visible' as methodologies, and 'connection' as a moralising force in agri-food relations, by contrast with 'distancing', encouraged both the more than (or non-) human and moral turns in BE.

The defining intellectual challenges

As well as presenting a situating genealogy of the book and introducing many of its protagonists, the previous section suggests that BE emerged from local and global reactions to changing materialities as well as scholarly endeavour, but faced push-back from established critical traditions. It points to the cognitive barriers that are often met and have to be dealt with when proposing a different knowledge approach. However, it also articulates the more general challenge that researchers in the emergent fields of PSPE, the more than human, and enactive research have faced, that of being asked to demonstrate through argument and illustration the knowledge gains that accrue from adopting a different lens, vocabulary, and interpretations. In this section we outline the three trajectories of thought that are privileged by contributors to this volume and that have been experienced by them as intellectual challenges.

Post-structural political economy

The very idea of 'post-structural political economy' (PSPE) speaks back to the huge intellectual battles in the agri-food world and other spheres of knowledge that dominated the 1990s and 2000s. Led by the iconoclastic 1997 *Globalising Food* book edited by David Goodman and Michael Watts, which confronted the divide in North American rural sociology around the adequacy of food regimes theory, researchers began to veer into alternative food networks and novel restatements of economy such as those penned by Jonathan Murdoch and Sarah Whatmore using actor–network theory. The *World of Foods* intervention in 2006 (Morgan et al. 2006) brought a more nuanced and enactive political economy and post-structuralist thought together in a highly productive encounter. In Australasia and elsewhere, Gibson-Graham's *A Postcapitalist Politics* (2006) and various interventions from Larner and Le Heron (2002a, 2002b) labelled PSPE had begun to shape a post-structuralist political economy that not only challenged the politics of established knowledge categories, but asked how academics might 'do the politics of knowledge' (Le Heron 2009). These directions resisted the structuralism of mainstream political economy and gradually forged an approach to agri-food scholarship more attuned to the practice of economy, the enactive politics of knowledge, and the emergent territorialities of scalar complexity.

In what way, then, is PSPE's interest in 'knowing economy differently' inscribed in the chapters of this book? First, its initial deconstructive move reveals and constructs productivist and political economy accounts of economy as macro, abstracted, disembodied and disembedded, agentless, focused on researching that which could be reduced into existing statistical measures and practices such as surveys, and so on; and it challenges their explanatory and political potentiality in this light. This meant rejecting uncritical acceptance of existing framings and scalings of economic activity (corporation, sector, region, nation) and related analytical approaches (input–output relations, growth/employment/investment measures) as the basis on which to identify problems, fund research (academic or otherwise), and investigate solutions. Scholars sought instead an approach that might reveal the practices, routines, and metrologies of assembling necessary to grasp empirically (and discern theoretically) the embodied and socio-ecologically embedded complexities of production–consumption relations PSPE encourages and licenses, and for which it demands alternative questions and approaches, and more open metaphors in place of definitive categories (Lewis et al. 2013): more agentic questions, micro-accounts, concepts like assemblage, open engagements, enactive and/or reflective knowledge making, ethnographic research, weak theorising, theorising away, and much more that we do not yet know of or how to do. It challenges scholars to break away from the impasses of existing and presumed framings, their categories, their interpretations of the world of production, and their politics.

Second, while PSPE joins political economists and contemporary policy makers to insist on the centrality, if not primacy, of investment and institutional structures, it also insists that these are made (and always in the making) in the relations of agency. To understand investment trajectories, then, necessitates new objects of analysis and theorisation and new methodological schemas such as non-human materialities, practices of market making, metrologies, assemblages of unlikely actors, and relational agencies of all kinds. If investments and institutions are thus more embodiments of alterable practices and contingent or uncertain agency, not only must economy be re-visioned but so too must politics.

Third, PSPE is set thoroughly in the wider relational turn associated with Latour, Deleuze, and others, which opens quickly and instinctively to the more than human turn. Again, scholars in this volume have grasped a licence to explore the connections, relations, and practices that shape and constitute agency – agency that must be stretched away from the purely human and understood very differently. This view diverges from the exclusive power of single hegemonic human agency and points towards the agentic assembling and reassembling of existing and possible worlds with multiple actors, many not previously recognised.

All this is extremely liberating, especially for agri-food scholars and economic geographers weighed down by the dead ends produced by critique of a monolithic neoliberalism and the weight of an older generation's measures, practices, and politics. Gibson-Graham (2006) narrate an account of their own embodied dance from feminism to Marxism to post-structuralism as an enriching co-constitutive journey rather than as a progressive enlightenment. However, the sharp step of recognising other actors and explanations, embracing unfamiliar and unorthodox objects of analysis, methodologies, and analytical categories, is uncomfortable for any scholar and never easy. Our argument is not that PSPE is a readily distinctive and self-contained approach or a decisive assault on extant paradigms that requires scholars to retool methodologically and theoretically to remain relevant. Rather it is that PSPE expresses, performs, and heralds a release from a certain paradigmatic constraint: one that is embodied and enabling even if it has yet to be institutionalised in discipline, journal publications, research funding, or policy.

Michael Carolan has on more than one occasion called himself a 'disgruntled political economist', an identity he attributes to his involvement with this project. Orthodox political economy approaches focus attention on the 'real' influence of state, capital, and their relations in ideology, regulation, and the transnational corporation. They have a critical richness that is intellectually satisfying and politically comforting or even consolatory, but frustratingly unproductive and methodologically and theoretically disgruntling. It is hard to properly grasp those political economic structures without understanding how they are constituted, co-created, and enacted/enacting. The movement of scholars from political economy to PSPE approaches is in part out of a concern that the former is not critical and constructive enough. The latter, you see, unpack many of the very categories the former takes for granted, revealing assemblages upon assemblages.

The world, according to PSPE frameworks, is composed not of objective, discrete, fixed things but of Things – phenomena too real to be representations but equally too disputed to play the role of stable, obdurate, and boring primary qualities that will furnish the universe till the end of time. In Michael's terms PSPE approaches offer an improvement in that they allow scholars to keep the baby of critique whilst throwing out the bathwater of Western thought's enduring essentialism. They point, in somewhat contradictory ways given the nomenclature, to both the dullness of political economy critique and the overly sharp-edged analytics of post-structuralism, in which critique is often an end in itself. Michael's thinking has evolved on this, thanks to the unsettling thought shown by the likes of Gibson-Graham (2006), Lewis (2009a), Le Heron (2009), and Campbell and Rosin (2011) toward convention when it comes to such subjects as social change, markets, and neoliberalism. Too often we confuse criticism, to the point of focusing only on what's bad and wrong, with gritty realism. There are opportunities for experimentation all around us, what Michael (Carolan 2013b) has called elsewhere 'difference-power'. One of Michael's contributions to this project is his constant reminder that the radical relationality underlying the biological economies approach does not make us pessimists but 'critical and constructive optimists'.

Assembling the human into relations with the non-human

What might be termed the non-human turn in agri-food has its origins in Latour, Harraway, Mol, Barad, and Bennett, and has emerged through the work of Jonathan Murdoch, Sarah Whatmore, David Goodman, Mara Miele, and Michael Carolan, among others. At heart are: the ontological challenge of ANT; the ethical challenge to redress the exclusions of a human-only focus and its consequent externalising of concern for the non-human; the empirical challenge of better accounting for what is really going on in agri-food worlds of production–consumption; and the political challenge of 'what to do', as Mol (2002) puts it, about both the consequences and the lost potential of our neglect. In each of these domains agri-food scholars have sought to disrupt established categories of knowledge. While much early work focused on an ethics of care, a new generation of agri-food researchers is calling for greater attention to the detail of more than human encounters (Miele 2011; Buller 2013; Latimer 2013; Krzywoszynska 2012, 2015).

Following these twists from New Zealand, members of the BE team had become involved in a series of their own disruptive domestic engagements with human structuring of the non-human in the early 2000s in the form of organic certification and sustainability auditing (Rosin and Campbell 2009; Campbell et al. 2012), the Royal Commission on GMOs (Le Heron 2003), and a review of work on pests, trees, and grasses in New Zealand's changing environmental landscape (Pawson and Brooking 2002). As the BE project developed, team members began to focus on the way in which economic value and networks were configured around market-making metrologies such as carbon pricing (Cooper and Rosin 2014) or Wagyu beef (Henry and Roche 2013). At the same time, in Australia, various more than human agents were beginning to animate meetings of the AFRN: the materiality and politics of food waste (Edwards and Mercer 2007), the environmental politics of GMOs (Cocklin et al. 2008), the transformative effects of nanotechnology (Scrinis and Lyons 2007), the relationships between disease, risk, and regulation in apple exporting (Higgins and Dibden 2011), the micron width of wool fibres (Pawson and Perkins 2013), and the lives of fruit flies and bees (Phillips 2013, 2014).

This volume extends the insights offered by the proliferating literature on human–non-human relationalities in relation to each of the challenges that the book offers to established knowledge (ontological, political, ethical, and empirical). These challenges are woven into many of the chapters and serve to strengthen accounts grounded more firmly in PSPE or enactive research. Those chapters driven primarily by more than human concerns respond enthusiastically to Krzywoszynska's (2012) Latourian challenge to transcend naïve empiricism and expose new Things, agents, and realms of agentic intervention. Caught in the legacies, attenuations, and lags of local encounters with more than human literatures the BE team over-emphasised the social at the expense of the non-human in its theorisations of value creation. This book offer a vicarious corrective.

Towards enactive dispositions in theory and practice

In his keynote address to the European Society for Rural Sociology conference in 2009, Philip Lowe called for rural sociologists to be more politically aware of the enactive power of the categories they use in research and policy advice (Lowe 2010). Michael Carolan's (2013b) appeal to the 'wild side of agrifood studies' makes use of the label 'enactive research'. This speaks not just to the kinds of unprojected research in the wild of which Michel Callon writes (Callon and Rabeharisoa 2003), but also the strong traditions of political engagement with diverse public audiences that his own multiple agri-food monographs exemplify so clearly. The BE group had also been practising forms of enactive research with institutional actors (Le Heron 2009; Lewis 2009b; Campbell and Rosin 2011), and the BE project was set up to extend this form of engaged research to co-producing knowledge with a wider range of community and business actors using the Chatham House workshop approach of Marsden and colleagues (see Ambler-Edwards et al. 2009). Researchers within BE were at the same time experimenting with other forms of what they too were beginning to label 'enactive research': an interest in participatory approaches of the community economies collective, and the 'wilder', performative research of 'journeying with' human and non-human actors at their invitation (FitzHerbert and Lewis 2010). In the spirit of PSPE, much of this interest in enactive research dovetailed with an exploration of the relationship between knowing and doing in coming to know, do, and be differently: what, following Carolan's (2009) provocation that 'I do therefore there is', Le Heron and Lewis (2011) term 'methodology as ontology'.

An enactive disposition presupposes normative and politicised questions – new categories for what and whose ends? If the idea of the value content has clarity that is linked to specific actors and contexts, then the question becomes: what values–means–ends pathways might be experimentally explored with such actors in their settings? Such questions recompose in a different, perhaps twenty-first-century manner, the political projects directed by political economy at global capitalism and by political ecology at environmental injustice. They presuppose a more multiple political project that recognises decidedly different capacities and capabilities to imagine and enact envisaged shifts in direction and changes in practices at very different scales, but not necessarily any less a critical concern for planetary processes.

The research presented in this book not only is aimed at being performative of new knowledge possibilities, but is about placing the academic body into very different and frequently uncomfortable settings. The enactive impulse written into BE's formative funding proposal was grounded in methodological experimentation, which in practice became a series of special purpose knowledge production experiments with thought leaders from the investment, institutional, and community worlds (see Lewis et al. 2013). This change shifted knowledge making from the pursuit of more knowing that could be represented, to positioning the academic as part of an assemblage of the capability of diverse actors. The 'workshops' broke away from extant models of engagement that try to get inside the problem of the day as understood by stakeholders to transcending the problem itself by reframing it critically in real time. The experiments confirmed enactive research to be composed of several co-constitutive moments: new category making, doing politics in 'rooms', and attaching the particular to enabling normative and political projects. There is an inherent wildness to this practice that allows for imaginative fusing and imaginative splitting, where agendas and the possibilities of enactment emerge from the conditions, style, and performance of engagement that enable different thinking to be done with the assembled and associated actors. It changes both the ontology and the politics of research processes. As Nigel Thrift (2007) said a decade ago, this constitutes an 'expressive field', which we argue prioritises the 'doing', but only by 'thinking differently'.

This new kind of positioning also changes us, as researchers, and as research subjects in co-learning experiments. The new experiences and expertise that spring from the re-formed capacities and capabilities open quite new horizons and strategies and ways of trying to make food futures. We believe there is something inherently hopeful about this style of scholarship. Once you start thinking in terms of verbs – doings, thinkings, and feelings – rather than nouns – structures, subjects, objects – you cannot help but grasp multiplicity, in terms of not only what 'is' but what 'could be'. In that spirit, we believe the biological economies approach is good to think with as we contemplate food futures.

The assembled book

The BE project was at the outset an opening or probing device that was framed to explore value creation and extend a recognition of the biological underpinnings of rural economies in ways that troubled orthodox understandings and policy-investor practices. This book in many ways explores how BE became far more disruptive by responding to the contingencies of the intellectual challenges posed by shifting intellectual and material terrains, the glimpse of political potentiality afforded by its experimental methodology, and its own internal turn to the moral. It is these shifts that we align and name in this chapter as PSPE, the more than human, and enactive research. They are of course wider trajectories, but have become increasingly familiar to the BE group and its interlocutors in these terms, to the point where they form a constantly changing, invigorating, and often frustrating conceptual space. As with the other authors in this volume, we, the authors of this chapter, have commenced an urgent move into what is a new knowledge formation about agriculture, food, and regional development that all of the authors have discerned in their exploration of the material vitalities of agri-food and the normative and political projects to which they have linked them.

The chapters that follow respond enthusiastically to Carolan's prefiguring of them as mind-melting. We reflect on just how and how far they may melt minds in our conclusion (Chapter 18). Safe to say we are more than pleased by the challenge that they have provided us in interpreting them. Individually and collectively they give an entirely different shaping and content to the metaphor of 'biological economies', which creates spaces for acting 'in and on' the biological and 'in and on' economy. Before we started the book, there was no broad and deep engagement with linkages between the biological and the economic and/or, as Marsden and colleagues would have it, the political possibilities that might emerge from knowing economies as either biological or ecological, or both at the same time. We conclude by arguing that collectively the chapters do cohere around a shared commitment to a new political project in agri-food research, which leaves us to finish here by outlining how the book is structured.

The book has both this extended introduction and a conclusion that explores the possibilities of biological economies as a political project. Between these two reflections on the state and potentiality of agri-food research, the book is organised into two parts. The first assembles a disparate suite of experimental empirical engagements with biological economies, primarily at micro scales of investigation that afford an unfamiliar privilege to more than human agencies. Their objects and frames of analysis eschew conventional scalar accounts of industry in place and even the now familiar framings of alternative food networks adopted in recent collections of agri-food scholarship. They explore the particularities of biological economies through situated framings in what is very much a remaking of agri-food knowledges from the empirical out. This mode of opening up the world crafts and colours a rougher empirical canvas upon which the chapters in Part 2 of the book more or less explicitly elaborate methodological and conceptual possibilities for enacting a new politics of knowledge making in agri-food. The authors in Part 2 build platforms that rework ontological, methodological, and moral domains in agri-food scholarship in relation to enduring political questions about social and ecological justice. Together the book's many and varied contributions sharpen the moral gaze, individual and collective ethical dispositions, political technologies, and methodological tools necessary to enact new and disruptive knowledge of agri-food worlds. They resource us to reimagine 'biological economies' as a political project.

This chapter has laid out the institutional networks that have defined and enabled the development of the book, often in unexpected and refreshingly new and novel ways. As the book really began to take shape in the early months of 2015 we began to see the fruits of the co-production of knowledge. Contributors and national and international colleagues gave generous intellectual suggestions as part of the reviewing process of book chapters. We are very conscious of how the book stands as a generational shift in theoretical priorities and modes of empirical emphasis and methodology in especially agri-food research. This exciting feature of the book opens many directions for agri-food research and scholarship. The book is made possible by the Biological Economies research project funded by the New Zealand Marsden Fund (Contract UoA0924). In the New Zealand context, this funding source gives researchers freedoms to pursue imaginative and innovative research, without disciplinary or institutional restraints. We are indebted to the fund and its administrators at the Royal Society of New Zealand. We are also indebted to the skills, patience, and tolerance of our copy-editor, June Logie, and to the guidance and support extended us by Tim Hardwick, then Routledge commissioning editor, and later Ashley Wright, from the Taylor & Francis team. Above all we extend our gratitude to all those scholars with whom we have engaged over many years and to the very many participants in our research (human and non-human) without whom it could not exist. The book is composed of interpretations and reworkings of traces of conversations, observations, experiences, and entanglements, all of which have involved the participation and insights of others. Thanks.

References

Ambler-Edwards, S., Bailey, K., Kiff, A., Lang, T., Lee, R., Marsden, T. and Tibbs, H. (2009) *Food Futures: Rethinking UK Strategy*, Chatham House report, Chatham House (Royal Institute of International Affairs), London.

Buller, H. (2013) 'Individuation, the mass and farm animals', *Theory, Culture and Society*, vol. 30, nos 7–8, pp. 155–175.

Callon, M. and Rabeharisoa, V. (2003) 'Research "in the wild" and the shaping of new social identities', *Technology in Society*, vol. 25, no. 2, pp. 193–204.

Campbell, H. and Rosin, C. (2011) 'After the "organic industrial complex": an ontological expedition through commercial organic agriculture in New Zealand', *Journal of Rural Studies*, vol. 27, pp. 350–361.

Campbell, H., Burton, R., Cooper, M., Henry, M., Le Heron, E., Le Heron, R., Lewis, N., Pawson, E., Perkins, H., Roche, M., Rosin, C. and White, T. (2009) 'Forum: from agricultural science to biological economies?', *New Zealand Journal of Agricultural Research*, vol. 52, no. 9, pp. 1–97.

Campbell, H., Rosin, C., Hunt, L. and Fairweather, J. (2012) 'The social practice of sustainable agriculture under audit discipline: initial insights from the ARGOS project in New Zealand', *Journal of Rural Studies*, vol. 28, pp. 129–141.

Carolan, M. (2009) '"I do therefore there is": enlivening socio-environmental theory', *Environmental Politics*, vol. 18, no. 1, pp. 1–17.

Carolan, M. (2013a) 'Doing and enacting economies of value: thinking through the assemblage', *New Zealand Geographer*, vol. 69, no. 3, pp. 176–179.

Carolan, M. (2013b) 'The wild side of agrifood studies: on co-experimentation, politics, change, and hope', *Sociologia Ruralis*, vol. 53, no. 4, pp. 413–431.

Carolan, M. (2015) 'Adventurous food futures: knowing about alternatives is not enough, we need to feel them', *Agriculture and Human Values*, DOI: 10.1007/s10460-015-9629-4.

Castree, N., Adams, W., Barry, J., Brockington, D., Büscher, B., Corbera, E., Demeritt, D., Duffy, R., Felt, U., Neves, K., Newell, P., Pellizzoni, L., Rigby, K., Robbins, P., Robin, L., Rose, D., Ross, A., Schlosberg, D., Sörlin, S., West, P., Whitehead, M. and Wynne, B. (2014) 'Changing the intellectual climate', *Nature Climate Change*, vol. 4, pp. 763–768.

Cocklin, C., Dibden, J. and Gibbs, D. (2008) 'Competitiveness versus "clean and green"? The regulation and governance of GMOs in Australia and the UK', *Geoforum*, vol. 39, no. 1, pp. 161–173.

Cooper, M. and Rosin, C. (2014) 'Absolving the sins of emission: the politics of regulating agricultural greenhouse gas emissions in New Zealand', *Journal of Rural Studies*, vol. 36, pp. 391–400.

Crist, E. (2013) 'On the poverty of our nomenclature', *Environmental Humanities*, vol. 3, pp. 129–147.

Deleuze, G. and Guattari, F. (1988) *A Thousand Plateaus*, Athlone Press, London.

DuPuis, M. (2015) *Dangerous Digestion: The Politics of American Dietary Advice*, University of California Press, Berkeley.

Edwards, F. and Mercer, D. (2007) 'Gleaning from gluttony: an Australian youth subculture confronts the ethics of waste', *Australian Geographer*, vol. 38, no. 3, pp. 279–296.

Elder-Vass, D. (2015) 'Disassembling actor-network theory', *Philosophy of the Social Sciences*, vol. 45, no. 1, pp. 100–121.

Enticott, G. (2012) 'The local universality of veterinary expertise and the geography of animal disease', *Transactions of the Institute of British Geographers*, vol. 37, no. 1, pp. 75–88.

FitzHerbert, S. and Lewis, N. (2010) 'He Iwi Kotahi Tatou Trust: post-development practices in Moerewa, Northland', *New Zealand Geographer*, vol. 66, no. 2, pp. 138–151.

Gibson-Graham, J. K. (2006) *A Postcapitalist Politics*, University of Minnesota Press, Minneapolis.

Gibson-Graham, J. K. and Roelvink, G. (2010) 'An economic ethics for the Anthropocene', *Antipode*, vol. 41, no. s1, pp. 320–346.

Gibson-Graham, J. K., Cameron, J. and Healy, S. (2013) *Take Back the Economy: An Ethical Guide for Transforming our Communities*, University of Minnesota Press, Minneapolis.

Goodman, D. and Watts, M. (1997) *Globalising Food: Agrarian Questions and Global Restructuring*, Psychology Press, London.

Goodman, M. K. and Sage, C. (eds) (2014) *Food Transgressions: Making Sense of Contemporary Food Politics*, Ashgate, Aldershot.

Henry, M. and Roche, M. (2013) 'Valuing lively materialities: bio-economic assembling in the making of new meat futures', *New Zealand Geographer*, vol. 69, pp. 197–207.

Higgins, V. and Dibden, J. (2011) 'Biosecurity, trade liberalisation, and the (anti)politics of risk analysis: the Australia–New Zealand apples dispute', *Environment and Planning A*, vol. 43, pp. 393–409.

Jackson, P., Ward, N. and Russell, P. (2009) 'Moral economies of food and geographies of responsibility', *Transactions of the Institute of British Geographers*, vol. 34, no. 1, pp. 12–24.

Krzywoszynska, A. (2012) 'We produce under this sky: making organic wine in a material world', Ph.D. thesis, March, Department of Geography, University of Sheffield.

Krzywoszynska, A. (2015) 'What farmers know: experiential knowledge and care in vine growing', *Sociologia Ruralis*, DOI: 10.1111/soru.12084.

Larner, W. and Le Heron, R. (2002a) 'From economic globalisation to globalising economic processes: towards post-structural political economies', *Geoforum*, vol. 33, no. 4, pp. 415–419.

Larner, W. and Le Heron, R. (2002b) 'The spaces and subjects of a globalising economy: a situated exploration of method', *Environment and Planning D: Society and Space*, vol. 20, no. 6, pp. 753–774.

Latimer, J. (2013) 'Being alongside: rethinking relations amongst different kinds', *Theory, Culture and Society*, vol. 30, nos 7–8, pp. 77–104.

Latimer, J. and Miele, M. (2013) 'Naturecultures? Science, affect and the non-human', *Theory, Culture and Society*, vol. 30, nos 7–8, pp. 5–31.

Lee, R. (2014) 'European food governance: the contrary influences of market liberalisation and agricultural exceptionalism', in T. Marsden and A. Morley (eds), *Sustainable Food Systems: Building a New Paradigm*, Earthscan, Abingdon, pp. 62–83.

Le Heron, R. (2003) 'Cr(eat)ing food futures: reflections on food governance issues in New Zealand's agri-food sector', *Journal of Rural Studies*, vol. 19, no. 1, pp. 111–125.

Le Heron, R. (2009) '"Rooms and moments" in neo-liberalising policy trajectories of metropolitan Auckland, New Zealand: towards constituting progressive spaces through post-structural political economy (PSPE)', *Asia Pacific Viewpoint*, vol. 50, no. 2, pp. 135–153.

Le Heron, R. and Lewis, N. (2009) 'Theorising food regimes: intervention as politics', *Agriculture and Human Values*, vol. 26, pp. 345–349.

Le Heron, R. and Lewis, N. (2011) 'New value from asking: "Is geography what geographers do?"', *Geoforum*, vol. 42, no. 1, pp. 1–6.

Lewis, N. (2009a) 'Progressive spaces of neoliberalism?', *Asia Pacific Viewpoint*, vol. 50, pp. 113–119.

Lewis, N. (2009b) 'Thinking/learning about policy to enact different food futures', *Regional Science Policy and Practice*, vol. 1, no. 2, pp. 187–192.

Lewis, N., Le Heron, R., Campbell, C., Henry, M., Le Heron, E., Pawson, E., Perkins, H., Roche, M. and Rosin, C. (2013) 'Assembling biological economies: region shaping initiatives in making and retaining value', *New Zealand Geographer*, vol. 69, no. 3, pp. 180–196.

Lowe, P. (2010) 'Enacting rural sociology: or what are the creativity claims?', *Sociologia Ruralis*, vol. 50, no. 4, pp. 311–330.

Marsden, T. (2010) 'Mobilizing the regional eco-economy: evolving webs of agri-food and rural development in the UK', *Cambridge Journal of Regions, Economy and Society*, vol. 3, no. 2, pp. 225–244.

Marsden, T. (2013) 'Sustainable place-making for sustainability science: the contested case of agri-food and urban–rural relations', *Sustainability Science*, vol. 8, no. 2, pp. 213–226.

Marsden, T. and Farioli, F. (2015) 'Natural powers: from the bio-economy to the eco-economy and sustainable place-making', *Sustainability Science*, vol. 10, no. 2, pp. 331–344.

Marsden, T. and Morley, A. (eds) (2014) *Sustainable Food Systems: Building a New Paradigm*, Earthscan, Abingdon.

Maye, D., Holloway, L. and Kneafsey, M. (eds) (2007) *Alternative Food Geographies: Representation and Practice*, Elsevier Science, Amsterdam.

Miele, M. (2011) 'The taste of happiness: free-range chicken', *Environment and Planning A*, vol. 43, no. 9, pp. 2076–2090.

Miele, M. and Evans, A. (2010) 'When foods become animals: ruminations on ethics and responsibility in care-full practices of consumption', *Ethics, Place and Environment*, vol. 13, no. 2, pp. 171–190.

Mol, A. (2002) *The Body Multiple: Ontology in Medical Practice*, Duke University Press, Durham, NC.

Morgan, K., Marsden, T. and Murdoch, J. (2006) 'Beyond the placeless foodscape: place, power, and provenance', in *Worlds of Food: Place, Power, and Provenance in the Food Chain*, Oxford University Press, Oxford.

Pawson, E. and Brooking, T. (2002) *Environmental Histories of New Zealand*, Oxford University Press, Melbourne.

Pawson, E. and Perkins, H. (2013) 'Worlds of wool: recreating value off the sheep's back', *New Zealand Geographer*, vol. 69, no. 3, pp. 208–220.

Phillips, C. (2013) 'Living without fruit flies: biosecuring horticulture and its markets', *Environment and Planning A*, vol. 45, no. 7, pp. 1679–1694.

Phillips, C. (2014) 'Following beekeeping: more-than-human practice in agrifood', *Journal of Rural Studies*, vol. 36, pp. 149–159.

Rosin, C. and Campbell, H. (2009) 'Beyond bifurcation: examining the conventions of organic agriculture in New Zealand', *Journal of Rural Studies*, vol. 25, pp. 35–47.

Scrinis, G. and Lyons, K. (2007) 'The emerging nano-corporate paradigm: nanotechnology and the transformation of nature, food and agri-food systems', *International Journal for the Sociology of Food and Agriculture*, vol. 15, no. 2, pp. 22–44.

Thrift, N. (2007) *Nonrepresentational Theory*, Sage, London.

Whatmore, S. (2006) 'Materialist returns: practising cultural geography in and for a more-than-human world', *Cultural Geographies*, vol. 13, pp. 600–609.

PART 1

Re-making knowledges of agri-food

2 Biological economies and processes of consumption
Practices, qualities and the vital materialism of food

David Evans

Introduction

The themes assembled under the umbrella term 'biological economies' (see Chapter 1) represent an exciting development in the study of food and agriculture. A cursory glance at the genesis of this term, and its execution and application in the chapters gathered here, suggests that it is primarily orientated towards re-thinking understandings of food production. This is not surprising given the intellectual tensions from which it emerged – principally the challenges posed to agri-food scholarship by post-human approaches to economic life (Callon 1998; Whatmore 2002; Bennett 2010) and post-structural approaches to political economy (Gibson-Graham 2006; Morgan et al. 2006). There is, however, a risk that the study of consumption will be left out of these developments or else black-boxed and tacked on to an otherwise complex, sophisticated and nuanced approach to the study of agri-food economy and its different social worlds. Of course, agri-food scholars have long recognised the importance of integrating better understandings of consumers (for example, Goodman 2002), the so-called 'invisible mouth' (Lockie 2002), into their analysis of food production–consumption relations. In practice, however, accounts remain lopsided, and consumption is often reduced to nothing more than the study of shopping, purchasing and 'consumer behaviour'. Alternatively, discussions of consumption (for example, Marsden et al. 2000) may be couched in the rhetorical tropes – identity, freedom, manipulation, desire, seduction – that once characterised cultural analysis and its engagement with 'consumerism'. While interesting in its own terms, and a step in the right direction, such research fails to engage with the apposite developments in consumption scholarship – many of which have direct implications for re-thinking the study of food.

At issue here is the proclivity for compartmentalising research on food production and food consumption, and the academic division of labour that this implies (Murcott 2011, 2013). Put crudely, agri-food scholars study production, politics and economy, whereas scholars of food and eating study consumption, culture and everyday life. This chapter considers processes of consumption in relation to the development of biological economies perspectives. I am writing from the vantage point of consumption scholarship, but let me make perfectly clear that I do not consider it the panacea for understanding agri-food worlds of production–consumption. Despite acknowledging the importance of understanding the various systems, modes and infrastructures through which food is provisioned (for example, Fine and Leopold 1993; Warde 1997), scholars of food and eating (consumption) do not engage sufficiently with contemporary developments in agri-food scholarship, and less still with sites and spaces of food production. Beyond simply stating, then, that the biological economies project ought to properly acknowledge processes of consumption, I am suggesting something rather more subtle and perhaps more ambitious. My starting point is that contemporary consumption scholarship has faced similar challenges to those identified by the editors of this volume, and so I take the view that understandings of food consumption should be engaging with the responses that have emerged under the auspices of the biological economies perspective. Further, I suggest that recognition of these shared challenges opens up the possibility of bridging the false and facile divide between production and consumption research.

In order to make these claims, I proceed as follows. I begin with a theoretical discussion of contemporary approaches in consumption scholarship that have engaged with more-than-human perspectives. With this in place, I demonstrate the application of these approaches through reference to my own empirical research on household consumption and food waste. By explicating the processes through which 'food' becomes 'waste', I am able to zoom in on the vital materialism (Bennett 2007) of food and the performativity of conventions around 'freshness' (Freidberg 2009). From here I move to a speculative discussion around the negotiation of freshness as a quality of food (Callon et al. 2002) and conclude with reflection on the ways in which a 'biological economies' sensibility might allow for better understandings of the recursive relationships between processes of food production and food consumption.

Consumption

In recent years, consumption scholarship – at least in Northern and Western Europe – has been heavily influenced by the so-called 'practice turn' in social theory (Schatzki et al. 2001). This is not the place to survey the variation in and variety of practice theories currently in circulation (see Nicolini 2012). However, it is sufficient to note they are held together by the ontological position that practices – as opposed to individuals, social structures or discourses – are the basic unit of social analysis. This shift in emphasis is intended to overcome some of social theory's irksome dualisms, such as structure and agency, or human and non-human.

Whilst definitions of what constitutes a practice vary, there appears to be a degree of consensus that they are recognisable and intelligible bundles of 'doings and sayings' that encompass practical activities and their representations (Warde 2005). They take the form of routinised behaviours (Reckwitz 2002) that are carried out by individuals without too much in the way of conscious deliberation. In the normal running of things, different individuals (including those who have never met one another) will enact these activities in accordance with shared understandings of normality and appropriate conduct. Practices are thought to be organised via the integration of disparate elements, including: skills and competence; affective know-how; meanings and images; bodily activities; and objects, materials and technologies (Reckwitz 2002; Shove et al. 2012). A useful distinction can be drawn between practices as entities and practices as performances (Schatzki 1996). Practices exist 'out there' as discernible entities, have a historical trajectory, and are configured by the intersection and alignment of their various constituent elements. For practices to survive, however, they need to be performed consistently and faithfully across time and space. While this can and does happen, people also 'adapt, improvise and experiment' with different ways of doing things such that practices are 'dynamic by virtue of their own internal logic' (Warde 2005). It is through performances – the doing of 'doings' – that practices as entities are reproduced, modified or otherwise changed by practitioners.

The decisive statement on the application of these ideas to consumption scholarship can be traced to the publication of Alan Warde's paper 'Consumption and theories of practice' (2005). In it, Warde convincingly argues that 'consumption is not itself a practice but is, rather, a moment in almost every practice' (Warde 2005: 137). The consequences of this manoeuvre are not trivial. Principally, it provides a corrective to approaches that place the sovereign individual at the centre of their analysis – as exemplified by notions of 'consumer choice'. By demonstrating that moments of consumption occur within and for the sake of practices (Warde 2005: 145), it follows that explanations should look beyond the discretion of individuals in order to explore the shared requirements of accomplishing a satisfactory performance of a particular practice. A corollary of this is that it broadens the gaze of consumption scholarship to encompass a focus on activities beyond the parameters of behaviours that are typically – and colloquially – understood as 'consuming'. For example, while shopping is almost certainly an activity that involves moments of consumption, there are a great many more examples of activities in which consumption is a moment, but we may not intuitively think of them as such. Activities as diverse as commuting to work, walking in the countryside, caring for loved ones and playing the cello are all examples where moments of consumption arise in the course of doing something else.

From a slightly different angle, theories of practice offer up the possibility of exploring phenomena that are obscured by or concealed in the biases of cultural analysis (Warde 2014). The once prevailing orthodoxy was modelled after Veblen's foundational account of conspicuous consumption, leading to an overemphasis on the role of consumption as social communication. The emergence and application of theories of practice can be viewed as part of a larger series of interventions in these core axioms of consumption scholarship. For example, against the rather heady language of meaning, identity, desire, representation and ideology that is (or was) typically deployed to theorise consumption, Gronow and Warde (2001) suggest that a good deal of what passes for consumption is rather more mundane or, as they put it, *ordinary*. Similarly, Shove and Warde (2002) coined the term *inconspicuous consumption* in recognition of the paucity of these dominant accounts when faced with the task of explaining escalating levels of environmentally significant consumption (such as the energy and water used in people's homes). As Warde (2014) points out:

> Against the model of the sovereign consumer, practice theories emphasise routine over actions, flow and sequence over discrete acts, dispositions over decisions, and practical consciousness over deliberation. In reaction to the cultural turn, emphasis is placed upon doing over thinking, the material over the symbolic, and embodied practical competence over expressive virtuosity in the fashioned presentation of self.
>
> (Warde 2014: 286)

Taking these points together, theories of practice intimate a radical re-think of how we define and approach the study of consumption.

Beyond the simple assertion that theories of practice offer a better and more up-to-date account of consumption than those currently deployed in studies of agri-food worlds, a number of important points can be made. Firstly, theories of practice represent a clear plea for consumption scholarship to engage with more-than-human approaches. For example, Elizabeth Shove's *Comfort, Cleanliness and Convenience* (2003) explicitly brings together insights from the sociology of consumption with those from science and technology studies to reveal the interdependence between, and co-evolution of, practices and technical systems. In this view, changing patterns of household food consumption (such as the rise of ready meals in the UK) can be explained *inter alia* by the adoption of domestic technologies such as the freezer (Shove and Southerton 2000), associated devices (such as the microwave), the frozen food infrastructure, shifting retail landscapes, the legacy of urban planning, labour market trends, and changes in the domestic division of labour. This sense of distributed agency and the configuration of practices by human and non-human agents resonates strongly with the actor–network theory (ANT)-inspired approaches to assembly and assemblage (Latour 2005) that have proven influential in agri-food scholarship.

Secondly, the domain of food and eating is an example *par excellence* of routine and ordinary consumption. It attends to the core concerns of practice theories, including corporeality, materiality, habits, skills, sociality, shared understandings and sequences of activity. Practice theories and their invocation to focus on the dynamics of what people do suggest that studies of food consumption should not stop at the point of purchase, nor should they rest at theoretical abstractions and hyperbolic inferences. They necessitate an empirical encounter in which food is followed beyond the point of acquisition to trace the various associations and relationships in which it becomes entangled through processes of appropriation, the procedures to which it is subject (such as cooking) and the machinery and devices that accompany its transformations (both biophysical and non-biophysical). I turn now to an illustration of this approach.

Household food waste

Food waste is rapidly emerging as an issue of political and cultural fixation. Estimates (for example, FAO 2013) suggest that one-third of global food production goes to waste, and so it is surprising that food scholarship has been slow to engage with this topic (Evans et al. 2013). Hitherto, the bulk of policy attention has been focused on household and consumer food waste, and in response to this some of my earlier work set out to develop a social scientific account of domestic food waste. As a study of material culture, my fieldwork explored how stuff that is understood as 'food' ends up as stuff that is 'waste'. I focused on the ways in which households plan and shop for food, how they prepare and eat it, the ways in which they store it and, ultimately, how they get rid of what they do not use. It involved a focus on the very literal movements of food – following it from the supermarket, to the home, to the saucepan, back to the fridge and, eventually, into the bin. It also involved a focus on the ways in which food moves between categories and evaluations – from raw ingredients, to a cooked meal, to leftovers, to 'past its best' and, eventually, to waste. My approach was broadly ethnographic, involving sustained and intimate contact (in 2009–10) with the residents of two 'ordinary' streets in and around south Manchester (UK).

The results of this study have been published extensively elsewhere (notably, Evans 2014), but by way of overview Figure 2.1 represents my account of how 'food' becomes 'waste' as it passes through people's homes. Without wishing to explicate all of the points that could be drawn from Figure 2.1, a number of key arguments can be discussed. The first is that, in order to understand how food becomes waste, it is important to first appreciate how it becomes *surplus*, or why households consistently acquire it in quantities that exceed their perceived and immediate requirements for consumption. My analysis suggests that this happens for a number of reasons, such as the quantities in which food is made available (for example, having to buy a bag of carrots when only a few are required), shared understandings of what it means to cook and eat 'properly' (meals cooked from scratch using a variety of fresh ingredients), the enduring convention of the family meal (including the persistent associations between household food provisioning and care), where and when people do their grocery shopping (for example, a 'big weekly shop' at large out-of-town supermarkets), disruptions to household routines (events that throw meal plans, however tacit, out of balance) and relationships with significant others (for example, differences in taste within a household). Taken together this suggests that people do not make deliberate and 'irresponsible' choices to purchase too much food when they know that they may end up wasting it. Surplus is

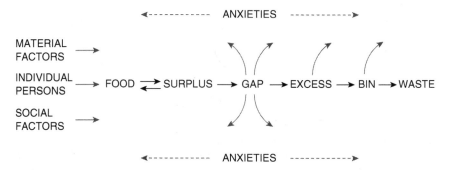

Figure 2.1 How 'food' becomes 'waste'

embedded in the flow of everyday life and, although it means that food may end up being wasted, it often arises for good reasons (for example, in response to the imperative to eat healthily) and from the best of intentions (such as caring for one's family).

The second point is that, although a good deal of surplus food ends up as waste, this is by no means inevitable, and the transmutation of 'surplus food' into 'food waste' is rarely simple. Surplus food is inherently ambiguous insofar as it serves no immediate purpose but has the potential to be useful given a different set of circumstances. Accordingly, it is not disposed of straight away; rather, it is placed somewhere else – typically the fridge – to deny its wastage and keep open the possibility that it will be eaten at some point in the future. Upon entering this 'gap' in disposal (Hetherington 2004), the trajectory of surplus food remains undecided. In addition to the possibility of 'surplus' becoming 'food' again, there exist multiple conduits (Gregson et al. 2007) through which its disposal may be enacted, and many of these do not route it in the direction of the waste stream. For instance, it could be re-circulated through gifting, it could be 'handed down' and used to feed domestic animals, or it could be transformed and used as something other than food (for example, compost). Although households can and do make use of these conduits, my analysis suggests that they do not operate consistently or effectively to dispose of surplus food or to save it from wastage (see Evans 2012).

In contrast, the conduits that connect surplus food to the waste stream provide a reliable mechanism for getting rid of surplus food. To illustrate: placing food in this gap allows for it to be quietly but actively forgotten as it slips from the category of 'surplus' (when it could be eaten) to 'excess' (when it has deteriorated to the point that it is no longer edible). Upon exiting the gap, it becomes appropriate to place it in the bin. The bin acts as an interface between private households and public systems of waste management (Chappells and Shove 1999) that connects the excess matter to its final resting place in landfill, where it can finally be consigned to the category of waste. In contrast to the shifting gradients and contours that prevent the consistent operation of most conduits of disposal (ranging from concerns around social respectability to differential levels of access), the trajectories connecting surplus food to the waste stream appear relatively stable. This stability derives, at least in part, from the various non-human actants that hold it together and the alignment between food as an unbecoming material (it is prone to rapid spoilage), domestic technologies (for example, Tupperware and refrigerators acting as coffins of decay), the bin itself, and infrastructures of waste collection and disposal.

The third point is that food becomes waste as the result of a complex and anxiety-laden process. For reasons of brevity, I'll stop short of discussing the concept of anxiety in any detail (although see Jackson et al. 2013) and instead note that, in addition to anxieties about wasting food, a whole host of food-related anxieties (for example, around eating properly or managing household budgets) and many more besides (for example, around identity and social position) are in circulation and have some bearing on this process. The more important point, at least for the purposes of this chapter, is that notions of 'food choice' do not adequately explain why households waste so much food. There is a need to look beyond the individuals who occasion and enact the various movements through which 'food' becomes 'waste'. Figure 2.1 captures the contextual factors that provide the backdrop to these performances. I have categorised some of these as 'material' (for example, bins, domestic technologies, food packaging and microbial life) and others as 'social' (for example, tastes, conventions, time and relationships with significant others). The distinction between 'social' and 'material' is entirely artificial and only made here for the purposes of practical representation. Following Latour (2005), I would rather view 'the social' as that which is held together by the assembly of humans and non-humans.

It is particularly useful to home in on the performative role of food and its variable materiality in configuring practices of household waste generation. Food – unlike most consumer objects – is susceptible to rapid spoilage and decay. As such, it is particularly well suited to claims that objects do not have fixed properties or qualities (Ingold 2007) and that they are in constant flux or becoming (Bennett 2007). Generally speaking, when food becomes mouldy, goes off or has otherwise 'gone bad', people take the view that it cannot be eaten and has to be thrown out. These processes of self-alteration suggest an active vitalism (Bennett 2010) that animates (Bennett 2007) food and, in doing so, creates certain affordances in practices of disposal. If the presence of surplus food in the home is anxiety inducing (for example, owing to its representational effects and connotations of bad household management), then its transformations – such as the appearance of mould, discoloration, changes in texture, altered taste or unpleasant smells – allow people to dispose of it with an easier conscience. The changes that food undergoes whilst being held in the 'gap' serve to legitimate the act of wasting it by bringing its intrinsic attributes closer in line with extrinsic household categorisations of its status. The performativity of food – particularly in states of transformation – strikes me as an important topic of enquiry and a useful mechanism for traversing the production–consumption divide. By way of example, I turn now to a discussion of how it might be applied to the study of 'freshness' in food systems.

Freshness

Conventions around the consumption of 'fresh' food were a major theme in my analysis of household food waste. However, the requirement and expectation of 'freshness' in food systems seem relevant to broader debates around agri-food economies and their social worlds. This section draws on a number of conceptual resources to offer some rather speculative reflections on how the relationships between production, consumption and 'freshness' might be theorised.[1] Of interest here are the associations between freshness and the turn to 'quality' in food production and consumption (Murdoch et al. 2000) and the processes through which foods are qualified (Callon et al. 2002; Harvey et al. 2004) as 'fresh'.

When applied to food, the word 'freshness' is almost always seen as a good thing, its importance self-evident. It carries connotations of purity, naturalness, authenticity, health, wholesomeness and virtue. To eat fresh, it seems, is to eat right, and in contemporary Western societies fresh foods are generally available year-round. It doesn't take much digging beneath this observation to realise that the systematic availability of 'fresh' produce is anything but natural (Jackson 2013). For example, the availability of 'fresh' pineapples on the shelves of UK supermarkets is a consequence of complex trade routes and negotiations. Similarly, the ubiquity of 'fresh' coffee – as compared to the freeze-dried varieties that were very much the norm in the UK until relatively recently – is reliant on increasingly globalised supply chains. In order to secure the 'freshness' of foodstuffs as they move through time and space, they need to be protected from spoilage by a sophisticated technical apparatus (such as cold chain technologies) and/or subjected to transformations by processes such as irradiation or chemical treatment. Even produce that doesn't have that far to travel is subject to these contradictions. For example, most people do not consider it controversial to drink milk from a refrigerator and call it fresh, even though it has most likely been pasteurised. The meaning of 'freshness', then, is a matter of some contestation and negotiation.[2]

This ambiguity suggests that positioning and qualifying (Callon et al. 2002) food as fresh is an active accomplishment of those involved in the production and consumption of food, and of other stakeholders (such as nutritionists and campaigning groups). Indeed, Susanne Freidberg's magnificent *Fresh: A Perishable History* (2009) takes a tour through an 'ordinary refrigerator' (p. 3) – focusing on beef and fish, fruit and vegetables, and milk and eggs – to explore not only what 'fresh' means but also what else it means. She suggests that the industrial production of freshness is the result of a series of sociotechnical transformations that took place during the mid- to late twentieth century, including streamlining crop varieties and technological advances in food storage, preservation and refrigeration. This transition marked a shift in the meaning of freshness from one of time and distance to the technology that secures it. Freidberg demonstrates how these developments evolved in tandem with changes in how people live their lives and how they value perishable food. These include the changing discourses of health and nutrition that underpin the idea that fresh food is good for us as well as the role of marketing campaigns in positioning freshness as a quality associated with wholesomeness, taste and nature. The industrial production of freshness is clearly profitable in so far as its associations with quality allow for the addition and extraction of value – see, for example, the price premium of 'fresh' orange juice (Foster et al. 2012). Similarly, processing and packaging food and then selling it as fresh (for example, cubed pineapples or sliced apples) create opportunities for the extraction of yet more value. On these points, Freidberg invokes the familiar frame of alienation from the food system and suggests that people are now more susceptible to accepting industrially produced freshness as natural.

Once food has been positioned as fresh, it will not remain there indefinitely. Actors throughout the food chain will necessarily be involved in the continuing measurement, monitoring and assessment of 'freshness' through a variety of technical, institutional and informal means. Some of these will be related to concerns around food safety, whereas others will be driven by concerns around aesthetics, display and profitability. Similarly, the categorisation of food as 'fresh' is reliant on – and open to negotiation by – processes of consumption. Food consumers are likely to continually measure, monitor and assess 'freshness' in the course of performing food-related practices such as grocery shopping or meal preparation. These qualification trials may involve the use of codified knowledge (such as date labelling) or more tacit and embodied forms of know-how (such as feeling for changes in texture or sniffing for changes in smell). At this juncture it is instructive to recall work by Callon and colleagues (2002) on the economy of qualities. They note:

> All quality is obtained at the end of a process of *qualification*, and all qualification aims to establish a constellation of characteristics, *stabilized* at least for a while, which are attached to the product and transform it temporarily into a tradable *good* in the market.
> (Callon et al. 2002: 199, emphasis added)

The 'constellation of characteristics' that configure a product's qualities are both *intrinsic* (the material properties of food itself, its taste, its smell, its appearance and so on) and *extrinsic* (shaped by evaluations and judgements that are subject to change and vary from one actor to the next). The crucial distinction here is between products and goods; the qualities associated with the former are open to negotiation, whereas those associated with the latter are temporarily closed in order to enable market exchanges. When food qualifies as 'fresh' it has value, and the qualification of food produce as fresh goods depends on the alignment of evaluations and judgements by actors throughout the food system, including final consumers. These in turn will depend on the devices used to assess and communicate freshness, but the intrinsic characteristics of food – and its unique capacity for material transformation – will also play a vital role in these qualification processes. When food no longer qualifies as 'fresh' it loses value.

Implicit in the discussion above is the idea that, in categorising food as fresh, fresh food is simultaneously categorised as quality food. Just as the qualification of food is variable, it would be a mistake to view these associations as a *fait accompli* or as the triumph of agri-business over the manipulation of consumer demand. For a start, they can be traced to the efforts of actors and organisations – such as social movements and public health campaigners – who are unlikely to be acting on behalf of the food industry. More pointedly, the value of freshness is reliant on sufficient consumers making and sustaining its associations with quality. Sociological analyses of taste (following Bourdieu – see Warde 1997) are instructive here. In addition to re-iterating the point that consumer dispositions or 'preferences' are shared, they draw attention to the class distinctions that are performed through the purchase of fresh food. The associations that have been historically attached to fresh produce are compatible with middle-class ideas of 'health' and what it means to eat properly (Plessz and Gojard 2015). By extension, the consumption of fresh produce is associated with good taste, and so there is reason to suspect that consumers may wish to collectively uphold the distinction between food that is fresh and that which is not. By way of example, note the clear differences between vegetables that are sold as 'fresh frozen' (such as a bag of peas) and those that are distributed through the cold chain but then sold as 'fresh' in chiller cabinets (such as a packet of 'ready-shelled' garden peas). These demarcations serve the interests both of producers (in the opportunities for value creation) *and* of consumers (in the symbolic distinctions that can be performed), and so both are invested in sustaining them. However, shifts on either side of the counter – for example, a producer campaign to promote the idea that frozen peas are fresher, or consumers collectively refusing 'freshly cut' produce such as ready-shelled peas – could lead to these tacit agreements being broken.

When consumption is taken seriously – that is, beyond notions of individual choices and the biases of cultural analysis – it makes little sense to think of 'consumers' passively accepting the imposition of fresh produce in their everyday lives or that they are duped into believing the associations between freshness and food quality. It would be equally misguided to view consumers as entirely active in forging these associations, or that the industrial production of freshness is nothing more than a response to 'consumer demand'. A comprehensive and sophisticated account of the role played by processes of consumption is necessarily beyond the scope of this short book chapter and these speculative reflections. With this caveat in mind, and in the hope of prompting just such scholarly endeavour, I end this section with some suggestions on how one might go about generating proper understandings of the relationships between consumption and the industrial production of freshness.

It would be sensible – indeed, necessary – to explore the trajectories of the practices for which the consumption of fresh produce occurs and to trace the various factors that have shaped their development. The actions and strategies of the food industry will no doubt be part of the story, but these would need to be understood in relation to patterns of technological development, broader societal trends and the recursive interactions between production and consumption.

Inspiration might also be drawn from conventions theory (Boltanski and Thevenot 2006). This perspective highlights the existence of multiple 'orders of worth' that serve as reference points for the legitimation and justification of action, and the basis for agreement and co-ordination (or not) in social and economic life. It suggests that, in addition to the market conventions that equate worth with economic value, there are grounds for locating worth in terms of collective interest (civic conventions), productivity and efficiency (industrial conventions), trust (domestic conventions), reputation (opinion conventions) and creativity (inspired conventions). A useful avenue of enquiry[3] might be to explore and systematically unpack the ways in which these 'grammars of worth' combine in various configurations to give rise to agreements on what constitutes 'quality' food and the mutual expectation of 'freshness'. For example, there may be a role for domestic conventions (drawing upon perceived attachments to locality) and inspired conventions (drawing on non-conformity *vis-à-vis* the perceived homogeneity of industrial food production), as well as economic conventions (the potential to add value) and industrial conventions (the efficiencies of pre-prepared but still 'fresh' produce). Typically, this approach has focused on the combination and alignment of conventions in networks of production – and it has been deployed to great effect (see, for example, Storper 1997; Murdoch et al. 2000). However, the significance of consumption and consumers is missing and has been all but neglected. Having argued that processes of consumption play an active role in maintaining the associations between freshness and food quality, it is important to properly theorise their place in the co-ordination of agri-food worlds, including points of alignment and differences of interpretation, and to acknowledge their generative role in assembling the conventions and expectations that emerge from these negotiations.

Conclusion

The preceding sections represent a plea for the biological economies project to acknowledge consumption. I started with the observation that consumption scholarship has been responding to the same conceptual challenges that have confronted the study of agri-food worlds. To illustrate this point, I gave a précis of theories of practice and their application to contemporary understandings of consumption. In addition to intimating a shared interest in post-human approaches to economic life, my suggestion is that agri-food scholarship could profit from paying greater attention to processes of consumption. In order to demonstrate what this might entail, I discussed the case of household food waste, and this in turn brought the vital materiality of food into focus. Beyond simply suggesting this as a theme that is ripe for exploration from a biological economies perspective, my argument is that food as vibrant matter does not respect the academic divisions of labour that underpin the compartmentalisation of production and consumption. In this spirit, my discussion segued into an exploration of the associations between freshness and quality, and the qualification of food as 'fresh'. This necessitated consideration of insights from conventions theory and actor–network theory – theoretical terrain that has been well trodden by new directions and developments in studies of food production. While I re-iterated the point that theories of practice offer the means of better analysing consumption, my conclusion is that studies of food consumption need to properly acknowledge food production and the theoretical resources that have been brought to bear on its analysis. More generally, it may well be intellectually more productive to start from the recognition of shared theoretical orientations – for example, towards post-humanism and practice (broadly defined) – than it is to work on one side of the production–consumption divide or the other and then attempt to bring lopsided analyses together. My hope is that the biological economies agenda represents a suitable vehicle for achieving this, as well as producing more comprehensive understandings of food and the multiple relationships in which it is embedded.

Notes

1 These reflect a research agenda that I have been developing in collaboration with Peter Jackson and Monica Truninger.
2 Despite the broad consensus around the positive connotations of fresh food, there are unintended consequences of the socio-technical infrastructure involved in securing freshness in food systems. These range from the energy burden of the cold chain to the unfavourable labour conditions endured by those involved in the production of fresh produce. For reasons of brevity, I do not discuss these issues here.
3 While offered as a suggestion, these are prospects that I would also like to pursue myself!

References

Bennett, J. (2007) 'Edible matter', *New Left Review*, vol. 45, pp. 133–145.
Bennett, J. (2010) *Vibrant Matter: A Political Ecology of Things*, Duke University Press, London.
Boltanski, L. and Thevenot, L. (2006) *On Justification: Economies of Worth*, Princeton University Press, Princeton, NJ.
Callon, M. (1998) *The Laws of the Markets*, Wiley-Blackwell, Oxford.
Callon, M., Meadel, C. and Rabeharisoa, V. (2002) 'The economy of qualities', *Economy and Society*, vol. 31, no. 2, pp. 194–217.
Chappells, H. and Shove, E. (1999) 'The dustbin: a study of domestic waste, household practices and utility services', *International Planning Studies*, vol. 4, no. 2, pp. 267–280.
Evans, D. (2012) 'Binning, gifting and recovery: the conduits of disposal in household food consumption', *Environment and Planning D: Society and Space*, vol. 30, no. 6, pp. 1123–1137.

Evans, D. (2014) *Food Waste: Home Consumption, Material Culture and Everyday Life*, Bloomsbury, London.
Evans, D., Campbell, H. and Murcott, A. (eds) (2013) *Waste Matters: New Perspectives on Food and Society*, Sociological Review Monographs, Wiley-Blackwell, Oxford.
FAO (2013) *Food Wastage Footprint: Impact on Natural Resources*, Food and Agriculture Organization of the United Nations, Rome.
Fine, B. and Leopold, E. (1993) *The World of Consumption: The Material and Cultural Revisited*, Routledge, London.
Foster, C., McMeekin, A. and Mylan, J. (2012) 'The entanglement of consumer expectations and eco-innovation pathways', *Technology Analysis and Strategic Management*, vol. 24, pp. 391–405.
Freidberg, S. (2009) *Fresh: A Perishable History*, Harvard University Press, Cambridge, MA.
Gibson-Graham, J. K. (2006) *A Postcapitalist Politics*, University of Minnesota Press, Minneapolis.
Goodman, D. (2002) 'Rethinking food production–consumption: integrative perspectives', *Sociologia Ruralis*, vol. 42, no. 4, pp. 271–277.
Gregson, N., Metcalfe, A. and Crewe, L. (2007) 'Moving things along: the conduits and practices of divestment in consumption', *Transactions of the Institute of British Geographers*, vol. 32, no. 2, pp. 187–200.
Gronow, J. and Warde, A. (eds) (2001) *Ordinary Consumption*, Routledge, London.
Harvey, M., McMeekin, A. and Warde, A. (eds) (2004) *Qualities of Food*, Manchester University Press, Manchester.
Hetherington, K. (2004) 'Secondhandedness: consumption, disposal and absent presence', *Environment and Planning D: Society and Space*, vol. 22, pp. 157–173.
Ingold, T. (2007) 'Materials against materiality', *Archaeological Dialogues*, vol. 14, no. 1, pp. 1–16.
Jackson, P. (2013) 'Fresh', in P. Jackson and the CONANX group, *Food Words*, Bloomsbury, London, pp. 85–86.
Jackson, P., Watson, M. and Piper, N. (2013) 'Locating anxiety in the social: the cultural mediation of food fears', *European Journal of Cultural Studies*, vol. 16, pp. 24–42.
Latour, B. (2005) *Reassembling the Social: An Introduction to Actor-Network-Theory*, Oxford University Press, Oxford.
Lockie, S. (2002) '"The invisible mouth": mobilizing "the consumer" in food production–consumption networks', *Sociologia Ruralis*, vol. 42, no. 4, pp. 278–294.
Marsden, T., Flynn, A. and Harrison, M. (2000) *Consuming Interests: The Social Provision of Foods*, UCL Press, London.
Morgan, K., Marsden, T. and Murdoch, J. (2006) *Worlds of Food: Place, Power and Provenance in the Food Chain*, Oxford University Press, Oxford.
Murcott, A. (2011) 'The BSA and the emergence of a "sociology of food": a personal view', *Sociological Research Online*, vol. 16, no. 3, p. 14.
Murcott, A. (2013) 'A burgeoning field', in A. Murcott, W. Belasco and P. Jackson (eds), *The Handbook of Food Research*, Bloomsbury, London, pp. 1–26.
Murdoch, J., Marsden, T. and Banks, J. (2000) 'Quality, nature and embeddedness: some theoretical considerations in the context of the food sector', *Economic Geography*, vol. 76, no. 2, pp. 107–125.
Nicolini, D. (2012) *Practice Theory, Work, and Organization*, Oxford University Press, Oxford.
Plessz, M. and Gojard, S. (2015) 'Fresh is best? Social position, cooking, and vegetable consumption in France', *Sociology*, vol. 49, no. 1, pp. 172–190.
Reckwitz, A. (2002) 'Towards a theory of social practices: a development in culturalist theorizing', *European Journal of Social Theory*, vol. 5, no. 2, pp. 243–263.
Schatzki, T. R. (1996) *Social Practices*, Cambridge University Press, Cambridge.

Schatzki, T. R., Knorr-Cetina, K. and Savigny, E. von (2001) *The Practice Turn in Contemporary Theory*, Psychology Press, London.

Shove, E. (2003) *Comfort, Cleanliness and Convenience: The Social Organisation of Normality*, Berg, Oxford.

Shove, E. and Southerton, D. (2000) 'Defrosting the freezer', *Journal of Material Culture*, vol. 5, pp. 301–319.

Shove, E. and Warde, A. (2002) 'Inconspicuous consumption: the sociology of lifestyles, consumption and the environment', in R. Dunlap, F. Buttel, P. Dickens and A. Gijswijt (eds), *Sociological Theory and the Environment: Classical Foundations, Contemporary Insights*, Rowman & Littlefield, New York, pp. 230–252.

Shove, E., Pantzar, M. and Watson, M. (2012) *The Dynamics of Social Practice*, Sage, London.

Storper, M. (1997) *The Regional World: Territorial Development in a Global Economy*, Guilford Press, New York.

Warde, A. (1997) *Consumption, Food and Taste*, Polity Press, Cambridge.

Warde, A. (2005) 'Consumption and theories of practice', *Journal of Consumer Culture*, vol. 5, pp. 131–153.

Warde, A. (2014) 'After taste: culture, consumption and theories of practice', *Journal of Consumer Culture*, vol. 14, pp. 279–303.

Whatmore, S. (2002) *Hybrid Geographies*, Sage, London.

3 The borderlands of animal disease

Knowing and governing animal disease in biological economies

Gareth Enticott

Introduction: the borderlands of disease control

One consequence of the ever-greater global flows of livestock has been the spread of disease (King et al. 2006). Highly pathogenic avian influenza; foot and mouth disease; Schmallenberg virus: all are examples of livestock diseases that threaten agriculture's global mobility. The international governance of animal health attempts to circumvent these outbreaks. Symbolised most by the aftermath of the outbreak of foot and mouth disease in 2001 in the United Kingdom, the result has been a proliferation of biosecurity strategies, tools, methods and technologies. Yet the work of controlling animal disease is not an easy feat, either on the ground or in the offices in which the practices and materials of biosecurity are formulated. Normative beliefs and institutional logics of appropriate action shape how biosecurity is done. In her ethnography of disease control within the UK government, for instance, Wilkinson (2011) recounts the stories policy makers tell of doing biosecurity work. These stories act as 'modes of ordering' (Law 1994), justifying actions whilst enacting a material and spatial geography to biosecurity policy. In Defra – the government department responsible for animal disease control – a rational mode of ordering neatly divides up the policy process into bounded parts. Rationalism supports the separation of policy from science: the two sides are kept apart by memos discouraging attendance at certain meetings, and housing the two sides in separate buildings. Bureaucracy is a second mode of ordering in which the materials of government – endless standards, forms and processes – bring biosecurity to life (Donaldson 2008) whilst allowing policy makers and scientists to believe they are contributing to a necessary service (Wilkinson 2011: 968). Finally, expediency as a mode of ordering justifies departing from standard operating procedures. During disease outbreaks, what matters is 'getting things done' by 'any means possible'. On this 'wartime' footing, organisations change: rules and regulations are remade and applied flexibly, hierarchies are broken down and everyone crowds round maps for short briefings. Disease management is not always like this: in 'peacetime', mundane bureaucracy dominates, but the stories of fighting disease give meaning to policy makers' lives.

These modes of ordering say much about neoliberal modes of governing agriculture and animal disease. On the one hand, the stories that policy makers tell about doing biosecurity allow them to make sense of and cope with disease management. On the other, modes of ordering reinforce the material and spatial organisation of neoliberal biosecurity work. The bureaucracy of universal standards reflects the 'anti-politics' of neoliberal biosecurity governance (Higgins and Dibden 2011), whilst creating material forms of power and control allowing policy makers to 'act at a distance' (Latour 1988). A distinct spatial organisation is enacted too, which seeks to maintain boundaries between disciplines and activities. But, as agriculture becomes so tightly coupled around these spatial and material practices, so is their failure spectacular if not unexpected (Law 2006). When disease strikes, getting things done by any means possible reflects the vulnerability of neoliberal agriculture and the potential for an alternative set of biosecurity logics.

Similar divisions exist between the three broad disciplines of animal disease control, each with their own distinctive spatial styles (Law and Mol 2011). Epidemiology, for instance, attempts to quantify objective risk, picturing agricultural space as a placeless flat surface. The laboratory requires precision and universality, allowing it to draw places together that are far apart. Finally, the clinic has an immediate and situated logic, fracturing standards and imagining a variegated agricultural spatial plane in which disease can look, sound and feel different depending on context. What distinguishes clinical practice from epidemiology is its spatial attunement and adaptability, which makes clinical practice highly mobile (Mol and Law 1994). Together, these different practices construct 'ontological variants' of disease such that diseases are not singular but a composite of different practices (Law and Mol 2011).

Whilst these disciplinary boundaries may be firmly patrolled (Bickerstaff and Simmons 2004), can the strict divisions between them be constantly maintained? In fact, recent studies of animal disease suggest replacing a focus on the maintenance of disciplinary boundaries with a focus on disciplinary 'borderlands' – the zone of 'intense entanglement' between different actors, materials and practices (Hinchliffe et al. 2013: 13). In these borderlands, new ways of working and doing biosecurity emerge to challenge old orders. Much the same is true of scientific disciplines as a whole. Kohler (2002), for instance, argues that distinct disciplines do not live in isolation: they pay attention to each other, meeting in a 'zone of active interaction and exchange' or a 'trading zone' (Galison 1996). These 'border crossings' provide space to combine and create novel practices, containing mixed practices and ambiguous identities that are as much of one place (for example the scientific laboratory) as of another (for example the policy makers' office, or the veterinarian in the field).

Borderlands can be created from dissatisfaction and anxieties with old scientific regimes (Kohler 2002). They reflect changes in the socio-political landscape of scientific life, made more or less important by institutions, social values and the deployment of scientific practices in new contexts (Sturdy and Cooter 1998; Leach and Scoones 2013). Successful exchanges across borderlands can depend on who is attempting to mix disciplines: navigating disciplinary borderlands requires geographical 'know-how' and judgement in order to identify which border practices are 'do-able' (Kohler 2002: 131–133). Thus, biosecurity might be better thought of as 'dynamic configurations of practices and ideas which, under appropriate conditions, can be combined – more or less successfully – with other configurations' (Amsterdamska 2004: 505).

How the borderlands of disease control are crossed and transgressed is the focus of this chapter. First, I turn to the practices of diagnosing cattle with bovine tuberculosis (bTB) in England and Wales. For the UK governments, bTB is one of the most challenging animal diseases, costing the government £100 million each year (see Enticott 2008). In following vets in practice, I show the skills required to successfully diagnose bTB, their social origins and how they cross a borderland between opposing veterinary traditions. Second, I turn to the practices involved in diagnosing bTB in New Zealand. Here a different borderland is described in which farmers came to directly shape the conduct of epidemiology, transforming it beyond its purely scientific origins. Each case speaks to the complicated, ambiguous and 'almost but not quite' nature of disease control. In doing so, these cases raise questions about current and future neoliberal approaches to governing animal disease.

Veterinary borderlands in managing bTB in the UK

As levels of bTB have increased in the UK, governments have become increasingly reliant on private vets to conduct diagnostic tests to check for the presence of disease, whilst the number of government vets conducting tests has also declined. Shifting regulatory activity to the private sector reflects wider public sector reform agendas, such as cutting costs and de-professionalising the civil service. However, these changes also affect the social and material practices of regulation. Firstly, private vets became responsible for the regulation of their own clients, introducing the potential for regulatory capture and imperfect regulatory practices (Black 1976). Secondly, responsibility for training vets to conduct tests also shifted to the private sector: whilst government vets provided initial theoretical training, practical on-farm training was provided by each vet's employer. Government vets were concerned that private vets would conduct regulation in ways that minimised the impact to their clients. Private vets responded by suggesting that government vets were too distant from the problem of bTB. The testing protocol was seen as unrealistic, a product of bureaucracy, and reflected how government vets stuck behind desks were unable to appreciate the realities of 'real' veterinary work.

This new social organisation to disease regulation highlights the pervasiveness of the bureaucratic mode of ordering disease. But disease control still needs to be conducted: new practices have therefore emerged that combine both bureaucratic and expedient forms of working. In short, the practices of disease control are products of both the government and the private sector, and support the aims of each.

Although the rules for bTB testing are formally laid out in European Union Directive 64/432, and an operations manual from the UK government (Animal Health 2010), in practice vets develop practical solutions to cope with the difficulties of conducting bTB tests (see Table 3.1). This does not mean completely replacing bureaucratic protocols with a different style of diagnosing disease, but it does involve learning to situate and adapt the bureaucratic order to a more flexible style. This style of working is referred to as 'local universality' (Timmermans and Berg 1997), reflecting how standards are always transforming and emerging in and through localised negotiations and pre-existing material relations. In short, the bureaucratic mode of ordering never fully succeeds: people – least of all vets – do not submit easily, but actively manage contingencies. This means deploying ad hoc interventions designed to keep modes of ordering more or less on track. In this way, protocols can

Table 3.1 Formal and informal versions of the bTB testing protocol

Formal bovine TB testing protocol	*Informal bovine TB testing protocol*
Day 1	Day 1
– Restrain each animal.	– Attempt to restrain those animals that can be restrained or need restraining. Help farmer set up a race and crush and herd cattle into a holding pen.
– Confirm identity of animal and presence of a clip mark.	– Restrain calves by hand. Farmer will advise when it is safe to test unrestrained or excited cattle.
– Identify animal – read ear tags (beware of multiple ID!).	– Check ear tag. Mistakes can be corrected or made up at a later date. If raining, don't bother unless help is available on the farm.
– Record in testing notebook – breed, age, sex.	– Make note of other lumps.
	– Clip only if necessary: long-haired cattle should be clipped, but dairy cows can be left.
At each injection site:	– Estimate skin thickness at one site by pinching with fingers and/or by assessing the age/breed of the cattle.
– Ensure no blemishes/pathological conditions.	– Inject tuberculin. Palpate skin only if you don't feel the injection go in.
– Clip hair at both sites *separately*.	
– Raise skin fold, measure (callipers) and record in millimetres in notebook (avian on top, bovine below).	
– Upper site for avian – left side of neck for young cattle.	
– Inject 0.1ml intradermally – palpate a nodule ('pea').	

Day 2 (72 hours later)	Day 2
– Restrain each animal.	– Trust farmer to present all cattle tested.
– Confirm identity of animal and presence of a clip mark.	– Help farmer set up crush and race and bring cattle in.
	– Run cattle through the crush – there is no need to restrain each one.
At each injection site:	– Look for reaction lumps or use hand and fingers to feel for lumps.
– Observe, palpate.	– Interpret initial result of test on sight and warn farmer of potential reactors.
– Re-measure skin fold at each site across swelling.	– Only stop and measure using callipers those cattle with suspicious lumps or lumps at both injection sites.
– Record measurements in notebook and describe reaction, e.g. oedema.	– Record skin measurements for reactors, inconclusive reactors and borderline cases.
– Interpret result using official interpretation charts, inform farmer, and spray mark indicating reactor or inconclusive reactor.	– Results for individual animals may be changed depending on the level of disease in the herd.

Source: formal bovine TB testing protocol: Animal Health (2010, chap. 23); informal bovine TB testing protocol: ethnographic fieldwork.

work in 'several locales at the same time', yet they are 'always also located as a product of contingent negotiations and pre-existing institutional and material relations. In sum local universality depends on how standards manage the tensions among transforming work practices while simultaneously being grounded in those practices' (Timmermans and Berg 1997: 297–298). The workings of a protocol therefore emerge from a seemingly chaotic interaction of multiple trajectories which transforms both the expertise of veterinary personnel and the rules of the protocol.

The practices of local universality are located in a biosecurity borderland – not quite bureaucratic, but not anarchic either. As vets test regularly, their bodily interactions with animals and technologies play a significant role in shaping the way they test. Handling hundreds of different animals each day, vets come to understand that the protocol is contingent and can be accomplished by dispensing with some elements or developing new practices to cope with different contexts. For example, cattle do not usually stand still when they are herded into a crush (a restraining device) to be tested. Testing is stressful, and cattle react suddenly and violently. It is not unusual for vets to be injured whilst clipping hair, measuring skin thickness and injecting – as demanded by the protocol. Instead, these steps of the protocol are often ignored and workarounds developed. For some vets, the routine of injecting leads to an embodied understanding of when the tuberculin enters the skin by feeling the feedback in the injecting gun. Only when this feeling is absent do they palpate the skin as required by the protocol to check whether the injection was successful. Other embodied skills are developed through physical interaction with cattle, rendering the use of callipers as specified in the protocol redundant. Take the following example:

> I'm on my way back from testing 400 cattle with Michelle. It's taken all day, but not because she was rigidly following the protocol. At first Michelle started to test the cows using the callipers, but after 10 minutes or so she starts to use her fingers, squeezing the skin together, slightly rolling it between her fingers and then shouting out a skin thickness measurement for me to write down. In the car on the way back I ask her when did she first stop using the callipers and why? Michelle says that she hadn't actually been testing that long, but she could soon tell the skin thickness simply by the sensation of her grip on the callipers. It was as if her hand had become the callipers, but the measuring scale was no longer required. With her sensitive fingers, she now only used the callipers to calibrate her fingers at the start of each test.
>
> (Excerpt from author's field diary)

Vets who adopt these procedures still want to be sure their finger measurements are in some way 'right'. For borderline results, several neck measurements will be taken using callipers close to the reaction site to ensure that the neck thickness taken by hand was accurate. Using the callipers like this to help interpret the test results takes less time and helps ensure the cattle are less agitated. The constant repetition of testing can lead to the conclusion that there is no significant difference in skin thickness at different sites across the neck, meaning there is no need to measure or feel the skin in both places. However, this rule only applies to female cattle: bulls and steers have thicker and more variable necks. Finally, the repetition of testing leads vets to learn the likely skin thickness of cattle according to their age, breed and sex. Some vets normalise skin measurements for cattle – for example, for some vets a Holstein dairy cow is always 7 millimetres, so there is no need to measure each one.

Learning about these methods is not just an individual embodied achievement, but accomplished collectively. Stories of testing are shared at the end of the day in a veterinary practice, sometimes openly, sometimes secretly. These stories celebrate the achievements of the veterinary profession, define its identity, and criticise those they are up against. Accounts of how to manage perceived exceptions to the test results may also be shared.

The accuracy of all medical tests is always subject to some degree of error. In the case of the skin test, there is an extremely low likelihood of false positive results, but between a 20 and 33 per cent chance of a false negative result: the test leaves behind a lot of infection. Reading the test at 'severe interpretation' reduces false negatives but increases false positives. At the same time, vets' on-going relationship with the farmer implicates them in the trajectory of the farm and its future. When judging test results, it is not just what the test tells them that is important, but a complex entanglement of relations taking in the history of disease on the farm, the type of cattle, their locations and the social characteristics of the farmer. Knowing the test means being aware of all the uncertainties, the implications of the test for farmers and their cattle, and being able to make an informed judgement of the likelihood of disease – a kind of 'situated epidemiology'. In this relationship, universalities do not apply; there are always other things to think about, other things to take into account. Care is situated in immediate localised relations, and the ability to make these judgements is what distinguishes veterinary care from the subjectivities of the protocol. Take this instance:

> John is testing 200 cattle on a farm on which the farmer wants to sell up, but the farmer's been down with bTB for the last two years and he can't sell up until he's clear. He needs to have two clear tests before he can get the all-clear, and today is that second test. The dairy cows are tested first on the home farm. The test is being interpreted at standard, but if a reactor is found then all the results will be re-interpreted at severe interpretation. John knows all the interpretation charts like the back of his hand, and as each one comes through he automatically logs whether the cow will be a pass, fail or inconclusive reactor (IR) at both standard and severe. All the cows are clear, but towards the end one walks in and turns out to be an IR on severe, but only just by 1 millimetre. The rest of the cows are clear, and John heads off to a separate group of steers. But here he finds a reactor – there's no getting away from it; the bovine reaction is huge. This means the sale of the farm is off – perhaps. The group of cattle with the reactor had been separated from the main dairy cows for several months – they could be treated as a separate epidemiological unit. In that case, the dairy cows can be interpreted on standard and they are clear to be sold. John thinks about the farm: is there really a problem there? If there was, he would have seen more lumps; there would have been something else to see. But there wasn't, nothing at all. And an IR by 1 millimetre on severe interpretation, when it would have been clear on standard – does that really mean it has bTB? So what to do? John decides to change the measurements for the severe IR, making it clear. This is a practical judgement, based on a veterinary assessment of the likelihood of disease, but connected to the social circumstances of the farmer.

Disease is always indefinite: results may be downgraded or upgraded to suit contingencies. New classifications of disease are developed: the cow that is 'nearly a reactor', 1 millimetre away from becoming a reactor. Vets make a note of these 'near reactors' and depending on the results of other cattle may adjust them accordingly. If there are many reactors on the farm, there is clearly a problem of disease and it is better that the 'near reactors' are reclassified as 'real reactors' and removed as soon as possible. Instead of a linear trajectory, the protocol becomes recursive. New skin measurements may be taken to double-check the measurements taken on the first day; lumps may be measured again and again, and individual results compared to those of the herd as a whole. This process of running through the protocol again and again is required to ensure that the cow and the farmer receive a fair chance.

Testing for bTB leads to a range of borderland practices, resting on situations and contingencies. Vets may complain of the bureaucratic procedures of the protocol, but there is never total rejection, just adaptation. In this way, vets reveal how bureaucracy comes to work through the process of 'local universality': to get something to work, there must be opportunities for leeway and discretion to ensure actors' cooperation. Implicitly, too, this biosecurity borderland is created and supported by government. Government vets are not unaware of these borderland practices, but have done little to prevent them. In relying so heavily on private regulation, governments have found themselves locked into one mode of delivery. In these veterinary practices, income from bTB tests plays a significant role in supporting the provision of veterinary services in marginal rural areas. The entrenchment of bTB testing within private veterinary practice has meant that government faces a dilemma: withdrawing bTB testing from private practices would compromise their ability to maintain not only animal disease surveillance for bTB, but also the wider provision of farm animal veterinary services. The biosecurity borderland of bTB therefore survives because of the need to live with these uncertainties rather than insisting that regulation must be ordered by rationalism.

Veterinary borderlands in New Zealand

The history of bTB control in New Zealand also reveals how a borderland was important to disease control. A New Zealand-wide eradication programme began in 1961, but from the outset farmers expressed concerns about the accuracy of the diagnostic tests being used. In the South Island, resistance to the testing regime was such that farmers refused to test in some areas. For instance, in August 1963, farmers in Tadmor–Matariki called a strike based on the fact that animals were testing positive but at slaughter no evidence of the disease could be found. The same problem was encountered on the West Coast of New Zealand. Farmers in the Karamea area were upset by what they referred to as the 'heifer reactor problem' or 'heiferlumps' – a disproportionate number of heifers reacting to the bTB test but failing to disclose disease at a post-mortem. The loss of these animals was causing financial hardship amongst farmers: it was unsurprising that farmers became disillusioned with the testing regime and refused to test their cattle.

The farmers in Karamea were supported by their vet, Peter Malone, who raised farmers' concerns at a meeting of vets in February 1963, and requested that these heifers be retested six months later rather than slaughtered. In comparison to the government vets running the bTB testing programme, Malone adopted a more pragmatic view to veterinary practice. For Malone, the testing rules laid down by the government left little room for interpretation, yet this was what was required in order to determine whether there were any anomalies to the test, such as the heiferlumps in Karamea. In fact, unbeknown to the government, Malone had already adopted such an approach. At a meeting with government vets, Malone described this method as 'reading light' – taking into account wider environmental and epidemiological factors in deciding the result of a test. These skills took time and experience to develop, but were not unlike those described above in the UK.

When the Department found out about Malone's methods, he was suspended from bTB testing. The Department subsequently sent its assistant director, George Adlam, to investigate the heiferlump problem in Karamea. Reporting back, Adlam suggested that farmers in Karamea

> feel they have been neglected, exploited and forgotten over the years. They are convinced that they cannot expect help and understanding from the central government, and this persecution complex has been strengthened further by the knowledge that the one man who has helped them, and tried to bring their difficulties over high losses from TB testing to the attention of Wellington, has been penalised by having his licence cancelled.

Adlam concluded his report by suggesting that the Department needed to show concern for the fate of farmers and investigate the problem of high reactor rates among young adult cattle.

The government response was to commission a large-scale scientific trial of the bTB test. The 'Flock House' experiment involved testing and slaughtering 500 cattle to determine the specificity of the bTB tests used in New Zealand – in other words, the rate of false positives and false negatives. When the experiment was over and the results published, the government celebrated that the results vindicated their faith in the test. However, for vets like Peter Malone, the fact that the experiment was not conducted in 'field conditions' invalidated the results. Farmers, meanwhile, pointed to the still not inconsiderable number of 'healthy cattle' – that is, false positives – that would end up slaughtered. If the aim of the trial was to change people's minds, it failed.

As Adlam had described, a significant problem was the relationship between government vets and farmers and vets on the ground. The government's view was a paternalistic and autocratic one in which a universal view of disease dominated. Led by Dr Sam Jamieson, the government view was that any approach that was not backed up in science was wrong: clinical interpretations of the meaning of test results, variation, flexibility and accommodation of difference were meaningless. For Jamieson animals either had the disease or did not have the disease; there were no borderlines and certainly no borderland of veterinary practice. Farmers' experiences were dismissed as local myths, whilst vets like Peter Malone were dismissed as troublemakers. In this rational terrain, there were no veterinary borderlands to speak of.

However, the 1970s saw changes to the way disease was managed by the New Zealand government, which precipitated the development of new forms of epidemiology. With Sam Jamieson retiring, new staff with formal training in epidemiology began to influence how the Department should look at and think about bTB. One such change was the development of the 'West Coast rules', a way of accommodating the West Coast's problem of non-specificity responsible for the heiferlumps. The rules reflected the development of a veterinary borderland in which farmer knowledge and experience combined with veterinary practice to make sense of disease in new ways. Until then, various theories had been proposed about the non-specific reactions causing heiferlumps: they might be down to age-related biological changes in cattle, or the interaction of cattle with sphagnum moss, which supported mycobacteria that could sensitise cattle to the bTB test.

The posting of new veterinary staff to the West Coast also led to a new way of dealing with these problems and exploration of these theories. Led by Paul Livingstone, epidemiological analysis of cattle ages testing positive for bTB confirmed the extent of the heiferlump problem. Explaining to the government in Wellington that this was 'wiping farmers out', Livingstone developed an alternative set of testing rules in which any cattle under three years old displaying heiferlumps would be retested after six months. The approach saved the slaughter of around 70 per cent of heifers reacting to the bTB test.

The creation of the West Coast rules was not simply a technical or epidemiological decision. Instead, it reflected a veterinary borderland made possible by a changing relationship between government vets and farmers. There was a growing feeling that disease control could only be successful if it was based on social as well as technical decisions. The recognition of heiferlumps as 'real' therefore went hand in hand with reframing bTB as a social problem requiring 'social work'. This would require listening to and addressing farmers' concerns. In forging a relationship with farmers to understand bTB, government vets on the West Coast had recognised a moral duty of care in getting disease control to work for farmers as much as the government.

Moreover, this 'social work' also involved taking on board ideas from farmers themselves. During his time on the West Coast, Paul Livingstone attended many 'very uncomfortable' meetings with farmers. Until his arrival, farmers' knowledge had been denied as unscientific, with Jamieson expressing his discomfort that farmers could influence the bTB testing regime. Yet for Livingstone farmers' knowledge – what he called 'gumboot epidemiology' – was crucial in redefining how bTB could be recognised and dealt with. Listening to and accepting farmers' 'gumboot epidemiology' were central to the development of the West Coast rules, but also contributed to the development and use of new diagnostic tools and risk-based trading mechanisms to stem the spread of disease. This new style of disease control therefore reflected a shift from a disciplinary style of disease control to one in which the government was a 'moral manager' (cf. Sinding 2004), where the social became as important as the scientific. The resulting hybrid approach balanced different forms of expertise, styles of thinking and geographical biological variations in the way bTB could be made visible. In this balanced approach to disease control, no single view of bTB dominated, but its definition remained a matter of contingencies.

The creation of this veterinary borderland combining technical and farmer expertise was reinforced by the increasing participation of farmers in the management of bTB during the 1970s and 1980s. The Department's original paternalistic scheme had gradually been replaced with an approach in which it acted as an adviser to help farmers find solutions to problems. Regional committees consisting of local farmers were established to contribute to the management of disease and propose their own solutions to keep areas of New Zealand bTB free. The 1980s financial crisis in New Zealand accelerated this approach, as the government withdrew from funding disease control, leading to the creation of a new organisation, the Animal Health Board (AHB) in 1994, to replace the work of the Department (Enticott 2014). The AHB was funded mostly by farmers, with some support from government, and its chairman was a farmer who governed by the maxim 'Farmer pays, farmer says.' In this neoliberal model of animal disease governance, regional committees provided farmers with elected representation and a voice in the national governance of bTB in New Zealand. With farmers now steering the disease control programme, the 1990s therefore saw the AHB further refine and develop the ways by which bTB was made visible by diagnostic tools, reflecting the relationship between disease control and the social environment in which it was situated.

Conclusion: the borderlands of biological economies

These accounts of biosecurity borderlands and the work that goes on within them reveal similar stories about the nature of disease and attempts to prevent its spread. At the same time, they raise broader questions about the most appropriate ways to manage animal disease in biological economies. In particular, this chapter has raised three key points.

The first point is that, in biosecurity borderlands, the nature of animal disease is not fixed or unchanging. Disease is defined not just by different veterinary disciplines but by their interactions with wider social and governmental structures. In looking for disease, relations between the social, the material, the technological and the biological all come to shape how disease is made visible. In the UK, the physical relationship between vets and cattle, and the difficulties of using technologies – like callipers – in dangerous places, shapes how disease comes to be known. In New Zealand, the West Coast heiferlump problem challenged the government's view that disease was universal, leading to protests that refined diagnostic testing. Finally, the ways in which governments organise the conduct of disease control create and legitimise the methods of understanding disease. In the UK, veterinary borderlands emerged in relation to the decision to contract out disease control to the private sector, whilst in New Zealand farmers became part of the government of disease control as neoliberal models of governance replaced a paternalistic model.

Secondly, these accounts reveal that, in the borderlands of biosecurity, no one mode of ordering or discipline dominates. Whereas Wilkinson (2011) sees the rational and expedient modes of ordering disease control as in opposition, in biosecurity borderlands these seemingly opposing ways of approaching disease management are necessarily, if not subtly, part of the same approach. Bureaucratic modes of ordering disease, involving written protocols and paperwork, are central to disease control. In practice, however, the contingencies of disease control mean these bureaucratic modes of ordering fail to fully function, becoming disrupted by the heterogeneous relations that configure how disease control unfolds in practice. Yet neither is this mode of ordering fully replaced. Instead, modes of ordering become 'locally universal' – adapted to the situation at hand to get the job done. Whilst these practices are reminiscent of the expediency talked about by government officials at times of disease emergencies, they are fully neither one nor the other. Protocols are never fully jettisoned, just as the need to get the job done does not lead to a complete free-for-all.

The same is true in New Zealand, where boundary crossings between different approaches to disease management result in an approach which never fully aligns itself to one or another discipline. So-called 'gumboot epidemiology' combines quite traditional elements of veterinary epidemiology, whilst reflecting the value of farmers' own understandings of disease. At the same time, 'gumboot epidemiology' reflects the need to take farmers' experiences of disease into account. In this view, disease control cannot be simply an exercise in scientific control, but must be equally an exercise in social work. This then is the borderland of biosecurity: a zone of intense entanglement where sides and perspectives are bound together, making them impossible to break apart. As Kohler (2002: 308) suggests, navigating these borderlands involves an art of borrowing, adapting and blending, whilst always remaining aware of the limits to cultural borrowing.

The final question is what to make of this biosecurity borderland: where should it sit in attempts to manage disease in biological economies? Should borderlands be encouraged and valued? Or is the role of social science to note their presence as a way of highlighting alternative ways of biological governance? Certainly, in exploring the work of biosecurity, the chapter reveals the value of social science in contributing to an understanding of the work of biosecurity. In one sense, social scientists enter their own borderland when investigating animal disease, traditionally the preserve of veterinary epidemiologists, revealing that the messy nature of disease control can be unsettling just as much as it requires working across disciplinary boundaries. For biological economies there is much to be gained by social scientists contributing to this new disciplinary borderland. Moreover, the value of exploring borderlands lies in uncovering what is lost when some modes of ordering come to dominate approaches to disease control. In this case, the reliance on centralised government control and bureaucratic processes silences other ways of knowing and dealing with disease. Unpacking the borderlands of biosecurity may help lead to new approaches to managing disease in the biological economy. One such approach – 'participatory epidemiology' (Catley et al. 2012) – recognises the value of different forms of knowledge found amongst different disciplines and communities. Arguably, the experiences of the West Coast in New Zealand represent an early form of this approach. Despite its promise, such an approach is not straightforward, calling for reflexivity and humility amongst disease control experts (Leach and Scoones 2013) and raising questions over which farmers and kinds of farming are able to reshape disease and for what purpose. It may be that, by involving farmers in the management of disease, some types of farming and types of diseases are prioritised over others for the purposes of profit over animal welfare. Yet, as Kohler (2002) suggests, crossing boundaries and engaging in the complexities of the borderland have always required careful thought and reflexive awareness. Developing forms of disease control that open up rather than silence conversations between different disciplines and communities may raise awkward questions, but, as the history of disease management suggests, flexible and place-specific practices have more chance of success. From the stories from the UK and New Zealand presented in this chapter, what is clear is that disease management belongs to no one discipline, but its practices are constantly in the making, varying from place to place across a veterinary borderland.

References

Amsterdamska, O. (2004) 'Achieving disbelief: thought styles, microbial variation, and American and British epidemiology, 1900–1940', *Studies in History and Philosophy of Science Part C: Studies in History and Philosophy of Biological and Biomedical Sciences*, vol. 35, pp. 483–507.

Animal Health (2010) *Operations Manual*, Animal Health, Worcester.

Bickerstaff, K. and Simmons, P. (2004) 'The right tool for the job? Modeling, spatial relationships, and styles of scientific practice in the UK foot and mouth crisis', *Environment and Planning D: Society and Space*, vol. 22, pp. 393–412.

Black, D. (1976) *The Behaviour of Law*, Academic Press, New York.

Catley, A., Alders, R. G. and Wood, J. L. N. (2012) 'Participatory epidemiology: approaches, methods, experiences', *Veterinary Journal*, vol. 191, pp. 151–160.

Donaldson, A. (2008) 'Biosecurity after event: risk politics and animal disease', *Environment and Planning A*, vol. 40, pp. 1552–1567.

Enticott, G. (2008) 'The spaces of biosecurity: prescribing and negotiating solutions to bovine tuberculosis', *Environment and Planning A*, vol. 40, pp. 1568–1582.

Enticott, G. (2014) 'Biosecurity and the bioeconomy: the case of disease regulation in the UK and New Zealand', in T. Marsden and A. Morley (eds), *Sustainable Food Systems: Building a New Paradigm*, Routledge, Abingdon, pp. 122–142.

Galison, P. (1996) 'Computer simulations and the trading zone', in P. Galison and D. J. Strump (eds), *The Disunity of Science: Boundaries, Contexts and Power*, Stanford University Press, Stanford, CA, pp. 118–157.

Higgins, V. and Dibden, J. (2011) 'Biosecurity, trade liberalisation, and the (anti)politics of risk analysis: the Australia–New Zealand apples dispute', *Environment and Planning A*, vol. 43, pp. 393–409.

Hinchliffe, S., Allen, J., Lavau, S., Bingham, N. and Carter, S. (2013) 'Biosecurity and the topologies of infected life: from borderlines to borderlands', *Transactions of the Institute of British Geographers*, vol. 38, pp. 531–543.

King, D. A., Peckham, C., Waage, J. K., Brownlie, J. and Woolhouse, M. E. J. (2006) 'Infectious diseases: preparing for the future', *Science*, vol. 313, pp. 1392–1393.

Kohler, R. E. (2002) *Landscapes and Labscapes: Exploring the Lab–Field Border in Biology*, Chicago University Press, London.

Latour, B. (1988) *The Pasteurization of France*, Harvard University Press, Cambridge, MA.

Law, J. (1994) *Organizing Modernity*, Blackwell, London.

Law, J. (2006) 'Disaster in agriculture: or foot and mouth mobilities', *Environment and Planning A*, vol. 38, pp. 227–239.

Law, J. and Mol, A. (2011) 'Veterinary realities: what is foot and mouth disease?', *Sociologia Ruralis*, vol. 51, pp. 1–16.

Leach, M. and Scoones, I. (2013) 'The social and political lives of zoonotic disease models: narratives, science and policy', *Social Science and Medicine*, vol. 88, pp. 10–17.

Mol, A. and Law, J. (1994) 'Regions, networks and fluids: anaemia and social topology', *Social Studies of Science*, vol. 24, pp. 641–671.

Sinding, C. (2004) 'The specificity of medical facts: the case of diabetology', *Studies in History and Philosophy of Science Part C: Studies in History and Philosophy of Biological and Biomedical Sciences*, vol. 35, pp. 545–559.

Sturdy, S. and Cooter, R. (1998) 'Science, scientific management, and the transformation of medicine in Britain *c*. 1870–1950', *History of Science*, vol. 114, pp. 421–466.

Timmermans, S. and Berg, M. (1997) 'Standardization in action: achieving local universality through medical protocols', *Social Studies of Science*, vol. 27, pp. 273–305.

Wilkinson, K. (2011) 'Organised chaos: an interpretive approach to evidence-based policy making in Defra', *Political Studies*, vol. 59, pp. 959–977.

4 Re-shaping 'soft gold'

Fungal agency and the bioeconomy in the caterpillar fungus market assemblage

Janka Linke

Introduction

Caterpillar fungus (Lat. *Ophiocordyceps sinensis*) is definitely not one of the 'cuddly' non-human actors with whom humans have built long-standing sympathetic relationships. Rather, it is a parasitic sac fungus feeding on the larvae of ghost moths (*Thitarodes* and other species) at altitudes between 3,000 and 5,000 metres in eastern areas of the Tibetan plateau and adjacent regions of the Himalayas. Usually, the host larvae of *O. sinensis* resist the low temperatures of the Tibetan winters in underground tunnels. Once a larva is infested, however, the fungus takes control and steers the larva close to the surface, where the fungus resumes dining on the body of the insect, ultimately leading to the death of the latter. In the end, the body is completely filled with mycelium, while the exoskeleton of the larva is left intact (Winkler 2009). In May or June, the fungus develops a fruiting body from the head of the former insect, resembling a blade of grass when it protrudes from the ground. This is the point of the life cycle when thousands of human gatherers start crawling through the high-altitude pastures in search of 'soft gold' (*ruan huangjin*).

In July 2013, one kilogram of premium-quality caterpillar fungus (*chongcao*)[1] fetched RMB 580,000 at retail stores in the megacity of Chengdu (Sichuan province), by far exceeding the price of gold.[2] Dried specimens are added as an ingredient to exquisite dishes at dinners and banquets, claimed to cure all kinds of ailments from hair loss to cancer, and given as a gift to others who might return a favour at some time in the future. Far from being a staple, it is nevertheless placed within agri-food networks as a luxury item by routines and practices which surround the distribution and consumption of caterpillar fungus. Meanwhile, its collection is 'inextricably linked' (Gertel and Le Heron 2011: 7) to the livelihoods (Chambers and Conway 1991; DFID 1999; Bohle 2001) of farmers and herders in or adjacent to caterpillar fungus-producing pastures of the Tibetan plateau. Thus the fungus bridges the economic gap between the industrialized, fast-developing eastern metropolises of the country and the 'poor' and 'backward' areas of the Chinese west.

The thriving market network which has evolved around the fungus provides the major source of cash income for more than 300,000 inhabitants of the Tibetan plateau (GMMC 2010: 89). Harvest sales can contribute up to 80 per cent of household income (Gruschke 2012: 367) in areas which traditionally have been characterized by agrarian and (semi-)nomadic subsistence strategies.

The relatively new rush for 'soft gold' has resulted in a growing complexity in terms of market participants, marketing strategies, and practices. Recently, biopharmaceutical companies have started to compete with informal kinship enterprises consisting of ethnic minority members; and researchers equipped with biotechnological devices and knowledge promote artificial mass production, while Tibetan nomads have commercialized the access to those pastures where natural caterpillar fungus can be harvested. In this chapter I focus on the competing actions of human and non-human players, and particularly on investigating the relationship between bioeconomic forces and the commodity itself within the caterpillar fungus market assemblage. Particularly, I ask how the marketization of a natural medicinal foodstuff (that is, caterpillar fungus) is enacted in a bioeconomic setting embedded in the Chinese political agenda.

Approaching fungal–human relationships in the caterpillar fungus market assemblage

China's rapid economic growth over the past two decades has resulted in severe challenges: major environmental problems, concerns about depleting resources, and food safety. To address these issues, China has taken several initiatives to develop its bioeconomy. The appliance of biotechnology in fields such as agriculture, waste treatment, energy and health care is intended to expand economic growth in sustainable ways.

The shift towards a bioeconomy, which is happening within China as well as on a global scale, is characterized by new forms of control over nature such that reproductive processes within nature itself (for example in the form of genetic modification) are manipulated. Based on Kitchen and Marsden (2011: 757), I suggest that entities promoting and realizing the bioeconomy are defined through: (1) their domination over the laws of nature itself; (2) control over biotechnology, knowledge and practices related to bioeconomic processes; and (3) their link with the political agenda of tackling the (global) issue of resource scarcity. This chapter considers the alignment of biopharmaceutical enterprises as relatively new actors and related bioeconomic knowledge within the distinct setting of the Chinese caterpillar fungus market. Following Çalışkan and Callon (2010), I draw on the concept of markets as 'socio-technological agencements', encompassing elements as heterogeneous as rules and conventions, material and technical devices, texts, knowledge, and human and non-human actors bearing various skills and competencies. This notion of markets resonates strongly with the Biological Economies research group's understanding of how 'value is generated within relations among products, people, places, animals and plants . . . without prioritising the role of specific actors and plants' (Rosin and Lewis 2013: 175).

Departing from Callon and colleagues, however, and arguing in line with recent research by Krzywoszynska (2015), I hold that its special features render caterpillar fungus a commodity that comes with many uncertainties in regard to its qualities and economic value from the point of view of consumers, entrepreneurs, scientists and traders. Human actors struggle to render caterpillar fungus a secure and passive commodity, which, according to Çalışkan and Callon (2010: 5), is a necessary precondition for the creation of a stable market network. In contrast, caterpillar fungus is approached here as an actor with the ability 'to *make* other actors *do* unexpected things' (Latour 2005: 129, original emphasis), centring human agency and attracting control in the process of market making. Many of the outcomes of the assemblage are thus the results of the combined characteristics of the caterpillar fungus itself. It takes, I argue, an active part in re-configuring the caterpillar fungus market and shaping notions of value (cf. Robbins and Marks 2009: 176).

The merger between my particular understanding of the bioeconomy, marketization and more-than-human approaches (in the spirit of FitzSimmons and Goodman 1998; Goodman 2001; Whatmore 2002) reveals how much human labour goes into disciplining and controlling the 'lively materialities' of caterpillar fungus (Henry and Roche 2013: 205) and highlights the central role of emerging practices of knowledge and the development of scientific methods and techniques in pursuing the goal of taming caterpillar fungus as a product ready to sell (cf. Atkins 2010).

In this chapter, I trace the trajectories of knowledge, expertise and capital which are constantly emerging but are also vulnerable to a range of contextual influences. By this I mean that caterpillar fungus as a commodity is an 'intrinsically cultural construction' (Bestor 2004: 129) whereby the creation and realization of value take place in a complex web of cultural and social dynamics. Entangled in this variety of relationships, it is constantly being charged with symbolic and material meaning through social practices and discourses (cf. Zader 2012: 56) in what could be called a high-risk environment where, at the same time, administrative regulations are largely absent, and food scares prevail in a society which has been unsettled by many food scandals over the past years. Against this background, I shed light on some of the many aspects of the cultural, scientific and lay politics of knowledge which bridge the worlds of production and consumption in the making of the caterpillar fungus market. The surrounding discursive entanglements are constantly re-framing caterpillars, fungus, humans, technology and science into an apparently stable market system.

The empirical data provided in this chapter are based on nine months of fieldwork conducted in the Chinese provinces of Qinghai (mainly Xining and the Tibetan autonomous prefectures of Golok and Yushu), Guangdong (Guangzhou, Shenzhen) and Sichuan (Chengdu) from 2009 to 2012. My methods included qualitative (such as participant observation, expert and biographical interviews, and group discussions) as well as quantitative approaches (such as a household questionnaire with 124 participants at the caterpillar fungus wholesale market in Xining). For this chapter I have also consulted an array of Chinese secondary literature and films available on the internet. Chinese quotes have been translated into English by the author, and key Chinese terms have been inserted into the text using the pinyin transcription.

Valuing caterpillar fungus

The application of caterpillar fungus as a tonic and aphrodisiac in traditional Tibetan medicine can be traced back to the fifteenth century. The two main traditional Chinese treatises *Bencao Congxin* (New Compilation of Materia Medica) and *Bencao Gangmu Shiyi* (Supplement to the Compendium of Materia Medica), from the eighteenth century, document its efficacy against lung and kidney problems as well as its special effect in the treatment of coughs (Winkler 2009: 294; Liang 2011: 3ff.). In the mid-1990s, 1 kilogram of caterpillar fungus, on average, cost about RMB 2,000 to RMB 4,000 in the harvest areas before prices mounted to tens of thousands of US dollars per kilogram in 2003.

Caterpillar fungus is marketed as a panacea, although its medical efficacy is still contested. Ignoring the fact that many scientific reports on its pharmacological functions appear to contradict each other (Buenz et al. 2005; Liang 2011: 5), some Chinese publications are quite confident in promoting its medicinal value. They suggest its use for combating lung and liver problems, high blood pressure, coughs and asthma, male and female infertility, cancer and more (GMMC 2010: 50). My interview partners would often refer especially to stories they had heard about someone who had been cured from cancer by regular doses of caterpillar fungus or whose life had at least been significantly prolonged by it, a narrative also fostered by popular television shows. Closely linked to the construction of caterpillar fungus as a wonder drug is the emergence of the global functional food industry. According to one Chinese saying, 'Food is better than medicine', and Chinese reference books on caterpillar fungus often encompass a whole section devoted to food recipes to promote health (Chen et al. 2010; Zhang 2011).

However, to understand the current 'hype' and rise in prices, one has to take into account other factors, such as the growing number of wealthy people in China. To them, caterpillar fungus serves as a status symbol and an object of pride, signifying the rapid economic development of their country. Buying, exchanging and consuming the species are actions of prestige and give face to each party in the exchange. Caterpillar fungus has come to play an extremely important role in the exchange of gifts among Chinese people, where presents act as lubricators of social ties (*guanxi*) (Nojonen 2003). Interview partners often associate the practice of giving caterpillar fungus to others with corruption (*fubai*). It is also often referred to as an alternative form of 'currency' (*huobi*).[3]

Another dynamic which has fuelled demand for caterpillar fungus is the construction of the narrative of the fungus being a scarce resource close to extinction.

Clearly, with thousands of people rushing to high-altitude pastures every year in the hunt for the 'soft gold', caterpillar fungus has been subject to mass exploitation in recent years, all the more since it cannot be cultivated. However, *chongcao* has proven to be quite resilient to its large-scale exploitation so far (Winkler 2009). Advertisement and business cards – essential items in any kind of business relationship and exchange – often use images of unspoiled Tibetan lands, snowy mountains and the traditional nomadic lifestyle, which is thought to reflect an ideal way of humans living in harmony with nature. The 'mysterious' caterpillar fungus evokes images of 'purity' and 'nature', and an exotic, harsh environment, which stands in sharp contrast to years of increasing Chinese urbanization, environmental pollution and never-ending food scandals.

Procuring safe caterpillar fungus in China

Food safety has been of great concern to consumers and producers alike over the past few years in China. In reaction to the ever-growing list of tainted foodstuffs, a new Food Safety Law was introduced in 2009. However, in their fight against the illegal use of prohibited ingredients and additives, and the 'recycling' of expired foodstuffs, government authorities have been struggling to implement an effective food safety system. The lack of overall binding and transparent regulations, and stable meanings of labels such as 'green' and 'organic', as well as ambiguities and overlap between overseeing departments, remain major obstacles to the implementation of better food safety standards. Understandably, the recent series of severe food safety scandals has 'created distrust in the Chinese food system' (Ortega et al. 2011). People buy foreign baby food and German milk in Chinese supermarkets because they place more trust in them than in domestic products, and the Chinese public 'consistently considers food safety a top concern' (Yan 2013: 248).[4]

Despite the high prices and unbroken demand, a certain atmosphere of distrust and uncertainty also prevails in the caterpillar fungus market. Basically, two sources of uncertainties can be distinguished. The first stems from the agency of the commodity itself. As the Grassland Monitoring and Management Center, Chinese Ministry of Agriculture, puts it, 'Since there is no consensus on the distribution and bioactive components of *Ophiocordyceps sinensis*, uniform grading standards have never been agreed at the central level. On the market, *Ophiocordyceps sinensis* is graded basically in line with its size and appearance' (GMMC 2010: 74). In other words, although dealing with one and the same species, its appearance can be very diverse according to its place of collection, altitude and maturity. Owing to the absence of official quality regulations and standards for caterpillar fungus, over time traders have established their own informal grading system, which basically aims at identifying how many pieces make up one pound (*jin*), the standard measuring unit on the wholesale market, which is mainly according to size, humidity content, colour and intactness. Still, dealers struggle to discipline it into a passive commodity. These kinds of instabilities naturally translate across to the behaviour of consumers, who often don't know how to judge the quality of the caterpillar fungus offered to them.

The second source of anxiety is human 'manufactured' risks. During my work on the wholesale caterpillar fungus market in Xining, capital of Qinghai province, traders used to complain about the 'chaotic' (*hunluan*) condition of the market and the lack of standardization (*guifanhua*) and management (*guanli*). Many were calling for better governance and monitoring of market activities. Indeed, the absence of a legal framework in combination with the profitability of the trade has led unscrupulous harvesters and dealers to become quite inventive regarding techniques to adulterate the weight and increase profits from the sale of caterpillar fungus. Several television shows documented these market 'secrets' (*mimi*) or 'chaotic conditions' (*luanxiang*),[5] warning consumers about how to protect themselves from contaminated goods.

These conditions have led to the growing focus of traders on gaining their customers' trust through a form of bottom-up self-standardization. This might involve the acquisition of scanners, voluntary registration as private enterprises, the acquisition of hygiene certifications and, if possible, the direct purchasing of 'first-hand' products, that is, caterpillar fungus that is directly procured from gatherers in the harvest areas. By contrast, a more top-down approach to food safety is demonstrated in the elaboration of biotechnologies intended to solve related problems in China.[6]

The growing body of literature on food safety usually focuses either on legal and management systems intended to improve Chinese food safety control systems and reduce public and international concerns (Jia and Jukes 2013) or on Chinese consumer perceptions of issues related to food safety (Ho et al. 2006; Liu et al. 2014). In what follows, I focus on a few biopharmaceutical companies in the caterpillar fungus industry navigating within this framework of a public unsettled by food scares and the official policy of using biotechnology to enable sustainable use of caterpillar fungus resources and secure food safety for this 'stubborn' commodity.

Translating bioeconomy

Systematic scientific study of *O. sinensis* dates back to the 1950s. Especially since the 1980s, there has been much progress with regard to strain identification, mycelium fermentation, moth feeding, and artificial cultivation of strains. Other fields of interest have involved research into chemical components and molecular biology and the development of products derived from caterpillar fungus strains. Research is carried out by various Chinese research institutes and – since the rise in demand at the beginning of the 2000s – also by private biopharmaceutical companies.

Modern research and biotechnological innovation, undertaken with the aim of mass cultivation of caterpillar fungus, is supported by the recurring narrative of limited natural caterpillar fungus resources and the environmental damage caused by harvesting practices. It is argued that natural resources are declining, owing to the severe imbalance between supply and demand in the caterpillar fungus market. Among other measures, increased artificial cultivation research is seen as a suitable approach towards the solution of these pressing issues (Han 2009).

That being said, any breakthrough regarding the artificial mass cultivation of *O. sinensis* isn't anywhere near. Humans are not able to control the infection of the host larva with the fungus and the subsequent creation of a reproductive stroma (Han 2009: 51) and, according to the estimates of Professor Shen Nanying, pioneer of biological research on *O. sinensis*, won't achieve this step before 2030.[7] However, Chinese pharmacies offer a broad range of products derived from fermented *O. sinensis* fungal strands (hyphae), based on the patented 'technique of *O. sinensis* production by fermentation' of Shen Nanying. Advertising and literature on caterpillar fungus suggest that these products contain similar chemical components and, thus, possess the same medical efficacy as natural caterpillar fungus. It is suggested that products derived from cultivated fungal strains could serve as a substitute for caterpillar fungus on a large scale and, thus, help to ease the huge pressure on the natural resource (for example Han 2009).

Qinghai Everest Aweto Pharmaceutical Company, Ltd is striving for 'the harmonious coexistence between man and nature'. Founded in 2005, this biopharmaceutical company produces *O. sinensis* fermented hypha powder,[8] creating an 'artificial substitute for the natural rare' product. This is based on Shen Nanying's patent and uses bioengineering technology. The company says that it wishes to protect Qinghai Tibetan plateau's rare medicinal resources of *O. sinensis*, and also maintain the ecological balance in the region, which acts as the source of the Yangzi, Yellow and Mekong rivers: 'Because of growing consumer demand, natural *O. sinensis* resources are increasingly being diminished. . . . Consequently, the industrialized production of natural *O. sinensis* substitutes, such as *O. sinensis* hypha powder and finished goods, has become inevitable' (QEAPC 2010a). In a brochure aimed at attracting domestic investors, the company highlights the congruence of its project with the official Chinese policy: 'The Chinese government promotes research and development of artificial plants or substitutes in regard to rare medicinal herbs. This is why our concept of replacing natural caterpillar fungus with artificially grown hypha powder is suitable to the requirements of Chinese resource management' (QEAPC 2010a). In this spirit, the company works on its capacity to produce 110 tons of artificial caterpillar fungus powder per year (QEAPC 2013). The powder is used to produce a series of products, such as soft capsules, film-coated tablets, powder, hard capsules, pills and a special teabag. The company claims that the artificially produced powder is significantly richer in regard to its biochemical compounds, and reports a much higher proportion of amino acids, polysaccharides and adenosine than in natural caterpillar fungus (QEAPC 2010b).

This biopharmaceutical case study illuminates the intertwining, overlapping and colliding interests of human and non-human actors within the setting of markets as 'socio-technical agencements'. Biopharmaceutical companies that produce artificial fungal substrates draw on the discourse of depleting caterpillar fungus resources.[9] They also have command over the appropriate technology and knowledge to intervene in the reproductive cycle of caterpillar fungus. Theoretically, they possess attributes that should render them competitive within the caterpillar fungus economy. Yet, at the most, they serve a market parallel to the market for natural caterpillar fungus, with hardly any influence on pricing mechanisms or demand for *O. sinensis*, thus failing to accomplish one of their major stated goals, that is, to protect natural resources and the environment. This is, for instance, reflected in the very low prices for the artificial substitutes, which hardly reach one-tenth of natural caterpillar fungus prices (Yuan 2012). Cultured *chongcao* products are dismissed as cheap imitations (Liang 2011: 6), while natural caterpillar fungus is appreciated even more in the eyes of consumers, owing to the fact that it cannot be artificially produced. Similar to Callon's scallops (1986), the process of translation within the bioeconomic paradigm, to date, has failed. Rather, *O. sinensis* has to be judged as an actor in its own right within the market setting, 'escaping' biotechnological control. This may in part explain the comparative lack of corporate control over the commodity network. However, this setting is undergoing continuous change, as elaborated in the following section.

Creating new values

> When I visited Qinfen Alley[10] in the summer of 2004, I started thinking: "Such a precious thing, more precious than gold, how can it be that it is traded and stored in such a backward [*luohou*] way?" I was shocked, actually. . . . ' Voice-over: . . . *At home, he discovered even more scary things.* 'I encountered many fake products, such as *Cordyceps hawkesii*,[11] pieces that had been kitted manually, pieces that had been smeared with heavy metals or others with inserted iron or lead wires. . . . When I examined my purchase under the microscope I was shocked further when I discovered how much polluted it was by sediments, and other substances, such as pathogenic bacteria, parasites. . . . I would never have expected it to be that dirty. . . . Now, people could say: "Just wash it, and that's it!" But after many experiments I found out that it loses many of its active ingredients during the process of washing.[12]

The man talking quietly about his alleged first encounters with caterpillar fungus has regularly appeared on Chinese television shows since 2006, telling roughly the same story. He is the founder of a private sci-tech company (Qinghai Chuntian Medical Resource Utilization[13]), which has notched up major successes regarding sales figures of its caterpillar fungus products in the last few years. Founded in 2003, it claims to be one of the central leading high-tech and industrializing enterprises in Qinghai province. The company's marketing strategy is made clear in the recurring messages being sent out to consumers, such as in the quoted television documentary, which can be summed up as the following. Consuming natural caterpillar fungus is not safe. It either is polluted by dirt, bacteria or parasites or has been contaminated in the 'backward' caterpillar fungus trade.[14] Washing is not a good option, since it destroys valuable nutritional ingredients. Adulteration on the other hand is not easily detected by ordinary consumers. However, the solution is at hand, in the form of '100 per cent pure caterpillar fungus powder pills' which are gained from natural caterpillar fungus by means of an 'ultra-micro cell disruption technique' and allegedly are 'seven times more efficient' than natural, unprocessed caterpillar fungus. The company considers this an achievement towards overcoming the 'inefficient and lavish' consumption of natural *O. sinensis*[15] and a rational exploitation and sustainable development of caterpillar fungus resources by means of high-tech methods.

While initially placing emphasis on the so-called 'cell disruption technique', which is, strictly speaking, a physical processing method, and other technical data, the company's focus has undergone a shift towards stressing the safety of its products:

> [The company] continues to provide *safer*, more efficient and more economic caterpillar fungus products for consumers. . . . Through its strict *quality control system* it has advanced the overall *standardization* level in the caterpillar fungus industry, accelerated the pace of transformation and upgrading of the entire industry . . . and realized . . . a *stabilization of product quality*.[16]

The company's web presence documents how much effort is put into creating the quality of 'safety' for Chinese consumers. Much room is given, for example, to the 'promise' that caterpillar fungus pure powder tablets are made of 100 per cent natural caterpillar fungus only. In the event of non-compliance, the company agrees to compensate consumers by 100 times the purchase price. Furthermore, all the production staff are held liable regarding the 100 per cent purity of the company's products, and cooperating partners and teams are equally held responsible for the upholding of the promise.

This marketing strategy seems to be paying off, at least for those who can afford these products. The caterpillar fungus pure powder tablets, in particular, seem to be very popular with Chinese consumers as gifts. These products come in boxes of 27 or 81 tablets. The 81-piece box, for instance, contains 28.35 grams of processed caterpillar fungus and is sold for a nationwide standard price of RMB 29,888. Making a projection on the price of RMB 1,054 per gram, we thus arrive at the astronomical figure of RMB 1,054,250 per kilogram.[17] In 2014, Qinghai Chuntian announced on its company website that it planned to process about 30 tons of caterpillar fungus over the next few years,[18] which, if accomplished, would mean control over a massive share of the available market supply.

All in all, the company has managed to create new margins for the economic value of caterpillar fungus by merging the narrative of the scarce resource with

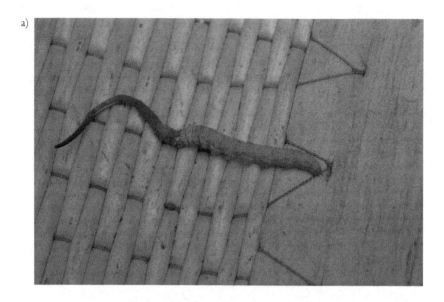

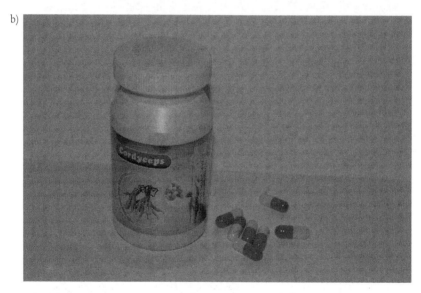

Figure 4.1 a) 'Soft gold': fresh caterpillar fungus (*Ophiocordyceps sinensis*) specimen; b) caterpillar fungus product from cultivated fungal strains

sci-tech innovation to create 'food safety'. In alternative food networks, the conditions under which a product is grown and the diversity (or uncertainty) linked to these can be valuable attributes for consumers (Krzywoszynska 2015). In China, however, where the social, political and cultural contexts differ dramatically, 'food safety' seems to be a value which is placed above all others, given the constant threat of new food scandals.[19] The high-tech processing of O. *sinensis* allows definite standards and quality monitoring. The tools of science and technology have rendered caterpillar fungus a passive thing which is always the same and can always be quantified and qualified by anyone.

The case study demonstrates the important role of trust, transparency and information in the processes of qualification and marketization, in this case accomplished through an extensive and clever marketing campaign through which the company has put itself in direct competition with the traditional market system. In Qinghai, the site of my empirical fieldwork, people with access to pastures, that is, primarily (former) Tibetan pastoralists, are in control of the harvest. Harvesters bring small amounts of O. *sinensis* to local markets, where larger quantities are pooled by middlemen. Almost all of the harvest is channelled through the caterpillar fungus wholesale market in Xining, the capital of Qinghai province. The market is dominated by Chinese Muslim minorities, who organize the trade based on informal kinship and family enterprises. Significantly, caterpillar fungus harvesters, middlemen and wholesalers tend to depend on it as their single source of income, while the mainly Han-Chinese retailers in major Chinese cities have considerable diversification of their businesses. With the alignment of new actors in the assemblage, it remains to be seen how they are going to react to the challenge of a possible shift of the current power relations, and who might benefit or lose out in the end.

Conclusion

In this chapter I have discussed the interactions between society, politics, technology, economy and nature through the specific lens of marketization in the Chinese bioeconomic setting. This approach allows us to consider how quality and values are constructed in an environment where the commodity, people and their technical tools, guided by specific discourses, knowledges and emotions, continue to shape one another.

Thinking through the assemblage as being co-constituted by humans and non-humans alike lays bare dimensions and entanglements which would otherwise have been neglected. Chinese consumers, for instance, often don't have the faintest idea about how crucial a role caterpillar fungus plays for several thousand people as the main, and sometimes only, source of income. The approach has proved helpful in confronting the empirical messiness and complexity of what makes up the caterpillar fungus market, and for exploring how relations are 'modified and modify further productive, managerial and sales practices' (Krzywoszynska 2012: 42). Producing knowledge has turned out to be a crucial practice of how assemblying is achieved (cf. Le Heron et al. 2013: 222).

Bringing the biological economies approach and marketization into tension and intellectual scrutiny brings back into focus the goal-orientedness of human action in market settings. The post-humanist reading allows human agency to be seen 'as an effect as much as a cause of particular materialisations'

(Krzywoszynska 2012: 42). Many outcomes of assemblages may thus be temporary and contingent, since the webs of relationships are always too complex and performative to be fully understood. This, however, must not distract from the fact that, in market contexts, humans act based on their own inherent logics, that is, within the demanding context to 'sell their stuff', as caterpillar fungus traders put it in their market language. In order to achieve this goal, humans seek to eliminate sources of uncertainty. The multiple ontologies of the assemblage, elements in association, and attempted hybridities are thus revealed as being stabilizations that are returned to time and time again. At the same time, they mutate and are mobile in the sense that they are re-deployed (cf. Rosin et al.'s 2013 notion of provenance and its role in creating stability).

The assemblage approach sharpens our understanding of the fact that stability, in regard to either food safety or corporate control, may never be achieved. Flows of knowledge, expertise and capital, as well as value, are not objectively given and stable (cf. Carolan 2013: 177). After all, the fungus has proven to be difficult to control. Its many entangled stories demonstrate once more that 'the material interactions that underpin the power of experts, capital, development, and planning also subvert the exclusive control upon which such people and arrangements depend. In the socio-material structures upon which power rests lie the seeds of their own collapse' (Robbins and Marks 2009: 190). New technologies are developed as responses to problems caused by earlier techno-scientific projects (cf. Mitchell 2002: 42; Stuart 2011). The assemblage approach, thus, allows a 'decentering of power' (Bear 2013: 24) and a focus on the question of how certain actors get others to comply with them: when and how do players emerge that adhere to the wider capitalistic forces and develop the power to put regulations and constraints on others in a way that threatens their livelihoods? And when and how, amidst the 'lightness of becoming' (Carolan 2013: 178), are disruptive processes initiated which end up in irreversible changes owing to the tendency of people to superimpose projects on 'complex interdependencies that are not – and cannot be – fully understood' (Scott 1998)? How do players who don't display much interest in restructuring the status quo stay 'in the knowledge and power game' (Haraway 1988: 577)? And, even if we take the entanglements of human and material worlds into account, how can policies be designed which 'attend to immanent change' (Bear 2013: 36)?

There may be no widely applicable conclusion or general answer, as I suggest that any assemblage is 'deeply contextually situated and highly experimental' (Le Heron et al. 2013: 222). Chinese policy makers have so far eschewed decision making in the context of the caterpillar fungus market, exactly because it is charged with too many elements such as issues of ethnicity, Chinese minority politics, rural and urban development in China's western regions, environment protection goals, and education standards. Practices of market management stay 'in construction', which reminds us more of a mode of experimentation where taking risks is welcome (Whatmore 2006: 606). After all, the making of values in the caterpillar fungus market is undergoing a constant process of re- and co-construction and therefore will be disrupted and re-shaped with changing courses of interaction.

Notes

1 *Chongcao* is short for the Chinese *dongchong xiacao*, meaning 'winter-worm-summer-grass', an allusion to the distinct life cycle of the species. In this chapter, I use all three of the terms, caterpillar fungus, *Ophiocordyceps sinensis* (*O. sinensis*) and *chongcao*, to refer to this unique commodity.
2 Corresponding to €73,000 (http://www.onvista.de/devisen/Euro-Yuan-EUR-CNY). One kilogram of gold cost about €34,000 in February 2015 (http://goldprice.org/, accessed 25 February 2015).
3 The observations from this section show considerable overlap with Liang's (2011) research, which investigates the socio-political and historical background of value construction in the emerging caterpillar fungus market.
4 Additionally, I recommend a case study on Chinese consumers and their increasing concern about the quality and safety of pork products (Barcellos et al. 2013: 445). Another recent study shows how Chinese consumers gain information on food safety and what kind of information sources they most likely trust the most (Liu et al. 2014).
5 For example 'Food safety in action: the secrets of caterpillar fungus' from the popular show *Consumer Viewpoint*, released on 31 May 2011, http://jingji.cntv.cn/20110531/111060.shtml, accessed 24 February 2015.
6 http://www.cncbd.org.cn/News/Detail/4856, accessed 25 February 2015.
7 Interview, 18 June 2010.
8 Fermentation here refers to the controlled bulk growth of *O. sinensis* hyphae (*Hirsutella sinensis*) on a growth medium under lab conditions. Genetic analyses show very similar genetics (97 per cent) between the natural and the substitute product.
9 Harvest is subject to annual fluctuations owing to varying precipitation, temperatures and so on. Annual production ranges from 100 to 200 tons – reliable data on this topic are rare. Overall, the species seems to have proven remarkably resilient to its mass exploitation so far (Winkler 2009).
10 The world's biggest wholesale market for caterpillar fungus is situated in Xining, capital of Qinghai province.
11 A caterpillar fungus species which looks very similar to *O. sinensis* but lacks medicinal values.
12 From 'Caterpillar Fungus Knows My Heart' (*Cun cao zhi wo xin*) from the series 'A Life Devoted to Science and Technology' (*Keji rensheng*), first on screen in 2010, http://tv.cntv.cn/video/C10562/7a5ddb60091944f814fe2db0db53e2d0, accessed 27 February 2015.
13 *Qinghai chuntian yaoyong ziyuan keji liyong youxian gongsi* in Chinese; see www.verygrass.com.
14 In an interview on 24 June 2010 the founder of the company stated to me personally that 100 per cent of caterpillar fungus in the real market is tampered with, having a negative impact on its quality. Indeed, the profitability of the caterpillar fungus trade had attracted a considerable amount of fraud. However, his kind of normative statement was clearly an exaggeration.
15 http://www.verygrass.com/show_qhct.php, accessed 1 June 2013. Meanwhile, this version of the internet page is no longer available, but can be accessed via www.archive.org:

https://web.archive.org/web/20130801200712/http://www.verygrass.com/zyzw.php, accessed 27 February 2015.
16 http://www.verygrass.com/about.html, accessed 19 February 2015, emphasis added.
17 Compared with the prices for natural caterpillar fungus given at the beginning of this chapter, the kilogram price for processed caterpillar fungus corresponded to €150,195 on 28 February 2015 (http://www.finanzen.net/devisen/euro-renminbi_yuan-kurs). Also note the intentional use of the number 8 to denote the price, as it sounds much like the Chinese word *fa* (generating wealth). Telephone numbers, car number plates and the like with the number 8 are considered lucky by the Chinese.
18 http://www.verygrass.com, accessed 21 July 2014. This information is no longer available on the website.
19 This is an observation which has also been made in the Chinese pork industry, where the authors conclude that, 'to the modern Chinese consumer, the large-scale, industrial food production system is generally well accepted, as it seems to be a way leading to food safety, a highly valuable attribute to consumers' (Barcellos et al. 2013: 450).

References

Atkins, P. W. (2010) *Liquid Materialities: A History of Milk, Science, and the Law*, Ashgate, Burlington, VT.
Barcellos, M. D. de, Grunert, K. G., Zhou, Y., Verbeke, W., Perez-Cueto, F. J. A. and Krystallis, A. (2013) 'Consumer attitudes to different pig production systems: a study from mainland China', *Agriculture and Human Values*, vol. 30, no. 3, pp. 443–455.
Bear, C. (2013) 'Assembling the sea: materiality, movement and regulatory practices in the Cardigan Bay scallop fishery', *Cultural Geographies*, vol. 20, no. 1, pp. 21–41.
Bestor, T. C. (2004) '*Tsukiji: The Fish Market at the Center of the World*, University of California Press, Berkeley.
Bohle, H. -G. (2001) 'Neue Ansätze der Geographischen Risikoforschung', *Die Erde*, vol. 132, no. 2, pp. 119–140.
Buenz, E. J., Bauer, B. A., Osmundson, T. W. and Motley, T. J. (2005) 'The traditional Chinese medicine *Cordyceps sinensis* and its effects on apoptotic homeostasis', *Journal of Ethnopharmacology*, vol. 96, nos 1–2, pp. 19–29.
Çalışkan, K. and Callon, M. (2010) 'Economization, part 2: a research programme for the study of markets', *Economy and Society*, vol. 39, no. 1, pp. 1–32.
Callon, M. (1986) 'Some elements of a sociology of translation: domestication of the scallops and the fishermen of St Brieuc Bay', in John Law (ed.), *Power, Action and Belief: A New Sociology of Knowledge?*, Routledge, London, pp. 196–223.
Carolan, M. (2013) 'Doing and enacting economies of value: thinking through the assemblage', *New Zealand Geographer*, vol. 69, no. 3, pp. 176–179.
Chambers, R. and Conway, G. R. (1991) *Sustainable Rural Livelihoods: Practical Concepts for the 21st Century*, IDS Discussion Paper 296, https://www.ids.ac.uk/files/Dp296.pdf, accessed 16 May 2014.
Chen, H. et al. (eds) (2010) *Dongchongxiacao yangsheng daquan* [Caterpillar fungus health encyclopaedia], Guangzhou chubanshe [Guangzhou Press], Guangzhou.
DFID (Department for International Development) (1999) *Sustainable Livelihoods Guidance Sheets*, http://www.eldis.org, accessed 16 May 2014.
FitzSimmons, M. and Goodman, D. (1998) 'Incorporating nature: environmental narratives and the reproduction of food', in Bruce Braun and Noel Castree (eds), *Remaking Reality: Nature at the Millennium*, Routledge, London, pp. 194–220.

Gertel, J. and Le Heron, R. (2011) 'Introduction: pastoral economies between resilience and exposure', in J. Gertel and R. Le Heron (eds), *Economic Spaces of Pastoral Production and Commodity Systems: Markets and Livelihoods*, Burlington, VT: Ashgate, pp. 3–24.

GMMC (Grassland Monitoring and Management Center, Chinese Ministry of Agriculture) (ed.) (2010) *Ophiocordyceps Sinensis in China: Zhongguo dongchongxiacao*, Xinhua chubanshe [Xinhua Press], Beijing.

Goodman, D. (2001) 'Ontology matters: the relational materiality of nature and agro-food studies', *Sociologia Ruralis*, vol. 41, no. 2, pp. 182–200.

Gruschke, A. (2012) *Nomadische Ressourcennutzung und Existenzsicherung im Umbruch: Die osttibetische Region Yushu (Qinghai, VR China)*, Reichert, Wiesbaden.

Han, F. (ed.) (2009) *Zhongguo chongcao de xiandai yanfa yu yingyong* [Modern research and development on caterpillar fungus and its application], Qinghai renmin chubanshe [Qinghai People's Press], Xining.

Haraway, D. (1988) 'Situated knowledges: the science question in feminism and the privilege of partial perspective', *Feminist Studies*, vol. 14, no. 3, pp. 575–599.

Henry, M. and Roche, M. (2013) 'Valuing lively materialities: bio-economic assembling in the making of new meat futures', *New Zealand Geographer*, vol. 69, no. 3, pp. 197–207.

Ho, P., Vermeer, E. B. and Zhao, J. H. (2006) 'Biotechnology and food safety in China: consumers' acceptance or resistance?', *Development and Change*, vol. 37, no. 1, pp. 227–254.

Jia, C. and Jukes, D. (2013) 'The national food safety control system of China – a systematic review', *Food Control*, vol. 32, no. 1, pp. 236–245.

Kitchen, L. and Marsden, T. (2011) 'Constructing sustainable communities: a theoretical exploration of the bio-economy and eco-economy paradigms', *Local Environment*, vol. 16, no. 8, pp. 753–769.

Krzywoszynska, A. (2012) '"We produce under this sky": making organic wine in a material world', Ph.D. thesis, University of Sheffield, UK.

Krzywoszynska, A. (2015), 'Wine is not Coca-Cola: marketization and taste in alternative food networks', *Agriculture and Human Values*, vol. 32, no. 3, pp. 491–503.

Latour, B. (2005) *Reassembling the Social: An Introduction to Actor-Network-Theory*, Oxford University Press, Oxford.

Le Heron, E., Le Heron, R. and Lewis, N. (2013) 'Wine economy as open assemblage: thinking beyond sector and region', *New Zealand Geographer*, vol. 69, no. 3, pp. 221–234.

Liang, Y. (2011) 'Making gold: commodification and consumption of the medicinal fungus *chongcao* in Guangdong and Hong Kong', *Hong Kong Anthropologist*, vol. 5, pp. 1–17.

Liu, R., Pieniak, Z. and Verbeke, W. (2014) 'Food-related hazards in China: consumers' perceptions of risk and trust in information sources', *Food Control*, vol. 46, pp. 291–298.

Mitchell, T. (2002) *Rule of Experts: Egypt, Techno-Politics, Modernity*, University of California Press, Berkeley.

Nojonen, M. (2003) 'The competitive advantage with Chinese characteristics: the sophisticated choreography of gift-giving', in John B. Kidd and Frank-Jürgen Richter (eds), *Corruption and Governance in Asia*, Palgrave Macmillan, Houndmills, pp. 107–130.

Ortega, D., Wang, H., Wu, L. and Olynk, N. (2011) 'Modeling heterogeneity in consumer preferences for select food safety attributes in China', *Food Policy*, vol. 36, no. 2, pp. 318–324.

QEAPC (Qinghai Everest Aweto Pharmaceutical Company) (not specified, procured 2010a) 'Qinghaisheng Xining shi shengwu chanye yuanqu dongchongxiacao chanyeyuan: Zhaoshang shouce' [Caterpillar Fungus Industrial Park in Qinghai Xining Bioindustrial Park Area: investment guide], Xining.

QEAPC (Qinghai Everest Aweto Pharmaceutical Company) (not specified, procured 2010b), Zhufeng Yaoye, Everest Pharmaceuticals, Xining.

QEAPC (Qinghai Everest Aweto Pharmaceutical Company) (2013), 'Qinghai zhufeng chongcao yaoye' [Qinghai Everest Aweto Pharmaceutical Company], http://www.zfchongcaoyaoye.com/js.html, accessed 27 February 2015.

Robbins, P. and Marks, B. (2009) 'Assemblage geographies', in S. J. Smith, R. Pain, S. A. Marston and J. P. Jones III (eds), *The Sage Handbook of Social Geographies*, Sage, London, pp. 176–194.

Rosin, C. and Lewis, N. (2013) 'Introduction', *New Zealand Geographer*, vol. 69, no. 3, p. 175.

Rosin, C., Dwiartama, A., Grant, D. and Hopkins, D. (2013) 'Using provenance to create stability: state-led territorialisation of central Otago as assemblage', *New Zealand Geographer*, vol. 69, no. 3, pp. 235–248.

Scott, J. C. (1998) *Seeing like a State: How Certain Schemes to Improve the Human Condition Have Failed*, Yale University Press, New Haven, CT.

Stuart, D. (2011) '"Nature" is not guilty: foodborne illness and the industrial bagged salad', *Sociologia Ruralis*, vol. 51, no. 2, pp. 158–174.

Whatmore, S. (2002) *Hybrid Geographies: Natures, Cultures, Spaces*, Sage, London.

Whatmore, S. (2006) 'Materialist returns: practising cultural geography in and for a more-than-human world', *Cultural Geographies*, vol. 13, no. 4, pp. 600–609.

Winkler, D. (2009) 'Caterpillar fungus (*Ophiocordyceps sinensis*) production and sustainability on the Tibetan plateau and in the Himalayas', *Asian Medicine*, vol. 5, no. 2, pp. 291–316.

Yan, Y. (2013) 'Food safety and social risk in contemporary China', in Perry Link, R. P. Madsen and P. G. Pickowicz (eds), *Restless China*, Rowman & Littlefield, Lanham, MD, pp. 247–271.

Yuan, Y. (2012) 'Zuo qiang Qinghai tese chanye – ji Qinghai zhufeng chongcao yaoye youxian gongsi dongshizhang Wang Hui' [Strengthen Qinghai's special industry – record of Qinghai Everest Aweto Pharmaceutical Company's president Wang Hui], *Qinghai ribao* [Qinghai Daily], http://www.tibet3.com/news/content/2012-10/23/content_943365.htm, accessed 25 February 2015.

Zader, A. (2012) 'Understanding quality food through cultural economy: the "politics of quality" in China's northeast japonica rice', *Agriculture and Human Values*, vol. 29, no. 1, pp. 53–63.

Zhang, Q. (2011) *Dongchong xiacao* [Caterpillar fungus], Guangzhou chubanshe [Guangzhou Press], Guangzhou.

5 Enacting Swiss cheese

About the multiple ontologies of local food

Jérémie Forney

Beyond radical criticism in food localisation

Environment, localisation and fairness are no longer the uncomplicated defining characteristics of alternative food networks. Instead, they have been integrated into the vocabulary of marketers and are now efficient tools for positioning products in the market. Largely inspired by political economy approaches, agri-food scholars have produced very critical interpretations of this kind of transition in food systems. This dominant epistemological posture has produced a binary framing of the question of what is genuinely alternative. With concepts such as bifurcation and conventionalisation, orthodox agri-food political economy questions the capacity of such alternative patterns to transform the conventional food system, building on an implicit opposition between 'real alternatives' and 'conventional appropriations'.

In this chapter, I argue that we have to look beyond an underlying binary opposition between true alternatives and perverted and sterilised mutations. To do so, I draw on a research project focusing on what could be called a conventionalisation of food localism in Switzerland.[1] However, this framing is highly unsatisfactory and of little use in describing what is happening in the emerging food networks I observed in my research, mainly because, following Rosin and Campbell (2009: 43–44), it offers 'an overly structured analysis of what is an evolving and volatile process'.

This dominant binary framework was initially developed in the critical study of the evolution of organic food networks (for example Guthman 2004). However, the same kind of framework can be found in the literature on local food. Originally, the virtue of localism – small scale, renewed proximity between actors, and specific connection with places – was central to the study of alternative food networks, as it embodied a rejection of a capitalised, industrialised and globalised hegemonic system: the 'food from nowhere regime' (for example McMichael 2002). However, after a short period of somewhat naïve enthusiasm, the literature on food localism has become more critical and has revealed a more complex and questionable reality. Scholars have shown how the 'local trap' (Born and Purcell 2006: 195) or an 'unreflexive localism' (DuPuis and Goodman 2005) conflates characteristics of food networks, assuming that 'local' automatically equals 'alternative' or 'sustainable', while being sometimes 'defensive' and reinforcing social and identity boundaries with little attention paid to ecological or social justice (for example Winter 2003). The mainstreaming of 'local food label', led by the big retail and supermarket chains, brings into the discussion another group of critics, who point to the conventionalisation argument, whereby food labels (for example local, organic) actually enable the neoliberalisation of environmental governance and nature (for example Guthman 2007).

My case studies involve the development of dairy products led by farmers' cooperative structures, which are using localness and provenance as a central claim. While drawing largely on 'alternative' values, such as localism, solidarity and environmentalism, these initiatives are fully entangled within the conventional food system, with close relations with big supermarket chains and large dairy companies (Forney and Häberli 2015; Häberli and Forney forthcoming). Mindful of the afore-mentioned discussion, I choose, in this chapter, to look beyond the imperfections of such networks and explore the transformational potential they might nevertheless contain. In doing so, I want to answer Gibson-Graham's (2008) call to 'read for difference' in the exploration of diverse economies (see also Wynne-Jones 2014). In other words, while most of the literature looks at how dominant actors subsume alternative values, I look for the cross-contaminations that might potentially transform food networks. To do so, I draw on a body of scholarship developing around the concept of 'enactive research'. This implies making a little detour to some fundamental insights inspired by actor–network theory (ANT), such as the agency of non-human actors and the multiplicity of ontologies. I use these concepts to describe the development of local dairy products in Switzerland. The identification of multiple ontologies of one of these local cheeses will enable us to think about the enactiveness of social sciences, first as an unveiling of a 'side-effect' of doing research, and then and above all as a fundamental question: how do I integrate this liveliness in a consciously enactive research programme?

Current transformation of the Swiss dairy sector

Milk production is an important element of Swiss agriculture, with about 24,400 dairy farms from a total of 56,575 farms (FOAG 2014: 262). In Switzerland, the dairy industry is usually divided into two sectors: the 'industry milk' chain and the 'cheese milk' chain. In the first, farmers supply a few big processing companies that produce mainly dairy products for direct consumption (yogurts, butter, milk and pasteurised industrial cheese) and for the food industry (for example milk powder, butter). In the second, farmers supply cheese dairies with high-quality (produced without silage feeding) raw milk. This premium cheese production is characterised by the existence of several 'protected designation of origin' (PDO) labels. Both sectors have been facing challenging times in the last decade, mainly because of a progressive programme of market deregulation initiated by the federal state. A significant step in this process has been the removal of federal milk quotas, which resulted in decreasing prices, overproduction, and discord among actors (Forney 2012). In the 'industry milk' chain, farmers have to choose between dealing directly with a dairy company as a 'direct producer' and joining a 'producers' organisation' (PO), whose main task is to purchase milk from farmers and sell it to the industry. POs' nature and strategies are diverse (Häberli and Forney forthcoming), and there is little unity among them. As a consequence, deregulation has led to an increase in national competition among milk producers. In contrast, in the cheese milk chain many small-scale production facilities exist, while a few large PDOs, organised around inter-professional boards, lead the sector. The progressive deregulation of agriculture has gone hand in hand with its ecologisation under the guidance of the federal agricultural policy. Since the 1990s, Switzerland has adopted a multifunctional paradigm based on farmers' cross-compliance with environmental schemes within a system of direct remuneration. This political reorientation parallels an evolution of the markets for food products, which is characterised by the multiplication of food labels. For products issuing from Swiss agriculture, these labels refer mainly to two kinds of justification: the environment (for example organic) and provenance and localisation (for example PDOs). In this chapter I will focus mainly on the latter, as they play a central role in our case studies.

Data and methods

This chapter is based on a research project that explored the evolution of the Swiss dairy industry, in particular its 'industry milk' chain, after the removal of the national quota system in 2009. The project was divided into two phases. From the beginning, the intention was to draw on the results of phase one to build up the second, using a more participatory approach, following an inductive and iterative research process. In the first phase, we studied several cases of food relocalisation initiatives that had been launched by farmers' cooperatives with the general aim of improving the situation and position of the dairy farmers. More precisely, we developed three case studies. One is located in the canton of Vaud and is about the development of local cheese specialities by Prolait, the regional federation of dairy cooperatives. Another is located in the north-west part of Switzerland and is about the revival of an own brand of the regional dairy farmers' federation, MIBA. And the last one is in the canton of Glarus and describes the new partnership between a local dairy farmers' cooperative and a local cheese factory. In these three case studies we looked at how the local had been reinterpreted and reformulated and at the kinds of changes that resulted from these new strategies (Forney and Häberli 2015). Furthermore, it appeared that at least two of these initiatives had been developed as an answer to a fundamental questioning of the structural character of the POs. Consequently, the second phase developed a broader reflection on the present evolution of cooperative structures in a context of deregulation and liberalisation (Häberli and Forney forthcoming). This chapter draws more directly on the first phase of the project and specifically on one of its case studies: the Prolait federation and its new cheese initiative.

Our data came out of 49 semi-structured interviews and a range of informal interviews and direct observations during meetings, assemblies and public events. From these interviews, 19 directly concern the Prolait case study. The interviews were directed at gaining an understanding of the strategies, the historical background of the cooperative structures and the changes that result (or should result at a later stage) from the new initiatives. They were conducted with members of the management boards of the cooperatives, with farmers and with representative of several stakeholders (for example retailers, dairy companies, authorities).

The project applied classical qualitative research methods. However, from conception to the last phases of the project, the intention was to remain receptive to significant shifts in connections, relations and practices. *A posteriori*, it might be said that this methodological posture coupled the following developments with an enactive research approach.

Non-human actors, multiple ontologies and enactive research

Three main theoretical sources inspired this chapter and its reflection on the 'enactiveness' of research. Firstly, a very basic notion of ANT is central: social life is made by human and non-human actors in their numerous connections. What interests me here more precisely is how acknowledging this changes our perception of agency and action in a (food) network. Secondly, the notion of 'multiple ontologies' emphasises the processes in which different sets of relations result in coexisting ontological variants of what something is. Finally, by developing enactive research approaches, we try to integrate these first two insights into the practice of social science.

Non-human actors and agency

Agri-food chains can be understood as wide networks of human (for example agro-merchants, farmers, retailers) and non-human (for example animals, soil, water, tractors, laws, labels) actors engaged around the production, processing, marketing and consumption of food products. In the study of agri-food networks, one of the key contributions of ANT has been to emphasise the role played by these non-human actors (actants) (for example Latour 1996). Non-human beings are not to be understood as being only passive recipients of human action. They have an active role in the production of social life and reality, 'in interaction that is simultaneously material and social' (Law and Urry 2004: 395). What interests me more specifically here is the application of this approach to the definition of agency and action (Dwiartama and Rosin 2014). Non-human actors act because of and through their connections with others actors, by being part of a network. Obviously, the capacity to act does not depend on the actant alone, but on its 'co-actors' within the network. Moreover, agency has a collective dimension and, following Law and Mol (2008: 72), 'it is not always clear who is doing what. Action moves around. It is like a viscous fluid.'

Consequently, the outcomes of action within an actor–network are never limited to what human consciousness has planned. Non-human actors have their say as well, and the interactions within the networks might have unexpected results. Paraphrasing Law and Mol again, we can say that what results is hard to predict, 'for assemblages, like actors, are creative. They have novel effects and they make new things' (2008: 74). Coming back to food networks and marketing strategies, we can conclude that the motivations and narratives developed by human actors are perhaps not the best criteria for assessing the transformative potential of a strategy, for example the development of a local food network. Non-human elements, such as a speciality cheese, the sets of standards for a food label, or the nutritional needs of cows, will interfere and contribute to the production of the final outcomes.

Enacting multiple ontologies

Multiple ontologies result from multiple enactments of things in multiple networks of belonging. What is referred to as the same 'thing' exists simultaneously in diverse ontologies. This multiplicity of ontologies is more easily demonstrated for highly complex phenomena such as climate change (Esbjörn-Hargens 2010). However, it is valid for 'simple' things as well, like a sheep, as brilliantly illustrated by Law and Mol (2008), or a cheese. Law and Mol describe how 'the' Cumbrian sheep is involved in different practices in the context of the foot-and-mouth disease crisis in the UK. These practices enact this sheep in different ways that are not only about diverging 'interpretations' of the animal but about ontologies: 'In each of these practices "a sheep" is something different' (Law and Mol 2008: 59). The same approach can be applied to more abstract actors too, like concepts or inanimate beings such as the foot-and-mouth disease itself (Law and Mol 2011). Similarly, in our research, we explored the multiplicity of the 'local' in our three case studies (Forney and Häberli 2015), looking at how diverse configurations of actors resulted in varying definitions (ontologies) of 'local food'. Looking for multiple ontologies gives a powerful framework for understanding how things are constructed and identities are created within networks of human and non-human actors.

Enactive research

Taking stock of the enacted dimension of reality, Law and Urry, among others, insist on the role of social sciences in the process of enactment. In particular, they highlight the role played by the method, with 'the prospect that it [the method] helps to produce the realities that it describes' (Law and Urry 2004: 397). In other words, the multiplicity of ontologies also relates to the multiplicity of methods and, it should be added, theories, for concepts, metrologies and other scientific artefacts are non-human actants like others and are therefore enactive. These considerations were first formulated as part of a reflexive analysis of sciences (STS) in the aftermath of constructionism and postmodern theories. However, the enactive dimension of social analysis has quickly gained a more programmatic dimension: given that our work as social scientists participates anyway in enacting specific ontologies, can we choose how we want to be enactive by rethinking the methods and epistemologies in our practice of research? Lowe reframed this question in the context of rural sociology and agri-food studies by claiming that social sciences should contribute to 'enact[ing] novel realities', through discursive and methodological creativity (Lowe 2010: 312).

As clearly stated by the editors, most of the contributors to this book join this *enactive turn* (Lewis and Rosin 2013), which embraces the work on enactment as described above, but also other scholarship such as that around the work of Gibson-Graham on performative knowledge (Gibson-Graham 2008) and the so-called ontological turn (Carolan 2009). Gibson-Graham firstly suggested that, by focusing on the power of capitalism, critical scholars have participated in the realisation of an omnipotent capitalism by obscuring all alternatives and despising them for their capitalist taint. The authors suggest that we should think differently and look for glimpses of differences that glow within a context dominated by capitalism, rather than always focusing on a radical and pure alternative. By doing so, we would not only allow the identification of diverse economies and diverse logics, but also empower them and this, per se, would 'generate new possibilities' (Gibson-Graham 2008: 623). Carolan says something similar when he claims that writing now about what was once 'beyond the imaginable' on one hand proves that things have changed and on the other hand contributes to 'enliven[ing]' the world in a way that will sustain this change (Carolan 2013: 424). In other words, this suggests that we have to work at the level of ontologies in order to put forward a new economic ontology that might allow space for new economic practices and experiments.

Consequently, this range of scholarship adds one important (if not totally new) argument to Law and Urry's (2004) analysis of the enactive role of social sciences. It might be hard, if not impossible, to assess and control how the concepts and methods we use in our research enact multiple realities. However, it is easier to reflect on how we 'read' the world and what might be the consequences of this (not always) conscious choice. Moreover, this fundamental reflexivity appears to be absolutely necessary to engaging knowingly and with full awareness in enactive efforts.

The enrolment of local cheese specialities in the struggle for better milk prices

I want to go back now to one of our case studies, located in the French-speaking part of Switzerland. There, a regional dairy farmers' federation, Prolait, had recently taken over the local production of cheese specialities in the town of Moudon in the canton of Vaud (see Figure 5.1). Historically this range of five types of soft cheese specialities was related to the cantonal school for cheese making and was developed mainly for teaching purposes. These somewhat 'French-style' cheeses offered a relatively atypical profile in the Swiss cheese landscape, largely dominated – qualitatively and quantitatively – by hard cheese varieties. The school closed in 2004, endangering their production. At this time, Prolait was looking for innovative solutions for the milk produced in its 'industry' chain. These specialities had one interesting characteristic: using 'industry milk' to produce them does not adversely affect their basic qualities. This is not the case with the long-lasting hard Swiss cheeses. New connections were then possible. Prolait's project involved the creation of a new brand (Le Grand Pré) for regional dairy products, the construction of a new cheese factory and the creation of a small limited company (Le Grand Pré SA) to run it. Prolait fully owns Le Grand Pré SA. Building the cheese factory required significant investment, which was financed jointly by public money, borrowing and the

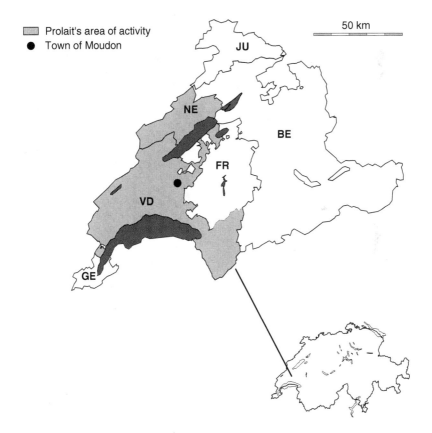

Figure 5.1 Prolait's area of activity in the canton of Vaud

Note: Swiss cantons: JU = Jura; NE = Neuchatel; BE = Bern; FR = Fribourg; VD = Vaud; GE = Geneva.

Prolait investment fund (consisting of members' contributions). Theoretically, when the company becomes profitable, the profits will be transferred to all the members of Prolait (dairy farmers) by means of a higher milk price.

This enrolment of the Moudon cheese specialities in the federation's activities took place within a longer-term reflection and strategy. After the deregulation of the milk market, Prolait was directly confronted with the general unsustainability of the food system in which it was embedded, above all regarding the economic and social sustainability at the level of the dairy farms. For a few years, possibilities of improvement of the milk price paid to members were explored. The federation mandated an extension organisation to develop an analysis of the market perspectives of different strategies based on the relocalisation of milk production. At the same time, research into the provenance of the fodder and feed given to the dairy cows on farms of the federation was co-developed in collaboration with a research institute. The main idea was to find a position on the market by assuming a strong and 'coherent' localisation. Such a position was developed in opposition to retailers' labels for regional products, which are, in the eyes of the federation, in many ways 'inconsistent' and often do not benefit the farmers. The investment in the cheese factory and in the new brand was the first concrete step in this process, after years of thinking and planning. The production of the Moudon cheese specialities, renamed under the new brand Le Grand Pré, started in 2013. While several small retailers were involved, a partnership with one of the major Swiss supermarket chains was crucial to reaching significant quantities. However, Prolait processes only a small portion of its milk through this channel, and production will still have to grow significantly to reach profitability.

In retrospect, the most significant effect of this initiative has probably been, so far, the creation of new relations and assemblages around the federation activities. In the preparatory phase, Prolait collaborated with actors from research and extension, with the regional authorities and with specialists in branding and marketing. In order to organise the retailing of its products, it developed closer partnerships with supermarkets and retailers. More generally, the whole process impacted on its relations with its usual partners, especially the dairy company Cremo.

The multiple ontologies of the local cheese

The enrolment of the Grand Pré cheese specialities in Prolait's strategies results in multiple translation processes and production of meanings. We have described elsewhere (Forney and Häberli 2015) how the 'local' was enacted and produced in multiple parallel ways in our case studies. Here, I want to focus on the multiple ontologies of the cheese itself. More precisely, I will describe now two dominant enactments: the market cheese and the cooperative cheese (see also Table 5.1). Both are of particular interest in the analysis of the transformative potential of such initiatives, as they illustrate two political paradigms often considered in opposition, solidarity and market competition.

Table 5.1 Two ontologies of Moudon cheese

	Market cheese	Cooperative cheese
Characteristics	– Local as market positioning – Competition for market shares	– Symbol of identification – Solidarity – Collective investments
Critical look	– Neoliberal inspiration	– Conservative localism
Seed of change	– New knowledge – Empowerment	– Reconnections – Actual autonomy

The market cheese: local food as neoliberalism in disguise?

A critical approach to the localisation strategies implemented in our case studies indicates that their inspiration comes first of all from a neoliberal rationality. Economic actors (farmers as entrepreneurs) regroup to maximise their power in the market and thus their profit. Because they identified a growing demand from consumers for localised food products, they used their own potential as providers of local products through proximity between, as example, consumers and producers, or between distinct regional identities. Consequently, they decided to invest and target this niche market through collaboration with big retailers. The operation and the change implied were only located at the level of marketing and investments. No change was made at the farm level in the farm practices, and no alternative retailing system was developed. The cheese was mainly integrated into the conventional food system with an aura of localness. In short, the main – if not only – purpose of the development of this cheese production was to obtain better prices for the farmers by exploiting a new trend in the market. This is what the actors involved in these new networks explicitly told us. For the federation board, membership has to become more attractive through a higher milk price. For the farmers, the investment has to be profitable. For the retailer, the cheese must first and above all sell.

Many are sceptical when evaluating this initiative's chances of success: the investment is high; the quantities remain limited. Still, the criteria that are mobilised to assess this success are economic and market related. Even if they were to fail, these local cheese specialities are market cheese.

As emphasised both by the board members and by their retail partners, developing such a strategy for the federation implies developing important new skills and knowledge at the marketing and trading level. The federation board members have to learn how to sell and how to behave with trade partners. This new situation initiated a process of knowledge – and competence – building in the federation to improve its overall ability to act in the food network. At the same time, the farmers' role has been reframed, and the assemblage of actors involved has been reshaped. Farmers are no longer the 'simple commodity producers' (Friedmann 1978) subsumed in the agro-industrial complex; they have something more to sell than just raw material for the agro-industry:

a brand, their image and their localness. They can actually start to negotiate with other actors. As an example, the board of Le Grand Pré SA was surprised by its success in negotiating with one of the big Swiss retailers: the supermarket chain wanted to integrate the cheese under its own brand for local products, putting on the side the name Le Grand Pré. At the end of a long discussion, the board members of Prolait and Le Grand Pré managed to maintain the name and the brand on the packaging, which was central to their marketing strategy. Arguably, then, the market cheese ontology results in the relative empowerment of farmers within the food network.

The cooperative cheese: alternatives in narrative and strategy?

The development of the new cheese factory and the launch of the Le Grand Pré brand were based on a typically cooperative principle: joint investment and shared benefits. This constitutes the basis of the cooperative cheese ontology. The explicit use of the values of solidarity and autonomy (from the big companies) by Prolait has been amplified by the general context of an industry characterised by disagreement and competition between producers' organisations. The cooperative cheese has turned into a symbol of solidarity among dairy farmers, at least at the regional level. It provides new opportunities for collective identification with the federation and with the region. As stated by one of our interviewees from another case study, 'You need a symbol to build up identification.'[2] This identification is part of a process of collective autonomisation that offers interesting parallels with actual autonomy as described by Stock et al. (2014), as a way of creating solidarity and collective action despite a hegemonic narrative based on individualism and competition.

Consequently, the localisation process enables reconnection in the food network: farmers' reconnection with the final food product and consumers' reconnection to a place through the cheese specialities. With the enactment of the cooperative cheese, solidarity develops not only among dairy farmers but also between consumers and local producers. The cooperative cheese questions the stereotype of the supermarket customer looking above all for low prices. In a way, the cooperative cheese also mitigates the identity of the big retailers. They are often described, notably by farmers, as heartless and greedy in business. Interestingly, the board of Prolait started to speak differently of them, as real partners. Simultaneously, a representative of one of the two big supermarket chains highlighted that their interest in dealing with a farmers' cooperative could be to gain access to the farmers and make possible renewed dialogue.

The reconfiguration of the network developing around the cooperative cheese leads to the re-negotiation of what was previously taken for granted: the role of the producers, the total dependence on the big dairy companies and retailers, and the passivity of consumers. This process will potentially result in a better situation for dairy farmers. What the cooperative cheese emphasises is that this empowerment of farmers in the food network is only possible through acts of collaboration.

The (en-)active cheese

If I were to adopt an orthodox critical perspective, I would look at the ways in which these experiments might offer alternatives to the current state of the food system. On one hand, and following the logic of the market cheese, the Moudon specialities can be easily related to a process of neoliberalisation of agri-food networks, where market instruments developed by the private sector (certification and branding) replace former state regulation of the sector (milk quotas). The localisation strategy parallels other labels and food standards for more sustainable food that have long been related to a neoliberal mode of governance of food and natural resource management. Indeed, they rely on market logic and consumer choice rather than democratic regulation and state intervention (for example Moberg 2014). I would conclude that the most significant effect produced by these cheese specialities is the implementation of neoliberal principles in the strategies of dairy cooperative structures. On the other hand, the focus set by the cooperative cheese on farmers' empowerment rings some familiar bells from the literature on food localism. The Prolait initiative aims mainly at improving the situation of local farmers, without more ambitious goals at the level of the food system. We are close here to an *unreflexive* localism (DuPuis and Goodman 2005).

While being very different, these two ontologies of the Moudon cheese would then suggest a similar conclusion: Prolait's initiative does not produce very significant change in the food system. Narratives of autonomisation and empowerment of the farmer could well be criticised as illusory: since dependencies are too deeply rooted in the food system and the production of cheese specialities is too restricted to shift this balance of power. The cooperative cheese arguably denies this interpretation, but at the same time confirms that the main goals have always been, above all, economic benefit for the farmer and not broader sustainability of the food system. My conclusion could well be that this is all smoke and mirrors and that there is no real alternativeness about the Moudon cheese. In so doing, I would just be adding another set of cases to theories demonstrating the conventionalisation of food alternatives in the context of food localism.

However, drawing on the emerging enactive research approach, I choose a more nuanced and optimistic conclusion. It begins by acknowledging that the choices I make as a researcher participate in enacting the world. This means that the 'real' transformative potential of such imperfect alternatives depends partly on us as researchers, and on the ontologies we contribute to create. This is close to what Gibson-Graham (2008) call 'reading for difference'. Furthermore, their potential cannot be reduced to the actions of human individuals. Moreover, it comes out of an ever-repeated process of negotiation and translation within a network, where non-human actants play a significant role. This complex set of relations participates in the wider creation of new meaning and social processes by producing multiple ontologies. As I am writing these lines, the members of the Prolait management board are working on the further development of their new brand. They are discussing projects for applying a stronger definition of the local, including the origin of the fodder given to the dairy cows. They are thinking about what kind of product would best fit their concept of fairer and more sustainable trade in the Swiss dairy industry. These developments go further than what they had in mind at the beginning of the process. However, once they had enrolled the cheese specialities in their new initiative, they opened the door to the new rationalities and experiments these new elements brought with them. As expressed in an interview, the management board of Prolait is half aware of this enactive capacity of the new products:

> I'm convinced that, once we have created the market, this is something that will stay, even develop, because the consumers' interest goes in this direction: with environmental practices . . . food security problems around the world . . . there are many elements that go in the direction of regional products.

What is more – thinking differently about the same idea of the enactive and transformative power of cheese – this initiative occasioned several learning processes. The creation of new forms of knowledge means a lot more than the acquisition of technical or practical skills and know-how. Knowledge influences how we *see* the world, and changing how we 'see' is a prerequisite for changing what we 'do' (Carolan 2006). New learning and understanding in marketing strategies, negotiations with trade partners, and fundamental questioning, as well as opportunistic thinking, changed how the actors involved in the initiative saw their world. Consequently, what they saw to be unthinkable at the beginning (that is, this whole process) became possible. The quest for better prices is progressively being replaced by one for a fairer and more sustainable industry. In other words, and referring to Marsden's (2013) work on reflexive governance and learning, the enrolment of the cheese specialities provoked 'awareness of and change to interpretive frameworks', which is typical of what he calls 'second order learning'. Such fundamental changes are the first conditions for the emergence of different, and hopefully more sustainable, food futures.

A third ontology and the enactiveness of the research?

In this chapter I have identified two coexisting ontologies of a regional cheese: the market cheese and the cooperative cheese. Both are very different. Both are enacted in networks of relations through repeated processes of meaning, attribution and translation. Neither is truer than the other. Multiple ontologies do exist simultaneously and are all part of what is 'real'. Acknowledging this coexistence of multiple ontologies allows us to 'read' for the transformative potential of new developments in food networks without dismissing any critical examination of these two ontologies: the neoliberal cheese might well introduce neoliberal logic within cooperative structures, and the cooperative cheese possibly leads to a relatively conservative interpretation of food localism. Still, looking at the multiplicity of ontologies leaves room for other interpretations. None alone offers a satisfying understanding of what *is* Le Grand Pré cheese. Firstly, this opens new spaces for the 'alternative' within the 'conventional', casting away a binary opposition between these two categories. Doing so, it allows imperfect actants, such as our local cheese specialities, to act as symbols of alternative values too. Secondly, this implies combining reflexivity and criticism by developing careful reflections on the impact of radical criticism. Far from naïve optimism, such positioning brings criticism one step deeper into the research process. Thirdly, by looking at the positive side of imperfect initiatives that draw on 'alternative' values, the research produces encouraging input for further developments. As nicely formulated by one of my interviewees, 'Because all these people are so interested in what we do, this means . . . we must be right . . . somewhere.' In this sense, I argue that adopting such a critically positive approach is a promising way of doing enactive research. Indeed, the fundamental question beyond these considerations, for us as scholars and researchers, is to define our particular role in this production of multiple ontologies. We cannot control the ontology we produce through our research practice, as we are not the only actors involved in the process. Le Heron and Lewis put it nicely when they underline the necessity of translation: 'For acting to become enacting translation has to take place. There are multiple moments of this and we should not regard translating as only an active choice' (Le Heron and Lewis 2011: 1). Because we cannot know how and when exactly this translation will happen, adopting an enactive research posture should firstly take place through careful reflexivity towards our contributions in the collective production of ontologies. This includes a critical examination of how we set up our research questions, how we present our research objectives and how we choose to 'read' the social processes we observe. Consequently, developing enactive research does not necessarily imply reinventing how we do research; rather it implies changing how we think about how we do research. In this sense, and as stated by the editors, it challenges the usual concepts and frameworks of research in order to do better by adopting an epistemological and theoretical orientation towards new possibilities rather than sterile pessimism.

Notes

1 I gratefully acknowledge the financial support of the Swiss National Science Foundation, which financed this research (project PZ00P1_142481).
2 While this quotation is related to one of the other case studies, it perfectly reflects this aspect of Prolait strategy.

References

Born, B. and Purcell, M. (2006) 'Avoiding the local trap: scale and food systems in planning research', *Journal of Planning Education and Research*, vol. 26, pp. 195–207.

Carolan, M. S. (2006) 'Do you see what I see? Examining the epistemic barriers to sustainable agriculture', *Rural Sociology*, vol. 71, pp. 232–260.

Carolan, M. S. (2009) '"I do therefore there is": enlivening socio-environmental theory', *Environmental Politics*, vol. 18, pp. 1–17.

Carolan, M. S. (2013) 'The wild side of agro-food studies: on co-experimentation, politics, change, and hope', *Sociologia Ruralis*, vol. 53, pp. 413–431.

DuPuis, M. and Goodman, D. (2005) 'Should we go "home" to eat? Toward a reflexive politics of localism', *Journal of Rural Studies*, vol. 21, pp. 359–371.

Dwiartama, A. and Rosin, C. (2014) 'Exploring agency beyond humans: the compatibility of actor-network theory (ANT) and resilience thinking', *Ecology and Society*, vol. 19.

Esbjörn-Hargens, S. (2010) 'An ontology of climate change: integral pluralism and the enactment of multiple objects', *Journal of Integral Theory and Practice*, vol. 5, pp. 143–174.

FOAG (2014) *Rapport agricole 2013*, Federal Office for Agriculture, Bern.

Forney, J. (2012) *Eleveurs laitiers: Peuvent-ils survivre?*, Presse Polytechniques et Universitaires Romandes, Lausanne.

Forney, J. and Häberli, I. (2015) 'Introducing "seeds of change" into the food system? Localisation strategies in the Swiss dairy industry', *Sociologia Ruralis*, early view online.

Friedmann, H. (1978) 'Simple commodity production and wage labour on the American plains', *Journal of Peasant Studies*, vol. 6, pp. 71–100.

Gibson-Graham, J. K. (2008) 'Diverse economies: performative practices for "other worlds"', *Progress in Human Geography*, vol. 32, pp. 613–632.

Guthman, J. (2004) 'The trouble with "organic lite" in California: a rejoinder to the "conventionalisation" debate', *Sociologia Ruralis*, vol. 44, pp. 301–316.

Guthman, J. (2007) 'The Polanyian way? Voluntary food labels as neoliberal governance', *Antipode*, vol. 39, pp. 456–478.

Häberli, I. and Forney, J. (forthcoming) 'Cooperative values and hybridity of farmers' organisations in the Swiss dairy sector'.

Latour, B. (1996) 'On actor-network theory: a few clarifications', *Soziale Welt*, vol. 47, pp. 369–381.

Law, J. and Mol, A. (2008) 'The actor-enacted: Cumbrian sheep in 2001', in C. Knappett and L. Malafouris (eds), *Material Agency: Towards a Non-Anthropocentric Approach*, Springer Science+Business Media, New York, pp. 57–77.

Law, J. and Mol, A. (2011) 'Veterinary realities: what is foot and mouth disease?', *Sociologia Ruralis*, vol. 51, pp. 1–16.

Law, J. and Urry, J. (2004) 'Enacting the social', *Economy and Society*, vol. 33, pp. 390–410.

Le Heron, R. and Lewis, N. (2011) 'New value from asking "Is geography what geographers do?"', *Geoforum*, vol. 42, pp. 1–5.

Lewis, N. and Rosin, C. (2013) 'Epilogue: emergent (re-)assemblings of biological economies', *New Zealand Geographer*, vol. 69, pp. 249–256.

Lowe, P. (2010) 'Enacting rural sociology: or what are the creativity claims of the engaged sciences?', *Sociologia Ruralis*, vol. 50, pp. 311–330.

Marsden, T. (2013) 'From post-productionism to reflexive governance: contested transitions in securing more sustainable food futures', *Journal of Rural Studies*, vol. 29, pp. 123–134.

McMichael, P. (2002) 'La restructuration globale des systems agro-alimentaires', *Mondes en développement*, vol. 30, pp. 45–54.

Moberg, M. (2014) 'Certification and neoliberal governance: moral economies of fair trade in the Eastern Caribbean', *American Anthropologist*, vol. 116, pp. 8–22.

Rosin, C. and Campbell, H. (2009) 'Beyond bifurcation: examining the conventions of organic agriculture in New Zealand', *Journal of Rural Studies*, vol. 25, pp. 35–47.

Stock, P. V., Forney, J., Emery, S. B. and Wittman, H. (2014) 'Neoliberal natures on the farm: farmer autonomy and cooperation in comparative perspective', *Journal of Rural Studies*, vol. 36, pp. 411–422.

Winter, M. (2003) 'Embeddedness, the new food economy and defensive localism', *Journal of Rural Studies*, vol. 19, pp. 23–32.

Wynne-Jones, S. (2014) '"Reading for difference" with payments for ecosystem services in Wales', *Critical Policy Studies*, vol. 8, pp. 148–164.

6 Understanding agri-food systems as assemblages
Worlds of rice in Indonesia

Angga Dwiartama, Christopher Rosin and Hugh Campbell

Introduction

Agri-food 'systems' are exemplary of multiple realities, from that of traditional to modern, to alternative, among which contestation often occurs in a fight for political power. In a political economy narrative – mobilized by right- or left-leaning scholars – the credit (or blame) is by and large put on humans and institutions as the sole source of agency. These points of view, however, fail to address the complexity of human–nature relationships and often end up with monolithic frameworks and outcomes framed by essentialist categories that obscure as much as they reveal. As an alternative, we will elaborate on previous arguments regarding agency as a force distributed across multiple entities, both human and non-human (Dwiartama and Rosin 2014), informed by a vibrant materialist approach (Bennett 2007). In this work, we reveal the extent to which characteristics of a non-human actor (in this sense, a crop) shape the way agricultural practices and policies can be enacted. To do this, we engage with Mol's (2002) concept of multiplicity to suggest that the political objective of a vibrant materialist approach in agri-food studies is to nurture a diversity of actions and practices shaped by the nature of non-human actors, and their alignment with the rest of the actors within an assemblage.

In order to elucidate this argument, this chapter discusses the worlds of rice, a commodity that lies at the heart of Indonesia's agriculture and food systems. Different from the people of many other countries outside South-East Asia, in which rice is merely an alternative to other sources of carbohydrate (such as maize, wheat and potato), for South-East Asians, and Indonesians in particular, rice has long been a part of their culture, the symbol of prosperity, and is used in many ways to exercise power. In Indonesia, public officials, politicians and governors all brandish rice as a political weapon, often symbolically harvesting rice to demonstrate their full commitment to the well-being of society. It thus has a long history, being central to Indonesian politics and society since before the era of the longest-ruling president, Soeharto, until the current president, Joko Widodo. But how has rice become such a powerful crop to the majority of Indonesians, and how are its many powers to be understood?

In answering this question, we refer initially to C. Peter Timmer (2005: 14), one of the most influential political economists studying Indonesia, who stated that 'rice is different, and the difference has powerfully influenced economics and politics throughout much of Asia'. The difference, he argued, lies in the multiplicity of rice: as a staple food, a crop and a commodity. As a food, rice supplies 35–67 per cent of the total calorie intake of the population, and its consumption has been increasing over the last four decades (Gerard et al. 2001; BPS 2012). As a crop, it is the source of income for more than 100 million farmers, farmworkers and retailers in Indonesia, and accounted for an area in 2009 of 12 million hectares, and a total production of up to 64 million tons (BPS 2012). In commodity terms, Indonesia has become both the third largest producer of rice and, at the same time, one of the largest importers of rice in the world (Hill 2000; Dawe 2002; FAO 2011). Therefore, rice price fluctuations have a serious impact on the livelihood of the majority of farmers and urban poor in Indonesia, causing the government to buffer its citizens from the fluctuating world price (Dawe 2001; Timmer 2005). It is, thus, not surprising that rice has become so pivotal to the politics of Indonesia's agri-food worlds.

What comes as a surprise is that there has been no single policy able to be applied effectively to Indonesia's rice agriculture. It is, evidently, an unruly and ungovernable crop. The history of Indonesia's rice agricultural development has been coloured with controversies and political turmoil surrounding what does and does not need to be done with rice production (Hill 2000). First, we will show how the current understanding of rice production has been focused too much on achieving a structured, singular and coordinated policy, which in the end results in political deadlock and inefficiency. This approach has overlooked the multiple realities and practices of rice agriculture, which implies the need for entirely different policy approaches.

Second, we attempt to look beyond the current understanding of political economy so as to see things differently. This is raised through the next question: how might a post-human political economy contribute to the practical understanding of agri-food systems? We employ what Mol (2002) terms 'multiplicity' in respect of rice: to see rice being enacted not only as an economic commodity but also as a political instrument and cultural artefact,[1] which intricately shapes different 'worlds of rice'.

A political history of rice in Indonesia

The history of rice in Indonesia has been characterized by the interplay of political power, even before the rise of its nation-state. Reid (1999), for instance, documented that, between the ninth and tenth centuries in ancient Java, rice became not only a major subsistence crop for the society but also a market commodity, and the basis of agricultural tax systems in several small kingdoms in the region. During Dutch colonialism, the Dutch East Indies had become one of the centres of production of tropical commodities – for example sugar, coffee and copra – and peasants were forced to plant those crops in combination, or rotation, with rice (Husken and White 1989). This, as it turned out, helped to shape how rice farming was practised, demonstrating a shift from subsistence to semi-intensive and finally industrialized agriculture.

After its independence in 1945, and following a series of political crises over the next two decades, Indonesia, with the help of the Food and Agriculture Organization, entered the era of the Green Revolution, in which it restructured its rice agriculture through the introduction of high-yielding rice varieties (HYVs), subsidization of agricultural inputs and credit, and stabilization of farm-gate prices (Gerard et al. 2001). With these strategies, rice agriculture in Indonesia showed consistent increases in yields in the early 1980s, only to be followed, within a decade, by a rapid decline in production. After 1990, Indonesia's economic growth began to stagnate and its resources were depleted, owing to an over-subsidized agriculture sector and a highly corrupt government (Gerard et al. 2001; Sumarto and Suryahadi 2007), reaching its worst point during the Asian Financial Crisis in 1997. This economic crisis was relieved by the International Monetary Fund (IMF)'s financial assistance; but it came at a large cost. Indonesia was forced to rescind all tariff and non-tariff barriers, as well as direct subsidies of its agricultural commodities.

More than 17 years have passed, and yet Indonesia's agricultural policies and strategies still show a lot of inconsistencies. For example, Indonesia liberalized its agriculture as a loan requirement made by the IMF (Gerard et al. 2001), but a few years later increased import tariffs and banned imported rice during harvest periods (Fane and Warr 2009). The government also experimented with contradictory agricultural policies, such as organic/hybrid rice (Dwiartama 2014) and food sovereignty/industrial food estates (Neilson and Arifin 2012). A critical political economy analysis, such as that set out by Neilson and Arifin (2012), might address the current state of inconsistencies as stemming from many familiar categories – political strategies and corruption among elites (and a role for peasants), which undermine food security, amidst the wider global economic and political shocks – and this kind of critique would almost certainly end with a prescription to rearrange elites, peasants and food system governance towards the most economically and politically effective policy approach to ensure food security and sustainable livelihoods. In this chapter, we laud these ends, but offer a different argument as to how we might get there.

A look beyond political economy

The ongoing, and sometimes harsh, political contests that drive towards hegemony of an agricultural paradigm (traditionalism, industrialism or an alternative) seem to show that the government has failed to acknowledge the multiple realities of rice agri-food systems in Indonesia. To date, traditional rice production is still operated by many local communities in rural areas for subsistence purposes. After the Green Revolution, industrialized agriculture grew significantly, engulfing the smaller and marginalized traditional farmers, although not entirely eliminating them. Along with the growth of agro-industry, there is also the growth of organic and alternative rice farming systems, which meet consumer demand from middle- to upper-class society in urban areas. These different agricultural systems extend beyond the farm level along the agri-food chain and, in the end, significantly influence how rice agricultural policies are being enacted in different worlds of rice.

We understand this from the realization that there are multiple meanings attached to rice, acquired through the assemblages formed with other actors, as shown in Figure 6.1. This figure does a particular kind of ontological work by avoiding the normal categories that are used to describe industries, sectors or economies. It does this by demonstrating the lines, relationships and assembling that 'make' the worlds of rice. Community groups attach themselves to particular rice varieties owing to cultural and dietary preferences, and thus bring meaning to rice as a cultural artefact. Pests, diseases, climate, water and soil all influence farmers and research centres when they are determining which rice should be planted in a particular area. Consumers, traders and technology negotiate the tastes, qualities and quantities of rice being produced. The government and political parties negotiate with rice as a commodity, establishing rice in a different role: rice as a political tool, influencing the many networks of Indonesian society. Assembling this alternative narrative, and building on Timmer's (2005) assertion of the three facets of rice (a food, a crop and a commodity), demands that we interrogate a new set of theoretical frameworks in ways that can take account of the multiplicity of rice revealed in Figure 6.1.

Rice in its multiplicity

Many authors who study rice start their introduction with an expression of amazement at the adaptability of rice (for example see Hanks 1972; Bray 1986). Rice grows in a very wide spectrum of conditions. Although it is known mainly as a semi-aquatic plant that thrives in swampy areas, it can also grow in dry areas (Lu and Chang 1980; Bray 1986). In fact, certain varieties of rice are not only tolerant to water, but also benefit from flooded conditions. Mikkelsen and de Datta (1980) note that precipitation and water enhance nutrient availability, help with nitrogen fixation, and create favourable microclimatic conditions for rice growth. Some varieties have also adapted to the extent that the water level flooding the stem of rice acts as an indicator for the initiation and ripening of its fruits (Vergara 1980).

Domesticated by the early Asian settlers in about 10000–15000 BC, the annual forms of rice are thought to originate from East India, South-East Asia and South-West China (Lu and Chang 1980; Bray 1986). It is estimated that, 10,000 years later, rice had successfully replaced root crops and other cereals as the staple food of people living in Asia. In its places of origin, rice formed three eco-geographic variety groups based on their affinities to specific ecological

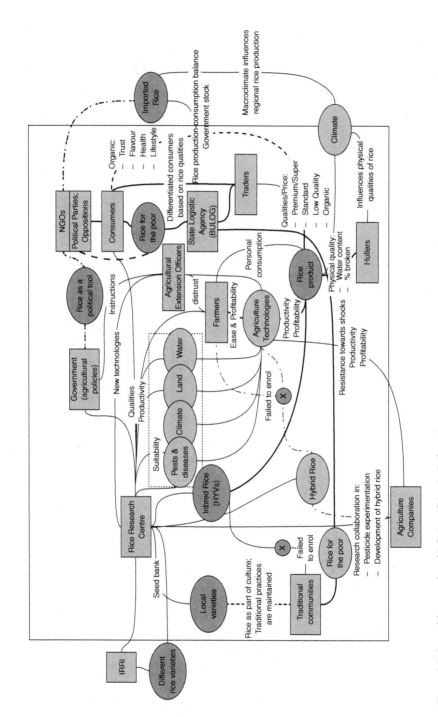

Figure 6.1 Assemblages and multiplicity of rice in Indonesia

and geographic characteristics. The first was the *sinica* (*japonica*) subspecies, its name reflecting its origin in temperate Asia (China and Japan). The second was *indica*, including the tropical rice varieties from India and the South-East Asian region (Hanks 1972; Lu and Chang 1980). The third subspecies had only been identified in 1958 as *javanica* to designate a similar variety group to *japonica*, but with significant differences in its affinity to a tropical environment (Bray 1986).

At this point, it is necessary to detail the characteristics of two relevant subspecies of rice in Indonesia, the *javanica* and *indica*, as these are vital for our subsequent analysis of the agency of rice that contributes to its multiplicity. The *javanica* subspecies, commonly known as the traditional variety group (TV), has broad, thick-culmed grains, low tillering, tall plant stature, low grain-shattering, and hard plant tissue (Bray 1986). It is somewhat less sensitive to sunlight and temperature, and thus has a good reputation for its ability to grow on dry upland areas of swidden agriculture (Asai et al. 2009).

The *indica* subspecies, from which the modern high-yielding rice varieties (HYVs) are derived, has longer grains, profuse tillering, low to intermediate plant stature, easy grain-shattering, and a soft plant tissue. It is more responsive to temperature and often found in lower altitudes. These characteristics made *indica* rice the perfect candidate for the Green Revolution in lowland tropical areas in Indonesia, which cover a very wide area with good irrigation systems and very fertile, alluvial soil. The profuse tillering means that it has more capacity to capture sunlight for grain production; the easy shattering means it is more energy efficient when separating the grain from the straw; the long and thinly culmed grain makes it easier to hull. It is apparent that these characteristics have shaped the way in which modern agriculture is practised in Indonesia, rather than it being a mere coincidence that the technology fits with the characteristics of *indica*. The following is an elaboration of how the two subspecies shape different worlds of rice in Indonesia.

Rice as an economic commodity

From the early 1950s, the Malthusian dilemma had oriented agriculture and food research and development to align with the productivity rhetoric and goals of the Green Revolution. The main objective of such research was to produce food commodities with higher yields and shorter growing periods. For rice, the perfect candidate was *indica*, as the once local varieties had already spread across tropical Asia (including Sri Lanka, Taiwan, Malaysia and Indonesia) (Herdt and Capule 1983). Simultaneously, many national-based research institutes in the region were developing new rice varieties; hence, the *indica* variety group provided a plethora of genetic resources for the development of HYVs.

Through *indica* rice, the HYVs introduced a new spirit of agriculture under the Green Revolution and re-oriented rice farming towards a more industrialized agriculture, directly connected to the domestic, and also international, rice markets (Dawe 2001). This has brought various shocks and changes to the system. Pests and diseases emerge in various forms. Climatic change, in combination with global economic crisis, exacerbates crisis conditions (Neilson and Arifin 2012). In response to these shocks, within the last 50 years the Indonesian Centre for Rice Research (ICRR) has developed more than 200 new varieties of *indica* rice from local and regional seed banks on the basis of their resistance to pests and diseases, their suitability to extreme environments (flood, drought, saline tolerance), their productivity, and taste preferences. The first three characteristics help farmers to better adapt to climate variability than the extent to which farmers traditionally had done so. This last characteristic, furthermore, is particularly useful for creating a variety of products within the rice market and, to some extent, a flexible and diverse economy for farmers.

The majority of farmers grow 'regular' varieties to produce a household-consumption standard of rice grain (although variation in quality exists owing to the different environmental conditions in which rice is grown). Others use varieties that are less desirable for household consumption, such as IR42 and glutinous rice, which, as raw materials in the food processing industry, have higher prices in the market. In the southern region of West Java, most of the farmers own very small plots of land, decreasing the commercial feasibility of their agricultural activities. Because of limited land and low soil quality that results in lower productivity, those who farm commercially often choose to plant premium varieties, which taste better and consumers prefer, such as the aromatic *pandanwangi* rice.

This variability also impacts on the dynamics of the rice market. The premium rice such as *pandanwangi* is limited in availability, resulting in a price that is more than 50 per cent higher than that of the regular rice in the same market. It follows that the premium rice only serves a particular market segment of upper-class consumers. Meanwhile, the regular rice constitutes more than 90 per cent of all traded rice. Therefore, the regular rice acts to shape the overall price in the market.

Interestingly, because the quality distinction is evident in rice only once it is cooked, there are no clear boundaries for the identity of rice in the market. Rice grains bear certain physical qualities (for example colour, moisture and size) that are often indistinguishable from the point of view of the typical consumer, which, however, result in very different cooking qualities (taste, texture, stickiness and so on). Different combinations of various types of rice cooked in the same pot may result in different cooking quality. In the market, retailers often mix multiple varieties of rice grains in countless combinations to formulate, in a way, new brands of rice. Between the regular and the premium rice, combinations of both in various proportions act as the intermediate qualities bridging the price points of both rice types. This creates a continuum of rice qualities and prices, and consequently also stabilizes prices.

Consumers do not necessarily select for the 'better' rice, and so we may see the qualities of rice as preferences instead of ranks. Based on a survey by Damardjati and Oka (1992), consumers in Java preferred traditional rice varieties over the modern ones, and the price premium for the traditional far exceeded the price of the 'better-tasting' modern varieties. This is because the traditional rice varieties provide a different taste and texture (particularly as a result of their high fibre content) from those that the modern varieties have to offer. Labourers commonly also paid less attention to taste, but more to rice varieties that could give 'an enhanced feeling of satiation' (Damardjati and Oka 1992: 60). These multiple dimensions of rice cooking and taste qualities illustrate the necessity of using an economic framework that accounts for much more than just the observable market of standardized rice varieties and the logic of supply and demand.

Rice as a political commodity

The intricacies of the engagement between rice and people, whether they be farmers, traders or consumers, show the importance of rice to the whole of Indonesian society. This fact supports the belief that social and political stability could not have been achieved without stability in the rice agricultural sector (Dawe 2001; Timmer 2005). The extent to which rice has become so important to both farmers and consumers has given rice another meaning: that is, as a lucrative political commodity for the government and political elites.

As a political commodity, rice is recognized as having been a key foundation of social and political stability during the 32 years of Soeharto's authoritarian regime (1966–98). Similarly, the realization of self-sufficiency in Indonesia that coincided with the 2008 World Food Crisis (Neilson and Arifin 2012), as well as some formative regulatory moves (Fane and Warr 2009), might be considered as much a political success as a significant agricultural achievement. It is evident from this study's observations that rice is embodied within political activities in Indonesia to a greater extent than any other commodity. The material and symbolic embodiment of rice, as a native plant of South-East Asia, staple food for the population, and commodity for the farmers, is evidenced in its strong attachment to, and influence upon, the region's geopolitics.

Rice as a political commodity serves as a means to cater to the needs not only of farmers and the agricultural sector, but also of a wider group of people, including the rural and urban poor. This has been achieved through a government project called the Rice for the Poor programme (*Beras untuk Keluarga Miskin*, RASKIN). RASKIN is a targeted subsidy of discounted rice distributed every month to poor families throughout Indonesia. The rice is sold to the beneficiaries for a quarter of the average rice price. As rice purchases account for more than 50 per cent of disposable income amongst the urban poor, affordable rice offers significant relief to such families, and helps in alleviating the impact of economic shocks (Irhamni and Nuryakin 2009; Neilson and Arifin 2012). The RASKIN programme has expanded, not only in urban and suburban areas, but also, and most importantly, in rural areas, in which the number of poor families is greater and they are known to be net consumers of rice (Irhamni and Nuryakin 2009).

Interestingly, in traditional communities RASKIN is not necessarily seen as the rice for the very poor. It has acquired an entirely different meaning. In traditional communities, which are most often self-sufficient in rice, some people are lured to purchase RASKIN because buying rice means that they do not have to work hard to produce and prepare it, which occupies much of their time and energy. As not many people in the traditional communities have money to purchase the rice, RASKIN rice has instead become a commodity for elites in the community. In a way, consuming RASKIN rice in these traditional communities is seen as a privilege for the affluent, evidence that they can have what the poor cannot.

What interests us in understanding this is that rice, in the form in which it was intended to be, can be translated into an entirely altered meaning, given its attachment to different actors. Rice brings within itself qualities that in the end can be perceived differently by every actor. Here, even RASKIN – a rice that through its quality embodies a symbol for the poor – is translated into an object of affluence and privilege as other actors attach themselves to it.

Rice as a cultural artefact

Rice in traditional communities helps to enact an entirely different world. This is not only the result of the way that traditional communities practise different ways of farming, but also because of the characteristics of traditional rice varieties that have rendered this traditional agriculture relevant to the people. The focus of this section shifts from the *indica* to the *javanica* rice variety group, more commonly known as the 'traditional' varieties. As implied by its name, *javanica* rice was, and in some areas still is, the most acceptable variety of rice in the island of Java. As an integral element of local lifeways, it helps to shape how farming and culture are practised in pockets of local communities in upland areas in Java. The traditional *javanica* rice has been deeply entangled with the life and practices of Javanese people. For centuries, rice has influenced Javanese culture in many ways – through their foods, ceremonies, agricultural practices and philosophies (Soemarwoto 2007).

The Javanese people recognize Dewi Sri, the rice or prosperity goddess, as of central importance to their agricultural activities (for more details see Wessing 1988). In their culture, Dewi Sri is not an external power regulating the performance of rice in the paddy (as most cultures perceive the influence of their deities). She herself is the rice, or the embodiment of rice. Thus, it is not peculiar that the traditional Javanese farmers treat rice in a very deferential manner, through a set of rituals and taboos surrounding this particular product, even around the ways of cooking and consuming it. For them, rice is irreplaceable; as they say, 'Without rice, we could not live.' The way they engage with rice is shown in their attempt to conserve its landraces.[2]

In one traditional community in West Java, the community leader informed us that they had more than 500 landraces, classified according to their sacredness (*buhun*, ancient; *biasa*, regular), their affinity to water–soil regimes (in wetland or dryland), and the elevation at which they are planted (as also noted in Soemarwoto 2007). The sanctity of rice also influences cultural protocols. For example, *buhun* rice, more so than the regular rice, has to be planted as a prerequisite for farming, using *huma* (the dryland rice farming) and with very stringent rules on the procedures of planting. In that sense, *buhun* rice is maintained as a constant reminder of the community's cultural values.

The people–rice relationships emerge not only through those symbolic interactions, but also through the materiality of rice. The physical features of traditional *javanica* rice – hard stem tissue, a long growing period, and low-shattering grains – have shaped traditional agricultural practices. The first two features impact on the way traditional farmers in South-East Asia use small 'finger knives' to cut the rice stalks off the straw (Hanks 1972). For traditional farmers, rice harvesting is a personal process between farmers and their crops. The 'finger' knife allows them to treat each stalk in a respectful, cautious manner, while, from a practical perspective, also giving them the opportunity to distinguish good rice varieties from bad for the purpose of selecting breeding stock.

Another physical feature of the traditional rice is its low-shattering grain. This characteristic is useful for storage, because farmers store the dried rice in stalk bundles, and an easy-shattering rice variety is impractical for this type of storage method. The stalk bundles are put in a small barn designed specifically for storing rice, which retains a particular temperature and humidity. Storing rice in stalk bundles inside this barn helps to lengthen the shelf-life of the rice for years. In many traditional communities in West Java, for instance, community members also allocate some portions of their harvest to be put into a communal rice barn. In circumstances where rice production is compromised owing to climatic shocks, the community relies on this communal barn, from which anyone can borrow rice at any time, and return it with the same amount he/she has borrowed after the next harvest period. With rice providing the basis of their local knowledge, a strong relationship of rice and people has created a system, or network, adaptive enough to withstand environmental shocks (such as climate change and pest infestation) through practices of maintaining the variability of rice varieties, and making use of the durability of rice for risk-sharing.

These examples of cultural practices (landrace conservation, traditional rice harvesting, and communal barns) are enacted on the basis of the multiplicity of rice, as a symbol, crop, food and cultural artefact. This assemblage is inextricably woven into centuries of co-assembly between humans and nature. The examples also illustrate the co-production or embedded nature of rice with local communities and how these exist in addition to (and should be equally valued and promoted along with) the forms of economy and production that fall under more orthodox categories of explanation.

Conclusions

To conclude, we would like to make the point that acknowledging the diversity and multiplicity of rice also demands facilitating a diversity of actions. The case presented here has demonstrated that each meaning of rice (economic and political commodity as well as cultural artefact) is manifested in different agri-food assemblages, or worlds, of rice. In regard to these multiple realities, this chapter follows the discussion initiated by Mol (2002) on the multiplicity of a disease. In her account, multiplicity is never simply a matter of recognizing different perspectives. Multiple realities are produced by particular practices that relate to each other and that adhere to distinct assemblages of human and non-human actors. These multiple realities also raise the possibility of conflicting practices that hinder a given political performance. The manner through which multiplicity enhances the agri-food systems depends on how these realities 'dovetail together . . . or include one another in complex ways' (Law 2008: 152).

The argument in this chapter also challenges many economic and political analyses that favour navigating Indonesia away from a rice-centred to a more export-oriented agricultural policy (McCulloch and Timmer 2008). Instead, this chapter has suggested that rice is indeed irreplaceable to Indonesians, as evidenced by the complex interconnectedness of rice and society in multiple practices. The fact that, through its multiple meanings and practices, rice is so deeply embodied and intertwined with Indonesian society implies that separating rice from society is practically impossible, and that all of the actors connected to rice will do whatever it takes for the continuance of rice agri-food systems in Indonesia. There should be no single paradigm for Indonesia's rice agriculture, nor for other agricultural commodities. It has been proven with rice that different policies and strategies cater to the needs of different groups, and are in line with the characteristics of different rice varieties. Without acknowledging that rice is multiple, agricultural policy will always invite tensions and deadlocks located in the realties that have been ignored. In the end, we suggest that the role of a post-human research agenda in political decision making comes as a shift from 'controlling' to 'working with' the non-human actors. Our acknowledgement, as social scientists, of the multiple realities of the materiality with which we engage is a political act that encourages more diverse and aware policy making and an openness to other pathways towards resilience, survival and security.

Notes

1 In Latourian terms, 'artefact' implies embodied actions and knowledge within a material object (see Latour 2005).
2 We agree with Rini Soemarwoto (2007) in using the term 'landraces' instead of 'varieties' or 'cultivars', as they are identified based on the community's traditional method, and a further analysis might determine that two or more landraces represent a single variety, or vice versa.

References

Asai, H., Saito, K., Samson, B., Sungyikhangsuthor, K., Homma, K., Shiraiwa, T., Kiyono, Y., Inoue, Y. and Horie, T. (2009) 'Yield response of *indica* and tropical *japonica* genotypes to soil fertility conditions under rainfed uplands in northern Laos', *Field Crops Research*, vol. 112, pp. 141–148.

Bennett, J. (2007) 'Edible matter', *New Left Review*, vol. 45, pp. 133–145.

BPS (Badan Pusat Statistik) (2012) *Statistik Indonesia*, http://www.bps.go.id/tnmn_pgn.php?kat=3, accessed 30 December 2013.

Bray, F. (1986) *The Rice Economies: Technology and Development in Asian Societies*, Basil Blackwell, Oxford.

Damardjati, D. S. and Oka, M. (1992) 'Evaluation of urban consumer preferences for rice quality characteristics in Indonesia', in L. J. Unneveher, B. Duff and B. O. Juliano (eds), *Consumer Demand for Rice Grain Quality*, International Rice Research Institute, Manila.

Dawe, D. (2001) 'How far down the path to free trade? The importance of rice price stabilization in developing Asia', *Food Policy*, vol. 26, pp. 163–175.

Dawe, D. (2002) 'The changing structure of the world rice market, 1950–2000', *Food Policy*, vol. 27, pp. 355–370.

Dwiartama, A. (2014) 'Investigating resilience of agriculture and food systems: insights from two theories and two case studies', doctoral dissertation, University of Otago.

Dwiartama, A. and Rosin, C. (2014) 'Exploring agency beyond humans: the compatibility of actor-network theory (ANT) and resilience thinking', *Ecology and Society*, vol. 19, no. 3, p. 28.

Fane, G. and Warr, P. (2009) 'Indonesia', in K. Anderson and W. Martin (eds), *Distortions to Agricultural Incentives in Asia*, World Bank, Washington, DC.

FAO (Food and Agriculture Organization) (2011) *FAOStat*, http://faostat.fao.org/site/342/default.aspx/, accessed 21 August 2011.

Gerard, F., Marty, I. and Erwidodo (2001) 'The 1998 food crisis: temporary blip or the end of food security?', in F. Gerard and F. Ruf (eds), *Agriculture in Crisis: People, Commodities, and Natural Resources in Indonesia, 1996–2000*, CIRAD, Montpellier.

Hanks, L. M. (1972) *Rice and Man: Agricultural Ecology in Southeast Asia*, Aldine Atherton, Chicago, IL.

Herdt, R. W. and Capule, C. (1983) *Adoption, Spread, and Production Impact of Modern Rice Varieties in Asia*, International Rice Research Institute, Manila.

Hill, H. (2000) *The Indonesian Economy* (2nd edn), Cambridge University Press, Cambridge.

Husken, F. and White, B. (1989) 'Java: social differentiation, food production, and agrarian control', in G. Hart, A. Turton, B. White, B. Fegan and L. T. Gheen (eds), *Agrarian Transformations: Local Processes and the State in Southeast Asia*, University of California Press, Berkeley.

Irhamni, M. and Nuryakin, C. (2009) 'The rice sector in West Java', in A. L. Stoler, J. Redden and L. A. Jackson (eds), *Trade and Poverty Reduction in the Asia-Pacific Region*, WTO and Cambridge University Press, Cambridge.

Latour, B. (2005) *Reassembling the Social: An Introduction to Actor-Network-Theory*, Oxford University Press, Oxford.

Law, J. (2008) 'Actor network theory and material semiotics', in B. S. Turner (ed.), *The New Blackwell Companion to Social Theory*, Blackwell Publishing, Malden, MA, pp. 141–158.

Lu, J. J. and Chang, T. T. (1980) 'Rice in its temporal and spatial perspectives', in B. S. Luh (ed.), *Rice: Production and Utilization*, AVI Publishing Company, Westport, CT.

McCulloch, N. and Timmer, C. P. (2008) 'Rice policy in Indonesia: a special issue', in *Bulletin of Indonesian Economic Studies*, vol. 44, no. 1, pp. 33–44.

Mikkelsen, D. S. and de Datta, S. K. (1980) 'Rice culture', in B. S. Luh (ed.), *Rice: Production and Utilization*, AVI Publishing Company, Westport, CT.

Mol, A. (2002) *The Body Multiple: Ontology in Medical Practice*, Duke University Press, Durham, NC.

Neilson, J. and Arifin, B. (2012) 'Food security and the de-agrarianisation of the Indonesian economy', in C. Rosin, H. Campbell and P. Stock (eds), *Food Systems Failure: The Global Food Crisis and the Future of Agriculture*, Earthscan, London.

Reid, A. (1999) *Charting the Shape of Modern Southeast Asia*, Silkworm Books, Chiang Mai.

Soemarwoto, R. (2007) 'Kasepuhan rice landrace diversity, risk management, and agricultural modernization', in R. Ellen (ed.), *Modern Crises and Traditional Strategies: Local Ecological Knowledge in Island Southeast Asia*, Berghahn Books, New York, pp. 84–111.

Sumarto, S. and Suryahadi, A. (2007) 'Indonesia', in F. Bresciani and A. Valdes (eds), *Beyond Food Production: The Role of Agriculture in Poverty Reduction*, FAO, Northampton, MA.

Timmer, C. P. (2005) 'Food security and economic growth: an Asian perspective', *Asian-Pacific Economic Literature*, vol. 19, no. 1, pp. 1–17.

Vergara, B. S. (1980) 'Rice plant growth and development', in B. S. Luh (ed.), *Rice: Production and Utilization*, AVI Publishing Company, Westport, CT.

Wessing, R. (1988) 'Spirits of the earth and spirits of the water: chthonic forces in the mountains of West Java', *Asian Folklore Studies*, vol. 47, pp. 43–61.

7 Materialising taste

Fatty lambs to eating quality – taste projects in New Zealand's red meat industry

Matthew Henry and Michael Roche

Introduction

In October 2013 the New Zealand (NZ) meat processor Silver Fern Farms (SFF) announced the implementation of a new Eating Quality (EQ) grading system for some of their beef products. In launching the EQ programme SFF's then chief executive Keith Cooper indicated that it had emerged from the company's 'pasture to plate' strategy, which involved trying to understand what consumers wanted and working backwards to shape the practices of farmers to meet those desires. Materialising and quantifying taste are central to the aspirations of the EQ programme, and SFF is not alone in that aspiration. SFF's main New Zealand competitors, principally Alliance and ANZCO, are engaging in similar work, while emerging companies such as Firstlight Foods have explicitly shaped themselves around a concern with taste, and how it can be altered via genetics, feed and processing. The story among NZ's international competitors is similar. For example, in Australia, the Meat Standards Australia (MSA) grading system has been developed by Meat and Livestock Australia to make the link between eating quality and farm, processing, and cooking practices in ways that echo SFF's EQ programme. Placed in this context SFF's EQ programme is not unique, but rather represents one example of much wider work that is placing taste at the core of reimagining and remaking the relationship between meat, consumers, processors and farmers.

This chapter takes SFF's EQ programme as a strategic aperture through which to explore how taste is being mobilised in the creation of these new meat relationships. We approach this task in two specific, but complementary, ways. First, much of the talk about eating quality is promissory in so far as it looks forward to economic futures that might happen. Where this talk does look back, it almost inevitably compares past practices unfavourably with what is promised. Our approach is to argue that the future trajectory of the NZ meat industry cannot be effectively gauged without understanding how that future is still materially embedded in work on taste spanning over a century. Second, animating the mobilisation of taste is the desire to materialise it as an attribute able to be stabilised and calculable in order to perform new economic work. Framed in this way our attention to taste has been shaped by Michel Callon's work that has sought to explore those processes of assemblage through which things are made economic (for an overview of this work see Çalışkan and Callon 2010). In approaching taste as having a materiality subject to, and enactive of, economic work we open up a realm of actors, devices and work that constitute the 'boring things' described by Star and Lampland (2009), but whose bringing together renders possible the making of taste as an economic object.

This twinning of a genealogical concern with ideas of economisation is framed by the broader project of poststructural political economy (PSPE) charted by Le Heron (2007) and others. Beginning with the destabilisation of economic categories, and ways of ordering in the meat industry, as articulated by the industry itself, the chapter focuses on the material fabric of those categories, and the ongoing play of stability and instability that makes up that fabric. The chapter brings into sight a myriad of actors and devices hitherto unseen, and in doing so expands our understanding of what constitutes an economic actor or object. It also, by asserting the significance of the more-than-human and material, asks us to consider those situated, material fixes that evolve in order that economies can accommodate the materialities embedded in previously created economic objects, and the ways those fixes shape economic trajectories in quotidian and uncertain ways.

We begin by elaborating on our approach to taste. We suggest that taste is characterised by a profound mutability that provides both an opportunity and an implement to taste's economisation. The chapter then briefly returns to SFF's EQ programme as our point of departure, before looking backwards to prior taste projects enacted at various times by NZ's meat industry. Here we examine taste work associated with Canterbury Frozen Meat prior to the First World War, the standardising work carried out by the New Zealand Meat Producers Board during the 1920s and 1930s, and the gradual dissolving of the assumed link between grading and taste in the 1960s and 1970s. We eschew a neat, chronological narrative so as to destabilise the teleological assumptions that are often implicit in such linear narratives, and to highlight the problematisation of taste's unstable materialities that has prompted, in multiple iterations, investment in new taste projects. The results of this, as we shall show, remain deeply embedded in the bodies of animals, farm management and processing practices, and cooking traditions. Such an approach forces us to consider the inadequacy of considering taste projects as *de novo* experiments in the enactment of new meat futures. Rather, we suggest that part of the uncertainty of the fashioning of taste assemblages is the relationship between the assembling work of the new, and that work which has already been rendered material and is embedded in existing taste assemblages.

Making taste

In her introduction to *The Taste Culture Reader,* Carolyn Korsmeyer (2005) points to the complexity that accompanies talk of taste. On one hand, she argues, the functional value of taste in helping sustain the body has resulted in its dismissal as a 'bodily' rather than 'intellectual' sense. On the other hand, taste has also been positioned as a signifier, and tool of civilisation, and of the difference between refinement and its 'other'. Given the extremes traced by these approaches, Korsmeyer warns us to avoid the lure of generalisation when it comes to thinking about taste: a point sharpened by her observation that the experience of taste is characterised by complex relationships of (in)commensurability, where the subtleties of individual sensory perception are entangled with dense associations of meaning, overlaid with the drift of time. Similarly, Mark Smith's (2007: 90) synthesis of work in sensory history argues that taste as a sense has been a key anchor of identity and distinction, but simultaneously subject 'to frequent and important redefinitions of what taste meant and how it functioned as an authenticator of truth and generator of reliable knowledge'. Consequently, in talking about taste we need to denaturalise the taken-for-granted stability of what we experience as taste, and instead start to examine how tastes are assembled and made to perform particular types of work.

Taste is an unstable sense, and Michael Carolan (2011) asks us to reflect on how this instability has been shaped as food has increasingly been mediated by preservation technologies such as canning and refrigeration. For Carolan industrial food has been accompanied by work to 'tune' taste, and here he draws our attention to Martin Bruegel's (2002) examination of the gradual acceptance of canned food by the French during the nineteenth and early twentieth centuries. As Bruegel recounts, the process of tuning French tastes to accept canned food involved multiple strategies, including the conditioning of soldiers to the taste and use of food, the linking of canned food with patriotism, widespread taste testing, and ongoing product calibration to make canned food 'good enough' for consumers. Here, the gradual melting away of resistance to canned food, and the acceptance of its palatability, required the fashioning of new food associations to stabilise the relationships between consumers, food and taste. What is evident in Bruegel's account is that there was no mysterious force behind the acceptance of canned food, but rather it was enacted by continual work designed to simultaneously tune both consumers' taste for canned food, and canned food itself. The varied dimensions of this taste work can be seen in other scholarship. Freidberg (2009) has explored the transformative possibilities for taste offered by refrigeration, while Horowitz's (2006) work shows us how the place of meat in American diets was continually reshaped by the complex, evolving assemblage of family routines, cooking practices, and technological changes in the meat-packing industry. Simultaneously responding to and enabling this evolution has been the transformation of the living tissue of animals, such as the fashioning of leaner pigs to accommodate consumer desires for less fat in their meat (Anderson 2009), the transformation of chickens into quotidian meat (Godley and Williams 2009), or the breeding of sheep for the intersecting demands of colonial environments, the frozen meat trade, and the specific tastes of British consumers (Woods 2012).

One of the characteristics of the changes that these studies highlight is that understanding the process of transforming taste requires attention to the assemblage of people, animals, plants, markets and technologies. In the context of the taste projects discussed in the chapter, we argue that an integral part of an attention to the assemblage of taste is the need to think about how taste is made economic (Çalışkan and Callon 2009, 2010), and argue that one of key moments in the making of markets is the creation of economic objects imbued with degrees of 'pacified agency' (Çalışkan and Callon 2010: 5). By 'passive', they are not denying agency to those objects, but rather they are referring to the ways in which the qualities of objects are stabilised so as to prevent the emergence of unexpected qualities that might disrupt calculations as to their performance or value. For example, in relation to canning, botulism was a quality that remained resolutely wild; until it was tamed it made canned food's qualities dangerously unstable, and significantly delayed canned food's emergence as an economic object. In this context, standardising work has historically represented a key way of producing passivity by abstracting the qualities of objects, making them precise, quantifiable, and commensurable across space and between communities of practice (Espeland and Stevens 1998; Timmermans and Epstein 2010).

Yet, as V. Higgins and Larner (2010) point out, the stabilisation work embedded in processes of standardisation is itself subject to instability. Çalışkan and Callon (2010) recognise this instability by pointing out that rendering things passive requires framing objects in terms of the qualities that are to be included in or excluded from the requirements of passivity, which in turn always creates the possibility of the overflow of the categories that have been constructed: one possibility that is doubly evident in the context of efforts to pacify the vibrant materialities of biological objects (Bennett 2010), and a possibility that is also alluded to by Calkins and Hodgen (2007), who make the point that hundreds of chemical compounds contribute to the taste of meat, and that the relationship between these compounds and taste is constantly altered through environment, diet, handling and cooking.

Framed by these ideas, and in particular an attentiveness to the assemblage of passivity in the creation of taste as an economic object, the chapter returns to sketching the development of SFF's EQ programme and the taste work which is at the core of that programme.

Silver Fern Farms Eating Quality programme

Central to SFF's EQ programme is a hoped-for congruence between a consumer's taste of EQ graded beef and the criteria upon which that meat is assessed. In broad terms the EQ system can be understood as the effort to try to fashion a niche standard for SFF's beef that defines its specific character in Olympian terms (Busch 2011). In making this specific connection between taste and grade, the EQ programme represents a distinctive reimagining of meat grading, since in NZ the tendency from the 1970s onwards has been to try to avoid embedding ideas of implied quality within grading categories.

The EQ system has been developed from taste tests involving tasters and researchers from Otago University and Texas Tech University. Speaking at the system's launch, SFF's chief executive, Keith Cooper, said that it reflected the company's strategy of working from consumer desires back to farmers, and its aspiration to develop a more systematically scientific means of determining consumers' taste preferences (Bishop 2013). Based on this testing the EQ system grades beef according to seven criteria that are believed to signal desired taste attributes: pH levels; the quantity and distribution of marbling within the meat; the degree of ossification within the carcass; the amount of rib fat; meat colour; fat colour; and the area of eye muscle. Notwithstanding the aspirations for scientific certitude in gauging taste, the grading process revolves around the expertise of graders and an array of prosthetic objects (meat and fat colour charts, marbling charts and so) in an assemblage that cannot simply be reduced to what Daston and Galison (2007: 115–190) term 'mechanical objectivity'.

As taste is made visible as a potential economic object, firstly through consumer testing, and more routinely through the grading assemblage, it is used to enact other economic relationships. Farmers supplying animals under SFF's various Backbone Programme contracts (contracts designed to standardise quality and ease stock procurement concerns) whose animals meet the EQ standard receive a premium over the standard market rate. More broadly all farmers supplying animals to SFF receive feedback reports based on the grading scores of their animals' carcasses. The expectation is that these feedback reports will shape farmers' land use and stock management decisions. The increasing entanglement of farmers' practice and SFF can be been in the light of SFF's involvement in the FarmIQ project. FarmIQ has been described elsewhere (Henry and Roche 2013), but it essentially represents the effort to create a farm management model that can enable the niche production of animals with particular carcass (and taste) attributes. Central to this model is the envelopment of farms in more systematic flows of quantitative and qualitative information that range from pasture tests to taste attributes. Information flows it is hoped will enable farmers to exploit emerging economic markets through the more intensive and disciplined management of the vibrant materialities of animals and farms.

Both FarmIQ and SFF's EQ programme have their genesis in the problematisation of economic returns in NZ's red meat industry (Deloitte 2011). A concern with the economic returns associated with agriculture has not been confined to the red meat industry, but has been sharpened by the historical significance of the red meat industry and its relative decline vis-à-vis a rapidly growing dairy industry. In 2009 the New Zealand government announced funding for a new suite of business-led programmes (primary growth partnerships, PGP) intended to foster innovation in the primary industry value chain. Currently there are 17 active PGP programmes, with total funding from government and industry of NZ$708 million. Of that money, almost half of it,

NZ$326 million, is wrapped up in five red meat-orientated projects. FarmIQ is one of the PGP programmes, and the largest (NZ$150 million) of the red meat projects. Started in 2010 and designed to conclude in 2017, FarmIQ promises an estimated economic benefit to NZ of approximately NZ$1.1 billion, while the government estimates for the whole PGP programme total economic benefits to New Zealand of $4.7 billion by 2025. Much then is expected of making taste visible as an economic object. Taste is being mobilised to more closely bind together consumer, processors and farmers. When metrologised it will provide a means for farmers to rework their farm and stock management practices, and it will be one of the mediators of national economic development. Yet we are not convinced that the making of taste visible as an economic object represents a *de novo* project and, perhaps more importantly, that it can be a *de novo* project disentangled from already existing assemblages and materialities. In the following sections we sketch a series of taste projects, beginning with the early origins of NZ's meat industry, the assemblages required to make them, and the material legacies of those taste projects. We conclude by reflecting on the limitations that the materialities of taste impose on the ability to render taste an economic object.

Canterbury Frozen Meat and carcass grading

The Canterbury Frozen Meat (CFM) company was founded in 1882 in Christchurch, NZ. As one of the first of a group of NZ-owned public meat companies it offers an excellent window into an emerging industry. It also provides a prequel to the recent EQ programme in so far as SFF was formed in 2008 out of the Primary Processing Co-operative Society (PPCS), which dated from 1948 and which from 1982 to 1986 had acquired CFM.

The NZ frozen meat industry was founded on mutton, and as late as 1913 mutton shipments still exceeded those of lamb (7.2 million to 3.6 million carcasses), though by 1927 lamb sales to the United Kingdom (UK) were double those of mutton (Barton 1984). The scale and nature of processing quickly assumed industrial food proportions, but one of the challenges, akin to that of canned food in France, was to tune the taste of frozen meat to British palates. NZ sheep meat was originally regarded as too fatty, a problem with quality that was accentuated by the fact that the first shipments were also 'heterogeneous assemblages of carcasses from sheep of varying ages, levels of fatness and weights' (Barton 1984: 58). The earliest 'taste' projects were thus dedicated to making NZ's frozen sheep meat conform to British expectations through visual appearance and measurement.

A major issue was that the initial shipments were of merino carcasses, a sheep bred for wool rather than meat production. Peden (2011) charts how the 'colonial' Halfbred and Corridale were subsequently bred as dual-purpose meat and wool breeds. The instability of meat in Carolan's (2011) terms can therefore be extended right back to the importation of pedigree stock from the UK in order to create animals that would produce meat palatable for the British consumers, and the success of that was 'testament to the power of imperial ties to remake taste, breeds and bodies' (Woods 2012: 308). The expert eye and ideas about the relationship between breed conformation and meat quality that guided these breeding efforts were crucial to this part of the earliest taste project.

By 1896 CFM had registered 'CFM' as a brand and developed a grading system for carcasses based around weight classes. There were early benefits, and by 1887 Canterbury meat was sought out 'in preference to that sent from other parts of the Dominion' (MacDonald 1957: 19). By the 1890s CFM's grading system was codified around five weight classes for mutton carcasses and three for lamb (Critchell and Raymond 1912: 107).[1] The increasing popularity of smaller-weight classes was attributed to working-class consumer preferences for smaller joints, 'because the wife of the English artisan and labourer is not skilled in making tasty dishes out of cold meat' (Critchell and Raymond 1912: 107): a perennial concern, and one that has, we show later, prompted the development of techniques such as cooking demonstrations. Even so CFM in the 1880s suffered financially because of the practice of selling small consignments from individual farmers through Smithfield, while the lack of central control in this, the major London meat market, meant there were delays in sorting, poor storage, and sometimes poor handling of carcasses. One result was the softening of meat – it was unstable in this sense as well. MacDonald (1957: 27), perhaps a little piously, in the CFM history observed:

> Much of the meat which was arriving lent support to the allegations of poor quality. South American meat was coarse and low-grade, and the same could be said of the North Island meat which was largely strong-woolled wether mutton. Australian merino wether mutton, however good it might taste, certainly wasn't much to look at.

Almost incidentally, this quotation reveals some of the attributes of meat that gave it a less than ideal taste. At Smithfield market local sellers confidently claimed to be able to distinguish home meat from colonial meat, with the colour of the defrosted carcasses being one distinguishing feature, and taste being directly inferred from the appearance of the carcass. Some New Zealand frozen meat was passed off as home meat by butchers, since the carcasses themselves were not individually identifiable as from New Zealand once the muslin casings were removed. On the other hand, poor-quality imported meat being sold as NZ meat did damage the country's reputation (Higgins, D. 2004).

Simultaneously another measurable taste project was under way. This was not initiated by the NZ meat companies, but emanated from the UK public health sector. Chapter 20 of Critchell and Raymond's (1912) comprehensive history of the early frozen meat trade is entitled 'The dietetics of frozen meat', and it neatly demonstrates Korsmeyer's (2005) view of the functional value of taste. Critchell and Raymond (1912: 290) avow that the amount of frozen meat consumed proved it was 'perfectly acceptable to all classes' – but they were sensitive to lingering criticism disputing its food value, even in 1912. Accordingly they cited results of comparative cooking tests of British and New Zealand mutton reported in the journal *Hospital*, including weight of slices, bone and gravy, along with other comparative tests of Australian and Argentine beef, and concluding with the testimony of medical officers of health.

As CFM's experiences suggest, the making of markets for New Zealand's sheep meat in the late nineteenth century is not reducible to a narrative of technological determinism associated with the development of refrigeration. Rather, these markets required experimentation with new forms of sheep breed, and learning about, and pacifying, the new materialities created by refrigeration. Driving this learning was the need to make New Zealand meat palatable, not so much a process of tuning the consumer, but rather a process of tuning meat producers to the tastes of Great Britain's consumers.

Standardising lamb: the New Zealand Meat Producers Board

The New Zealand Meat Producers Board (MPB) was established following the passage of the Meat Export Control Act in February 1922. The genesis of the MPB lay in the disastrous returns of the 1920–21 season as the supply agreement ('the commandeer') under which the British government had negotiated to buy all of New Zealand's meat came to an end, and the UK market was flooded with meat from South America as well as NZ (Hayward 1972). Provoked by this crisis, a vigorous debate within NZ canvassed the desirability of creating a meat pool to bring order to NZ's exports, and to improve returns to farmers.

The MPB's first report, in June 1923, articulated a set of problems that reflected the recommendations of a government-appointed inquiry into meat markets which had reported back to Parliament in December 1921 (*Hawera and Normanby Star* 1921). The inquiry's key findings concerned the uneven patterns of the arrival of NZ meat in the United Kingdom, and the costs associated with the handling of a multiplicity of meat grades and small packages of meat. Framed by these findings, the MPB emphasised, and would repeatedly emphasise, the importance of standardisation and grading in creating the confidence in buyers to buy meat in advance rather than off the hook at places such as London's Smithfield market (New Zealand Meat Producers Board 1923). Embedded in the MPB's advocacy of grading standardisation were two arguments about quality: firstly, the idea that adherence to a uniform grade system would maintain NZ meat's reputation for quality; and, secondly, the argument that the categories contained in the grade system reflected the eating qualities of NZ meat.

The link between grading and quality was codified in the standardised grade marks that the MPB developed during 1922 for lamb, mutton and beef (*New Zealand Journal of Agriculture* 1922). This system drew a distinction between 'prime' and 'seconds', with further subcategories based on weight. The purpose of this system was twofold: to give buyers an estimation of the quantity of meat in a carcass; and simultaneously to indicate the quality of the carcass's meat. The grading of meat into these categories was based on a range of criteria, including most significantly weight, fat content and conformation (shape) of the carcass. This system of grading, to use Busch's (2011) typology, represented the evolution of a hierarchical system that first filtered export-quality carcasses, and then ranked those carcasses based on the assumptions of eating quality associated with criteria such as fat and conformation. The systemisation of a national, uniform grading system represented a key moment of the pacification of carcasses, and the creation of a device through which ideas of taste could be subject to ongoing calculation and experimentation.

The grading system used by the MPB created what Barry (2006: 239) has termed a 'technological zone', which provided a space of commensurable expectations connecting meat buyers in the United Kingdom with farmers in NZ. In 1925 the MPB commented that, in order to maintain NZ's competitive position, 'we must not only increase our output, but we must also continue to improve the quality of our product' (New Zealand Meat Producers Board 1925: 6). To this end the MPB had announced in 1924 that it was offering prizes each year at the Royal Agricultural Show for lambs suitable for export. Lambs would be judged alive at the show, and then slaughtered and shipped to Smithfield for judging by the British Incorporated Society of Meat Importers.

This competition reflected the MPB's desire to make the quality expectations of meat buyers visible to lamb producers in the hope that the latter would embed those categories in their everyday farm management. At the 1924 Royal Agricultural Show hosted by the Manawatu and West Coast Agricultural and Pastoral Association (MWCA&P) in Palmerston North, the new class of competition was introduced as the 'Special London Freezing Class' and described as consisting of 'Fat lambs, most suitable for Dominion's export trade and the type most desired to keep up our reputation on the London market' (Manawatu and West Coast Agricultural and Pastoral Association 1924: 163). That this new competition, and its novel quality criteria, represented a challenge to the existing traditions of stock competitions was alluded to by the outgoing president of the MWCA&P, Leonard Wall, who complained that, unlike what applied to the freezing class supported by the MPB in other breed classes, 'there is too much notice taken of the get up of an animal instead of relying on real value – that is wool and mutton in a sheep' (Manawatu and West Coast Agricultural and Pastoral Association 1932, unpaged).

The prizes awarded by the MPB, alongside grading, represented parts of an ongoing effort to transform the materialities of NZ lamb to render them commensurable with the attributes of desirability articulated by meat buyers in the UK. Commensurability in this context was enacted through common expectations about weight, fat and carcass conformation, but also through how those expectations were translated into price variations across the grades. Implicit in, but never absent from, this effort was an assumption of the congruence between the attributes rendered visible and calculable in the grading system, and the eating qualities of NZ lamb.

Breaking the link between taste and grade

As the thicket of controls that had characterised the regulation of NZ's Second World War meat exports began to reach its end, the MPB congratulated itself that its policy of maintaining pre-war grading standards throughout the war had maintained the country's reputation for quality, and crucially secured the future of meat exports to the UK (New Zealand Meat Producers Board 1950). However, notwithstanding this sense of success, the assumptions of taste and quality embedded in the grading system introduced after the First World War would become disconnected from consumer ideas of taste and quality in the recovery from the Second World War, and increasingly the subject of concern and intervention.

In October 1965 the MPB published a report from its Meat Export Grades Investigation Committee, which had conducted the first major review of the grading system since its establishment in 1922. The committee did not recommend profound changes to the grading system, but it did recognise the limitations of the assumed link between grading and eating quality. It noted that, while names such as 'prime', 'choice' and 'good' were widely used to denote a quality hierarchy, 'consumer demand may decide that Choice or Good is preferable to Prime' (Meat Export Grades Investigation Committee 1965: 1). Consequently, the committee indicated a growing preference for the use of non-descriptive terms to distinguish different grades. This philosophical shift was reflected in the growing dissonance between the judging standards of Smithfield's meat buyers and consumer buying patterns. While meat buyers at Smithfield routinely judged the Southdown breed, which dominated the MPB's freezer-class competitions, as ideal, 'distributers have difficulty in selling them to a large section of the trade' (Meat Export Grades Investigation Committee 1965: 2–3). In preference to the award-winning Downs, buyers and consumers were increasingly favouring, as better-quality, the leaner 'Y'-classed lambs that had been passed over as seconds in the past (Anonymous 1975).

The shift from a hierarchical system of implied quality to divisions based on categorical difference was given further impetus in the early 1970s with the announcement of a further meat-grading inquiry. The purpose of the second inquiry can be found in the rationale behind the MPB's abolishment of its sponsored lamb export competitions in 1973. In announcing the demise of these competitions, the MPB stated that, while they had served their purpose in educating farmers about the requirements of the UK market, the changing preferences of that market, as well as other markets, meant that 'there was no one, "ideal" type of lamb universally acceptable to all markets' (Anonymous 1973: 1).

Simultaneous with the shift away from grades based on implied quality, the 1974 grading inquiry was also critical of the existing system of grading, which was largely based on the expertise of meat graders in visually assessing carcasses. Instead what the inquiry hoped for would be the development of 'a more objective operation, governed by scientific measurement standards' (Anonymous 1974: 3).As the report demonstrated, however, while it might be possible to specify measurement standards, actually fashioning a measurement system able to cope with the physical demands of a freezing works was an altogether different matter. Thus, despite the aspiration for mechanical objectivity and ongoing research and development of measurement systems to enact this objectivity, human graders in alliance with other actors remained central to grading systems through to SFF's contemporary EQ programme.

Persuading consumers to purchase lamb meant changes to its presentation and pricing, and the development of tenderness as a desired material quality of lamb. Because tenderness was unstable, however, it meant that it could not be guaranteed via the grading system. This realisation was reflected in the shifting logic behind grading. Fixing taste meant attempting to stabilise other relationships through which taste was being made. For instance, it meant paying attention to the evolving cooking practices of consumers, because those could significantly affect the taste of meat. Here it was argued that complaints about the toughness of NZ lamb were caused by a combination of factors, including the practice of cooking frozen rather than thawed lamb. Cooking from frozen was being recommended by freezer centres, but contradicted what the MPB recommended in its promotional literature. To counter this, Wood (1974: 7) reported that the 'Board's promotional department in London continues to sponsor cooking demonstrations to housewives and has produced special literature to assist consumers purchasing New Zealand lamb from freezer centres'. Taste could also be stabilised by the more effective ageing and conditioning of meat by processors in NZ. Stabilising taste through ageing and conditioning arrangements, such as squat-posture hanging or electrical stimulation, had implications for farmers because they were expensive. But, argued Wood (1974), making tenderness a taste attribute of NZ meat that would be stable regardless of cooking method would be instrumental in helping to maintain the potential value of that meat in markets that were becoming increasingly contested.

Conclusion

As a sense, taste is enormously mutable, and liable to constantly overflow the categories that we construct for it. In significant part, this is due to the complex materialities of objects such as meat, and the ways in which materials such as fats and proteins relate to one another, and are transformed by actions such as cooking. Consequently what we have argued is that the taste projects we have described simultaneously work with the opportunities provided by the richness of material complexity, and work to pacify that richness in order that the ephemerality of taste may be made durable, and able to be stably valued as an economic attribute of meat. In order to corral taste, we have suggested, using

SFF's EQ programme as the entry point, that what is fashioned is assemblages of taste characterised by varied actors and technical devices designed to do different work on taste. Through these assemblages, which brought together such things as refrigeration, fat lamb competitions, grading reports and practices, cooking demonstrations and so on, taste in the NZ meat industry was made visible, calculable, and deeply embedded in the practices of farmers and processors, the bodies of animals, and the palates of consumers.

The identification of these myriad assemblages leads us to conclude with two thoughts that might give us cause to reflect upon the enactment of new meat futures.

First, there is the absence of taste from our understanding of the development of the meat industry. We do not see systematically discussed anywhere the taste-making work that this chapter has shown exists. Yet, as we have demonstrated, the work to enact taste as an economic object has been enduring and concerted, and has seen the fashioning of complex arrangements of people, objects, technologies and animals. To pay no regard to that work, to perhaps assume that it safely rests in the realm of the settled, stable, 'boring things', is to ignore vibrant worlds of economic practice that have profound implications for understanding meat industries both historically and also as new meat futures are being enacted.

Second, what the extant sensory histories of taste have shown us is that taste is enormously unstable. In other words, our sense of taste is always in the process of changing. The agencements that we have discussed represent then contradictory efforts to mobilise the mutability of taste and to fix taste. Focusing on the latter we argue that these assemblages discussed here represent collective projects to stabilise the taste of NZ's meat, by knitting together and aligning the unstable materialities of animals and meat, as well as the technologies of meat production, and the practices and subjectivities of farmers and consumers. It is, in other words, an assemblage of assemblages, the effect of which has been the creation of a momentum that is hard to shift because it is deeply embedded in the routine understandings, materials and practices of meat worlds. Consequently, we remain pessimistic about the promise of programmes such as SFF's EQ to enact new meat futures, because such an enactment is not simply an act of will, but rather requires the patient work of piecing together new 'boring things' in circumstances where those things are buffeted between the material instability of meat itself and the embedded momentum of those already existing materialities, created and transformed in previous efforts to mobilise taste and make it economic.

Note

1 In New Zealand, Australian and UK usage, 'lamb' broadly refers to meat coming from sheep less than one year old, 'hogget' or 'teg' to meat from sheep between one and two years old, and 'mutton' to meat coming from sheep older than two years.

References

Anderson, J. (2009) 'Lard to lean: making the meat-type hog in post-World War II America', in W. Belasco and R. W. Horowitz (eds), *Food Chains: From Farmyard to Shopping Cart*, University of Pennsylvania Press, Philadelphia, pp. 29–46.

Anonymous (1973) 'Meat field days as alternative to lamb competitions', *New Zealand Meat Producer*, November, vols 1–2.

Anonymous (1974) 'Meat grading report released', *New Zealand Meat Producer*, vol. 3, no. 3.

Anonymous (1975) 'Board pays premium for Y grade', *New Zealand Meat Producer*, vol. 3, February.

Barry, A. (2006) 'Technological zones', *European Journal of Social Theory*, vol. 9, pp. 239–253.

Barton, R. A. (1984) 'New Zealand export carcass grades of lamb, mutton and beef: past, present and probable', in R. A. Barton (ed.), *A Century of Achievement*, Dunmore Press, Palmerston North.

Bennett, J. (2010) *Vibrant Matter: A Political Ecology of Things*, Duke University Press, Durham, NC.

Bishop, D. (2013) 'Grading system gives an edge', *Southland Times*, 28 November.

Bruegel, M. (2002) 'How the French learned to eat canned food, 1809–1930', in W. Belasco and P. W. Scranton (eds), *Food Nations: Selling Taste in Consumer Societies*, Routledge, New York, pp. 113–130.

Busch, L. (2011) *Standards: Recipes for Reality*, MIT Press, Cambridge, MA.

Çalışkan, K. and Callon, M. (2009) 'Economization, part 1: shifting attention from the economy towards processes of economization', *Economy and Society*, vol. 38, pp. 369–398.

Çalışkan, K. and Callon, M. (2010) 'Economization, part 2: a research programme for the study of markets', *Economy and Society*, vol. 39, pp. 1–32.

Calkins, C. and Hodgen, J. (2007) 'A fresh look at meat flavor', *Meat Science*, vol. 77, no. 1, pp. 63–80.

Carolan, M. S. (2011) *Embodied Food Politics*, Ashgate, Farnham.

Critchell, J. T. and Raymond, J. (1912) *A History of the Frozen Meat Trade*, Constable & Co., London.

Daston, L. and Galison, P. (2007) *Objectivity*, Zone Books, New York.

Deloitte (2011) *Red Meat Sector Strategy Report*, Deloitte, Auckland.

Espeland, W. N. and Stevens, M. L. (1998) 'Commensuration as a social process', *Annual Review of Sociology*, vol. 24, pp. 313–343.

Freidberg, S. (2009) *Fresh: A Perishable History*, Belknap Press, Cambridge, MA.

Godley, A. and Williams, B. (2009) 'Democratizing luxury and the contentious "invention of the technological chicken" in Britain', *Business History Review*, vol. 83, pp. 267–290.

Hawera and Normanby Star (1921) 'Meat pool scheme', *Hawera and Normanby Star*, 21 December.

Hayward, D. (1972) *Golden Jubilee: The Story of the First Fifty Years of the New Zealand Meat Producers Board*, Universal Printers, Wellington.

Henry, M. and Roche, M. (2013) 'Valuing lively materialities: bio-economic assembling in the making of new meat futures', *New Zealand Geographer*, vol. 69, pp. 197–207.

Higgins, D. (2004) '"Mutton dressed as lamb?" The misrepresentation of Australian and New Zealand meat in the British market 1890–1914', *Australian Economic History Review*, vol. 44, pp. 161–184.

Higgins, V. and Larner, W. (2010) 'From standardization to standardizing work', in V. Higgins and W. Larner (eds), *Calculating the Social: Standards and the Reconfiguration of Governing*, Palgrave Macmillan, New York.

Horowitz, R. (2006) *Putting Meat on the American Table: Taste, Technology, Transformation*, Johns Hopkins University Press, Baltimore, MD.

Korsmeyer, C. (2005) 'Introduction', in C. Korsmeyer (ed.), *The Taste Culture Reader: Experiencing Food and Drink*, Berg, Oxford.

Le Heron, R. (2007) 'Globalisation, governance and post-structural political economy: perspectives from Australasia', *Asia Pacific Viewpoint*, vol. 48, pp. 26–40.

MacDonald, G. R. (1957) *The Canterbury Frozen Meat Company Ltd: The First Seventy Five Years*, Canterbury Frozen Meat Company, Christchurch.

Manawatu and West Coast Agricultural and Pastoral Association (1924) *The First Royal (NZ) Agricultural Show Catalogue*, Palmerston North.

Manawatu and West Coast Agricultural and Pastoral Association (1932) 'Meeting of General Committee minutes, 15 March 1932', vol. 7, 17 September 1929 – 15 May 1932, Ian Matheson City Archives, Palmerston North.

Meat Export Grades Investigation Committee (1965) *Report to the New Zealand Meat Producers Board*, New Zealand Meat Producers Board, Wellington.

New Zealand Journal of Agriculture (1922) 'Standardized grade-marks for frozen meat', *New Zealand Journal of Agriculture*, 20 October, vol. 254.

New Zealand Meat Producers Board (1923) *First Annual Report and Statement of Accounts for the Period from 14th March 1922, to 30th June 1923*, New Zealand Meat Producers Board, Wellington.

New Zealand Meat Producers Board (1925) *Third Annual Report and Statement of Accounts for Year Ending 30th June 1925*, New Zealand Meat Producers Board, Wellington.

New Zealand Meat Producers Board (1950) *Twenty-Eighth Annual Report and Statement of Accounts for Year Ending 30th June 1950*, New Zealand Meat Producers Board, Wellington.

Peden, R. (2011) 'Pastoralism and the transformation of the open grasslands', in T. Brooking and E. Pawson (eds), *Seeds of Empire: The Environmental Transformation of New Zealand*, I. B. Tauris, London.

Smith, M. (2007) *Sensing the Past: Seeing, Smelling, Tasting, and Touching in History*, University of California Press, Berkeley.

Star, S. L. and Lampland, M. (2009) 'Reckoning with standards', *Standards and Their Stories: How Quantifying, Classifying, and Formalizing Practices Shape Everyday Life*, Cornell University Press, Ithaca, NY.

Timmermans, S. and Epstein, S. (2010) 'A world of standards but not a standard world: toward a sociology of standards and standardization', *Annual Review of Sociology*, vol. 36, pp. 69–89.

Wood, L. (1974) 'Cutting New Zealand lamb to cater to the demands of Continental Europe', *New Zealand Meat Producer*, 6 October.

Woods, R. J. H. (2012) 'Breed, culture, and economy: the New Zealand frozen meat trade, 1880–1914', *Agricultural History Review*, vol. 60, pp. 288–308.

8 Enactive encounters with the Langstroth hive

Post-human framing of the work of bees in the Bay of Plenty

Roseanna M. Spiers and Nick Lewis

This chapter explores the lively materialities of the work of honey bees and their keepers in New Zealand's Bay of Plenty. Drawing on a recent research project in which Roseanna followed 'a box of bees' and its beekeepers as they followed its bees (Spiers 2014), we ask what enactive, post-human research can contribute to fostering apiarian potentiality. In this account we concentrate attention on the 'box of bees' by narrating two encounters with everyday apicultural practices and their political and ecological economy that were staged as part of that research: being in the shed constructing Langstroth hives, and being with those hives in the field. The two vignettes allow us to recognise the hive as an assemblage of things, a significant biopolitical intervention in the management of honey bees (*Apis mellifera*) through which 'bees' come to be framed and mobilised to do particular work within New Zealand's broader biological economies and governing pastoral metrologies.

The chapter deploys the playful metaphor of 'speaking bees' to confront the ontological status of bees and develop a post-human account of apiarian potentiality. It demonstrates that it is through 'speaking bees' at sites such as the paddock and the smoko shed[1] that *A. mellifera* are enacted as material–semiotic entities and political–economic–ecological actors with a radical historical and ecological contingency. Here the phrase 'speaking bees' references an onto-storying (see Bennett 2004; Haraway 2008; Tsing 2010) and Deleuzian mapping of the conceptualisation and being of bees as an assemblage encompassing both content (machinic assemblages) and expression (collective assemblages of enunciation) (Deleuze and Guattari 2013). More simply, we attempt to emphasise the discursive materiality of bees, and how their situated assembling is no mere matter of discursive construction or material aggregation along some lines and not others. Rather, we point to the intra-activity of 'social' and 'natural' agencies encountered in the banal work of building and managing hives (where the distinction between 'social' and 'natural' emerges out of specific intra-actions), and to how 'bees' consequently emerge (in some forms and not others) through the resulting entanglement of matter and meaning. 'Speaking bees' and 'bees' (a general entomological category) therefore refer to beekeepers (and others) assembling the discursive materiality of 'bees' as a 'thing' which can be named, owned, and put to work.

This assemblage is brought into being through the co-constitutive acts, namings and framings of material objects, practices, and relations, in which bees are pivotal actors rather than plastic things subject to human directives from science and/or economy.

We make two arguments. First, not only do economy and ecology demand new ways of knowing the world of bees in the context of global environmental change,[2] but there is also a crucial ontological politics to knowing 'bees' as an enactive category and as worldly others. Second, the work of bees and of 'speaking bees' is always situated, and thus shaped technologically, economically, and socio-ecologically into a particular materiality that is vital, placed, and historical. This work has situated potentiality as well as consequences for the everyday lived realities-in-relation of pastures, pollinators, and people. Both arguments, we will suggest, take us beyond the worlds of bees to offer methodologies, an ontological politics, and a politics of representation for performing culture–nature interventions in what many are calling the Anthropocene, be they horticultural, agricultural, educational, or governmental.

Speaking bees in Aotearoa: a Langstroth framed radical historicity and vital materiality

Inspired by the work of Bennett (2004, 2010), Haraway (1988, 2008), and Barad (2007, 2010, 2012a, 2012b, 2013), our starting position is that apiculture in New Zealand has a radical historicity and a vital materiality in which the co-constitutiveness of human sociotechnologies and the reproductive sociality of *A. mellifera* have co-fabricated a complex and intra-active biological economy. Bennett (2010: 116) uses the term 'onto-story' as metaphor for how we might come to know and represent such a process of 'co-fabrication'. The standard narrative of the work of bees and bees at work in New Zealand fails to grapple with more lively, and risky, apicultural onto-stories. Our effort to do otherwise and to validate cosmopolitical attempts of knowing and doing 'bees' differently in New Zealand begins with the Langstroth hive, a movable-frame hive developed in the 1850s. Used exclusively by the beekeepers involved in this research and still the dominant hive used by commercial and backyard beekeepers in New Zealand and around the world, the Langstroth is understood to have a unique practicality in terms of cost, ease of construction, panoptical intervention, and colony manipulation (Hopkins 1916; Crane 1990, 1999). While represented in beekeeping discourse as an unproblematic 'box of bees' – 'a floorboard, a roof, and a variable number of boxes or hive bodies in between' (Matheson and Reid 2011: 29) – we explore the Langstroth as far more-than-human than a particular rationale and method for honey bee colony management.

Practical understandings of the 'hive' as human-made technology or physical architecture are tightly connected to its sociality and temporality as an event and a site of human intervention, as well as notions of 'colony', 'nest', and eusocial insect society. Broadly speaking, the concept of a superorganism is appropriate for any insect colony that is eusocial, or 'truly social'. More than an expansion of the 'organism' category, it poses a disruption or rejection of modernist categories. In entomology, the superorganism refers to an insect collectivity functioning as something more than the sum of its parts (Hölldobler and Wilson 2009). An *A. mellifera* colony (bees, brood, stores, and wax combs) is thus a composite being, in and of which the hive or nest is an integral constitutive component. The hive shapes honey bees, the work they do, and how they connect with their environment. As a sojourner in the Langstroth hive, the comb constitutes a uniquely accessible space for exploring apiarian potentialities – specifically the gathering and revealing of bee becomings. Our engagement with the hive does not seek to ontologically privilege the hive or argue that it is an ontological class in itself, separate from the broader environment. Rather, we highlight the hive and comb as a privileged site for post-human intra-action and engagements. The bees are here, constituting and being constituted through the enactment of the honeycomb nest.

A honey bee nest is part of, and plays a key role in, the visible expression of the bee superorganism. Its significance for the functioning of the bee colony is far greater than that which comes to mind for nests more generally – a shelter constructed of materials from the environment. The dominant feature of the hive or nest is the wax combs, which are in a sense a part of the bees themselves. They channel material, energy, and information in the hive (Tautz 2008; Seeley 2010). The nest is not only living space, food store, and nursery, but also an integral part of the superorganism: skeleton, sensory organ, nervous system, memory store, and immune system. It is an integral part of the larger superorganism entity, an environment constructed by the bees (and beekeeper) and one that has evolved with bees like any other organ or character, rather than one to which they have adapted. Even the forager bees that leave the comb on foraging flights spend more than 90 per cent of their lives within or on it (Matheson and Reid 2011). In beekeeping terms, the comb is where 'the magic' happens. This protracted amount of life spent on the comb provides countless possibilities for co-constitutive intra-actions between honeycomb, bee, colony, frames, and beekeeper, which (re)produce the honeycomb/wax frames/hive body as a site and event and shape the vital materialities coalescing through it.

Significantly, the hive lacks a distinct and discernible boundary between *milieu intérieur* (environment within organisms) and *milieu extérieur* (environment external to organisms) (Tautz 2008: 158). The hive body is very much an active site and event of emergent becoming. Far more than a human-made framing of bee lives, it is a site of multiple mundane and open-ended intra-actions among bees, beekeepers, flowers and pasture, wax comb, honey stores, wooden boxes, miticide-impregnated plastic strips, and more. Privileging beekeepers for a moment, the internal wax comb structure has presented them with an accessible and direct way of intervening in, and shaping, honey bee colony activity for more than 2,000 years (Crane 1983, 1999). They have mobilised specific colony management strategies, hive technologies, and bundles of apicultural knowledge to materially construct and channel bee bodies, activity, and agency along particular productive and extractive trajectories. For the past 175 years the Langstroth, which provides an artificial nest cavity (that is, stacked hive boxes) that restricts honeycomb construction to regular rectangular leaves or movable frames, has been the epitome of anthropocentric constructs for enabling these human interventions (Winter 1975; Crane 1990; Matheson and Reid 2011).

The Langstroth, then, is used by beekeepers quite literally to frame bees. Beekeeping literature and practice recognise this practical work of the hive but only in terms of standardised measures, sugar syrup ratios, seasonal management plans, do-it-yourself construction guides, and desirable production outcomes (Winter 1975; Matheson and Reid 2011). They focus less on 'interventions' beyond measurement of bee productivity, disease management, and ease of harvesting. 'Social' research on bees is largely restricted to: interest in literary tropes; economic potentiality in terms of supply chains, markets, labour, and (in recent years) alternative urban economies; and the implications for economy and society of the disappearance and latent work of bees (Crane 1983; Dobson 2005; Guthrie 2007; Benjamin and McCallum 2009; Horn 2011; Lahey 2012; McKibben 2013). There has been no critical attempt to explore the work of the hive as nature–culture in apiculture and biological economies more generally. The hive remains represented stubbornly as 'a box of bees', albeit a very useful and productive box, and not as a site of privileged human intervention that positions honey bees in the world and shapes their performance as a diffuse intra-active agency in the becoming of economic, agricultural, and ecological worlds. In the vignette that follows, we grapple with the ontological complexity of bees and the potential of research that explodes worldly apicultural relations to speak (of) bees more creatively, enrich stories of bees in circulation, and enact more lively futures.

The vignette narrates encounters with beekeeping practice in the daily (re)production of bees and the (re)structuring of the work they do. It gathers moments, sites, activities, and embodied experiences that are at once mundane and momentous, and allows us both to transcend the particular and to communicate some of the highly productive joy and passion experienced by 'proceeding from the middle' with honey bees (Haraway 1988, 2008; Gibson-Graham 2006: 194).

Roseanna at work in the shed (and field)

In the shed I come to know the hives, the bees that dwell within them, and the work they do through my own assembling of Langstroth hives. Gathering and composing hive components, measuring, threading, stapling, scraping, thrumming, and hammering Hoffman frames, I see the hive emerge as an apparatus for intervening in honey bee colony management. I come to know the knowing of the hive and the doing of the hive through this practice of constructing components in the company of experienced beekeepers. Being open to their guiding, my own practice in the shed engenders the beekeepers enacting the embodied logics of the(ir) hive, and the material–semiotic rationales choreographing our collective performance in the shed and through the hives.

August, a cool cloudy grey day with spatters of rain. David un-padlocks 'the shed', rolls up the corrugated iron door, and drags the heavy diesel generator out the front. It makes a horrible screeching sound on the concrete before I lock the wheels in place with a couple of stones. The generator is switched on to warm up: it will run the nail and staple guns, power tools, and portable lamps. To my nose the shed smells of treated wood, dust, paint, and damp. David corrects me: 'It stinks.' Now the sun is coming in through the open door. Inside is dim; the few small windows are dirty, and weak morning sun flints gold off dust in the air. Timber roof supports are cobwebbed and coated with bird droppings. Before relocating here in winter 2013, three beekeepers spent several days 'bird-proofing' the shed with corrugated plastic and wire netting. I can see completed hive boxes stacked 10 high at the far rear of the shed. There is a blackened kettle and gas burner: no mains electricity, no running water, no toilet facilities. Cardboard boxes of pre-cut eco-tanalised timber, hive frames, floors, and boxes at various stages of completion, a honey extractor, boxes of miticide strips, pails of paint, rolls of wire mesh, plastic propolis mats, and other beekeeping paraphernalia crowd three small workstations which are currently set up for building hive frames. This shed is where several hundred Langstroth hives and Hoffman frames are constructed over the slow winter season.

> The frames arrived at my workstation with David having assembled the basic wooden rectangle from pre-cut eco-tanalised wood. This frame consists of two equal sides with the wire holes pre-drilled, a bottom bar, and a top bar. Figure 8.1 summarises construction prior to the frame arriving at my workstation.
>
> Ten pairs of hive ends are slotted into a side splits construction box. The tops of the frame ends are dabbed with superglue and the top bar fixed in place. David staple-guns each top bar end straight down vertically into the side bar. The side splits construction box is flipped and the process repeated with the bottom bar. The box is placed on the floor; David kneels and hammers the staples level with the wood. This is necessary because of insufficient air pressure in the staple gun on this day. Each frame is then removed from the box and placed flat on the bench. A nail gun pumps four nails through the top and bottom of the side bars into the top and bottom bar. First stage complete, the frames are stacked two and two jenga-style in a tower next to the second workstation.
>
> *(continued)*

(continued)

Figure 8.1 Stage one of Hoffman frame construction: assembling the four sides

Source: Photos taken by R. Spiers, Paradise Valley, 9 September 2013.

The Hoffman frame is a movable, self-spacing frame wide enough to provide the correct bee space between combs when the frames are pushed together. Bee space is the space left between the leaves of comb: if the space is greater or less than the distance between the centre lines of adjacent 'natural' combs then the bees will construct comb or propolis across the gap. Hoffman frames are most common, as they can be used in both brood and honey boxes. The hives belonging to the beekeepers in this research feature 10 Hoffman frames per brood box and 8 per honey super: in honey boxes this works to encourage the bees to extend the comb beyond the frames and makes uncapping honey frames much easier. The end bars are scalloped to reduce the area of frames that can be propolised together, and to allow the bees to move around the ends of the frames: the 33 millimetre (as opposed to 35 millimetre) end bars are closest to the bee's natural comb spacing. These frames can be used comfortably at 10 per brood box, even after a season or two of use when bees have added propolis to the end bars.

Even in the middle of the day the shed is dim, cool, and noisy and smells strongly of diesel fumes: the generator rattles on the concrete and the power tools 'pfutt' continually. The partly assembled Hoffman frames arrive at my workstation, with David having secured the basic wooden rectangle (see Figure 8.2, top left). The workbench features a battery-powered lamp, staple gun, box of staples, wire cutters, and frame wiring board. The frame wiring board includes a roll of wire, a wooden outline securing the frame to be wired, and a wooden fastener arm used to hold the tension in the wire while the ends are fixed.

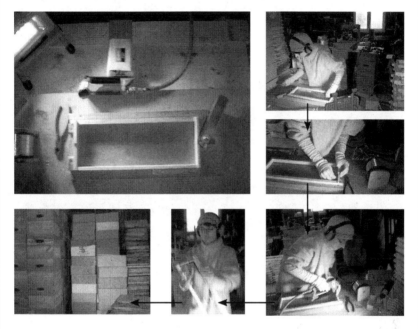

Figure 8.2 Stage two of Hoffman frame construction: threading wire

Source: Photos taken by D. Spiers, Paradise Valley, 9 September 2013.

The prepared frame is placed in the frame board. With my left hand I thread the wire through the bottom hole on the left end bar, and pull the wire through from left to right an armful and a bit. I thread the wire with my right hand through the right end bar bottom hole, pull the end through, up across the fastener arm, and feed it through the right end bar top hole. My left hand pulls the wire right to left back across the frame and through the top hole of the left end bar. I fold the end of the wire back over the staple right to left and staple. Excess wire is snipped. I roll excess wire back on to the wire feeder with my left hand to tighten the

(continued)

> *(continued)*
>
> threaded wire. I tighten it till the tension in the frame is high and I hear a low 'ting' as the wire clicks round the corners of the hole to tighten fully. With my left hand I hold the roll at tension, and with my right hand I pull the fastener arm all the way down to secure it. My body leans hard left as I do so to pull the arm down whilst holding the board in place on the workstation bench top. Scraping across the board, the fastener arm shaves off soft wood powder. Pinching the wire just right of the left end bar, I hold the tension whilst my right hand cuts the wire just left of the bottom left bar. I bend the end of the wire over the frame left to right and staple. I cut the excess wire and remove the frame from the board. Holding the frame in both hands, I 'thrumm' the wire with my thumb to confirm the tension, before stacking it jenga-style on the growing tower immediately right of my workbench. In the final stage, an electric current will be run through the wire to soften cut sheets of wax foundation, thus securing it in the frame. I am already reaching for another frame to thread.

The honeycomb is the largest organ in the honey bee superorganism. The Hoffman frame allows beekeepers to inspect the condition of the bees, manage disease and pestilence, and harvest bee products without destroying the colony. The comb can be removed without jarring, cutting, or agitating the bees; the bees are induced to build their combs with great regularity, and to accept additional frames; brood comb can be segregated from surplus honey storage; and surplus honey can be removed with convenience. The invention of the frame was a pivotal human intervention in the management of the honey bee colony, and it has remained the dominant hive technology for more than 125 years. It actively seeks to 'make' the hive in a way that gives the beekeeper control over all the combs, yet co-produces the hive with the bees. The frame is shaped by the biology and sociality of the honey bee superorganism and its instability, dynamism, and far from fully anticipatable set of intra-actions among human and non-human agencies; and it is not fully circumscribed by the Langstroth hive. A pivotal example is that of the constrained honeycomb.

Movable frames such as the Hoffman allow beekeepers to enclose the comb on all sides, but a frame that completely encloses the comb prevents, for instance, the horizontal displacement of the 'comb-wide web' seriously compromising communication (Tautz 2009). The motion of the surface network is restricted: it is not able to spread out across the rims of the cells, as there is no longer any free edge that can expand and contract. Bees have the capacity to intra-act with the human intervention, again, through the medium of the comb, bringing the being of bees by bees and the knowing of bees by humans (through the apparatus of the hive) into dynamic relation and potential conflict. Bees dance, a form of communication within the hive involving comb manipulation. While they do not disrupt framed honeycomb, on which they do not dance, leaving the combs intact as installed, on combs where dances do take place bees introduce large gaps between the wax and the wooden Hoffman frames. This restores signal transmission and the functionality of the comb as a lively materiality, even if the gaps interfere with the desired 'economy' of most beekeepers by weakening the structure of the combs and reducing the hive volume available for honey.

This example of human–technology–bee interplay suggests that the 'becoming' of the hive is more open than might be imagined within the shed where this colony life is imagined, plotted, and framed by human economic actors with the work of human hands and machines. The Langstroth hive comes into being as an ongoing non-human and human assembling. Rather than a planned set of human technologies (see Matheson and Reid 2011), 'the hive' as a thing produced is neither non-existent when its elements enter the shed nor 'complete' when it reaches 'the end' of the production line. The 'final product' is not the empty boxes stacked at the back of the shed, but the human design embedded in them and the shaping of bee lives embodied in them and about to be enacted in the field. It is in the field that the semiotic materiality of the hive becomes truly meaningful and the Langstroth hives are worked (positioned, repositioned, inspected, destroyed, fed, cleaned, supered up, divided, re-queened, harvested, and moved) in a far more lively, intra-active and messy nature–society engagement than might be imagined in a techno-instrumental account. There is little established prior to situated practice or exterior to bee being (no fully codified, fully technologised procedure) in the working of the hives in each of the moments from selecting fields to harvesting and repositioning. Rather, there are complex place-based calculations of likely human–human, bee–human, bee–bee, bee–(other) non-human intra-actions, which materialise with the intra-actions themselves and further rounds of measurement and calculation in the field. The 'box of bees' being assembled is inherently more lively than suggested by the linear, human-directed production line assembling hive parts in the shed.

The post-human work of 'bees'

In Roseanna's encounters, 'speaking bees' took place in armchairs in the beekeepers' homes and in the cab of the beekeepers' truck as they moved hives around fields across the Bay of Plenty and further afield, as well as in the shed as they assembled frames into hives and in the field as they worked hives. Speaking bees is a situated and ongoing interactive process in beekeeping practice and knowledge production, into which the researcher was temporarily positioned. The work of 'speaking bees' is at once the socio-political, economic, and ecological work of bees and 'bees' at work in New Zealand. Our vignette emphasises a recognition of bees as material–semiotic entities, but also of the hive as a networked intra-action of material–semiotic *and* nature–society intra-actions, what Latour (2002: 90) understands as 'Real as Nature, collective as Society, existential as Being'. The vignette examines the ontological politics at work in the intra-actions of making and working the Langstroth hive. In this section, we extend this discussion to three more specific practices embedded in, and co-constitutive of, the hive, its work, and apicultural relations in Aotearoa: the naming of the bee, the measuring of the work of the hive, and the disciplining of the practice of swarming.

Naming the bee and measuring the hive

There are approximately 40 species of bee in Aotearoa New Zealand, of which 13 have arrived since colonial European settler invasion. Colonies generally include a queen bee, thousands of workers, and several hundred drones. The primary commercial species is *Apis mellifera*, which includes multiple subspecies, races, breeds, or strains. In a New Zealand of bee immigrants (see Spiers 2014), the predominant breeds are generally termed 'races', the most important of which are the Carniolan, Italian, and European (German) bee. These races are understood to have defining phenotypic traits, and are put to work differently in the hive, in biological economies of honey production, and in pollination services more generally (see Table 8.1).

'Speaking bees' with beekeepers gathers the spatial and material constitution of *Apis mellifera* and reveals it as a particular thing (see Joronen 2013). It enacts and disrupts subspecies boundaries. In Roseanna's encounters, beekeeper participants used 'bees' in everyday discussion of their practices and their aspirations. The 'bees' to which they referred were common, commercial ('mongrel') bee stock in Aotearoa, that is, *Apis mellifera* of mixed race. Boundaries between particular races were erased, and the buzz of other bee species as pollinators and worldly others was dampened or concealed, performing a particular ontological politics that reinforces 'bee' potentials associated with the current political economies of beekeeping whilst closing off others. However, if the specifics of bee type had particular significance in the conversation, then the beekeeper would expand on 'bee'. During spring build-up preparation, David spoke 'bees' until he got to discussing the type of queen bee he wanted to acquire: a golden Italian, a material–semiotic entity which is said to have a golden beauty and the promise of producing honey during a strong nectar flow, yet still produce brood during a dearth (personal communication, D. Spiers and J. Knox, Rotorua, 12 August 2013). Specificity became important, and David abandoned the generic 'queen bee' phraseology.

The beekeepers with whom Roseanna engaged placed significant emphasis on what makes 'a good hive', a question that calibrates ethical and material purpose (making honey of particular qualities or pollinating crops in particular ways and to particular orders). It is a question that invites a calculation of qualities, and directs attention to how qualities are identified, attributed, measured, and made visible, and to the codes making possible performative

Table 8.1 Comparison of popular races of *Apis mellifera* and their traits

	Italian A. m. ligustica	German A. m. mellifera	Carniolan A. m. carnica
Colour	Light, golden	Dark	Black
Disease/pest resistance			
Varroa	–	–	–
Tracheal	–	–	–
AFB*	0	–	+
EFB**	0	0	0
Other	0	0	+
Gentleness	Moderate	Low	High
Spring build-up	Good	Low	Very good
Overwintering ability	Good	Very good	Good
Excess swarming	Moderate	Moderate	High
Honey processing	Very good	Moderate	Good
Propolis	Low	Moderate	Low
Robbing	Heavy		Low
Other traits	Usually large colony size. Extended periods of brood rearing, so queens lay all through the summer.	Hardy, able to survive long, cold winters. Do well in damp cold climates.	Rapid spring build-up to take advantage of early blooms; frugal for winter. Shuts down brood rearing during dearths.

Source: After Matheson and Reid (2011).

Note: *AFB = American foulbrood; **EFB = European foulbrood.

human–bee knowing and doing. In both shed and field, such calculations of qualities are made possible by measurement, and in turn embed measurement and its rationalities in the categorisation of hives, colonies, and bees, the construction of the Langstroth hives and their management in the field, and the material–semiotic assemblage of bee being. The measures enacted, including numbers of frames and bees, queen temperament, honey productivity, and disease prevalence, not only assume and privilege particular ways of knowing the world (Latour 2002), but become performative and constitutive of bee worlds. They categorise a hive, queen, and/or site as performing well or poorly, healthy or failing, productive or uneconomical, and resource poor or rich. Commercial beekeeping best practice rationales script measures and indicators in terms of economic efficiency, productivity, and niche value creation. As Mitchell (2008), Carolan (2009), Çalışkan and Callon (2010), and others suggest in other settings, these categories and measures constitute that which they speak of (bees) and frame the world and our capacity to enact it (speaking bees in the field and in the shed). Beekeepers thus enact hives, queens, and sites in the terms of their measures, think the field into both the shed and the market in those terms, and speak particular bees in particular ways.

Disciplining swarming

Beekeepers intervene in the lives of colonies to prevent bees from swarming. When a colony swarms, the original queen departs with two-thirds of the colony, leaving a daughter queen bee with a third of the worker bees, and combs filled with honey, pollen, and developing larvae. Swarming is reproduction through the body of a naked colony, naked of its hive comb exoskeleton as it were: workers gorge themselves before swarming, thereby taking with them the means for constructing their new nest. A colony occupying the same nest over an extended period will have changed itself, like a genetic chameleon, with each new queen. Swarming therefore ensures the disassembling and re-assembling of the colony; 'the superorganism is the same, and yet not the same' (Tautz 2008: 45).

In the nineteenth century, use of fixed-comb box hives and skeps encouraged swarming as a way of obtaining colonies and refreshing genetic 'colour', to replace hives that had died or been killed at the previous honey harvest, and to increase colony numbers in a new human colony with a rapidly growing pastoral economy in need of bee services (Cotton 1848a, 1848b; Hopkins 1916). Swarming was desirable and swarming season the highlight of the beekeeping year, as beekeepers hurriedly caught and hived swarms. In contrast, in a modern system of beekeeping, swarming is an unruly and undesirable performance that escapes the containments of the Langstroth hive and the economic disciplines of ownership, spatial organisation, surveillance, and profitability. It greatly reduces a hive's honey production and pollinating ability, often to the point of making the hive uneconomic, while absconding swarms from varroa-afflicted colonies threaten to spread the mite.

The Hoffman frames that Roseanna helped to assemble in the shed are part of a hive apparatus that disciplines swarming. Hoffman frames reduce the colony's propensity for making preparations for swarming. They provide room in the brood chamber, avoiding overcrowding and supporting the supply of fresh combs in the brood nest (personal communication, D. Spiers, Rotorua, 10–12 September 2013; Matheson and Reid 2011). The frames also provide room for honey storage. The first honey super (surplus honey box) added contains drawn comb, reducing the work that bees must perform to draw out the foundation before they can use it as extra space. Timing supering, and re-assembling the hive through addition or rearrangement of frames in the supers available, allows beekeepers to manage the hive in the field.

The Langstroth hive allows for the practice of dividing to discipline swarming through seasonal management practices that align the colony's 'natural' rhythms to beekeeping objectives (personal communication, D. Spiers,

Rotorua, 16 March 2013). Here, beekeepers split parts of a hive from the parent hive, with the divided portion used to increase numbers, or held in reserve as a replacement for a failing or dead colony. Dividing and/or uniting hives is also associated with the practice of raising queen bees *en masse* to be introduced to the new (split) hives or to replace a dead or failing queen. This is a colony management intervention at a genetic level and is a significant investment, financially and in terms of shaping the phenotype of future colonies, by selecting for demonstrated desirable traits such as productivity, varroa sensitive hygiene, or gentleness.

Beekeepers talk about these practices as the 'disciplining' of swarming. The term, of course, also has a troubling Foucauldian meaning in the context of post-human thinking. By using it here, we do not suggest a subjugation of the bee colony's agency to pre-modern human over-determination. Rather, we follow Valverde (2004) to emphasise the productive tensions between the Foucauldian categories of 'discipline' and 'biopolitics' in shaping unruly behaviour into more productive economic performance. In this instance, the disciplining involves a post-human framing of the productive agency of bee colonies. Swarming is a matter of concern in speaking 'bees', and its 'disciplining' enacts a change in the material–semiotic assemblage of the modern bee and in how the colony is known and made as a reproductive unit, in terms of both its biology and the political economy of beekeeping. The disciplining reworks the ontological status of bees in a politics that is both ethical and commercial as well as biological.

Conclusion

This chapter makes four key observations: humans and bees are always in community with others; 'bees' and 'hives' are situated discursive materialities co-fabricated by a multitude of lively materialities and diffuse agencies; the Langstroth hive is a dominant biopolitical intervention that contains space–time imperatives, such as swarming or profitability in constituting the lives of *A. mellifera*, and where 'modern' beekeepers mediate how matter comes to matter in a dynamic field of intra-acting agencies; and 'exploding' and 'following' hives as human–non-human intra-actions provide a richly nuanced and affective account of apiculture. The chapter demonstrates that, in coming to know and do bees, beekeepers articulate and perform situated and codified understandings that emerge from embodied practice, as well as performative *in situ* rationales of science and/or economics. The hive and colony are known and made in particular ways, from framing to naming/categorisation, measurement, and disciplining bee work in place (Aotearoa), but our account suggests that there are multiple openings for knowing–doing 'bees' and apiculture differently. Thus known, the hive is a particular gathering–revealing of what bees do as more-than-human agents enrolled in the (re)production of New Zealand biological economies. To this end 'speaking bees' in the field and shed with commercial beekeepers, working with bees, and unsettling the work of bees have come to be both the context for research approach and a crucial metaphor for knowing the processes of intra-action in which 'bees', 'beekeepers', and the work they do coalesce and fall apart.

We conclude by making a set of points about what these insights tell us about the values of such a post-human and enactive production of knowledge. First, the vignette of the shed (and field) (re)presents how we came to know of this intra-action and its vitality. It details an enactive research practice and an affective experience that, whilst in some sense staged, was also for Roseanna tactile and embodied. Engaged in the shed with the frames passing through her hands, she was able to grasp how situated narratives of human assembling of knowing might be enlarged upon to enable and reveal the co-productivity of non-human and human assembling, something which is silenced in beekeeping lore, apicultural science, and much agri-food scholarship. Coming to know through engaging in this way with the speaking of bees and the material construction and work of hives confirms that knowing is situated. Indeed, our coming to know is multiply situated in time, place, and Roseanna's experience. This includes the connections to the actors that presented the opportunity to stage the encounters described. David the beekeeper is Roseanna's father, and the struggles of making both bees and the enterprise work in particular ways are also those of Roseanna's lived life.

Second, these various layers of situatedness implicate our work in the ontological politics of speaking bees, just as they do in any other post-human intra-action through which scholars might attempt to come to know. Coming to know is, in such terms, enactive, and demonstrates that knowing can only be open-ended as well as situated. The point is neatly made by the observation that, since the encounter and subsequent assembling of this text, the beekeepers have acquired a line of rolling credit for expansionary purposes.[3] The shed now has mains electricity, running water, and a restored toilet facility. Ready-built hive frames are imported in bulk from Russia, along with pre-prepared hive components from national suppliers. The work of bees in 2013–14 cannot be encountered in the same way today, not least because the ready-made frames take away the opportunity for corporeal, productive, and tactile practices of knowledge production in the shed. Beekeeping practices are being remade and 'speaking bees' altered. That which emerged in the vignette above is already disassembling and being gathered into other configurings.

Third, honey bees and the work they perform are multiply framed. Their ownmost conditions of possibility for the different ontological modalities of their constitution and politics of their revealing are made finite through the hive apparatus. The hive is always, already and categorically, more than a mere box of bees. Nonetheless, while a site and thus, as Joronen (2013) suggests, a place of openness for the spatial differentiation and gathering of things, it may become enclosed and monopolised through apicultural interventions. Such human interventions perform what Barad (2007: 175) terms agentic cuts or a resolution of the ontological indeterminacy (within the phenomena) and agential separability. It is through such cuts that the boundaries and properties of 'components' of phenomena (a hive, honey bee colony, dairy pasture) become determinate and that particular articulations become meaningful (Barad 2007: 148). Humans may just as easily enact a concealing as a revealing of honey bees, their work, and place. Indeed, our account focused on human interventions in the hive, concealing non-human interventions such as those enacted by varroa mites, adulterated honey, and agricultural pesticides. Ours has been an enactive engagement with a hive that is always already coming to be known through the making of it, which as an apparatus makes known and knowable the place and work of bees as earthly others and ecosystem service providers. The 'box of bees' constructed is an emphatically lively bundle.

Fourth, as spacetimemattering (Barad 2007) that emerges through (re)making (dis)connections, the hive is brought into being by doing it, that is, by the connections and meanings made, and orderings imposed, on space, time, and matter by bees, beekeepers, and others. 'Exploding' the hive confirms that relata do not pre-exist their intra-active relations, but emerge through (re)making (dis)connections: through the enactive performance of doing the hive (by bees, beekeepers, and others), space, time, and matter not only are ordered and made meaningful, but come to be. This suggests that research must be attentive to the detail and relational agency of practice (for example naming, categorising, measuring, and ways of knowing and doing), and that researchers number among the constitutive others (perhaps prominently). It demands that we acknowledge and take responsibility for the cuts we enact.

Finally, this imposes ethical and political opportunities, and burdens. For Roseanna, following 'a box of bees' and coming to know and do the work of the Langstroth hive in the shed, field, cab, and armchair became less about inventorying, categorising, and accounting for the 'stuff' of the hive and more a knowledge making enmeshed in the intra-active relations of the hive and the family business. As well as revealing the vital materiality of the hive and promoting critical understandings of honey bee ontology with an embodied intensity, the experience highlights the consequences of such world making – human and non-human. It is in this conjunction that we see possibilities in material encounters for responding to Gibson-Graham and Roelvink's (2010) call for a new 'learning to be affected' as a platform for knowledge making in the Anthropocene. Engaging with the hive's vital materiality, and engaging in its ontological politics alongside the affecting politics of beekeeping as a human and economic activity, offers us a model for knowing that not only builds on post-human sensitivities to identify post-human relations, but leads us to ask how they might be remade.

The Langstroth hive confirms that producing knowledge is never innocent. Understood as assembling and mobilising material–semiotic boundary performances, this lack of innocence can be readily seen to have consequences for the everyday lived realities-in-relation of pastures, pollinators, and people. When you speak 'bees', you are inside political worlds of labour processes, health and dietary practices, regulatory apparatuses, and resilient economies and ecosystems. In granting radical historical contingency to the material–semiotic technologies we assemble and deploy in relation with others (including naming), we invite their participation in co-composing richly exploding worldly apicultural relations. There are always a plurality of other imaginings that might be storied, emergent orderings and possible futures that might be traced and reconciled, and different tools for knowing and doing beekeeping that might be conceptualised. Understood as post-human and relational, such sites present opportunities for post-human enactive research.

Notes

1 In New Zealand 'smoko' is a slang term used for a short coffee break or outdoor rest. The smoko shed is the utility shed where the beekeepers shelter to take their break.
2 We neither presume 'the Anthropocene' has a singular, ideological meaning, nor wish to reinscribe the anthropocentrism that generated it in the first place. Rather we recognise that honey bees find themselves located at the intersection of multiple crises (loss of foraging diversity, reduced disease resilience, environmental toxicity) that are increasingly attributed to the Anthropocene (see McKibben 2013). We choose to locate our account of the work of bees as localised compositions within what Crist (2013) terms the 'braided' discourse of the Anthropocene, a discourse that requires a richer enactive and post-human conception (see Gibson-Graham and Roelvink 2010; Castree et al. 2014).
3 Banks will not supply 'loans' for apicultural endeavours.

References

Barad, K. (2007) *Meeting the Universe Halfway: Quantum Physics and the Entanglement of Matter and Meaning*, Duke University Press, Durham, NC.
Barad, K. (2010) 'Quantum entanglements and hauntological relations of inheritance: dis/continuities, spacetime enfoldings, and justice-to-come', *Derrida Today*, vol. 3, no. 2, pp. 240–268.
Barad, K. (2012a) 'Nature's queer performativity', *Kvinder, Køn & Forskning*, vols 1–2, pp. 25–53.
Barad, K. (2012b) 'On touching – the inhuman that therefore I am', *Differences: A Journal of Feminist Cultural Studies*, vol. 23, no. 3, pp. 206–223.
Barad, K. (2013) 'Ma(r)king time: material entanglements and re-memberings: cutting together-apart', in P. R. Carlile, D. Nicolini, A. Langley and H. Tsoukas (eds), *How Matter Matters: Objects, Artifacts, and Materiality in Organization Studies*, Oxford University Press, Oxford.
Benjamin, A. and McCallum, B. (2009) *A World without Bees*, Guardian Books, London.
Bennett, J. (2004) 'The force of things: steps toward an ecology of matter', *Political Theory*, vol. 32, no. 3, pp. 347–372.
Bennett, J. (2010) *Vibrant Matter: A Political Ecology of Things*, Duke University Press, Durham, NC.
Çalışkan, K. and Callon, M. (2010) 'Economization, part 2: a research programme for the study of markets', *Economy and Society*, vol. 39, no. 1, pp. 1–32.

Carolan, M. S. (2009) '"I do therefore there is": enlivening socio-environmental theory', *Environmental Politics*, vol. 18, no. 1, pp. 1–17.
Castree, N., Adams, W. M., Barry, J., Brockington, D., Büscher, B., Corbera, E., Demeritt, D., Duffy, R., Felt, U., Neves, K., Newell, P., Pellizzoni, L., Rigby, K., Robbins, P., Robin, L., Rose, D. B., Ross, A., Schlosberg, D., Sörlin, S., West, P., Whitehead, M. and Wynne, B. (2014) 'Changing the intellectual climate', *Nature Climate Change*, vol. 4, pp. 763–768.
Cotton, W. C. (1848a) *A Manual for New Zealand Bee Keepers*, R. Stokes, Wellington.
Cotton, W. C. (1848b) *My Bee Book*, J. G. F. & J. Rivington, London.
Crane, E. (1983) *The Archaeology of Beekeeping*, Duckworth, London.
Crane, E. (1990) *Bees and Beekeeping: Science, Practice and World Resources*, Comstock Publishing, New York.
Crane, E. (1999) *The World History of Beekeeping and Honey Hunting*, Routledge, New York.
Crist, E. (2013) 'On the poverty of our nomenclature', *Environmental Humanities*, vol. 3, pp. 129–147.
Deleuze, G. and Guattari, F. (2013) *A Thousand Plateaus*, Bloomsbury, London.
Dobson, E. (2005) *A Box of Bees*, Victoria University Press, Wellington.
Gibson-Graham, J. K. (2006) *A Postcapitalist Politics*, University of Minnesota Press, Minneapolis.
Gibson-Graham, J. K. and Roelvink, G. (2010) 'An economic ethics for the Anthropocene', *Antipode*, vol. 41, no. s1, pp. 320–346.
Guthrie, J. R. (2007) 'Darwinian Dickinson: the scandalous rise and noble fall of the common clover', *Emily Dickinson Journal*, vol. 16, no. 1, pp. 73–91.
Haraway, D. (1988) 'Situated knowledges: the science question in feminism and the privilege of partial perspective', *Feminist Studies*, vol. 14, no. 3, pp. 575–599.
Haraway, D. (2008) *When Species Meet*, University of Minnesota Press, Minneapolis.
Hölldobler, B. and Wilson, E. O. (2009) *The Superorganism: The Beauty, Elegance, and Strangeness of Insect Societies*, W. W. Norton, New York.
Hopkins, I. (1916) *Forty-Two Years of Bee-Keeping in New Zealand 1874–1916: Some Reminiscences*, Auckland.
Horn, T. (2011) *Beeconomy: What Women and Bees Can Teach Us about Local Trade and the Global Market*, University Press of Kentucky, Lexington.
Joronen, M. (2013) 'Heidegger, event and the ontological politics of the site', *Transactions of the Institute of British Geographers*, vol. 38, pp. 627–638.
Lahey, S. T. (2012) 'Honeybees and discontented workers: a critique of labour in Louisa May Alcott', *American Literary Realism*, vol. 44, no. 2, pp. 133–156.
Latour, B. (2002) *We Have Never Been Modern*, Harvard University Press, Cambridge, MA.
Matheson, A. and Reid, M. (2011) *Practical Beekeeping in New Zealand* (4th edn), Exisle Publishing, Auckland.
McKibben, B. (2013) *Oil and Honey: The Education of an Unlikely Activist*, Times Books, London.
Mitchell, T. (2008) 'Rethinking economy', *Geoforum*, vol. 39, no. 3, pp. 1116–1121.
Seeley, T. D. (2010) *Honeybee Democracy*, Princeton University Press, Princeton, NJ.
Spiers, R. M. (2014) '"A good hive": diffractive cosmopolitical exploding of worldly apicultural relations in New Zealand', unpublished master's thesis, University of Auckland, New Zealand.
Tautz, J. (2008) *The Buzz about Bees: Biology of a Superorganism*, Springer, Berlin.

Tautz, J. (2009) *The Buzz about Bees: Biology of a Superorganism*, corrected 2nd printing, Springer, Berlin.

Tsing, A. (2010) 'Arts of inclusion, or how to love a mushroom', *Manoa*, vol. 22, no. 2, pp. 191–203.

Valverde, M. (2004) 'Experience and truth telling in a post-humanist world: a Foucauldian contribution to feminist ethical reflections', in D. Taylor and K. Vintges (eds), *Feminism and the Final Foucault*, University of Illinois Press, Urbana, pp. 67–90.

Winter, T. S. (1975) *Beekeeping in New Zealand* (revised and reprinted), Ministry of Agriculture and Fisheries, Wellington.

9 Ever-redder apples

How aesthetics shape the biology of markets

Katharine Legun

Introduction

In 2000, the US apple industry was in trouble. Washington State, a powerhouse of production, was unable to sell all its apples. The price of apples dropped, and many growers had fallen into debt. The federal government had to engage in 'the biggest apple bailout in history' (Egan 2000). Many placed blame on the Red Delicious apple; it had been the darling and then the bane of the industry.

The floundering industry placed a variety at the centre of the economic ills. Yet the Red Delicious story is about more than a particular apple. It is retold as a woeful illustration of the problems in the apple industry more broadly, and delivers a moral lesson about competitive ethics in pursuing 'the perfect apple'. In doing so, it also provides an insight into the complex environmental and social relations operating in modern capitalist agriculture. In particular, the centrality of redness to the Red Delicious narrative can tell us about how aesthetics operate at the interface between biology and economics in ways that shape the character of the industry.

The redness of apples is an aesthetic feature of a commodity. Redness can be sensed in a retail setting, and this gives it currency. While some niche markets such as 'Whole Foods' have championed the practice of in-store tasting in some lucky districts, for the most part the colour of produce is one of the only features that can provide distinction in the supermarket. The shiny surface of a dark red apple seems to sparkle in the human eye. It is demonstrable of a type of cult of colour in produce, where demands for red apples are matched by the bright orange hues of carrots, the vibrant yellow of lemons, or a triad of green, red, and yellow from the pepper section. The way in which colour has become a metric of value for producers and consumers is an important character in food industry narratives. Following the development of redness in apples can tell us something about distinction, competition, and the politics of aesthetics in the production of biologically based commodities.

Redness in apples interacts with the human body. In the market, size and colour are the main ways to separate apples into price categories, and differentiating price is a necessary feature of the market. Yet the pressure to develop redness generates a type of homogeneity across apples. As Gala apples become ever redder, they increasingly look like Red Delicious apples, and contribute to a block of indistinguishable fruit in the supermarket. The drive for greater aesthetic vibrancy is ultimately self-thwarting as those sensory features of food become concentrated and homogeneous, creating a sea of bright colour, and ultimately muting their effect. This chapter discusses the destructive drive for aesthetic idealism that underlies the commodification of produce, and the tension it creates can be considered a feature of modern food systems.

Redness is about materiality, aesthetics, and politics, and these features help in understanding the Red Delicious narrative and how it speaks to the industry. Drawing on interviews with apple growers in the Midwest, I'll discuss the ways that the drive for redness degrades the value of redness, while red, in a pure perfect form, is unachievable. The result is a cycling towards the perfect commodity form in an effort to achieve high economic returns, while that cycling in effect makes those economic returns less likely in the long term. The cycling processes are fuelled by the biological realities of apple production: the perfect harvest of red apples is something that must be continuously worked at and approached, but can never be fully realized. This undermining can be viewed in relation to work that describes late liberalism as characterized by systems of practice that inherently derail the goals they are designed to achieve, but produce value in the striving towards them.

Redness as a political aesthetic

> Colours range from near white to forgettable beige to the deep, waxy near black of a showroom limo. And that's not to mention the reds, in uncountable shades, patterns, and levels of opacity and luminosity. An apple's red coat overlies a layer of yellow or ochre or green that will either set the apple ablaze or mute it. A Stayman's red is transposed to a minor key by the green pigment below. But on Winter Banana or Ozark Gold, the red blush acts as a lens, incandescing with the light that reflects up through it.
>
> (Yepsen 1994)

The history of the Red Delicious apple is a history of redness. From the luminous apple that supplied Snow White with a dose of poison, to the apple that commonly illustrates the eviction from Eden, red apples have been culturally propagated as an idealized form of the fruit. The lavish production values of contemporary photography and cinematography add new depths of colour and suggestiveness to this trope. Foregrounded against the partial face of the heroine in promotional material for the television series *Once*, cradled in the hands of the heroine on the cover of the book *Twilight*, or forming a bed for the five seductively posed heroines of *Desperate Housewives* in a boxed set of Series 2 DVDs titled 'the extra juicy edition', velvety crimson or claret-red apples play on the fatal attractions of dangerous fruit and original sin. Moreover redness, and colour more generally, has a symbolic currency that enables it to be used in economic markets. That symbolic value is mobilized and can shape relationships in the food industry.

During a pivotal growth period in food retail, researchers conducted a variety of studies on the relationship between colour and palate (Kanig 1955; Hall 1958; Pangborn 1960). For example, an early study by Moir (1936) found that, when a raspberry jelly was dyed an inappropriate colour, people found it more difficult to identify the flavour, while Pangborn (1960) found that the colour of a solution influenced its interpreted sweetness. More recent work continues to emphasize that colour plays a role in shaping food perception and choices (Francis 1995; Downham and Collings 2000; Spence et al. 2010).

These connections between colour and taste are not stagnant or inherent, but can change over time and adopt overtly cultural and political messages. Bourdieu (1984) made this social feature of objects even clearer when he suggested that cultural symbols and their group affinities are an expression of class and group distinction. Just as the taste for music, literature, and art is a signifier of membership in a class or status group, alliances with various shades in produce can carry the same kind of communicative weight. The campaign against 'eating white', targeting refined bread, white rice, dessert topping, and even peeled apples, is a testament to how food colour comes to embody food politics (Belasco 1990; Levenstein 2003). The vibrancy of colour becomes even more evident with the aesthetic sensibilities that arise with foodie culture (Johnston and Baumann 2014) and new food movements that have strong aesthetic components (Murdoch and Miele 2004; Sassatelli and Davolio 2010). These movements pivot on sensory experiences of food, as well as the cultural enjoyment of food in particular sensory forms.

Many of the characteristics enjoyed in food, and many of the meanings attached to food aesthetics, are learned, created, and qualified. While the taste of strawberry flavours may be enhanced when delivered through a red product, this is because people have grown to associate that particular colour with the fruit. Let us note, also, the rise of the white pineberry, meant to contain hints of pineapple: transgressive in its rogue appearance and made sensible through an affiliation with an appropriately coloured sister-fruit. Carolan (2011) has described the development of sensory consumer experiences as a process of 'tuning' bodies to foods, and notes how industry actors have engaged in this process of tuning to create and secure markets. This is the 'political economy of tuning' (Carolan 2011: 36). How we identify food as food and the symbols that give it greater or lesser value are largely learned metrics (Murdoch and Miele 2004), and they're made particularly stable by commodity markets, where those metrics guide the parameters of production as well as the parameters of valuation confronting consumers. Advancing a symbolic lexicon around food valuation, and institutionalizing it through metrics, is then a political process. What gets defined as qualities in food in the market shapes competition by ascribing what actions will be valued, and who performs those actions (see Callon et al. 2002; Marsden 2004). The qualities of produce that are made salient through supermarket staging set not only what is seen by consumers, but what *can* be seen.

In apples, the mainstream aesthetic is a shiny, large, red apple. The development of that red aesthetic preference and its institutionalization are intertwined with the history of the Red Delicious, and examining that history as it is retold can reveal its political underpinnings. This history was raised repeatedly during my fieldwork in 2010–12, when I interviewed 43 people involved in the apple industry in the Midwest. In the Delicious story, standards were created around colour and instituted across the USA, the variety was made redder through biotechnology, and redness became a broad organizing ethic in apples. Yet the use of the Red Delicious narrative demonstrates ambivalence towards this process, creating a type of hesitant engagement with the pursuit of the ideal. This weariness is a pivotal feature of the contemporary apple industry, and demonstrates a shift from modernism to a type of late modernism in production. Work goes into getting apples as close as possible to an ideal red, and the pursuit of redness remains a point of competition. In this culture of production the future is a spectre never to be entirely realized. This arrangement can be seen to illustrate a character of our contemporary society: modernism functioning as an economic ideal, in the true sense of ideal – an unattainable fantasy. The real material practices of production exist in the striving towards the ideal, but are contingent on its unattainability.

The Red Delicious and its discontents

How did red become the forceful symbol of the 'appleness' of the apple? Some growers that I spoke to alluded to a relationship between redness and ripeness. However, the character of this relationship and its source were opaque at best. Colour and ripeness are only weakly linked. For apples that do go from green to red, or green to partially red, the redness does develop over time, but an apple can be ready to eat before it has reached a maximum level of possible redness, and more redness can mean over-maturity. The indication that an apple is ripe is more likely to be found in the background colour – for example, when the green portion of a bi-coloured apple turns more yellowish (Watkins et al. 1992; Plotto et al. 1995). The proportion of a bi-coloured apple that will turn red is largely determined by the variety and climate. For an apple that's typically 50 per cent red, it's ripe when 50 per cent red. Yet more redness has come to be valued as objectively better than non-redness generally. This assumption would propel the industry towards an ever-redder goal.

Redness became a dominant organizing feature in the narrative of the Red Delicious: it can be seen as both an instigator and a product of the variety. The original 'Red Delicious' apple was actually called the 'Hawkeye' and found on a farm in Iowa in 1872. It was purchased by Stark Brothers Nursery and renamed the Delicious. Purportedly, the apple was less than 50 per cent red. By 1921 there was a redder strain of the Delicious, which became 'Starking' Delicious, followed by a cluster of other redder strains, and a supercolour strain in 1951 called 'Starkrimson' Delicious (Hampson and Kemp 2003). There are now over 100 redder strains or 'sports' of the Delicious.

At present, there is no way simply to make a bi-coloured variety red through genetic engineering, so instead industry actors wait for biological processes to unfold and capitalize on mutational changes. Bill, an apple breeder, explained that growers may see a limb of a tree with redder apples on it, and 'In the perfect world, that's a mutation. They then reproduce that mutation clonally and basically have a red version.' Mutations happen in an unpredictable way, and thus it's an imprecise process that's highly dependent on the spontaneous behaviour of plants. Bill explained:

> As plants grow they grow as our bodies, the same way. Cells divide, they replicate themselves, they split in half and form pairs, and in the process maybe one in a million or a billion times that replication goes slightly awry, and that's a mutation. It's naturally occurring.... A tiny percentage of those mutations are something that we happen to see, and in the case of apples the ones that people look for is something that turns the fruit redder.

Red sports achieve redness imperfectly – that is, there will be an increase in colour, but it will never be a solid, perfect hue of red that silences the red pursuit. The observable changes may be marginal, but they grow after mutations upon mutations upon mutations. In the meantime, growers tread through cycles of replanting, as old strains and their lower-colour produce gradually become unmarketable. This is a pervasive process unfolding in the contemporary apple industry, and one that was seemingly ushered in by the Red Delicious.

The Red Delicious apple adopted almost fairy-tale-like features in its common narration among growers, and the lesson was often tied to the propagation of redder and redder strains. 'Red Delicious,' Bill explains,

> is my least favourite apple in the world. It's the result of over 200 mutations that have been discovered. It was originally found on a broken-down farm in Iowa and it was probably about 30 per cent red at the time, and now, 200 mutations later, you can't find a part of that apple that's not red. It doesn't mean it's ripe, but it's red.

Growers in Washington cite the cycle of strains as a reason for the collapse of the industry. In a *New York Times* article, Egan (2000) suggested that the search for the perfect apple had driven economic decline in the industry. He cited a long-term apple farmer who complained that 'for almost 50 years we've been cramming down the consumer's throat a red apple with ever-thicker skin, sometimes mushy, sometimes very good if done right, but a product that was bred for color and size and not for taste' (Egan 2000). The story of the Red Delicious is a story of over-zealously pursuing the redness of the apple in ways that support an industrial food infrastructure while eroding the price of the apple for growers and the taste of the apple for consumers.

The drive for redness cannot be explained as simply consumer preference. In a 1962 marketing research report, *How Color of Red Delicious Apples Affects their Sales* (Frye and Hoofnagle 1962), the authors divided colour categories of Red Delicious apples into three: the all-red, the high-red, and the part-red. While the solidly red apples sold the best, the part-red apples, which were less than 60 per cent red, sold better than the high-red and only marginally less than the all-red. In other words, redness wasn't something that people responded to as a scale, with sales improving as apples got gradually redder. Instead, people preferred fully red apples and fully bi-coloured apples, and did not like the apples with a redness in between. In 1962, consumers would have been happy with a bi-coloured Red Delicious, and yet grading standards were introduced that set grade based on a scale with price correlated directly to redness. Why redness became preferred has more to do with selling larger quantities of apples in an industrial food setting, and managing regional competition.

The drive for redness can be located in the organization of the industry and an attempt to mask apple imperfections. In Fry and Hoofnagle's (1962) study, there were fewer of the all-red apples discarded in store, because they more easily hid bruises and blemishes. At the time, this would suggest that redder apples afforded an advantage to retailers, who would spend less on spoilage. Moreover, the red sports of the Red Delicious meant that it could be picked and shipped earlier and stored for longer (Hampson and Kemp 2003). While consumers may have (marginally) preferred a redder apple, the real gain would be in selling more apples to consumers, and making apples more visually appealing, as consumers would be unable to detect the blemishes that would otherwise speckle the apple bin.

The grading standards associated with redness also have an effect in shaping inter-regional competition. Grading standards are used to value apples in the market. While the consumer may increasingly gravitate towards more varied sizes, shapes, and colours, the economic infrastructure of apple production is organized around particular aesthetic ideals. These ideals were built into the architecture of apple markets by categorizing the apple grade based on colour. Washington State was the first to introduce grades, in the late nineteenth century, partly as a way to develop markets for its apples (Jarosz and Qazi 2000; Dimitri 2002). By developing grades that standardized the qualities it could more easily produce, the state created a market advantage on the East Coast, where apples were smaller and coloured less easily. Washington State was also the more prolific producer of the Red Delicious, and unique standards would be made wherein the highest grade of the apple would be near purple. Many of the varieties most prized by the market become redder in specific regions characterized by warm sunny days and cold nights. The mobilization of redness in Red Delicious, as in all apples, privileges growers in particular regions over others, and shapes the structure of market competition.

These preferences for colour are built into packing technologies, further embedding colour into the industry. Sometimes an orchard will have its own packing line, where apples are sorted before being sold. Most growers send their apples to a packhouse, where a company acts as a broker, and where their apples are sorted, stored, and sold. In a packing line, apples will be set on to a river and floated down a buffer that cleans the apple and removes debris. The apples are loaded on to little cups that travel in lines, so that a packing line will have between 4 and 20 lines of apples, each apple in an individual place. The cups weigh each apple, toss off any that don't meet the minimum requirements, and track the weight of the others. A modern packing line will internally scan the apples, using UV light, to check for blemishes. Apples that have some internal defect will be ejected from the line. The apples then run through a scanner, and the cups vibrate and get the apples to rotate while a machine takes pictures – 25 pictures per apple. The percentage of redness on the surface is noted. The apples that have a higher percentage of redness are sorted for a higher grade, or they may go to a more expensive market, while the others will be sorted to different grades and often different markets. Apples that grace the bargain bins at the local value supermarket could conceivably be from the same orchard as ones that sell for a premium price at a high-end retailer.

Yet, according to common accounts, approaching that aesthetic and industrial ideal led to the collapse of the apple market in Washington. Red Delicious apples were oversupplied to the market, and the desire for the apple waned. The apples became too red, and hid blemishes too well. This narrative of the Red Delicious illustrates a paradox in the infrastructure. If apples could be easily and accurately made as red as the grower desired, there would be no need to sort them and the distinction between apples on the market would decrease, meaning a considerable expansion in competitors. Moreover, when apples are easily red, it would be expected that the premium for redness would no longer exist. The pursuit of redness, when approached, actually erodes its currency.

While the Red Delicious apple is held as an egregious example of the unfettered pursuit of colour, there is another story about the politics of modernist projects. Red apple ideals, and their institutionalization, served the desires of retailers and the expansion of commodity chains across space. And yet, while the Red Delicious is emblematic of problems associated with idealism in aesthetic aspirations, redness continues to play a dominant role in the industry.

Apples, redness, and political economies of insatiability

K: So are there red strains of Honeycrisp?
George: Yeah. Yeah, there are some strains, theoretically, and I'll just put it that way. They tend to be higher colouring strains. That's the normal evolution in apple varieties. I talked about the Jonagolds. You start with a strain and then, you know, the marketplace is looking for more colour, so then you find a limb mutation or some variation and you get a higher colouring strain that just packs out better, has better

profile in it. The same thing is happening in the Honeycrisp. We talked about northern Michigan being the ideal location for growing Honeycrisp. Well, now they've found a red strain. Not necessarily here, so maybe that will expand or allow, on the margins – Grand Rapids or the southwest or eastern Washington – allow them to grow Honeycrisp there because it's a more colouring strain. It gets to be kind of a treadmill thing. You keep going for more colour, more colour, and then the red strains here. It's not all bad; it's not all bad. As we evolve, it might be the thing to do. We do it constantly with McIntosh. We do it constantly with Gala. That's the history of the apple industry.

While growers I interviewed often criticized the ways that apples would rapidly become redder through mutations, they also oriented to redness generally in their production practices as a normative organizing element. Red sports in general were only rarely condemned outright, although many growers would note that the eating quality of a variety might be reduced with a new strain. This illustrates the anxieties around the pursuit of redness, particularly around the achievement of redness.

In this section, I'll firstly discuss the ways that the construction of redness as a pure commodity aesthetic symbolizes anxieties about the reach of the power of the market and secondly how the maintenance of some contextual resistance to wholesale redness generates an important competitive dynamic among apple producers. In this second sense, biological features of apple production, and particularly the animate nature of plants that tends to wilfully resist the dictates of the market, become a generator of value and a foundation for competition.

Some tree varieties produce apples that naturally turn a solid red on the tree, but the majority of apples that have redness are bi-coloured, meaning that they are red and green or yellow. Popular varieties that grace the supermarket shelves, such as the Red Delicious or Gala, have been *made* red, or at least *redder*. The road to red apples takes considerable effort, coordination, and finesse, and always remains imperfectly executed. Like Callon's (1986) scallops of St Brieuc Bay, the redness of apples is coaxed out by an arrangement of actors, networked together. Sometimes redness is produced in particular climates, or by planting the trees on a landscape in a particular way to capture the sun. Other options include bagging (Arakawa 1988), the use of sprinkler irrigation to cool the apples in a way that improves colour (Williams 1993; Iglesias et al. 2005, 2008), and the use of reflective film to reflect more light on to the apples (Ju et al. 1999). These other methods were less common than strains.

The production of red strains is a rather spontaneous and imprecise process. The breeder's comment, noted earlier, that apple mutations are random and rare is telling, as is his comparison between apple genes and human genes. In addition to the scarcity of mutations, those mutations can be chimeras, prone to switching back to their initial genetic make-up and original apple aesthetic after a few years (see Brown and Maloney 2003). This animacy or unpredictability in trees can be seen as a way in which the market commodity form is disturbed by plants, and that disturbance produces the types of variation that can generate value. A similar capitalization on the vibrancy of living matter was discussed by Henry and Roche (2013), who found that environmental conditions participated in the creation of a niche market for grass-fed Wagyu beef. For apples, these deviations are a precondition for the structure of the market, so that the red ideal, and maintaining it as an ideal, is the crux of market value. That is, profit is created by approaching this aesthetic ideal in the context of difficulty and resistance, and that resistance lies in the whimsy of biological matter.

While the Red Delicious was condemned, the shiny red apple remained the prototype of high-value commodity apples, and engaging with it remained a normative aspect of grower strategy. When asked why they were planting a red strain of McIntosh (Ruby Mac), Carol gave me a typical response: 'I think people tend to like really red fruit.' She also mentioned that the orchard manager, Adam, liked to try new varieties.

There was a fairly unchallenged idea that there was a preference for redness, and red sports were an acceptable way to achieve it, and part of any growing strategy. Yet they required caution. This caution could be linked to anxieties about detaching colour from other aspects of production that could decrease quality. Some growers I interviewed were interested in developing intellectual property mechanisms to make red sports of some varieties harder to develop (see Legun 2015). Yet even these growers accepted the general doctrine of colour. Jeff, for example, was still committed to colour as a general metric for the Honeycrisp, and interested in pursuing it in his own orchard, while being anxious about how it might affect competition in the industry more broadly:

> I know there are some redder strains of Honeycrisp in the nursery right now, and they're starting to ramp up production. That'll be a double-edged sword because, for somebody like me, that grows them in a climate that we can finish a Honeycrisp well, it will allow us to pick Honeycrisp in probably two pickings instead of four, and the quality of Honeycrisp, if they hang on the tree too long, goes downhill. They start to get soft, and they start to get growth cracks up around the stem, which lowers our pack-out and storability, but a lot of times we're waiting for that third or fourth pick to let those apples get some colour. They eat well, but they don't have enough colour yet, and so if we get some red strains I think we'll be able to pick them based on the background colour.
>
> The other side of the sword is, they could be grown in hotter climates, and Honeycrisp grown in hotter climates don't seem to have as good an eating quality as cooler climates. Right now, if you buy a nice red Honeycrisp, generally it's grown in the right place because in hot climates they can't get good colour.

An interesting aspect of Jeff's comment is the way he frames his own practices around the pursuit of colour as something that detracts from the quality of his apples, and a red strain could resolve that tension. But, if the red strain were used in other locations to alleviate the colour pressure, it would be seen as problematic. The quote illustrates the ways that red sports have the potential to liberate the individual from regional constraints, while being detrimental to the industry overall, because it would reduce the role of redness as a source of climate-based competition.

The problem with strains that approach a uniform redness is that it reduces the parameters through which growers can compete. Redness is no longer an economic tool for growers to practise and use to position themselves, but instead becomes an expression of pure capital investment, as those who can purchase and plant new red sports have a market advantage. The elevation of colour in the retail space becomes the economic silencing of colour for growers, and this can be exacerbated by the introduction of strains. Several growers described problems from the aesthetic convergence of Gala and Red Delicious apples, as Gala sports make them increasingly similar to the Red Delicious. What is lost in economic power for growers is gained by retailers who have a bigger pool of growers producing increasingly similar apples.

The Red Delicious apple is a testament to the detrimental effects of approaching redness in an apple variety, and how it can lead to economic failure in an industry. It serves mainly as a cautionary tale against the speedy pursuit of the perfect commodity form in ways that propel it forward as a fully marketized, qualitatively homogeneous (mute) object. There are red sports, there is a drive towards redness, and this aesthetic essentially leads to a devaluation of redness. Having the colour variably produced is useful for growers, as a group of economic actors, as an important point of competitive reference, and, while pursuing that redness is necessary and important for growers as individual producers, increasing the standards too much can undercut values on a more collective level. Having this ideal aesthetic that fuels an entire infrastructure to value its varying lack of achievement has important implications for thinking through how plant-based industries have developed and are evolving.

There is a way that the ideal aesthetic commodity form exists as an ideal: an organizing goal to be moved towards. Yet this approach must be managed, so that distance between the real and the ideal is maintained and people can strategize within the remaining space. We can see how there is an economic role of 'aesthetic becoming' in the plant commodities.

Once the Red Delicious apple has surpassed redness to achieve an almost purple hue, and once Gala apples, originally more yellow, have become so red they're indistinguishable from the Delicious, there is a type of finitude to the reddening process. There is also a reduction in price. The goal, in these cases, acts as a fantasy propelling the economic churning of the industry, and notably in ways that keep the industrial infrastructure alive, along with its grading systems and retail supply chains. These efforts mirror what both Povinelli (2011) and Berlant (2011) have described as features of our current society. There are ideals and economies built on the movement towards those ideals, but they can never be realized. A perpetual state of becoming and striving is the contemporary condition.

Redness is a property that is always becoming in apples, but the Red Delicious tale is about a more collective problem faced by the industry when that becoming reaches an end-point. We can see the drop in value with the Red Delicious, now the cheapest apple in the USA, and emerging anxieties around the Gala, which has rapidly transformed in colour. Without an area where there is differentiation, the apple becomes a mono-dimensional commodity, and all sellers are the same. But when the redness is a potential, or something that takes work to approach and never fully achieve, it allows for a project of redness for growers, and a point of movement or strategy. It also narrows the competitive pool. Striving for redness is a productive economic action for individuals, but amalgamated across growers it is threatening to the currency of redness and the industry overall.

It is rare for a popular bi-coloured apple to remain bi-coloured, in the sense that new strains of the apple are typically introduced. Yet the pursuit of redness, in particular, often has the effect of eroding the value of the variety. Growers suggested that this was because the quality of the apple would go down as colour became detached from the practices and environments that produced the colour. On the other hand, it also creates more competition among growers and generates less distinction in the market. Growers often mentioned that, as apples transformed in colour, they also came to look increasingly like one another, so there would be less distinction in the market. In the case of apples, and because those ideal types are challenging to achieve, there is an opportunity for growers to resist the increased commodification of the apple and maintain that colour diversity. The Red Delicious narrative serves to problematize redness and encourage the maintenance of colour diversity, while also allowing a project of redness generally to persist, along with its technological, economic, and cultural infrastructure.

Twenty-first-century food fantasies

Scholars have recognized that we are operating in a period of late liberalism (Berlant 2011; Povinelli 2011), reflexive modernity (Giddens 1990; Beck 1992), or meta-modernism (Vermeulen and van den Akker 2015). This ambivalence can be seen in emerging food industries that strive for authenticity and embeddedness, while also being driven towards mainstream commodity forms and aesthetics. Vermeulen and van den Akker (2015) suggest that emerging craft industries serve as a vehicle for a 'utopia, sort of'. A state of utopia is realized in the freedom gained through its immateriality and lack of structure. Similar forms of utopianism have been developing in food (see Stock et al. 2015).

In this cultural sphere, the promises of modern utopia have been rejected, the post-modern relativism has also been rejected, and what remains is an ambivalent engagement with modernist visions, and a new use of idealism as a reference point. In food, the case of the red apple can be telling. The ideal exists, it's critiqued, but not discarded, and what remains is the management of idealism in practice. The development of grower cooperatives in apples to manage the aesthetic qualities of varieties indicates that institutional organization is happening in this space (Legun 2015). New forms of semi-modern engagement, reliant on those infrastructures of industrial idealism, but managing them, can be seen in the produce aisle. Plants and other living matter, in some ways, can be seen as a perfect pivot point for these types of economic engagement, because their potential for wildness generates a space characteristically ambivalent. The apple tree is never fully committed to the commodity project, and perhaps this positions it as a perfect character of our contemporary economic moment.

The vision of the perfect aesthetic commodity, and the wilfulness of a world that fails to produce it, illuminates the role that biological materials play in betraying modernist projects, and the work that is generated through that betrayal. Money is made in managing the spaces between what is desired and what can be produced, and living vibrancy facilitates the opening of those spaces. This management of unattainable commodity aesthetics, and particularly the ways that perfection is pursued but destructive and derided, features in the culture of late liberal capitalism and its anxious modernism. These trends can help us make sense of new food movements that stock grocery shelves with a wider variety of produce, and new mosaics of botanically etched aesthetics.

References

Arakawa, O. (1988) 'Characteristics of colour development in some apple cultivars: changes in anthocyanin synthesis during maturation as affected by bagging and light quality', *Journal of the Japanese Society for Horticultural Science*, vol. 57, pp. 373–380.
Beck, U. (1992) *Risk Society: Towards a New Modernity*, Sage, London.
Belasco, W. (1990) *Appetite for Change*, Pantheon, New York.
Berlant, L. G. (2011) *Cruel Optimism*, Duke University Press, Durham, NC.
Bourdieu, P. (1984) *Distinction: A Social Critique of the Judgement of Taste*, Harvard University Press, Cambridge, MA.
Brown, S. K. and Maloney, K. E. (2003) 'Genetic improvement of apple', in D. C. Ferree and I. J. Warrington (eds), *Apples: Botany, Production and Uses*, CABI Publishing, Wallingford, pp. 30–59.
Callon, M. (1986) 'Some elements of a sociology of translation: domestication of the scallops and the fishermen of St Brieuc Bay', in John Law (ed.), *Power, Action and Belief: A New Sociology of Knowledge?*, Routledge, London, pp. 196–229.
Callon, M., Méadel, C. and Rabeharisoa, V. (2002) 'The economy of qualities', *Economy and Society*, vol. 31, no. 2, pp. 194–217.
Carolan, M. S. (2011) *Embodied Food Politics*, Ashgate, Farnham.
Dimitri, C. (2002) 'Contract evolution and institutional innovation: marketing Pacific-grown apples from 1890 to 1930', *Journal of Economic History*, vol. 62, no. 01, pp. 189–212.
Downham, A. and Collins, P. (2000) 'Colouring our foods in the last and next millennium', *International Journal of Food Science and Technology*, vol. 35, no. 1, pp. 5–22.

Egan, T. (2000) '"Perfect" apple pushed growers into debt', *New York Times*, 4 November, http://www.nytimes.com/2000/11/04/us/perfect-apple-pushed-growers-into-debt.html.

Francis, F. J. (1995) 'Quality as influenced by color', *Food Quality and Preference*, vol. 6, no. 3, pp. 149–155.

Frye, R. E. and Hoofnagle, W. S. (1962) *How Color of Red Delicious Apples Affects Their Sales*, Marketing Research Report 618, US Department of Agriculture, https://ia801609.us.archive.org/16/items/howcolorofreddel618smit/howcolorofreddel618smit.pdf.

Giddens, A. (1990) *The Consequences of Modernity*, Polity, Cambridge.

Hall, R. L. (1958) 'Flavor study approaches at McCormick and Co., Inc.', in Arthur D. Little (ed.), *Flavor Research and Food Acceptance*, Reinhold, New York, pp. 224–240.

Hampson, C. and Kemp, H. (2003) 'Characteristics of important commercial apple cultivars', in D. C. Ferree and I. J. Warrington (eds), *Apples: Botany, Production and Uses*, CABI Publishing, Wallingford, pp. 61–89.

Henry, M. and Roche, M. (2013) 'Valuing lively materialities: bio-economic assembling in the making of new meat futures', *New Zealand Geographer*, vol. 69, no. 3, pp. 197–207.

Iglesias, I., Salvia, J., Torguet, L. and Montserrat, R. (2005) 'The evaporative cooling effects of overtree microsprinkler irrigation on "Mondial Gala" apples', *Scientia Horticulturae*, vol. 103, pp. 267–287.

Iglesias, I., Echeverria, G. and Soria, Y. (2008) 'Differences in fruit colour development, anthocyanin content, fruit quality and consumer acceptability of eight "Gala" apple strains', *Scientia Horticulturae*, vol. 119, no. 1, pp. 32–40.

Jarosz, L. and Qazi, J. (2000) 'The geography of Washington's world apple: global expressions in a local landscape', *Journal of Rural Studies*, vol. 16, no. 1, pp. 1–11.

Johnston, J. and Baumann, S. (2014) *Foodies: Democracy and Distinction in the Gourmet Foodscape*, Routledge, New York.

Ju, Z., Duan, Y. and Ju, Z. (1999) 'Effects of covering the orchard floor with reflecting film on pigment accumulation and fruit coloration in "Fuji" apples', *Scientia Horticulturae*, vol. 82, pp. 47–56.

Kanig, J. L. (1955) 'Mental impact of colors in food studies', *Food Field Reporter*, vol. 23, no. 57.

Legun, K. (2015) 'Club apples: a biology of markets built on the social life of variety', *Economy and Society*, vol. 44, no. 2, pp. 291–315.

Levenstein, H. A. (2003) *Paradox of Plenty: A Social History of Eating in Modern America*, University of California Press, Berkeley.

Marsden, T. (2004) 'Theorising food quality: some key issues in understanding its competitive production and regulation', in M. Harvey, M. McMeekin and A. Warde (eds), *Qualities of Food*, Manchester University Press, Manchester, pp. 129–155.

Moir, H. C. (1936) 'Some observations on the appreciation of flavor in foodstuffs', *Journal of the Society of Chemical Industry*, vol. 55, no. 8, pp. 145–148.

Murdoch, J. and Miele, M. (2004) 'A new aesthetic of food? Relational reflexivity in the "alternative" food movement', in M. Harvey, M. McMeekin and A. Warde (eds), *Qualities of Food*, Manchester University Press, Manchester, pp. 156–175.

Pangborn, R. M. (1960) 'Influence of color on the discrimination of sweetness', *American Journal of Psychology*, vol. 73, no. 2, pp. 229–238.

Plotto, A., Azarendo, A. N., Mattheis, J. P. and McDaniel, M. R. (1995) '"Gala", "Braeburn", and "Fuji" apples: maturity indices and quality after storage', *Fruit Varieties Journal*, vol. 49, no. 3, pp. 133–142.

Povinelli, E. A. (2011) *Economies of Abandonment: Social Belonging and Endurance in Late Liberalism*, Duke University Press, Durham, NC.

Sassatelli, R. and Davolio, F. (2010) 'Consumption, pleasure and politics: slow food and the politico-aesthetic problematization of food', *Journal of Consumer Culture*, vol. 10, no. 2, pp. 202–232.

Spence, C., Levitan, C. A., Shankar, M. U. and Zampini, M. (2010) 'Does food color influence taste and flavor perception in humans?', *Chemosensory Perception*, vol. 3, no. 1, pp. 68–84.

Stock, P., Carolan, M. and Rosin, C. (eds) (2015) *Food Utopias: Reimagining Citizenship, Ethics and Community*, Routledge, London.

Vermeulen, T. and van den Akker, R. (2015) 'Utopia, sort of: a case study in metamodernism', *Studia Neophilologica*, vol. 87, no. sup1, pp. 55–67.

Watkins, C. B., Brookfield, P. L. and Harker, F. R. (1992) 'Development of maturity indices for the "Fuji" apple cultivar in relation to watercore incidence', *International Symposium on Pre- and Postharvest Physiology of Pome-Fruit*, vol. 326, June, pp. 267–276.

Williams, K. (1993) 'Part three: use of evaporative cooling for enhancing apple fruit quality', *Good Fruit Grower*, vol. 44, no. 11, pp. 23–27.

Yepsen, R. (1994) *Apples*, W. W. Norton, New York.

10 Value and values in the making of merino

Harvey C. Perkins and Eric Pawson

Introduction

In this chapter we explore and explicate the link between economic value and other-than-economic values in rural production (Miller 2008: 1123). 'Value' and 'values' in these terms have a number of meanings. They refer to assuring financial return for farmers and secondary producers, producing high-quality farm outputs, maintaining productive landscapes, protecting and conserving natural environments, owning and managing farms intergenerationally, enhancing rural community, sustaining relationships with value chain members, making stylish fit-for-purpose products, and increasing consumer demand for those products. We illustrate our discussion using the examples of fine merino wools in the high-fashion and 'against-the-skin' outdoor recreation garment industries and their associated organizational assemblages (Pawson and Perkins 2013). Our focus will be on business strategies designed to create assured value or price for New Zealand growers of fine wools and makers of garments. We shall show how, in the mid-1990s, through the agency of the New Zealand Merino Company and its allies in the farming and textile and garment manufacturing industries, merino was created as a niche product differentiated from the national wool clip. This represented a step-change in merino production, incorporating a wider range of uses for merino fibre, new practices in the countryside, and a greatly increased geographical extension of the networks of people, processes, objects, organizations, and places associated with assembling merino into marketable products.

The story of New Zealand merino sheep and the problems of both the New Zealand and the international wool industry since the late 1960s are at the centre of our argument. The merino is New Zealand's oldest sheep breed and also one of the world's oldest, originating in Iberia in the Middle Ages. While merino sheep were initially widespread, they had become marginalized to the high country of the South Island by 1900. Today they account for only about 5 per cent of New Zealand's 29.6 million sheep, most of which are bred for meat, with wool now being a low-value by-product (Beef and Lamb New Zealand 2015a). This is the case because most classes of wool have decreased in value industrially, having been superseded by synthetic fibres.

Some parts of the merino fibre clip have however proved an exception. While perhaps not generating the kinds of prices preferred by farmers, New Zealand-grown fibre in the superfine to ultrafine diameter range has always been in demand for garment manufacturing, particularly for expensive and high-status business suits for men, and more recently for women. This was not, at first, the case for coarser or stronger merino, in the fine and mid-micron diameter range, which until the 1990s was combined with merino of similar type from Australia and South Africa, and sold as a generic fibre. The potential for increased demand and prices for this class of merino grown in New Zealand changed with successful textile manufacturing experiments in the early 1990s, leading to the development of novel against-the-skin outdoor recreation garments made from fine and mid-micron wool. These are now manufactured and sold globally.

In discussing this significant change we will emphasize the tactics used successfully to identify and represent all merino as a high-value fibre, earning growers a premium price, albeit annually variable, when compared with coarse wool growers (Beef and Lamb New Zealand 2015a: 15). These tactics have included: multi-year contracts for merino farmers who adhere to strict metrological fibre diameter criteria; propositions promoting values associated with provenance, quality, fitness for purpose, and environmental and social sustainability; and marketing strategies in which merino clothing is represented as a natural extension of the human body and integral to a range of human activities. Our study has explored these tactics and their effects on merino production, price and manufacturing, and the next two sections outline the background to it and the research methods we used.

The merino story

New Zealand merino sheep (Figure 10.1) are mostly produced in the rugged, climatically extreme and sometimes remote environment of the South Island high country. Farms are usually large, in the order of several thousand hectares, and the prosperity of farmers has depended significantly on the market price of fine wool. Creating new opportunities to profit from this fine wool has therefore been crucial in sustaining value and values and their adherence in high-country places. In the last two decades there has been a transformation in the way this has occurred. New organizational forms have emerged that have substantially realigned relations between rural New Zealand primary producers, intermediaries in fibre purchasing and processing, textile manufacturing, garment design and marketing, and mainly wealthy global urban consumers.

Two events were central to this process: first, merino farmers broke away from the New Zealand Wool Board in the mid-1990s and established the New Zealand Merino Company;[1] and second, at about the same time, Icebreaker was established by entrepreneur Jeremy Moon as a New Zealand-based merino clothing design company. Both initiatives in combination have offered farmers an assured income through fixed-price multi-year contracts.

Value and values in the making of merino 143

Figure 10.1 Grazing merino sheep, Ahuriri Valley near Omarama, Otago
Source: Photograph by Harvey Perkins.

A number of accounts of these events have been written, typically from the perspective of the proponents and beneficiaries of change. John Perriam, a Central Otago wool grower and advocate for the breakaway of the merino farmers, describes how, up to the early 1990s, New Zealand merino was incorporated with 'unknown merino fibre from around the world. It had no identity past first-stage processing' (Perriam 2010: 235). He attributes this to the Wool Board and the generic promotional approach implicit in the Woolmark brand of the International Wool Secretariat, the latter of which was established in the 1930s to position 'wool' as a natural fibre against inexpensive synthetic competitors (Abbott 1998). As Table 10.1 shows, these competitors had dramatically undermined wool's market position since the 1960s. Roger Buchanan (2012), the last chief executive of the Wool Board, elaborated on this argument, pointing out that, as the International Wool Secretariat was largely funded by Australian wool growers, and because their merino is generally a coarser fibre, generic promotion did not suit the interests of New Zealand producers.

As Perriam puts it, those whom the Wool Board saw as 'rebels' 'were, in fact, simply a group of determined merino growers who wanted to take control of [their] future beyond the farm gate' (2010: 236). In order to do this, they had to create new markets and adopt new business practices. These contradicted the

Table 10.1 Global fibre consumption

	Wool %	Cotton %	Synthetics %	Cellulosics %
1960	10	68	5	18
1980	5	46	37	12
2000	3	38	54	5
2009	2	36	57	5

Source: Oerlikon (2010: 92).

established view that it was impossible to differentiate wool fibre categories, or to assure forward prices in excess of the commodity price that would, in turn, be honoured, and that value could be added through marketing and captured by growers (Stanford Graduate School of Business 2013). Within a few years of its establishment, the New Zealand Merino Company was handling about 85 per cent of all merino grown in New Zealand. Its methods include forward contracts with an expanding range of high-quality textile and garment manufacturers worldwide, who each demand a fibre of specific diameter (see for example Cronshaw 2015a), the use of an accreditation system to underwrite the quality and attributes of the product, and often clear sourcing and provenance of the fibre. There is widespread agreement that this fibre is known as 'merino', rather than as a form of wool.

Methods

We used a range of methods, during several years of fieldwork, to gather the data used to create the merino story we outline above and will elaborate below. We sought data that illustrated the active interplay between experimentation, institutions, value, values, measurement and the production of new environments, animals and technologies. In doing so we studied merino on farms, in consumer spaces and in the places in between. The significant historical literature on wool production and manufacture in New Zealand was a useful aid in understanding institutional and farming practices. The Internet provided data and commentary on recent developments, with examples of the ways merino products are advertised and presented to consumers. We also studied representations of merino products in retail settings, on packaging, in popular magazines, on television and on roadside hoardings on farms. The farming pages of the daily newspapers were a constant source of stories about institutional changes and new business practices in merino. These stories recorded ongoing experiments with animal production, the development of new alliances, and the creation of new products and market trends. Merino industry gatherings and associated workshops and conferences were also useful sources of information, and provided contacts and advice about the best people to speak with and interview.

To these data were added 20 interviews with farmers, stock and station agents, wool buyers, product manufacturers, retailers and marketers either resident in or linked to Central Otago in the high country of the South Island. All were either chosen by us or recommended by other interviewees for their capacity to add to our unfolding interpretation. Interviews generally took place at our research participants' places of work, giving us the opportunity to observe interactions between objects, people and merino. We organized a day-long exchange of views between participants in the industry, including farmers, manufacturers and service agencies. We also visited merino retail outlets, and wore various against-the-skin and outer-layer woollen garments in a variety of domestic, professional and recreational settings. Compilation and analysis of all of these data sources progressed iteratively across the three years, in what became a period of observation, periodic exchanges with participants, and regular face-to-face researcher meetings. These data were subjected to ongoing thematic analysis to elaborate the merino story more fully. Three theoretical constructs emerged as being centrally important to our analysis: metrology, provenance, and embodiment and co-constitution, and we discuss these below.

Metrology: wool, sheep and farms

The significance of the role of fibre diameter, measured in microns (micrometres), in the classification of merino for particular end uses has already been introduced. While other fibre attributes are also important, such as crimp (number of bends per unit length along the fibre), tensile strength, and colour, 'clear price differentials exist for different fibre diameters and in *almost* all cases the price increases as the diameter decreases' (New Zealand Wool Testing Authority n.d.: 1, original emphasis). It follows therefore that questions and techniques of measurement or metrology play an important part in the merino story, and link it to a much broader set of organizational arrangements worldwide. Metrology is the science of quantity systems and units of measurement. Its practitioners define, establish and promulgate standard units of measurement. The development of standard units of measurement is today coordinated as part of the International System of Units by the International Bureau of Weights and Measures, to which many countries, including New Zealand, are signatories. The Bureau's protocols in turn underpin the work of national metrological organizations interested in measurement standards (BIPM 2015).

The standards established by international and national metrological organizations have their counterparts in industry. There, measurement and calibration are often key technical factors in production and distribution, and in the methods by which processes and systems can be standardized and interpreted more uniformly by participants. The micro-computer and allied sensing, data storage and networking technologies have been fundamental tools in metrological development in many industries over recent decades: notably, in the context of this chapter, where hand-held or small-scale applications are useful. From reading about metrology in industry, one factor comes through very strongly: it is a dynamic field, marked by continuous technological innovation, the efficacy of which is often constrained by a range of complex and interacting bio-physical environmental, cultural and economic factors.

Nevertheless, the pursuit of accuracy in industries once mainly reliant on qualitative assessment of biological raw materials displaying the effects of considerable genetic and environmental variability, however difficult, has opened up important opportunities for product differentiation and established new discourses of communication, organization and practice within these industries. In wool, and merino specifically, fibre classing in its earliest forms, using the Bradford Count System, saw classification being conducted qualitatively by eye and touch to judge the spinning characteristics of a fleece (Ryder 1995). Qualitative classing, on the farm in the wool shed, and in wool stores in urban centres prior to sale, was based on a combination of tacit and codified knowledge built up by classers over lifetimes of work, and handed down intergenerationally. The significance of this knowledge and its transmission was illustrated in a 1916 newspaper article from Oamaru, North Otago, in the South Island:

> Wool-classing and study of wool
>
> An adult class for instruction in wool-classing and study of wool characteristics is again being formed at the Technical School. Mr J. McGregor, wool expert to the Otago and Southland Education Boards, will outline the syllabus and give the first lecture and demonstration next Monday evening. As Oamaru is now becoming important as a wool-classing centre, it is necessary that those employed by wool broking firms, should have a good knowledge of the staple product of the Dominion. . . . A lecture is given each evening on a subject relating to wool, such as the Bradford system of counts, condition in wool crimps and serrations, characteristics of a stylish ram's fleece, a faulty fleece, yolk or suint [a natural greasy substance in sheep's wool], qualities of various purebred wools, treatment of hogget wool, etc.
>
> (*Oamaru Mail* 1916: 6)

This form of classing is being increasingly replaced today by what is known as 'objective measurement' and more highly codified forms of quantitative data and analysis in commercial wool transactions (Roche 1995). Fibre is sometimes measured quantitatively on the farm in the wool shed using portable scanning machine techniques but also later in the laboratory (New Zealand Wool Testing Authority n.d.). The factors measured include fibre diameter, yield (including the amount of vegetable matter), staple length, staple strength and sometimes colour. Such measurements are important in processes of sampling, audit and accreditation (Australian Wool Exchange 2015; Australian Wool Testing Authority 2015).

The capacity to measure fibre accurately, and a general agreement to do so, allows classes of merino to be differentiated from each other more clearly. This differentiation process opens up opportunities for producers, designers and manufacturers to imagine new possibilities and markets for merino, each one meeting strict measurement standards, and linked by mediating organizational and contractual arrangements to product design, manufacturing and marketing. As illustrated in Table 10.2, particular micron ranges correspond to different end uses, and enable farmers to develop their product and sell it by using a number of brokerage techniques, including contract growing and sale at auction, for specific markets. These include socks manufactured by the US SmartWool company for active outdoor use, and Italian-made suits from super- and ultrafine fibre.

The corollary of this is that, aided by agricultural scientists, land management ecologists and agri-technologists, farmers are also applying additional metrological techniques to the development of the merino sheep and their farms. These techniques are being used to 'make better sheep' (Cronshaw 2015b) and also have an established history. As early as 1896 the New Zealand Sheep Breeders' Association published the first volume of the *New Zealand Flock-Book*. Its authors noted that 'Three hundred flocks [had] been entered' and expressed the view that 'The work should prove of great value to breeders of pure stock' (*New Zealand Official Yearbook* 1896: 372). The early merino sheep had a short fibre staple and a small carcass when compared to today's animal. The modern merino sheep has been produced over many years of intensive selective breeding, the practice of which by 2015 was based on computerized recording of flock data in order to meet specific development and production criteria. The redesigned merino sheep is managed on farms in new ways, and here too measurement is to the fore. Particular animal husbandry and land management methods are conducive to the production of specific types of fibre so that metrological 'monitoring of vegetation, soil health and stock health are regular and ongoing' (Forest Range Estate 2015). Animal breeding to increase sheep health and farm profitability is also a subject of metrological enquiry. A recent report on the Feetfirst initiative indicated that 'footrot is costing merino sheep farmers $NZ10 million a year in treatment and lost production and a [genetic] test is being developed [by a partnership of farmers, the New Zealand Merino Company and the New Zealand government] to identify more resistant sires' to help overcome the problem (Cronshaw 2015b: A10).

Table 10.2 Merino fibre diameter ranges and allied products

Description	Micron range	End use
Strong/broad	22.6 upward	Blending, seating fabrics
Medium fine/medium	19.6–22.5	SmartWool
Fine	18.6–19.5	Icebreaker, SmartWool
Superfine	17.6–18.5	Suits, Icebreaker
Ultrafine	less than 17.5	Suits

Source: www.merinos.com.au.

Note: A human hair is *c.* 60 microns in diameter.

Farmers use the metrological data derived from the types of activities discussed above to portray and distinguish the production characteristics of their farms, particularly stud operations, on their business websites (see for example data for Forest Range Estate 2015 and Earnscleugh Station 2015). Metrological differentiation is thus an essential vehicle for increasing fibre value. Such differentiation is also a feature of garment marketing, with measurement and classification incorporated in stories about product quality, the uses to which they may be put, and their fitness for purpose. As these stories have developed, links are also made to the attributes of the places in which merino fibre is grown, and the processes used to raise and harvest it, and in this way metrology becomes connected to provenance.

Provenance

The New Zealand Merino Company, its farmer shareholders, merino textile and garment designers, manufacturers and retailers have successfully identified and represented merino as a high-value fibre. They have done this by creating propositions or stories promoting values associated with provenance and, by association, quality, fitness for purpose, and environmental and social sustainability (Pawson and Perkins 2013). The essential idea in this approach is that classes of biological products such as types of fibre can easily be associated with positive marketing stories which transmit ideas about rural origins, qualities and practices. Such stories create value by seeking to 'fill the holes – epistemic, emotional, sensorial . . . created by [product standardization]' (Carolan 2011: 29–30). They do so because they appeal to the desires and needs of largely urban consumers globally (Miller 2008: 1130). The stories emphasize high-quality fibre which has the 'right kind of provenance', one that is represented as being authentic, as being in no way fake and as having at least a measure of uniqueness.

Thus provenance is partly to do with product attributes: such as garments made from fibre that is sustainably grown and manufactured in ways that are not exploitative of people and animals. It is also associated with the attributes of a product's place of origin. In the case of merino fibre and clothing, such places are represented as clean, green, wild, well treated, managed environmentally, home to viable and vibrant local communities, and also somewhat out of the ordinary. In marketing terms this appeal to provenance is bound up with the now all-pervasive culture of advertising. Purchasing a high-status, fit-for-purpose, sustainably made product, the constituents of which are traceable to a particular location with the attributes discussed above, 'promises the lucky purchaser special powers that they would otherwise not have' (Gottdiener 2000: 4) and distinguishes purchasers from others who cannot consume in this way (Bourdieu 1984). This allows a premium to be charged for the product. Traceability is a key element in this equation because it allows consumers to assess the attribution of values. The need to do so is heightened because, as expressed in Oerlikon's survey of the world textile industry, and its assessment of the rise of consumer sustainability concerns, 'An average consumer appears [otherwise] to be overextended in the tangle of labels' (Oerlikon 2010: 8).

Additionally, seen from the perspective of fibre producers, provenance stories are directly and indirectly performative, and influence the management of products and the places in which they are produced (Cloke and Perkins 1998; Pawson and Perkins 2013). Once established, farmers understand that it is crucial there is no obvious dissonance between proposition and practice: so those who are party to the development of merino provenance stories are bound to make their production practices conform as far as possible to the marketing representations contained in them. The risks of not doing so could be serious in reputational and financial terms.

In practice, the provenance stories about merino grown in New Zealand interweave messages about product and locational attributes, traceability, and the excellence of farming practices, some of them metrological, others associated with animal husbandry and ecological management. The New Zealand Merino Company, for example, has established an accreditation system known as ZQ (New Zealand Merino Company 2015) to which all of its contracted producers must adhere. The Company promotes ZQ in terms which emphasize value in the form of enhanced and assured financial return to farmers, but also focuses on 'animal welfare, environmental care, and social sustainability, along with delivering premium quality fit for purpose fibre' (New Zealand Merino Company 2015). It also distinguishes niche 'high-value' merino grown on contract in New Zealand from the remainder of the world's supply of merino, sold, it is suggested, as a generic undervalued commodity at auction:

> Not all merino is created equal. The global brands that partner with ZQ Merino have done their homework and taken the time to discover the difference.
>
> Most merino is a faceless commodity, sold through an adversarial supply chain whose ultimate goal is lowest price. ZQ Merino weaves human understanding with nature's brilliance to produce the world's premium fibre. Working in synergy with its partners at every level, ZQ Merino delivers on authenticity and provenance, amplifying a brand's reputation and the value it is able to offer to its customers.
>
> (New Zealand Merino Company 2015)

These claims are backed by on-farm accreditation programmes that seek to raise product quality and practices. They are illustrated on the Company's website with photographs of the wild high-country landscape in which merino sheep dwell. Icebreaker relies heavily on such claims and imagery in its advertising material. It has established close relationships with farmers, with these being publicly displayed on large roadside company signs (Figure 10.2), on the land of those participating stations located on popular tourist routes. Icebreaker has also introduced traceability and transparency for consumers

Figure 10.2 Icebreaker sign on Cluden Station, Lindis Pass, Central Otago
Source: Photograph by Harvey Perkins.

who, using each garment's 'baa code', can track the origin of the fibre used in their clothing to source on particular high-country stations (Pawson and Perkins 2013).

The approach taken by other participants in New Zealand merino textile manufacturing, and smaller-scale garment designers and retailers, replicates the provenance story, but also shifts its emphasis slightly to suit particular marketing goals. Tika Merino is an example of this. Its provenance proposition, set against a backdrop of snow-covered South Island high country, asserts that its garments are made from fibre that is 'natural, sustainable, bio-degradable, annually renewable, recyclable, and a good fit for retailers looking for eco chic apparel' (Tika Merino 2008).

Provenance stories are also an essential part of the way the New Zealand Merino Company and other smaller merino brokers link New Zealand merino farmers with overseas design and manufacturing clients. In an example of this intermediation, Rae (2008) reports the interpretation of the senior trader of a fibre brokerage firm, who had linked suit manufacturer Konaka Company of Japan with the owners of a merino farm, Closeburn Station in Central Otago. He indicated that, 'for the [overseas] client, the driver is twofold, telling the origin of the wool story as well as the quality of the fibre story', [and] 'for the grower, it is being rewarded for farming practices that often take years of investment to perfect' (see also Cronshaw 2015c). John Smedley, British garment manufacturer and New Zealand Merino Company ZQ partner, also emphasize the importance of the traceability aspect of the provenance story. They buy their merino from the New Zealand Merino Company, which in turn contracts the owners of 12,000 hectare Omarama Station to grow the fibre to metrological specification. John Smedley make a direct link in their marketing to Omarama Station, and in turn its owners, Richard and Annabelle Subtil, refer in the farming news media to 'the station as an original and loyal supplier of wool into John Smedley and Icebreaker contracts' (Beef and Lamb New Zealand 2015b). Cognizant of the importance of having a reputation for high-quality farming practices, a valuable adjunct to contractual relationships such as these, the Subtils recently entered and won the competition for the supreme Canterbury Ballance Farm Environment Award (Beef and Lamb New Zealand 2015b).

We have dealt so far largely with the representational aspect of provenance stories as illustrated in websites, advertising, print media and organizational interactions. It is important to mention that our fieldwork indicates that these stories are also evident in consumer discourse. Word-of-mouth and social media interactions about day-to-day and occasional specialist use of merino garments among members of social networks incorporate the positive elements of provenance but can also interrupt the stories if consumers are unhappy with their purchases. Recognizing the importance of building stronger face-to-face connections with consumers, Icebreaker has named its global chain of retail outlets 'TouchLabs' (Icebreaker 2015a), encouraging consumers to touch and try on their garments before purchasing. This is an indication of the ways the embodied, sensuous and material co-constitutive connections between merino and human experience and action are being harnessed in attempts to increase the value of merino.

Embodying and co-constituting merino

A key element in merino marketing strategies is therefore the ways in which garments made from the fibre are represented as a natural extension of the human body, and integral to a range of human activities. Theoretically, this emphasizes the role of bodily activity and sensation in social action, and the ways humans live through, and act in accordance with, their combined cognitive, bodily and worldly social and environmental interactions. In this theorization garments are an excellent example of embodiment: they are not separate from but blend with the human body and extend its capacities to engage with activities in the world. Specialist garment manufacturers and retailers understand this and, when combined with the knowledge that people's 'clothing practices are an important and pervasive form of appearance management that reflects the continued monitoring of their visual selves' (Frith and Gleeson 2004), then powerful value-enhancing advertising text and imagery can be created and enacted.

In the case of merino garments we have identified three overlapping types of embodiment: those associated with active bodies, fashionable bodies and protected bodies. All of the companies that produce outdoor recreational clothing from merino, for example, emphasize the connection between fit-for-purpose garments and enhanced recreational performance. Icebreaker (2015b) has this to say about the design of its clothing:

> When we're designing a new garment, the key question for us is always: how does this perform?
>
> It's all about functionality – better temperature regulation, mobility, sweat management, and fit. . . . The aim is to create styles so light and unrestrictive that people feel as free as if they're wearing nothing at all. . . .
>
> The design ethos is under-stated and elegant, and always has an element of surprise – interior stitching, or a print on a pocket. Icebreaker's roots are in nature, and our designers constantly use New Zealand's wild landscape as a source of inspiration.

Icebreaker clothing is made to be layered on the body, but, even when the against-the-body layer and its owner's skin are together soaked in perspiration, fashion and up-to-date style are clearly to the fore. The garments are accordingly priced at a premium.

Bodies looking fashionable in New Zealand merino may take other forms. The fibre is used to create NZ$25,000 high-fashion men's and women's business suits made from fabric woven in Italy (Cronshaw 2014). These very 'high-end' values are exceptional. Still expensive, but positioned in price nearer that of the outdoor recreational garment sector of the market, are clothes associated with lifestyle fashion designers. Untouched World is a good example. It uses images of slender fashion models and high-profile figures (such as former US president Bill Clinton and current president Barack Obama) wearing the company's clothing on its website to market a range of, again layered, merino casual home, office and street wear. Like Icebreaker, Untouched World relies on the provenance stories we have already discussed to underpin its marketing. Untouched World is:

> The first fashion company in the world to be recognized by the United Nations for sustainability. . . . Here at Untouched World™ our ethos is simple. We want to create beautiful, easy wear, easy care pieces you will enjoy for years to come. Pieces that not only make you feel good inside and out, but that are also easy on the earth. Quality and sustainability are non-negotiables for us, and we won't budge on either.
>
> (Untouched World 2015)

Whether designed primarily for active or fashionable bodies, all merino clothing protects to one degree or another. One brand focuses specifically on protecting the active body. Armadillo Merino is marketed as 'merino body armour for professional risk takers', 'a diverse range of professionals facing extreme and challenging conditions all around the world'. This company 'specializes in next-to-skin protective clothing made from innovative knit fabrics that utilise the natural benefits of superfine merino wool'. Armadillo Merino's marketing depends on images of humans in extreme environments, arguing that merino has 'built-in advantages, [which] combined with a natural softness and strength, make it the ideal fibre to enhance your *protection*, *performance* and *comfort* in extreme environments' (Armadillo Merino 2015, original emphasis). The marketing also makes specific reference to the New Zealand Merino Company's ZQ accreditation system.

There is a strong sense in each of these examples of merino and embodiment of the networked agency of humans and other-than-humans in the co-constitution (Cloke and Perkins 2005) of the fibre and merino garments under discussion. Figure 10.3 illustrates this point: merino garments are co-constituted in ongoing interactions between people, their technologies, economic and recreational activities, merino sheep, and the landscapes which merino sheep and humans inhabit. It is not possible to comprehend fully the merino story without incorporating all of these elements and the ways they interconnect and construct each other.

This is hinted at in the story of the New Zealand Merino Company where it is stated that: 'ZQ merino weaves human understanding with nature's brilliance to produce the world's premium fibre' (New Zealand Merino Company 2015). Similarly, the merino textile and garment manufacturing companies make mention of being 'inspired by and learning from nature' (in Icebreaker's case), with metaphorical comparison being made between the sheep's merino clothing and garments worn by humans produced from the sheep's fibre. Website and other imagery leans heavily on the interacting influence of landscape, merino sheep, clothing, activity and embodiment.

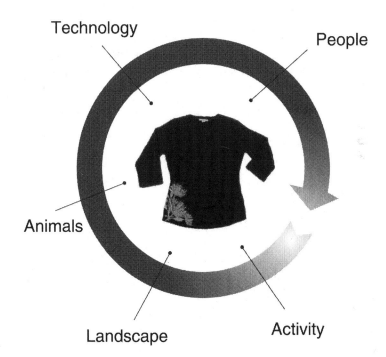

Figure 10.3 Garments as embodied and co-constructed

Conclusion

In this chapter, using the example of recent developments in the New Zealand merino industry, we have explored the link between economic value and other-than-economic values for both producers and consumers. The development of the merino contract system by the New Zealand Merino Company, and its engagement with a growing global assemblage of actors, has signalled a significant differentiation in the value accruing to fine wool producers in the South Island of New Zealand's high country, when measured over the long run. This, despite annual price variation, has been an important element in assuring those parts of farm profitability associated with merino sheep production. Similar value has accrued to companies that trade in aspects of merino garment manufacture. Part of assured value for farmer producers has arisen from more effective and efficient farming techniques and improvement in technologies and animal husbandry and production. A greater reliance on metrology has allowed fibre types to be more effectively matched to production possibilities.

The advancement of production possibilities has also been aided with skilful intermediation by the New Zealand Merino Company and other wool brokers. They have worked assiduously to link contracted New Zealand farmers to client companies in many parts of the world. This has had the effect of allowing farmers to see well beyond the farm gate, and to manage their farms and flocks in a way that is consistent with client and consumer desires and needs. The farmer accreditation schemes and provenance stories that have emerged in this process have found favour with a range of textile and garment design, manufacturing and retailing companies with global reach, keen to source their merino from well-managed and environmentally sound farms. These provenance stories are shaped to be attractive to consumers, and form the basis of marketing strategies emphasizing traceability of merino fibre to such farms. This marketing also takes advantage of the attractive imagery of the places in which merino sheep are farmed, and the possibilities inherent in representing merino clothing as being the embodiment of activity, fashion and protection.

In turn, these accreditation schemes and marketing strategies have a performative effect. Farmers are farming differently and engaging in a range of animal welfare and land management practices that were not high priorities in the past. Although practices undoubtedly vary, there is a keener sense that farmers' reputations, and that of their produce, are dependent on the improvement of day-to-day farm operations and on a focus on the long-term sustainability of their land and its product. But further to this is the realization that the networks of connections beyond the farm gate, symbolized and enacted through the three key elements we have examined here, namely metrologies, provenance, and consumer clothing practices, create the conditions for the generation of economic value as well as wider values in merino production. Amongst these are the maintenance of the livelihoods and places of farming families who produce a niche product that in turn satisfies some of the desires of distant and well-off urban consumers for fashionable, effective and storied garments.

Note

1 The New Zealand Merino Company was established after the McKinsey Report of 2000 proposed new commercial wool marketing companies for both strong wools and fine wools. The Company took over the assets of Merino New Zealand, the industry-good organization that had been established with the breakaway in 1996, and which was funded by transfer of the producer levy (since discontinued) from the Wool Board.

References

Abbott, M. J. (1998) 'Promoting wool internationally: the formation of the International Wool Secretariat', *Australian Economic History Review*, vol. 38, pp. 258–279.

Armadillo Merino (2015) *About Us*, https://www.armadillomerino.com/content/about-us, accessed 4 June 2015.

Australian Wool Exchange (2015) *Standards*, http://www.awex.com.au/standards/, accessed 26 May 2015.

Australian Wool Testing Authority (2015) *Specialised Wool Testing, Innovative Test Solutions, Trusted and Independent Results*, http://www.awtawooltesting.com.au/index.php/en/, accessed 26 May 2015.

Beef and Lamb New Zealand (2015a) *Compendium of New Zealand Farm Facts 2015*, Beef and Lamb New Zealand, Wellington.

Beef and Lamb New Zealand (2015b) *Case Study: Omarama Station, McKenzie County*, http://www.beeflambnz.com/news-events/News/2015/april/case-study-omarama-station/, accessed 28 May 2015.

BIPM (International Bureau of Weights and Measures) (2015) http://www.bipm.org/en/about-us/, accessed 26 May 2015.

Bourdieu, P. (1984) *Distinction: A Social Critique of the Judgement of Taste*, Harvard University Press, Cambridge, MA.

Buchanan, R. (2012) *Last Shepherd: Anecdotes and Observations from Five Decades in the Wool Industry*, Ngaio Press, Wellington.

Carolan, M. S. (2011) *The Real Cost of Cheap Food*, Earthscan, Abingdon.

Cloke, P. and Perkins, H. C. (1998) '"Cracking the canyon with the awesome foursome": representations of adventure tourism in New Zealand', *Environment and Planning D: Society and Space*, vol. 16, pp. 185–218.

Cloke, P. and Perkins, H. C. (2005) 'Cetacean performance and tourism in Kaikoura, New Zealand', *Environment and Planning D: Society and Space*, vol. 23, no. 6, pp. 903–924.

Cronshaw, T. (2014) 'Ultrafine merino set to deliver $25,000 suits', *New Zealand Farmer*, http://www.stuff.co.nz/business/farming/sheep/10627658/Ultrafine-merino-set-to-deliver-25-000-suits, accessed 30 May 2015.

Cronshaw, T. (2015a) 'Farmers flock to clothing deal', *The Press* (Christchurch), 17 April.

Cronshaw, T. (2015b) 'Better merino sheep in the making', *The Press* (Christchurch), 8 May.

Cronshaw, T. (2015c) 'Fine merino suits are hot seller in Japan', *The Press* (Christchurch), 22 May.

Earnscleugh Station (2015) *Merino Policy and Technology*, http://www.earnscleughstation.co.nz/merino-policy.htm, accessed 26 May 2015.

Forest Range Estate (2015) *Management*, http://www.forestrange.co.nz/management.html, accessed 26 May 2015.

Frith, H. and Gleeson, K. (2004) 'Clothing and embodiment: men managing body image and appearance', *Psychology of Men and Masculinity*, vol. 5, pp. 40–48.

Gottdiener, M. (ed.) (2000) *New Forms of Consumption: Consumers, Culture and Commodification*, Rowman & Littlefield, Lanham, MD.

Icebreaker (2105a) *Icebreaker TouchLabs*, http://nz.icebreaker.com/en/about-icebreaker/icebreaker-touchlabs.html, accessed 28 May 2015.

Icebreaker (2015b) *How We Design*, http://nz.icebreaker.com/en/about-icebreaker/how-we-design.html, accessed 30 May 2015.

Miller, D. (2008) 'The uses of value', *Geoforum*, vol. 39, no. 3, pp. 1122–1132.

New Zealand Merino Company (2015) *Discover ZQ Merino*, http://www.nzmerino.co.nz/discover-zq-merino/, accessed 28 May 2015.

New Zealand Official Yearbook (1896), New Zealand Government.

New Zealand Wool Testing Authority (n.d.) *Fibre Fineness*, NZWTA, Napier, http://www.nzwta.co.nz/docs/fibre_diameter.pdf, accessed 27 May 2015.

Oamaru Mail (1916) 'Wool-classing and study of wool', *Oamaru Mail*, vol. XLII, no. 12872, 14 June.

Oerlikon (2010) *The Fiber Year 2009/10: A World Survey on Nonwovens and Textile Industry*, issue 10, May, http://www.indotextiles.com/download/Fiber%20Year%202009_10.pdf, accessed 30 May 2015.

Pawson, E. and Perkins, H. (2013) 'Worlds of wool: recreating value off the sheep's back', *New Zealand Geographer*, vol. 69, no. 3, pp. 208–220.

Perriam, J. (2010) *Dust to Gold: The Inspiring Story of Bendigo Station, Home of Shrek*, Random House, Auckland.

Rae, S. (2008) 'Fine deal for merino farmer', *Otago Daily Times*, http://www.odt.co.nz/news/farming/204482/fine-deal-merino-farmer, accessed 28 May 2015.

Roche, J. (1995) *The International Wool Trade*, Woodhead Publishing, Cambridge.

Ryder, M. L. (1995) 'Fleece grading and wool sorting: the historical perspective', *Textile History*, vol. 26, no. 1, 3–22.

Stanford Graduate School of Business (2013) *The New Zealand Merino Company*, http://discoverzque.com/casestudy, accessed 26 October 2013.

Tika Merino (2008) 'Tika Merino to showcase eco friendly design', press release, *Scoop Business*, http://www.scoop.co.nz/stories/BU0808/S00138/tika-merino-to-showcase-expanded-eco-friendly-line.htm, accessed 28 May 2015.

Untouched World (2015) *Untouched World: Ethos*, http://www.untouchedworld.com/ethos.htm, accessed 30 May 2015.

11 Eating the unthinkable

The case of ENTO, eating insects and bioeconomic experimentation

Paul V. Stock, Catherine Phillips, Hugh Campbell and Anne Murcott

Introduction

The intentions of this chapter[1] are set squarely within the overall political and theoretical project of the idea of biological economies: examining those moments and sites of confluence of environmental and economic challenges in agri-food systems that also lead toward experimentation. Drawing on the evolving work in biological economies (Campbell et al. 2009; Le Heron 2009; Lewis et al. 2013; this volume, Chapters 1 and 18) as well as food utopias (Stock et al. 2015) and more-than-human agri-food studies (Phillips 2013, 2014), we examine both economic and cultural experimentation around the conceptualisation, and outcomes of trying to bring insect-based[2] foodstuffs to Western markets. In food utopias, the idea of experimentation aims to 'move away from expecting things and relationships to be in some finished state and therefore able to be explained' (Stock et al. 2015: 8; see also this volume, Chapter 15). By being utopian in both method and subject we enter the terrain of risk for both economic actors and researchers. On one hand, we hope to have identified something interesting and instructive for understanding novel ways of 'doing' food. On the other hand, our case might dissolve leaving nothing more than celebratory blog posts and an empty 'Upcoming Events' web page.

What follows takes exactly this kind of risk by doing agri-food research that tries to embrace the diversity of biological economies, food utopias and more-than-human studies. We do this by introducing and interrogating one such economic experiment that is responding to the question: 'How do insects, and the prospect of eating them, make us think about food and food security?' Further, as researchers into experimental economies, we ask 'What can we learn from what is already happening (Gibson-Graham 2008) as start-up enterprises work to remake insects into foods for global North consumers?' This is a venture engaged with the earliest stages of one experimental biological economy, directed both methodologically and through its subject matter towards the utopian and the more-than-human.

This chapter presents a case study of ENTO – a London-based start-up company using insects as the primary ingredient for novel foodstuffs.[3] As an example of experimentation ENTO illustrates important dynamics associated with novel and disruptive foods:

- First, the difficulty of bringing novelty to the shelf involves more than production, supply chain management and retailing. It also incorporates various ways of knowing the world or justifying or challenging the world as it is, including the cultural dynamics of palatability, edibility and visibility.
- Second, it reveals the need to account for more-than-human dynamics (Whatmore 2002; Bennett 2010) in experimentation around new agri-food assemblages (Carolan 2013a; Lewis et al. 2013). Insects' materialities and capacities are vital in the unfolding of this particular experiment.
- Finally, the case of ENTO challenges orthodox political economy framings of agri-food. The problems faced by ENTO, as well as the potential consequences of widespread adoption of insects in Western diets, involve regulatory dilemmas and re-categorisation of foodstuffs. They also prompt new ways of understanding utopian reassembling of agri-food systems.

The chapter enlarges on these three considerations via the case study of ENTO's experimental relations with insects, and their edibility, for Western markets. In so doing, it aims to reveal an enactive potential that both breaks existing frameworks and opens new opportunities for agri-food futures.

Before describing ENTO, we add a brief background observation to our proposal that, among other things, this chapter addresses the cultural dynamics of edibility. Although omnivorous, all human groups are selective in what they eat and thus what they recognise as food. None, as far as is known, eat everything available that is nutritious and safe – and there is evidence that avoidances are particularly strong in respect of animal food sources (Simoons 1961). Examples of such discriminations are well known – the Hindu avoidance of beef, dog relished in China – while less familiarly fox was once judged a delicacy in Russia. That these avoidances or preferences are aligned with cultural differences is readily apparent. Differing preferences and cultural importance, however, vary over time; marked, for instance, is a decline in Western diets of, and an apparent rise in disgust for, offal. Insects are no exception, as they 'supplied ... early humans [with] a substantial proportion of protein' (Farb and Armelagos 1980: 43), and they continue to do so in many non-Western diets – beetles, caterpillars, bees, ants, grasshoppers and crickets (among others) are all consumed in diverse ways and places (van Huis et al. 2013: 9–33). Our discussion, then, contributes to reflection on the circumstances surrounding change and the extent to which it may be consciously orchestrated.

ENTO and its context

ENTO originated when four postgraduate students who shared a concern for sustainability were studying design innovation in London. They collaborated on a course project intended to make eating insects more palatable – materially and culturally – for Western diets. The group was inspired by an emerging narrative about the feasibility and novelty of insect consumption as a solution to the twin problems of supplying enough protein globally and the environmental degradation of typical livestock production. As design students, they recognised that a major drawback to eating insects was one of perception, which they viewed as amenable to change in terms of design approaches and solutions. In turn this rendered food security fundamentally a problem that can be solved through design rather than the accumulation of technology and an assumption of progress. ENTO's response to the changing agri-food world is thus both political and highly pragmatic.

Drawing on their design backgrounds, the team converged on food security and food sustainability as their goals. Noting sushi's transformation from an unknown if not disgusting food for non-Japanese people to its current status as popular Western fare, the students brainstormed the idea of ENTO as a combination of entomophagy (insect eating) and the Japanese bento box in which food, such as take-out meals, is transported. The Asian subtext of ENTO, for the team, also hinted at the cultural acceptability of eating insects in other parts of the world. The team saw the elegant simplicity of the word ENTO as sleek and modern but also as connecting with the success of other food transformations: 'It was a really nice-sounding four-letter word that sounded like it already existed' comments Julene (one of ENTO's co-founders).

By experimenting with different insects, researching recipes, collaborating with chefs, interviewing customers and working through design issues, ENTO has tried to rethink the role of insects in agri-food as a way of contributing to promoting sustainability and food security. As Julene says, 'We're interested in introducing insects as a source of meat. They very often get used as a gimmick or as an extra detail or thing, and we think their value is that they're meat, and that they're substantial, and that they're good in their own right.'

Using the vocabulary of sustainability as a platform for collaboration, ENTO chose geometric shapes for foods to move away from direct reference to their animal origin: '*entocubes* aim to redefine insects as a type of food, not as a type of animal' (Core Jr 2012). This was intended as a transitional strategy to desensitise Western consumers to eating insects. Julene put it this way:

> The taboo is so great that not having the insects being visible helps people come to terms with it first as an idea, before being confronted by the visuals – it helps as a stepping stone. We have found that when people first try the pâté, pancakes or croquettes they are then much more likely to try a cricket or a locust on their full form.

Their design also relies on mimicking recognisable flavours. The cooking experiments involved testing taste matches:

> The database we used (www.foodpairing.com) did not contain insects, but we substituted them for close flavour matches (e.g. baked waxworms taste a lot like roasted pistachio nuts). Using this method, we collected over 70 ingredients that could be combined with insects, and began tasting every combination one by one (it was a very long day of eating insects . . .).

> At the end of this experiment, we had created a database of ingredients that could potentially be used with the insects to create new recipes.
>
> (Core Jr 2012)

ENTO have intentionally delayed moving into retailing via supermarkets. Instead they have focused on food fairs and festivals, pop-up restaurants, and strategic collaborations with notable chefs. They plan their first product launch for 2015 (at the time of writing, still in the future). Seen in this light, ENTO might be seen as either revolutionary or trivial, or both. Their phased plan prompted van Huis et al. (2013: 151) to suggest that 'The ENTO project is a roadmap for introducing edible insects to the Western diet . . . focusing on different groups of the public at different stages.'

ENTO are not alone in its pursuit of entomophagy experimenting. In 2014, a Dutch supermarket chain began selling edible insect products such as mealworm snacks and burger patties as 'a healthy and sustainable alternative to eating fish or meat' (Kaufman 2014), and places like food cart Don Bugito (USA) or online Edible Bug Shop (Australia) offer flavoured grubs, crickets and mealworms as part of main courses, snacks and desserts. Most commonly, however, insects are used as new food ingredients in the form of cricket powder or 'flour' for start-up experiments like high-profile palaeo-diet protein bars (produced by EXO, Chapul and Hopper), SixFoods' chirps (cricket-based crisps), BittyFoods' cookies or Crickers' crackers. Many of these products source their insect protein from places like Tiny Farms (USA) and Next Millennium Farms (Canada), which are certified to produce insects for human consumption.

The significant point here is that insects as food in the Western diet are moving beyond mere novelty and shows like *Fear Factor* (Kunitz 2001–06) or *Top Chef Masters* (Stone 2011). Whether insects become a staple of the Western diet remains to be seen. It is at this boundary between edible and inedible, culturally speaking, that ENTO provides a valuable case to examine the current moment of eating what for centuries in the West has been unthinkable. The timing of ENTO is associated with increasing regularity of food crises, the persisting inability to feed the world, increasing rates of food-borne illnesses, mounting concerns and growing trends around particular diet and lifestyle choices, and increasing environmental strains. All of these things combine to serve pro-entomophagy enthusiasts well in addition to representing a spur to their initiatives.

The rest of this chapter explores why experimentation like ENTO's does all sorts of important work in agri-food worlds, making it more important than its small scale and (at this point) limited commercial applicability suggest.

Disgust, design and future foodways

A documentary on insect eating suggests that, 'If we look beyond our disgust, we might realise we've been ignoring a food that could just possibly change the world' (Gates 2013). People's aversion to insect eating remains firm in

Western cultures (van Huis et al. 2013). While resistance may be weakening, at least as evidenced by the increasing popularity of documentaries and television shows, festivals and markets, cookbooks and initiatives such as ENTO, insects still represent the least acceptable protein (Schösler et al. 2012; de Boer et al. 2013).

Disgust toward insects as food may draw upon more general attitudes toward the creatures. Despite the importance of insects to ecologies, invertebrate extinctions garner little sympathy, and insects are regarded most commonly with fear or aversion (Kellert 1993). Lorimer (2007) explains how such aversions are manifest in corporeal, ecological and aesthetic terms, indicating that insects' feral charisma can engender disgust and even panic regarding whole taxa. ENTO and initiatives like it confront such negative feral charisma in their pursuit of reworking insect bodies into tasty food. As Julene explains, the ENTO group asks: 'How can we turn insects into an accepted source of sustainable protein in the West?' ENTO has adopted three main strategies as part of trialling insect eating to deal with what popularly has been called the 'yuck', 'eww' or 'ugh' factor.

The first strategy involves experimental tasting events. These events allow people to see, feel and taste insects in new ways in order to familiarise them with insects as food and expand acceptance. 'It's quite terrifying', one person commented at an ENTO tasting event, but as he ate he added: 'It tastes really nice!' (ENTO 2012). In his popular TedX talk (which has inspired ENTO), Dicke (2010) employs a similar strategy, beginning by asking the audience 'Who has eaten insects before?', and ending as carts of samples are rolled out for audiences to try. Recent studies suggest that anticipated negative sensations and reminders of foods' previous 'aliveness' are more likely to elicit disgust (Martins and Pliner 2006), while openness to new foods and familiar tastes and sensations offer strong predictors of willingness to adopt entomophagy (Megido et al. 2014; Verbeke 2015). Taking such insights as read, ENTO targets adventurous eaters at food festivals or pop-up events. Julene explains: 'We think that, if people try them in the right setting and if they have an experience around them, they'll be able to accept them and see them as food.' Experimenting at places with people most likely to be open to such experiences increases ENTO's chances of success, and avoids any challenge presented by relatively higher prices. Further, preparatory experiments with chefs, team tastings and focus groups contribute to ENTO's ensuring public experiences of their products are as positive as possible. In this way, ENTO has adopted a practical approach to re-tuning tastes (Carolan 2013a) to include those that come with ingesting insects.

Communication and re-education are the second strategy. As Julene notes, part of their challenge is 'to bring that message across' that insects are good and tasty food. Along with ENTO, connected media and emergent entomophagy enthusiast networks provide information on the benefits of using insects as food (and feed). In addition, promotions rebrand insects using comparisons with previously unacceptable foods that are now regularly eaten – like sushi and shrimp. In these tasks, ENTO and other advocates work to re-categorise insects, making them into food. Packaging also plays its part. EXO's co-CEO emphasises that their packaging has no 'cartoon cricket as our mascot or little legs in the logo', while Hopper's co-founder comments: 'You certainly won't be seeing any insects on our packaging' (cited in Krasney 2014). In both cases, while there is some reference to insects they are carefully not presented graphically on the packaging. While ENTO's logo includes insect visuals, they are abstracted forms.

The third strategy in remaking insects into food involves material transformation: simply making it difficult to recognise them. Julene observes: 'There's a weird thing with insects about how a live cricket looks very much like a fried cricket and a fried worm looks like very much a live worm', and unfortunately 'It's hard to imagine people jumping across that.' Schösler et al. (2012) confirm that visible insect forms are least acceptable to consumers, and suggest less obvious insect-based products as the best introductory path. Incorporation of insects as powder into protein bars or cookies versus snacks of whole insects is an example. For ENTO, the entocubes abstract the form of insects, signalling human control and cleanliness, as well as future food imaginaries (ENTO 2012). Transforming insects into ingredients and then into cubes distances the consumer from insects – from any reminder of insects' previous lives and their alterity – to allow the creation of new associations, thus easing the process of insects becoming food.

Although meant as a transitional strategy (as noted in the previous section), ENTO continues to mask insects as ingredients. This runs counter to trends of transparency and traceability in food, dilutes the encounter with insects themselves, and undermines ENTO's argument that insects should be known as 'good in their own right' as meat. This can result in consumer dissatisfaction. Reflecting on a high-end event, Julene indicates that 'They wanted, like, the hard experience, and then they came in and it was just a really nice dinner that happened to be made of insects . . . but I think they wanted more evidence that they had eaten insects.' This response may indicate attendees' desires to demonstrate 'adventurous' eating but may also point to an interest in encountering insects themselves as food – not just as hidden ingredients. Recognition here goes beyond seeing (or visibility) to achieve an embodied knowledge of having eaten insects intentionally and with a good conscience.

The yuck/yum discussion often offers a provocative beginning to debating eating insects. However, ENTO takes the possibility of entomophagy as given – not simply its acceptability, but more that it will be a part of the future – and proceeds toward accomplishing this reality. As enacting agri-food experiments this is inspiring, but this can also evade one of the most difficult aspects implied by such experiments in changing foodways: the need for rethinking the future of food production and consumption in a more thoroughgoing fashion than just the inclusion of new food resources. Two aspects are singled out for attention here.

First, the debates about consuming insects might shift beyond a human-centred analysis. Multispecies living and dying, eating and being eaten, are part of the unarticulated aspects of such debates. What might be gained by considering humans and insects together in questions about how to do consuming and producing well? In part, this raises questions of insect welfare, but beyond that it urges us, as we eat, to continue thinking, learning and feeling with, rather than just about, insects. What might the future hold if we ate together with insects, as 'messmates' (Haraway 2008)?

Second, insect-eating initiatives open possibilities to consider how to productively engage with disgust and other 'negative' associations instead of immediately focusing on overcoming them. How might the disgust about entomophagy provide a lens through which to understand how we live and what sustains us (Probyn 2000)? What do such visceral, affective responses reveal about relations with insects and about broader foodways – past, present and future?

This section has illustrated how ENTO's aim to shift foodways involves strategies that serve both to dilute and to refine aversions to insects and eating them. It has also highlighted some of the ways in which this debate might be developed to consider ethical and political implications for agri-food. This leads us to consider what might be said about ENTO in connection with food security and safety, a topic to which the next section turns.

Security, supply and safety

Previous sections wrestled with some of the philosophical and experimental aspects of ENTO transforming insects into a normalised part of Western diets. This section continues this exploration but focuses on entomophagy's relevance in renewed calls for food security, on achieving a consistent supply of insects for human consumption, and on regulation of food safety.

One source of recent political motivation and support for entomophagy and mini-livestock production stems from a renewed emphasis on food security more generally (van Huis et al. 2013). The discursive justifications for insects as food in the Western diet follow well-established food security narratives that seek to provide enough food. Much of the promotional information – including ENTO's – as well as research on entomophagy invokes the challenge of feeding the world's growing population (ENTO 2012; van Huis 2013). Carolan (2013b) is the most recent to argue that food policy since roughly the Second World War has aimed to secure enough food and calories via a system of productivism based on a simple metric of agricultural yield. This justification uses a moral framing of feeding the world to focus on the production of grain- and animal-derived calories without considering the environmental and social consequences of such systems (Rosin 2013). Julene explains that, for the ENTO team, 'taking that step back and looking at it from the angle of food security and a bigger sense of the food world and environment' represent their main motivation. This chimes with the key claim for insects as a solution in that the production and consumption of insects as food can offset some of the demand from a meat-hungry populace, as well as providing protein through a production system with a smaller ecological footprint (Dicke 2010; Vogel 2010; van Huis et al. 2013).

For advocates of entomophagy, insects provide two significant types of benefit regarding food security: dietary (they are nutritious) and environmental (in reduced requirements for water, energy and land, with a lower impact on adverse climate changes). First, those advocating and marketing insects as food to date have tended to emphasise insects as a high-protein, low-fat food source in a world needing both (DeFoliart 1999; Finke 2002; Raubenheimer and Rothman 2013; van Huis 2013). So cricket crisps, EXO bars and mealworm tacos are promoted as not just exotic, but also really good for you. Second, the production of insects is far more environmentally friendly, especially in comparison to most meat production (notably cattle, pork and poultry). In a review of literature on the nutritiousness and energy efficiency of insects for human consumption, Premalatha et al. (2011: 4359) estimate that 'more than 10 times more plant nutrients are needed in order to produce one kilogram of meat than one kilogram of insect zoomass'. Insects also produce far less waste and fewer greenhouse gases, and require less water (van Huis et al. 2013). ENTO's promotional video illustrates this in statements that 'Global food demand is accelerating and global food production cannot keep up', followed by comparisons of resource use, waste production, and nutrition involved in insect versus other animal production (ENTO 2012).

In pursuing their agenda of getting Western consumers to accept insect eating as part of a food-secure and environmentally sustainable future, in addition to shifting foodways, ENTO faces problems of securing supply and assuring safety. Certainly ENTO recognised – as have other start-ups seeking insect-based ingredients – that a ready-made supply chain for industrial-scale production of insects already exists in the pet-food industry. However, these facilities were not licensed to produce foods fit for human consumption. Van Huis et al. (2013: 155) deal explicitly with the lack of clear regulation for insects as human food, explaining for instance that the United States Department of Agriculture classified insects as filth, not food. In Europe, the Novel Food Regulations prohibit insect parts, but ambiguity remains regarding whole insects. Thus ENTO, among others, work to challenge the underlying assumption that insects contaminate rather than constitute food. Julene explains that while 'we know we're being very safe . . . we've always been very thorough about the purging, the washing and the cooking' and that 'everyone feels weird about feeding them to other people without that stamp and certification'. In some cases lack of regulation can allow for experimentation, but for ENTO this absence actually hampers the ability to experiment and attract investment, because the arena of agri-food can be so risky, at least from a regulatory standpoint.

Moreover, while insects might be made available by ensuring that procedures for food safety are developed and regulated appropriately, this does not necessarily reflect the ideals of production or of taste. As Julene explains, ENTO has:

sourced freeze-dried ones from the Netherlands, and that's like the safest thing to do because they have developed these processes for human consumption. . . . They've said 'What's meat production like for humans, how do we make that for insects, and let's follow that procedure.' But freeze-dried insects are . . . not the tastiest version. The fresh ones are just by far better.

So far, the cost and biosecurity of transporting live insects internationally have prevented ENTO from pursuing this possibility. Instead, at least for now, they have settled for less tasty versions – as powder or freeze-dried – that carry a larger ecological footprint (given international transport). In addition to seeking out local pet-food suppliers that might be interested in producing for humans, ENTO have recognised an opportunity rather than an obstacle in sourcing insects for human consumption. They have envisioned one utopian possibility for future insect supply – an urban farming network of small-scale producers, each using a system of self-contained cabinets housing insects at various stages of life (a prototype of which ENTO have designed[4]). ENTO have yet to address questions of animal welfare in production and transport. However, industry and governments are beginning to wrestle with this question, as evidenced by the Dutch Animal Act's inclusion of insects (see Erens et al. 2012).

Transforming insects into foods involves an assemblage of various experimentations, including more insect-oriented practices, regulatory changes, innovation, creative investment, altered cultural understandings, artefacts like new insect-appropriate farm buildings, clever design, timely marketing, and entrepreneurship among other factors. That said, the discussion so far proposes that, in treating the multiple crises of conventional agri-food as an opportunity, ENTO's experimentation is enacting a shift toward their envisioned future agri-food world.

ENTO as enactive experimentation

ENTO are not necessarily the most established (or perhaps even the most viable) of Western enterprises aiming to promote the value and accessibility of insects as food. However, their interest in sustainability and food security encourages a pragmatic experimentation. Drawing upon design and engineering, their perspectives confront the all-too-simple binary thinking associated with insects: pairs such as yuck/yum, edible/inedible or Western/indigenous. This also moves us past the dichotomy of success/failure (Stock 2014) so common to assessments of experiments and how much they upend (or not) status quo relationships in an agri-food system built upon power imbalances, cultural appropriations of food and foodways, the ecological overdraft, and dependence on fossil fuels. ENTO's cultural, political and economic awareness of these tension-filled areas makes them more than just an experimental food start-up with clever design.

As this chapter has shown, ENTO are disruptive as well as supportive of existing agri-food in several ways. There are certainly limits to what ENTO have accomplished thus far and what might even be expected. But ENTO illustrate the complexity of our contemporary dilemma of how to bring good food to the table while keeping in mind Salvador's (2014) definition of good food as 'healthy, affordable, green, and fair'. To ENTO, entocubes and food pairing experiments exemplify a playful hope, but also a pragmatic and experimental sensibility that regards food insecurity and disgust not as catastrophe, but a challenge to collective design sensibility for repacking 'the problem'. Contesting the very nature of what culturally constitutes food breaks open one of the enduring dualities that has long hindered debates in food security. Furthermore, rather than the usual abstract observation of the unintended consequences of edibility barriers in times of food security crisis, ENTO create a pragmatic politics of edibility.

The result of so much experimentation is a utopian project that is not designed to have as its primary outcome putting new food products into retail situations. It is a practical and political project with the intention of designing and mapping the alternative structures and foods needed to shift a key food source from inedible to edible, and from unavailable to available. In other words, ENTO's experimenting points to one possibility of how people might end up eating the unthinkable.

In many ways, this chapter finds itself in a genealogy of agri-food thought trying to make sense of significant social, geographic and economic changes related to identity, foodways, production/consumption and food movements since the Second World War (including Le Heron 2003; DuPuis 2015). Its brief view of new experimentation in entomophagy in Western societies suggests that something interesting and novel is happening at the borders of in/edibility and, with it, the consuming, provisioning and regulatory arrangements for 'alternative' foods. This chapter has focused on ENTO as one of these experiments, arguing that they deserve far greater attention than their size as an economic venture might warrant. At four levels, and with varying degrees of success, new experiments in entomophagy like ENTO reframe or subvert: cultural norms; the 'viable' options for global food security; exclusionary regulations associated with food safety; and the materialities of supply chains. In effect, ENTO manifest these subversions and reframings in their design for future consumption and production.

New start-up companies and projects like ENTO do important work by presenting scholars with new assemblages, materialities and economic experiments that move across, often in contradiction to, established economic categories and political intentions, thus enacting new ways of thinking and knowing worlds of food. Such a new entomophagic moment for Western societies illustrates the relevance of the biological economies approach to knowing, understanding and enacting new food futures while leading in novel cultural and political directions. In this sense, ENTO are already 'successful' in that they get people (including us) to consider what it might mean to become 'messmates' with insects – for eaters and agri-food systems more broadly.

The assemblage involved in normalising novel foods includes typical agri-food players like industry, infrastructure, food scientists, regulatory measures, eaters and taste (both sensory and aesthetic). Insects could merely be seen as a new ingredient of everyday foodways. Despite not questioning this role for insects, ENTO go further in other ways, representing an experiment knowingly and reflexively aware of the existing assemblage and its challenges while trying something new. In this way, ENTO's experimentation and our discussion offer something novel. ENTO provide an interesting set of informed solutions to address issues of food security and sustainability, while our academic commentary helps open spaces for dialogue between different case studies, and with agri-food scholars operating within different paradigms. Just as food utopias encourage dialogue among a variety of scholars, biological economies and wilding agri-food studies (Carolan 2013b) embrace the risk of experimentation. But the costs of maintaining narrow theoretical and methodological pursuits could be far graver. Rather than privileging that which has already run its course, our new pursuits privilege experimentation aiming to disrupt the status quo, look for the approaching messmates, and promote new ways of thinking and engaging. Thus, both ENTO and these new ways of studying agri-food reinforce one another and co-create 'spaces of incubation' (Carolan 2011: 145–148) promoting ethical food and ethical processes of research.

Notes

1 Thanks to Julene for her time and insight, which made this chapter possible. Thanks also to the rest of the ENTO team and Ikerne, Julene's sister. We are also grateful to the editors for their comments and valuable suggestions.
2 We use the term 'insect' here in a general sense encompassing groups of species such as beetles and termites as well as creatures such as caterpillars, maggots, spiders and so on.
3 ENTO's process, plan and product images are available on its website and Facebook pages; see also Core Jr (2012); ENTO (2012, 2015).
4 For example, see http://s3files.core77.com/blog/images/2012/02/Ento-CABINET2.jpg.

References

Bennett, J. (2010) *Vibrant Matter: A Political Ecology of Things*, Duke University Press, Durham, NC.
Campbell, H., Burton, R., Cooper, M., Henry, M., Le Heron, E., Le Heron, R., Lewis, N., Pawson, E., Perkins, H., Roche, M., Rosin, C. and White, T. (2009) 'From agricultural science to "biological economies"?', *New Zealand Journal of Agricultural Research*, vol. 52, pp. 91–97.
Carolan, M. (2011) *Embodied Food Politics*, Ashgate, Farnham.
Carolan M. (2013a) 'The wild side of agro-food studies: on co-experimentation, politics, change, and hope', *Sociologia Ruralis*, vol. 53, pp. 413–431.
Carolan, M. (2013b) *Reclaiming Food Security*, Routledge, London.

Core Jr (2012) *Case Study: ENTO*, http://www.core77.com/blog/case_study/case_study_ento_the_art_of_eating_insects_21841.asp.
de Boer, J., Schösler, H. and Boersema, J. J. (2013), 'Motivational differences in food orientation and the choice of snacks made from lentils, locusts, seaweed or "hybrid" meat', *Food Quality and Preference*, vol. 28, pp. 32–35.
DeFoliart, G. (1999) 'Insects as food: why the Western attitude is important', *Annual Review of Entomology*, vol. 44, pp. 21–50.
Dicke, M. (2010) 'Why not eat insects?', http://www.ted.com/talks/marcel_dicke_why_not_eat_insects?language=en.
DuPuis, E. M. (2015) *Dangerous Digestion: The Politics of American Dietary Advice*, University of California Press, Berkeley.
ENTO (2012) 'ENTO: the art of eating insects', http://vimeo.com/35846172.
ENTO (2015) 'What we do', http://www.eat-ento.co.uk/index.php/what-we-do/.
Erens, J., van Es, S., Haverkort, F., Kapsomenou, E. and Luijben, A. (2012) 'A bug's life: large-scale insect rearing in relation to animal welfare', University of Wageningen, Wageningen.
Farb, P. and Armelagos, G. (1980) *Consuming Passions: The Anthropology of Eating*, Houghton Mifflin, Boston, MA.
Finke, M. (2002) 'Complete nutrient composition of commercially raised invertebrates used as food for insectivores', *Zoo Biology*, vol. 21, pp. 269–285.
Gates, S. (performer) (2013) *Can Eating Insects Save the World?*, documentary, BBC, London, https://www.youtube.com/watch?v=GekDjhpnTU4.
Gibson-Graham, J. K. (2008) 'Diverse economies: performative practices for other worlds', *Progress in Human Geography*, vol. 32, pp. 613–632.
Haraway, D. (2008) *When Species Meet*, University of Minnesota Press, Minneapolis.
Kaufman, N. (2014) 'Edible insects hit grocery store shelves', http://www.foodandwine.com/fwx/food/edible-insects-hit-grocery-store-shelves.
Kellert, S. R. (1993), 'Values and perceptions of invertebrates', *Conservation Biology*, vol. 7, pp. 845–855.
Krasney, J. (2014) '6 startups that want to convince you to eat bugs', http://www.inc.com/ss/jill-krasny/boldly-going-where-no-foodie-has-gone-before.html.
Kunitz, M. (producer) (2001–06) *Fear Factor*, television series, National Broadcasting Company, New York.
Le Heron, R. (2003) 'Creating food futures: reflections on food governance issues in New Zealand's agri-food sector', *International Perspectives on Alternative Agro-Food Networks*, vol. 19, pp. 111–125.
Le Heron, R. (2009) '"Rooms and moments" in neoliberalising policy trajectories of metropolitan Auckland, New Zealand: towards constituting progressive spaces through post-structural political economy', *Asia Pacific Viewpoint*, vol. 50, pp. 135–153.
Lewis, N., Le Heron, R., Campbell, H., Henry, M., Le Heron, E., Pawson, E., Perkins, H., Roche, M. and Rosin, C. (2013) 'Assembling biological economies: region-shaping initiatives in making and retaining value', *New Zealand Geographer*, vol. 69, pp. 180–196.
Lorimer, J. (2007) 'Nonhuman charisma', *Environment and Planning D*, vol. 25, pp. 911–932.
Martins, Y. and Pliner, P. (2006) '"Ugh! That's disgusting!" Identification of the characteristics of foods underlying rejections based on disgust', *Appetite*, vol. 46, pp. 75–85.
Megido, R., Sablon, L., Geuens, M., Brostaux, Y., Alabi, T., Blecker, C., Drugmand, D., Haubruge, É. and Francis, F. (2014) 'Edible insects acceptance by Belgian consumers', *Journal of Sensory Studies*, vol. 29, pp. 14–20.

Phillips, C. (2013) *Saving More than Seeds: Practices and Politics of Seed Saving*, Ashgate, Farnham.

Phillips, C. (2014) 'Following beekeeping: more-than-human practice in agrifood', *Journal of Rural Studies*, vol. 36, pp. 149–159.

Premalatha, M., Abbasi, Tasneem, Abbasi, Tabassum and Abbasi, S. A. (2011) 'Energy-efficient food production to reduce global warming and ecodegradation: the use of edible insects', *Renewable and Sustainable Energy Reviews*, vol. 15, pp. 4357–4360.

Probyn, E. (2000) *Carnal Appetites: Food, Sex, Identities*, Routledge, London.

Raubenheimer, D. and Rothman, J. (2013) 'Nutritional ecology of entomophagy in humans and other primates', *Annual Review of Entomology*, vol. 58, pp. 141–160.

Rosin, C. (2013) 'Food security and the justification of productivism in New Zealand', *Journal of Rural Studies*, vol. 29, pp. 50–58.

Salvador, R. (2014) 'The food movement, public health and wellbeing', paper presented at Johns Hopkins Center for a Livable Future conference, Baltimore, MD, December, http://www.cornucopia.org/2014/12/ricardo-salvador-build-new-food-system/.

Schösler, H., de Boer, J. and Boersema, J. J. (2012) 'Can we cut meat out of the dish? Constructing consumer-oriented pathways towards meat substitution', *Appetite*, vol. 58, pp. 39–47.

Simoons, F. J. (1961) *Eat Not This Flesh: Food Avoidances in the Old World*, University of Wisconsin Press, Madison.

Stock, P. (2014) 'The perennial nature of the Catholic Worker farms: a reconsideration of failure', *Rural Sociology*, vol. 79, pp. 143–173.

Stock, P., Carolan, M. and Rosin, C. (eds) (2015) *Food Utopias: Reimagining Citizenship, Ethics and Community*, Routledge, London.

Stone, C. (presenter) (2011) 'Quickfire challenge, diners to donors', television series episode, *Top Chef Masters*, Bravo, Burbank, CA.

van Huis, A. (2013) 'Potential of insects as food and feed in assuring food security', *Annual Review of Entomology*, 58, 563–583.

van Huis, A., Van Itterbeeck, J., Klunder, H., Mertens, E., Halloran, A., Muir, G. and Vantomme, P. (2013) *Edible Insects: Future Prospects for Food and Feed Security*, FAO Forestry Paper 171, Food and Agriculture Organization, Rome.

Verbeke, W. (2015) 'Profiling consumers who are ready to adopt insects as a meat substitute in a Western society', *Food Quality and Preference*, vol. 39, pp. 147–155.

Vogel, G. (2010) 'For more protein, filet of cricket', *Science*, vol. 327, p. 811.

Whatmore, S. (2002) *Hybrid Geographies*, Sage, London.

12 Enacting BAdairying as a system of farm practices in New Zealand

Towards an emergent politics of new soil resourcefulness?

Richard Le Heron, Geoff Smith, Erena Le Heron and Michael Roche

Introduction: soils in question

As an object of scientific, social and agri-food research, soil has to be a Cinderella subject. Intriguingly, however, soil knowledge has changed dramatically over the past decade. The United Nations' declaration in 2015 of an International Year of Soils (IYS) (http://www.fao.org/soils-2015/about/en/) may, for example, go some distance to dissolving the paradox of something that is said to underpin human civilisations, and yet is largely invisible in popular thought. But its early impacts are more likely to be the global exposure of two differing dispositions about the nature of soil and its agency, how soil knowledge might be developed, and ultimately how soil's differentially created resourcefulness can add to or subtract from global initiatives in the name of the planet and humanity. Importantly, remarkably little has been written about soil as a category in multiple, a site of politics relating to different soil conceptions, agentic qualities and potentialities.

This chapter attempts to cut into these realities of soil knowledge by using a post-structural political economy (PSPE) lens (Le Heron 2007; Lewis et al. forthcoming) to investigate what happened in New Zealand when biological agriculture (BA) as a corpus of farming practice and knowledge, viewing soil as a living materiality of life forms, was gradually adopted by a segment of dairy farmers who transitioned from industrial-chemical (I-C) dairying systems. The urgencies over global soil governance (*Letter from Brasilia* 2015) that are exposed by the IYS and other initiatives mean that the distinctly New Zealand story of a new (to New Zealand) farming system, biological agriculture dairying (BAdairying) (Smith 2010; Masters 2014), which is centred on soil vitality, becomes an invaluable case study of attempts to 'actually make other soil futures' and promulgate alternative farming approaches. In focusing on BAdairying, we address a recent operational fusion of BA and dairying, an assembled approach to farming that is motivated by soil issues, and the future possibilities of soil tended differently. But to narrate dimensions of soil knowledge that might add to new pro-planet soil imaginaries, as the IYS and recent work appear to seek, requires breaks with conventional Western thinking about soil, and the framing of alternative farming understandings and knowledge frameworks.

This chapter's organisation reflects departures from standard socio-ecological knowledge building. It begins with the IYS as a globalisation project, where soils are being reconfigured by new metaphorical attachments that are generating new soil thinking, and introduces significant strands of recent narrative developments relating to soil. The chapter then situates the BAdairying phenomenon, by first moving to the contextual influences of international currents of alternative and sustainable agriculture (of which BA is one strand), and the long-established NZ I-C dairy scene into which an alternative model of dairying is set. This is followed by grounded empirical evidence from a survey of 30 BA dairying operations of observable and measurable practice changes, and their related effects and affects. These are examined through convention theory (Rosin 2008). These methodological steps are necessary because knowledge from alternative forms of doing agriculture was being developed concurrently, in many parts of the world, precisely when BAdairying was appearing in NZ's dairying context. The general limits of soil knowledge worldwide were that soil's productivity for plants and animals could be enhanced by the application of chemicals – fertilisers, pesticides and biocides.

We bring complementary perspectives to the ontological matters explored. Richard is concerned with assembling and enacting agentic and structural interplays in investment and governance domains, Geoff's farming experience embraces I-Cdairying and BA consulting, Erena's socio-cultural interests lie in the genesis and work of metaphors and narratives, and Mike has researched NZ's soil formation under colonisation and its history of soil conservation.

International Year of Soils 2015: realigning soil into a globalisation project?

Soil underwent a great displacement as a category in the mid-twentieth century, with the rise of industrialised chemical-centred agriculture. Hitherto it had been mostly seen as a category that stressed its importance to human life in particular contexts, and was something to be nurtured responsibly by attention to soil's living qualities. There were contradictions, such as tobacco and cotton plantations, with farmers moving on when soils were depleted. With the advent of the I-C farming paradigm, soil began to stand apart from life relations, as it became an object for the application of corporate and institutional science, especially in the form of fertilisers, pesticides, fungicides and weed killers. The shift in ontological recognition and emphasis was never complete, however, and often blurred, but despite pressures many farmers remained with the life-nurturing model. One enduring outcome was that residual agricultural conceptions morphed into alternative models of agriculture. The variants are many, and include agri-ecology, sustainable agriculture, biodynamics, biointensive agriculture, organics, alternative low input, permaculture, mulch farming and polyculture. Not surprisingly, the farm in industrialised countries became an immediate site of contest over soil's husbandry or utility. Widespread adoption of the practices of I-C agriculture enabled massive increases in land productivity, firstly in developed countries and then in developing countries from various aid programmes that directed farmers to modernise agriculture and switch away from subsistence, 'soil is living' farming, to export production, based on a package of I-C interventions.

By the twenty-first century, the ontological cleavage had begun to take on new dimensions, as the invisibilities of soil were being steadily detected and reinterpreted into crucial frontiers for alternative and I-C farming alike. Soil was still a multiple, but how it was being known was intimately linked to new instrumentation and tests that were guided by expanding theoretical knowledge about ecological and social systems. What is intriguing about these advances is that they were being forged at least initially in soil knowledge silos.

The IYS exemplifies the legacy of entrenched, and the emergence of fresh, understandings of soil. Interpretive material about soil is revealing profoundly new initiatives and, importantly, significant convergences in the twenty-first century driven by relentless observational and measurement imperatives in different agricultural paradigms. The IYS is unquestionably a call to give soils a great deal more attention. 'At the global level management of soils has been dismal'; indeed, in the lengthy outcome document outlining future directions (UN 2012) of the 2012 UN Conference on Sustainable Development, the word 'soil' appeared twice. The director-general of the Food and Agriculture Organization, in launching IYS, declared: 'Soils don't have a voice, and few people speak out for them. They are our silent ally in food production' (Graziano da Silva 2015). The IYS objectives and supporting documentation give three powerful reasons for promoting soil internationally: soil is important for human life, and therefore efforts must continue to prevent massive soil loss and erosion; soils can be aligned to normative projects such as food security, climate change adaptation and mitigation, essential ecosystem services, poverty alleviation and sustainable development; and policies for the sustainable management and protection of soil resources require urgent attention.

The idea that soil has the function of sustaining land uses, but widespread crusting, compaction and erosion impair its functionalities, harks back to twentieth-century concerns over productivity. The alignments to normative projects is where distinctively new knowledge work is under way. Metaphorical propositions describing soil look to the future. Nurturing soils as a living resource can be the basis for sustainable development. Soils are everywhere and are integral to ecosystems and the services they provide. Soils can, for example, withstand biophysical variations and contribute to food security.

Independently, in the two-year lead-up to the IYS, soil knowledge outside mainstream institutions has rapidly consolidated on some mega-narratives with further metaphorical triggers. A snapshot of such developments can be gained from an *Acres* interview with Australian soil ecologist Christine Jones (Frisch 2015), a frequent visitor to NZ to speak to biological farming (BF) groups. We outline a digest of narrative elements to complement the stretch in imagination discernible around the IYS initiative. The Jones interview upends traditional soil thinking. We italicise key concepts to emphasise the metaphorical content. She argues that *topsoil* can be rebuilt, and its rate of formation is 'breathtakingly rapid' (Frisch 2015: 2), a position counter to accepted wisdom. She stressed an old idea with a new interpretation: the flow of *liquid carbon* to the soil is the primary pathway by which new topsoil is formed. For carbon to flow there has to be a partnership or 'plant–microbial bridge' between plant roots and the soil microbes that will receive the carbon. The symbiotic relationship allows exchange of carbon for minerals and other microbe products. As Jones reflects, 'we inadvertently blow the bridge in conventional farming, with high rates of synthetic fertiliser, fungicides or other biocides', which alters soil potentialities enormously. This relies on the formation of *soil aggregates*, 'the fundamental unit of soil function' (Frisch 2015: 3) and agency. She contends that the *multi-species crop revolution*, which replaces single-crop cover or leaving the soil barren between saleable crops, can be shown to accelerate aggregate formation, the 'most significant breakthrough in modern agriculture' (Frisch 2015: 5). Moving the *ratio of bacteria to fungi* towards fungi further energises soil transformation. And, in a challenge to the status quo, she holds: 'The focus needs to be on transforming every farm that's a *carbon source into a net carbon sink*' (Frisch 2015: 7).

Mixed reactions in NZ to the launch of the IYS epitomise ongoing local contestation over soil and what ontological realities are being validated. Out of the corner of frustration with the antiquated nature of much soil knowledge in NZ, no-till exponent John Baker (2015) offers a damning judgement that too often 'New Zealanders treat soil like dirt. . . . New Zealand's rotation of arable crops and pasture land gives us more time but many arable farmers both here and around the world are still unknowingly but progressively destroying the soils.' In a similarly telling observation, university soil scientist Maria Camps (2015), freshly back from the Intergovernmental Technical Panel on Soils (a linked IYS project), stated: 'some of this sort of thinking is quite recent . . . soil scientists have paid little attention to the biodiversity of soil in the past'.

We have sought to highlight the expanding metaphorical field around soil, to set the scene for the chapter's attention to a farming system that embodies soil as its key tenet. We could not have written such an overview at the turn of the twenty-first century. This contrast in the domain of soil knowledge is significant to our purpose. When BA agriculture ideas were beginning to circulate in NZ, the system of ideas and practices was sharply, and even threateningly, different from understandings that prevailed locally. The 2015 overview enables a contemporary reflection on the energising intellectual and practical work of soil ideas, occasioned by the uptake of BA in an investment and institutional context that was not receptive to unfamiliar ideas about a more holistic approach to farming centred on soil. We can see for example, looking back, that many key ideas had not been articulated, and some ideas were hunches and dreams that nonetheless influenced people, yet new technical practices were being introduced and information was gradually being systematically gathered. Geoff's thesis was an attempt to link disparate farm-level and personal changes (around dairying) into a broader narrative, and it reflected farming and theoretical ideas and understandings that had currency in the 2000s. The investigation's interest in the interconnections involving soil meant it formed a significant empirical and interpretive resource in tracking actual transformations in soil-related knowledge and practice. In the next two sections we provide two sorts of contextual information to help depict the active material, and the discursive agency of the environment in which farmers were contemplating (or not) to commit to stewarding their soil, land and land uses differently.

Contextual trajectories, and silences around soil

Two frontiers have constantly strained the alternative and sustainable agriculture movements. The rise of global supply chains and large food chains meant that previously localised markets for produce were under pressure, and the aspirations of alternative agriculture were being reshaped. Developments in organic and sustainable agriculture have slowly impacted on dairying as a food category with generic product identity, with organic being defended by ties back to farm philosophy and, to a lesser extent, farm practices. In the US, for example, organic dairying was thrown into turmoil when, in 2006, WalMart announced it would give major space to organic products from its principal suppliers. The Cornucopia Institute, an organic NGO, surveyed organic dairy suppliers nation-wide, using an organic score card relating to what organic dairying sourced for inputs and how organic farming was conducted (Kastler 2006). Significantly, no question in the survey referred to or implied anything about soil biology! BA was of a different order in its soil emphasis.

The second frontier involved expertise, and BA figured in this trend. Broadly, BA practitioners and advocates advanced understandings of soil biology and loss of soil carbon by examining the scattered evidence of soil biology breakdown from excess application of inorganic fertilisers, reviewing evidence about the reliability of indicators of better soil biology performance (for example earthworms, importance of calcium to soil life, and base saturation influence on soil pH) and then attempting to frame more holistic summaries of soil characteristics (for example changes in mineral profiles of soil), with the recognition of the role of individual species of fungi and bacteria in soil, and evidence of some key interaction effects in soil complexes around humates, while steadily broadening the tool kit of tests that can be reliably used to measure and monitor soil biology performance. Pioneer research by Albrecht, Reams and Ingham, in particular, laid down reliable soil tests of great importance to BA.

The Albrecht Brookside test established the ratio of minerals in the soil, the Reams test established what access plants will have to the nutrition produced by specific microorganisms, and the Ingham test identifies which microorganisms are present, and so links the other two tests.

Thus, although by the late 1990s BA in the US was part of a vanguard of scientific and farming ideas, it lacked strong integrating narratives about the significance to consumers (the planet wasn't yet on the agenda), and simplified stories about its supporting science. This said, BA was there to be used *and* leading BA experts were travelling to other countries, with the techniques and understandings of the moment.

NZ dairy realities: constituting conformity, disabling difference or unrecognised co-existence?

NZ's experience with BA has always been intimately tied to BA developments elsewhere, some as early as the 1940s. A vigorous movement of multiple international strands appeared in the 1940s (Paull 2009). Yet in 2000 only a handful of dairy producers in NZ were organic, and none called themselves BAdairying farmers, though some farmers were experimenting towards this option. In contrast, by 2010, NZ's complement of 10,500 dairy farmers included 90 or so organic dairy suppliers to Fonterra, and an estimated 1,500 dairy farmers trying out some alternatives to the nitrogen phosphorus potassium (NPK) NZ variant of I-Cdairying, plus upwards of 100 small companies supplying innovative products to enhance soil qualities.

Several influences meant the 1990s NZ dairy scene featured competing advice about on-farm dairy practice options. Firstly, mainstream dairying was intensifying and expanding. This involved a switch to artificially sourced nitrogen, especially urea (instead of clover and biology). This shift remained publicly invisible until the early 2000s, when NZ dairying's off-farm effluent excesses were described internationally as 'dirty dairying'. Dairy expansion in the 1990s engendered optimism over economic productivity, dulled critique of environmental impacts, and encouraged dismissive attitudes towards alternative agriculture. Secondly, in the 1970s and 1980s, research arms of several government departments openly investigated alternative agriculture, with policy proposals being considered for organic agriculture (MAF 1991) and sustainable agriculture (MAF 1993). Although both Lincoln and Massey universities had major connections with alternative agriculture, deep tensions arose over how best to evaluate alternatives. NZ held the 10th IFOAM conference in 1994. The availability of knowledge and its promotion were curtailed under the NZ government's policy of minimal direct involvement in agriculture (Fairweather 1999), when Crown Research Institutes were formed out of government restructuring, with new goals (including making a profit). Thirdly, NZ's long-standing Producer Board framework was abolished, and replaced by an amalgam of the large dairy cooperatives, and the New Zealand Dairy Board. The new entity, Fonterra, inherited the statutory requirement to accept all milk offered by dairy farmers. Dairy farmers at large faced no obstacle to their milk entering the NZ dairy processing system. The wave of international interest in alternative and sustainable agriculture sparked a report (Christensen and Saunders 2003: ix), which concluded that:

> [Global market] modelling shows how the NZ dairy sector could benefit overall from some conversion to organics. Even very conservative estimates of organic consumption and consumers' preference for organic dairy products result in increases in NZ organic and total producer returns. We argue, therefore, that it is important for the NZ dairy sector to commit itself towards organic production and signal this to the NZ dairy farmers.

Notably, the discussion of organics practices was absent, and soil questions did not figure in the account.

We conclude that momentum and enthusiasm over alternatives to the intensive dairying model waned in the 1990s, partly reflecting the disappearance of friendly institutions, enthusiastic press coverage of the I-Cdairying model, and lack of 'acceptable' proof of alternative agriculture claims in the NZ research community. Intensified I-Cdairying continued, fuelled by upscaling through amalgamations and conversions from other land uses, especially in areas previously less favoured for dairying (for example Southland, South Canterbury). So what was it that stimulated and reinforced an emergence of BAdairying, a medium and messenger of alternative soil knowledge and stewarding?

Conditions of emergence of BAdairying in New Zealand

We emphasise conditions of emergence, as unless these were broadly favourable the prospects for spontaneous, independent and dispersed commitments of farmers to the new farming system would likely be fruitless. Further, we wish to stress that the decision to adopt a BA farming strategy was not an independent decision – it was always contextually informed, embedded and constrained. In keeping with our earlier contextual discussion that showed much was going on in BA outside NZ, we provide evidence of the manner in which the NZ dairy scene and its farmers were connected into the wider developments. As we indicate in this section, there was really no NZ capacity amongst farmers, and capability in an institutional sense, at the time, to initiate what became BAdairying.

Figure 12.1 provides a tentative trajectory-based genealogy (Le Heron 2013) of the emergent BAdairying segment of NZ's dairy industry. The figure is an artefact of research that prioritised setting farmer and soil agency into political economy developments. Crucially the figure's foundations are human actors in many settings and their purposive soil-directed decisions, multiple paths of interpenetrating economic and institutional development which most farmers were in no position to create alone, and power-expertise interplays that contained,

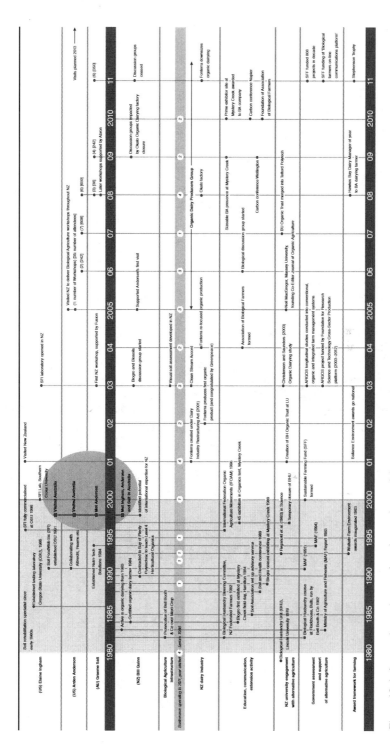

Figure 12.1 A tentative trajectory-based genealogy of the emergent BAdairying segment of New Zealand's dairy industry

but also facilitated, the BA initiative. The left-hand side (grey background) of Figure 12.1 details early initiatives and, by this exposure, their fate over the decade. The right-hand side (white background) summarises details of emerging BAdairying by the late 2000s. The figure does ontological work, detailing relationships that form the 'conditions of possibility' of BAdairying. It picks up on traces of the non-valuing and displacement of BA, evidence of the eventual social expression of BA, and the incorporation of BA into dairying, to become BAdairying. In Figure 12.1, we also locate the understandings and aspirations of the key experts and champions, and their ground-changing meeting in 1998 in Australia (see shaded ellipse in Figure 12.1).

An interview between Arden Andersen (US) and Graeme Sait (Australia) in 1998 (http://www.nofamass.org/seminars/pdfs/Arden_Andersen_interview.pdf) *before* they regularly visited NZ gives valuable perspective. In a candid reflection they say: 'More and more farmers are looking at sustainable agriculture, *biological agriculture or whatever you want to call it*, but, at the same time, the government agencies are finally admitting to problems that we were talking about fifteen to twenty years ago' (emphasis added). It sheds light on three aspects about BA: the category we are using in this chapter wasn't being discussed; BA's testing techniques were in their infancy; and the practices on offer had only recently been streamlined.

The schemata of trajectories making up Figure 12.1 indicate a steady annual addition of new BA infrastructure businesses, key individuals playing prominent roles, and the agency of visits of overseas experts and field days in transmitting knowledge on microbe, plant, mineral and pest management, and supplementary sessions on nutrition and human health. Speaking of the difficult early years, NZ pioneer Bill Quinn, for example, states that, although he began in organics in the early 1980s, he later established Biogro and BioSoil discussion groups 'to remove the organic word for those farmers that were a bit sensitive'. On his way to give a lecture in South Africa, he stopped in Perth to attend talks by Ingham and Andersen, where he realised they had knowledge missing from the NZ scene, and helped fund their early visits. But arguably most impact on public consciousness would come from farming award schemes, such as the Ballance Farm Environment Awards. BA farmers are now being shortlisted and, in 2011, a BA farmer was the Ballance national winner.

Figure 12.1 thus conceptualises the material and discursive world of NZ BAdairying, for the first time, into a series of local and trans-local ties and interpenetrating trajectories. Through placement in the figure, multiple trajectories can be seen as potentially in association. The absence of some links is as significant as the presence of links. Figure 12.1 departs from the usual analysis of industries, and in doing so allows the genesis of BAdairying to be examined *as an ongoing and open project*, involving contingent alignments. Representing these in Figure 12.1 through contextual documentation highlights where possibilities of emergence came from. In this respect Figure 12.1 is a technology for knowing both dairying and soils differently.

BAdairying as practice-led soil futures

The convention theory (CT) thinkers Boltanski and Thevenot (1991: 11) contend that researchers should be 'attentive to the relationships . . . produced by researchers and those produced by actors . . . *the researcher is obligated in her description, to adhere as closely as possible to the procedure the actors themselves use in establishing proof in a given situation*' (emphasis added). We adopt this non-standard approach. Through this method CT shows the architecture of difference, by giving credence to multiple and co-constitutive rationalities and disables I-Cdairying as a hegemonic but undifferentiated category, when content is given to its mix of usually unstated rationalities. The consequence of this is that BAdairying can be interrogated in its own right, because of its distinguishing differences, and in a knowledge framework that keeps such difference visible.

In order to analyse transition dimensions from I-Cdairying to BAdairying, we created a framework that meant I-C and BA were treated equivalently in terms of attributes that should be given attention. This meant both I-C and BA had to 'conform' to a similar metrology of knowledge, and the different features were each given light. This constructive move in knowledge politics was a deliberate strategy to sidestep the imposition of orthodox farm performance evaluations that were narrowly, if not exclusively, economic focused. This CT-inspired depiction is novel. The entries used were derived from published statements by practitioners, advocates and authorities in each knowledge system. The purpose of the collages was to reveal the wider milieu in which the dairy farmers found themselves – a milieu of competing, successful practice claims.

We now analyse, using a CT lens, what motivated farmers into BAdairying, and what kinds of transitions followed the decision to convert. Data are drawn from a telephone survey in 2009 of 30 BAdairying farmers, many of whom Geoff had previously met. The survey obtained histories of farmer engagement with and farm response to BAdairying. Farmers were identified from press and industry articles, introductions at field days and conferences, discussions with consultants and referrals by BAdairying farmers, and had to have attended a course or field day run by Andersen, or were named by consultants as practising BAdairying. Herd sizes ranged from 180 to 1,600 cows, with six herds of over 600 cows. No farmer withdrew from the survey. In 2011 all respondents were re-approached to update information.

Open-ended questions spanned topics ranging from their encounters with Andersen, what they learnt from his courses and field days, networking, and sources of information around making the decision to change, to why Andersen's message was compelling or not, how information was checked out, the decision processes engaged in over adoption, how to start, who was involved, including whether the decision process was protracted over several seasons or a sudden change, farm monitoring undertaken, the changes especially related to soil that were noticed on the farm, their temporality and location, links of monitoring to pattern identification, availability of innovative fertilisers and their reliability, the changes that followed adoption, problems encountered and what was done to resolve these, farmer statements about success and failure on their farms, and pride and satisfaction levels about system change to the Andersen system. The questions enabled probing of on-farm emergence of BAdairying practices, from the first commitment to them until the 2010–11 season. The survey findings allowed us to begin to know the *doing* of BAdairying in a particular manner. This took the form of an ex-post interrogation of the whole experience, as narrated by the respondents, through their ways of knowing the practices they were employing, as they persisted with moving towards full conversion. Schemata of changes are shown in Table 12.1. Its holistic conception accommodates the breadth of farmer–farming realities signalled by CT's multiple worths. It incorporates difference and variable pace of transition in contrast to a universal statement of determinate and linear process. Thus, instead of just a list of claims about what ought to happen, Table 12.1 identifies practice changes and affects or effects in each domain of worth, according to when they were made and noticed by those surveyed. We are conscious that there are many practices (hence the use of schemata instead of a summary) and that the schemata are an embodiment of BAdairying 'in multiple' (Law and Singleton 2005). The conditions of I-Cdairying, in the first column, form a base against which later affects or effects are benchmarked. Some affects or effects appear in a season, while others take longer to build up. Farmers may tire of their commitment and abandon their new practices, or banks and farm accountants may insist on a return to the I-C system. Importantly the transition schemata are built up from observation of altering soil features and related interdependent and cumulative agency of soil biota, grass and animals. There is a simultaneity of doing and knowing by doing, and redoing by knowing over the seasons. The transition can be understood as a journey, of at least three porous parts, or thought about in terms of initial experience with the paradigm, progress of various kinds from continuing commitment, and being able to think farming in quite new ways, because the transition is well advanced. This involves, we contend like Bell (2004), a remaking of self, household and family and business relationships, with the non-human actors in and of the soil. This can also spread to wider ecological consideration of the farm enterprise, and river catchment relations.

The interviews gathered fascinating transitional details. First-year biological farmers, who are usually male, recognise that their wives or partners have relevant views, knowledge and expertise on how farm operations could be managed according to biodiversity and habitat principles. Fears about the implications of reduced stocking rates (frequently construed elsewhere in the dairy industry as failing to contribute) are gradually outweighed by improved animal health, lower veterinarian costs and improved profits. A BAdairying farmer of five seasons is looking ahead to the benefits that accrue from trees and vegetation maturing, improvements from farm nutrient balance, and being able to narrate what is different in highly accessible terms. One BAdairying

Table 12.1 Schemata of changes in the doing of BAdairying

	I-Cdairying	BAdairying first year	BAdairying 2–4 years	BAdairying 5 years plus
Mode of farm management	Follow old methods as recommended by institutional advice.	Learn relationships between soil chemistry, biology and physics and flow on to plants, animals and food.	Keep learning initial lessons. Expand knowledge through research. Stimulated by new information.	Continue knowledge acquisition. Attend outside conferences, local conferences.
Soil	Shallow, very little microbe life. Topsoil 75–100 cm. Dries and pugs easily. Thick thatch.	Active with worms. Fungi more apparent. Topsoil 100-plus cm. Compaction lessening. Thatch starting to break down.	Top soil to 200-plus cm. Increase in humus. Thatch digested by microbes.	Top soil to 500 cm. Huge water-holding capacity, but not wet or dry. Very friable. Smells good.
Plant	Rye dominant. Grass 'pulling' as normal. Brix 2–5.	Colour changes in leaves to much darker. Brix 6–8.	Multiple species grow naturally. Some reseeding with clovers, chicory, plantain, cocksfoot, timothy. Good palatability. Plants grazed evenly. Brix 8–14.	Seasonal species to 20-plus. Brix 14-plus.
Animal	Poor reproduction: 10–23% empty rates. Replacement rate high. Bloat, eczema, feet problems.	Slow change depending on past land use, but positive difference.	Obvious improvements. Reproduction: only 4–7% empty rate. Animals more content. Do not have as much volume available but same volume of milk = more nutrient in grass.	Good levels of production. Milk tastes like food. Cream whips straight from cowshed. Much improved health of farm.

(continued)

Table 12.1 (continued)

	I-Cdairying	BAdairying first year	BAdairying 2–4 years	BAdairying 5 years plus
Environment	Trees as nuisance. Little water storage capacity in soil. No biodiversity.	Awareness of possibilities and time requirements to change. Planning stage.	Planting trees and vegetation. More birds and insects on farm. Effects on water quality decreased. Effluent composted or treated.	Fence line plantings for medicinal purposes, shelter, habitat for birds and insects. Effluent composted or treated with microbes or minerals.
Social	'Fixit' reactionary mode stresses farmer and family.	Become member of consultancy or discussion group to increase knowledge. Attend conferences and field days.	Attend conferences and discussion days. Stress reduced owing to appearance of farm. Soil, plant and animal coherence. Start to see achievements in farm structure and operation.	Become mentor for new entrants. Enjoy farming and family.
Business	Milk factory. Numbers game. High attrition rates of staff and objects of production.	Sometimes increased costs of fertiliser to right past mistakes, sometimes reduced costs.	Start to think about certifying to gain premium through organic farming. Bank manager and accountant happy.	Lower costs embedded in system = increased profit. Audit = increased profit. Invest in further processing or marketing. In business as a biological farmer.

farmer saw changed cow behaviour as a crucial sign of transition, stating in a manner resonating with Lorrimer (2005) that a visible non-human actor is a key performer of relations of soil-directed practice:

> Watch cows go into a paddock with low-Brix, urea-rich grass, and they'll walk right to the back of the paddock then slowly walk back again. They're looking for the best food. When they get to the end of the paddock, there is nowhere else to go, so they just start to eat!

When the beings of production are not performing as well as they can, yields and profits can be in jeopardy.

Conclusion: edging into a politics of soil resourcefulness?

We enacted a multi-faceted knowledge intervention, designed to give shape and dimensions to a series of individual and quasi-collective experiments in NZ, dedicated to applying soil transforming ideals and techniques. This has enabled us to begin to see aspects of soil-centred farming in transition and soil transformations from new connections, relationships and organisation. Whether we have decentred human agency through our efforts is less clear. Our approach sought to illuminate the breadth and depth of human with more-than-human agency involved, a knowledge production strategy that differs fundamentally from mainstream agricultural research in NZ, even if it only goes some steps towards foregrounding the potentialities of well-balanced soils. This is an attempt to see the rearrangement of socio-ecological coordinates of doing a new style of dairying. This investigative goal of course contains tensions over the empirical evidence we generate, and the conceptual ploys we used to come to know both BAdairying and soil's new persona in the new relations we outline. We were concerned with how and why soil ideas contra orthodox understandings in NZ were navigated into a NZ context, and the macro- and micro-politics that defined BAdairying's emerging path, especially the manner in which barriers were put in the way of farmers motivated to trial well-planned experimental farm management directions. In NZ the burden on change is that the system's economic productivity be upheld. The research has had to overcome the fact that BAdairying could be made to disappear by subjecting its farm-level initiatives to economic analysis, not scrutiny of soil transforming practices. BAdairying practitioners value soil, not as a directly exploitable resource, but as a 'potentiality' that with different attentions might (and usually does) confer new kinds of future possibilities. As researchers, we were cutting into an emergent BAdairying world. This was being made and known differently, through farm system experimentation, according to BAdairying principles. Our task became discerning as much as possible, of this soil-directed farmer and other actor methodology of experimentation, and its accompanying enactments, through our own enactive methodological experimentation.

We offer several reflections on the politics of ontology and ontological politics that knowing dairying and soil qualities differently exposes. In the refreshing contributions of the IYS, which we supplemented with a discussion of new metaphors powering soil imaginaries, the growth and productivity metaphors are both relatively muted, and noticeably displaced by other metaphors. The chapter's evidence gives perspective on what strategic interventions might help describe this more planet-friendly direction. We found that BAdairying was contested, and that lines of contest pivoted on a split between an *a priori* definition of soil and its qualities and an *a priori* commitment to helping soil's agency benefit from its own largely unknown and certainly unappreciated potentials.

An aspect of the reality faced by adoptive farmers was the cognitive and plausibility gaps between what they believed was going on in soil and what I-C farmers and others were prepared to believe. These gaps are ontological in their effects, highlighting differences in what soil is thought to be, and how humans should or could be in relation with the multitude of more-than-human actors that are now regarded as constituting and constitutive of soil and soil processes. BA farmers expressed much anxiety over the depreciation of their grounded ways of knowing a relational object that the mainstream world was simply not interested in, but still had strong and obstructive views about. At the 2nd NZ Biological Farming Conference in 2013, one sceptic present could only situate BF knowledge in 'his' framework, leaving no intellectual space to probe what other possible framings might open up (this was the problem that was averted by developing the CT equivalence framework). These sentiments and knowledge rigidities, which had been summarised in a letter to the editor in the NZ Soil Association *New Zealand Soil News* (Edmeades 2012: 10) some months before the conference, capture the restricted view being espoused: 'We can define soil quality in terms of the chemical, physical and biological properties of a given soil. Collectively these tell us what a soil IS. The concept of ecosystem services takes us further and instructs us what a system DOES' (original capitals).

Another concern among the surveyed farmers was the conundrum about where the commitment goes. Why isn't it valued economically? How can links to consumers be made? What of healthy food from healthy soils? These kinds of concerns echo those being expressed by most contemporarily involved in alternative and sustainable agriculture. In the case of BAdairying a 'profile of values' is integral to the making of milk. But does this translate into distinctive milk qualities from distinctive farming practices? BAdairy farmers would argue they do, in spite of this running counter to the model of I-Cdairying that standardises much farming practice throughout NZ *and* standardises the notion of milk itself. I-C milk is remade in a factory into a consumer product with diminished nutrient values. This general conundrum goes to the heart of the idea of values–means–ends pathways, seen by Castree et al. (2014) as essential to obtain meaningful imagining and comparative evaluation of futures, and which we have approached through our CT-based comparative worth framing. Participants at the BF conference stalled over this conundrum in at least three ways. Firstly, they could not disassociate themselves from the hope that they could connect into whole supply chains – a way to generate BF consumers. Secondly, there was much fixation on the oppositional politics of them (organics, I-C) and us (BF). Thirdly, there was considerable resistance to 'biological' being regulated like 'organic', 'sustainable' and 'natural'. These revealed behavioural positions indicate difficulties around imagining ontological futures embracing soil, as well as difficulties in trying to frame intervention strategies.

To conclude, the chapter gives a glimpse of the conceptual complexities and fluidity that typify different sorts of ontological tussles. Tanya Li (2014) has coined the word 'resourcefulness' to sharpen up the in-the-making nature of such contests, which she sees in the case of land as being over materialities and ecologies, relations, technologies and discourses. If soil resourcefulness is to lead a wellspring of ontological imagining and interventions informed by such efforts, then much work needs to be done to enact and further politicise experiments into soil futures.

References

Baker, J. (2015) 'Expert spills dirt on declining soil quality', *Hawkes Bay Times*, 16 April.
Bell, M. (2004) *Farming for All of Us: Practical Agriculture and the Cultivation of Sustainability*, Pennsylvania University Press, University Park.
Boltanski, L. and Thevenot, L. (1991) *On Justification: Economies of Worth*, English translation 2006, Princeton University Press, Princeton, NJ.
Camps, M. (2015) 'Growing concern', *Otago Daily Times*, 11 May.
Castree, N., Adams, W. M., Barry, J., Brockington, D., Büscher, B., Corbera, E., Demeritt, D., Duffy, R., Felt, U., Neves, K., Newell, P., Pellizzoni, L., Rigby, K., Robbins, P., Robin, L., Rose, D. B., Ross, A., Schlosberg, D., Sörlin, S., West, P., Whitehead, M. and Wynne, B. (2014) 'Changing the intellectual climate', *Nature Climate Change*, vol. 4, pp. 763–768.
Christensen, V. and Saunders, C. (2003) *Economic Analysis of Issues Concerning Organic Dairying*, Research Report no. 257, Agriculture and Economic Research Unit, Lincoln University, Canterbury.
Edmeades, G. (2012) Letter to the editor, 'Soil in the Big Smoke', *New Zealand Soil News*, vol. 60, no. 2.
Fairweather, J. (1999) 'Understanding how farmers choose between organic and conventional production: results from New Zealand and policy implications', *Agriculture and Human Values*, vol. 16, pp. 51–63.
Frisch, T. (2015) Interview with Christine Jones, 'SOS: save our soils – amazing carbon!', *Acres*, vol. 45, no. 3, pp. 1–9.
Graziano da Silva, J. (2015) 'Introduction to FAO website', http://www.fao.org/soils-2015/en/.
Kastler, M. (2006) 'Wal-Mart: the nation's largest grocer rolls-out organic products. Market expansion or market delusion?', White Paper from the Cornucopia Institute, 27 September.
Law, J. and Singleton, V. (2005) 'Object lessons', *Organization*, vol. 12, no. 3, pp. 331–355.
Le Heron, R. (2007) 'Globalisation, governance and post-structural political economy: perspectives from Australasia', *Asia Pacific Viewpoint*, vol. 48, no. 1, pp. 26–40.

Le Heron, R. (2013) 'Emerging neo-liberalising economic and governmental processes in New Zealand's land-based sector: a post-structural political economy framing using emergence diagrams', *Applied Geography*, vol. 45, pp. 392–401.

Letter from Brasilia (2015) http://globalsoilweek.org/wp-content/uploads/2015/04/Brazilian-Letter-Soil-Governance-Conference-2015.pdf.

Lewis, N., McGuirk, P. and Le Heron, R. (forthcoming) 'Practicing generative economic geography: a post-structural political economy approach', *Progress in Human Geography*.

Li, T. (2014) 'What is land? Assembling a resource for global investment', *Transactions of the Institute of British Geographers*, vol. 39, no. 4, pp. 589–602.

Lorrimer, H. (2005) 'Cultural geography: the busyness of being "more-than-representational"', *Progress in Human Geography*, vol. 29, no. 1, pp. 83–94.

MAF (Ministry of Agriculture and Fisheries) (1991) *A Proposed Policy on Organic Agriculture*, Policy Position Paper no. 1, Ministry of Agriculture and Fisheries, Wellington.

MAF (Ministry of Agriculture and Fisheries) (1993) *Sustainable Agriculture*, Policy Position Paper no. 2, Ministry of Agriculture and Fisheries, Wellington.

Masters, N. (2014) 'Benefits, threats and opportunities for biological farming', opening address to 2nd New Zealand Biological Farming Conference, Rotorua, 3 February.

Paull, J. (2009) 'The Living Soil Association: pioneering organic farming and innovating social inclusion', *Journal of Organic Systems*, vol. 4, no. 1, pp. 15–33.

Rosin, C. (2008) 'The conventions of agri-environmental practice in New Zealand: farmers, retail driven audit schemes and a new spirit of farming', *GeoJournal*, vol. 73, pp. 45–54.

Smith, G. (2010) 'A convention theory analysis of justifications for biological agricultural practices in New Zealand dairy farming', unpublished M.Sc. thesis, University of Auckland.

UN (2012) *Report of the United Nations Conference on Sustainable Development*, Rio de Janeiro.

PART 2
Enacting new politics of knowledge

13 In your face

Why food is politics and why we are finally starting to admit it

Michael M. Bell

There you are, at the end of your day, sitting down to tuck into your vittles. At the end of your day, when you try to slough off the mud and the grime that accumulated on the undercarriage of your mind after slogging through the dirty streets of daily life. At the end of your day, when you seek release and freedom, a measure of pleasure, some bit of delight to salve and soothe the little woes that nettle the spirit. You want taste. You want conviviality. You want a comforting feeling of gentle excess, swelling the belly just enough to warm you into restful sloth and ease. You don't want politics.

But if there is food before you, there are politics too. Seventeen minutes before I sat down to start to write this chapter – at 12.57 p.m., Central Standard Time, Friday, May 29th, 2015 – the *New York Times* posted on its website a Reuters story that, according to the United Nations World Food Programme, upwards of 200,000 people are facing starvation in northern Cameroon after Boko Haram stormed across the border from Nigeria, forcing villagers to flee their villages and abandon their fields (Reuters 2015). Earlier in the day, a *New York Times* story appeared about how Israel is overcoming water shortages through desalinization, waste-water recycling, and higher water prices for farmers and city-dwellers. "There was a lot of hydro-politics," the article quotes a faculty member at the Hebrew University as saying – and still is, as anyone familiar with Israeli and Palestinian politics will know (Kershner 2015). A third story for the day relates the struggles of Ariana Miyamoto, recently crowned Miss Universe Japan 2015 (Fackler 2015). Ariana is a *hafu* person, Japanese for someone born of mixed racial parentage – in her case an African-American sailor in the US Navy and a local Japanese woman. When she sits down to eat at a restaurant in Japan, where she was raised, Ariana apparently is commonly presented with an English menu and praised for her expert chopstick use. But, when she spent two years with her father's family in rural Arkansas during high school, "she found herself growing homesick and pining for Japanese food" (Fackler 2015). And two days before the *New York Times* ran a story about a new report from the UN Food and Agriculture Organization which finds that both the percentage and the absolute number of the world's hungry have declined over the last 25 years, from 23.3 percent to 12.9 percent, and from 991 million to 780 million. While noting much unevenness in improvement around the world, the report praises the new international political cooperation in hunger reduction since the establishment of the Millennium Development Goals in 2000 (Gladstone 2015).

That's only three days' news. I could go on and maybe expand my searches to the *Guardian* in Britain, *Le Monde* in France, the *New Zealand Herald* in New Zealand, or perhaps the *Sowetan* in South Africa. But I don't have to. Each day's papers, blogs, Facebook postings, and tweets bring a steady harvest of like kind, as the days since I did that search of the *New York Times* and wrote these lines I'm sure have shown.

We eat politics, literally. May I coin a slogan? Food: it's always in your face.

Food scholars are increasingly coming to accept this spiciness of the political. Food isn't so bland anymore. It's a hot topic, in so many ways, as the contributions to this volume abundantly show. Food fills us with contentedness, but also contentiousness. The more we look and listen, the more it seems that food isn't something we're going to solve anytime soon, whether we're trying to figure out what all of us can tolerate to eat together around a middle-class family dinner table or trying to figure out how we're going to manage to have anything for dinner at all around a cook fire outside the family hut. The more scholars fill up on the subject of food, the more we realize that there is a lot to digest – as well as a lot of perpetual indigestion of enduring conflicts, both human and non-human.

Herein lies one of the three main reasons I'll suggest for why we are starting to acknowledge the political taste of all food, and the most generous to the practice of scholarship: We're studying food way more now, and we have been empirically committed enough to recognize that it is profusely political, whether we like it or not. Good.

My second reason is less generous, and starts by asking why we weren't studying food with such seriousness earlier. How could we have missed such a fundamental aspect of human society and existence and our relationship with the rest of the world? To my mind, it surely can't be accidental that the rise of food studies across academe tracks so closely with the wide acceptance of the principles of feminism, albeit often by other names. We'd long been studying the production side of the equation, the culturally more manly act of yanking yields from the ground and selling them in the marketplace. We still study production, of course, as we should, and as this volume continues to do. But why do I teach in a college of agriculture, not a college of food – or, even better, a college of food and agriculture? Because when such colleges were being founded, prestige lay with men's concerns. Studies of food, such as they were, either became opportunities for burly industrialization through technological manipulation of nutrients or were relegated to women's scholarship in the distinctly lower-prestige colleges of "home economics," as they were then known before a wave of embarrassed renaming and reconfiguring in the 1970s and 1980s. What a loss. The phrase "home economics" is a lovely one, and is far more resonant of the broadness of vision and care that the term "biological economies" I think wants to connote. For a home should be understood as human and non-human and immediately ecological, given that the root of ecology, *ecos*, means exactly that: home. Let's bring home economics "back in."

But even if we don't, the embrace of food scholarship within the context of feminist ideas brought with it a crucial feminist point, even if not always recognized as such: the inescapably political character of human life and its institutions. To be alert to food within the context of the cultural changes wrought by feminism is to be alert to the political.

Bringing food "back in" went hand in hand with a broader shift away from a sense that scholarship is, or should be, politically neutral. (Feminism wasn't the only factor in that shift, although it was certainly a mighty one.) This leads me to my third reason for the widening acknowledgement of the political fiber of all food: the widening acknowledgement of the political fiber of all human relationships that has come with the critique of positivism, a critique so widespread that there can now be only a few neo-classical economists and evolutionary psychologists who have not heard the roar of its downpour from deep in their academic caves. For positivism, most fundamentally, was non-politicalism – which was itself a powerful politics, powerful in large measure because its politics were not openly acknowledged. They were not openly acknowledged because that lack of acknowledgement was precisely the mind-move of positivism: No politics here. Its brothers – modernism and structuralism – were part of the same movement of mind into the remotest caverns of human denial.

An emergence into the sunlight of the political – for all that is good and wicked, gratifying and frustrating, about politics – is central to the energies of this volume. To be a post-positivist, a post-modernist, a post-structuralist, a "post-structural . . . political economist," or a post-humanist means, if nothing else, that one understands that we live in an immanent world of conflicts and desires, as well as a world of the equally political phenomena of cooperation and bonhomie – plus bon-non-homie! We are all local to ourselves and our contexts, and thus have ambitions and values and needs and logics that differ. As we should. If nothing else, it makes for a much more varied and interesting menu of life.

That's all welcome. But I have something to complain about in this volume too: the continued appeal of metaphors and habits of thought that make it hard to admit the disconnections and conflicts that are as central to the political as any sweet connections and happy resolutions. (You knew I would. I've done it before [Bell 2008, 2011; Bland and Bell 2007, 2009].) Why do we continue to love the word *systems* and the various unlovely phrases built upon it, like *food systems*, *agricultural systems*, *agroecosystems*, and *agri-food systems*? And why do we rush to similar images of blissful respect and kind mutualism such as, I fear, assemblages and post-humanism?

Don't get me wrong. I'm all in favor of respect and mutualism, and also for building connections and finding resolutions. But that's not all life is about. Let's not lose the fullness of a political imagination about food and agriculture just as we are starting to finally get one.

Warning: I'm going to be a bit of a mosquito for a while, supping from our bloodlines of debate, to try to keep our political itch going.

Here's my first bite. Words and images like *system*, *assemblage*, and *post-humanism* are great for emphasizing cooperation and connection in a relational world that de-centers the self and the human. But they seem to take for granted the very matters they ask us to appreciate. In a relationship? Nice. Congratulations. But it takes work, constant work, if it is going to last. If you treat a relationship as something that is just there, pretty soon it won't be. The fact of a connection indicates a difference, not an easy unity of sameness. Otherwise there would be nothing to connect and relate. Connections don't just happen. And we can't just assert a system, an assemblage, or a post-human rejection of the arrogance of a Noah's ark view of ecology. You have to do it.

Here's my second bite. Not only do such imaginaries take connections for granted; they take them as unproblematic. The relationship becomes a love-fest, a happy unity of holism, diversity, and difference, where everyone and everything is respected for what they bring to the great assemblage of actants. "You see," we say with a friendly smile, "everything's connected, everything's important, and everyone and every perspective and every discipline is wanted and valued because we're all in this together. So let's have a hug." But don't go giving out hugs before others are ready for it. If there's some difference, there's some conflict, at least potentially. And that's not necessarily a bad thing. Difference and conflict can be immensely creative. That creativity is another reason why relationality takes work, because the relationship is always changing – a point I'll get back to in a minute.

But first I'll take a couple more bites. Here's my third: We actually don't want a world that is all connected up. Not only does connection imply disconnection. Many aspects of our world we definitely want to keep separate. We want disconnection as much as we want connection. Because we're not all one. We don't want fertilizer to get into the groundwater. We don't want pesticide residues in our food. We don't want smallpox. We don't want the NSA snooping in our email. We don't want mosquitos biting us. And mosquitos don't want frogs and barn swallows eating them – or us slapping them before they manage the momentary connection of skin to proboscis. Sometimes these disconnections are not easy to manage. Disconnections often take a lot of work to maintain, just as connections do. And disconnections can do good, just as connections can do bad. Deciding which are good and which are bad is, of course, a matter of the deepest politics of perspective and interest. I fully intend to slap the next mosquito that lands on my arm before what I take to be an unhappy unity can transpire, much as the mosquito might see it differently. I also regard Monsanto as altogether too well assembled into a connected-up system – one that is not the least bit post-human – that I would very much like to see disaggregated back into its bits.

My fourth bite is that I would ask us to be very wary of the tendency of metaphors of unity to universalize. Got a problem with your corn? Have I got a cropping system for you, say the scientist and the Monsanto chemical salesperson. Got a problem getting a CSA going that reaches more than the usual white, middle-class crowd? Set up a post-human assemblage as they did in my town and it will all work out. Universal unity quickly becomes a sales pitch, a science pitch, a moral pitch. But one situation's problems are always a little bit different from another's because, well, it is a different situation. And that situation's solutions are always a bit different too.

My fifth and last bite – for now anyway, if I can continue to dodge the swat of the academic hand – is that these happy metaphors provide little insight into why life is constantly changing. The circuit board image of hard systems theory is nice when I urge my fingers to the keys and hope to see the intended letters appear on the screen. A static view of life assembled is also nice when I try to persuade you of something that I claim will make your life (and mine) better. And it is nice when I am professing my unending ecocentric love for all of post-human creation, stating my commitment to all others in the presence of all others, a wedding of de-centeredness. But life never works out so easily. Computers break, and so do relationships. They do so because, try as unities might to assert a common commitment, there is always a multipleness of logics, a pluralism of purposes, a many-ness of situations involved in any connection or disconnection. Out of this unending variety comes unending variation, ever working out and re-working out the balances and imbalances of each new day.

That's not what you meant when you mouthed that hissing word *systems*, or those awkward words and phrases *assemblages, post-humanism*, and *biological economy*? Probably not. But read over my little caricature of the unwelcome mosquito and tell me you really don't see any of yourself there. Come on . . . I know I do – and not just as the mosquito! After all, I currently direct an academic unit called the Center for Integrated Agricultural Systems at the University of Wisconsin-Madison. I didn't name it, but nonetheless I do sometimes use the phrases *food systems* and *agricultural systems* and *agri-food systems*, especially when talking to natural scientists, college deans, and newspaper reporters about why the social sciences and humanities and post-humanities have something to offer to discussions about food and agriculture, and why the situation is more involved than some kind of techno-capitalist fix is going to handle. I don't say *assemblage* and *post-human* much, although I'm fine with it when I see others grappling for something to correct our reductionism and separatism and species arrogance. There is useful work, political work, relational work that we attempt with these words.

But I think we can do better, at least when chatting among ourselves as social and post-human scholars, awaiting the development of a conceptual language that might be both more accurate and yet still resonant with natural scientists and deans and reporters. I have a few suggestions of where to begin.

First, rather than relying on metaphors of connection, which then make it hard for us to talk about disconnection, difference, and conflict, I would urge us to focus more on two other *con-* words: *consequence* and *context*. The point I think we are really trying to get at when we fume over our reductionism, separatism, and arrogance is not so much the presence of connection as it is recognizing that life has consequences. Everything we do, if we've done anything at all, has consequences. We should not confuse the importance of recognizing consequence with proclaiming metaphors of connection. Have we thought those consequences all out? Probably not. Indeed, certainly not. There is too much in motion, and simply too much, for that. Plus connections that you thought were there often weren't, just as disconnections you thought were there weren't. Help doesn't come and listeria gets into the food. So a large measure of humility and openness to the unexpected is always in order, and thus always in disorder.

We open ourselves to a deeper appreciation of consequence when we start to think not in terms of the dream of universal fellow-feeling among non-hierarchical equals but in terms of context, with all its difference, dynamism, and disconnection – as well as connection. There is much about one context that extends to another, like a stream flowing down a mountain side. But there is always more than one stream washing through any one situation. They typically flow both ways at once. And they plash and play amid the rocks of their locality in ways that constantly re-erode the channels of flow and re-shape the standing waves of conflict (for more on the stream metaphor, see Orne and Bell 2015).

I like to think about it as a matter of grasping the *multilogics* of context and consequence (Bell 2011; Orne and Bell 2015). We don't need to think in terms of a single, universal logic to understand the world. And we don't, much as we have often tried to persuade ourselves that we should. You think differently than I, and my cat thinks differently than both of us. That's not because one of us is wrong, necessarily. It's because we are trying to understand contexts that are at least slightly different. I might be wrong, though. There might be something about your context that you can point out is actually flowing into mine, and that I hadn't noticed among all the various cross-currents. And vice versa. So we have a lot to learn from each other, a lot to connect about – precisely because we are not fully connected.

Plus I don't even think with one logic myself. For my context isn't a oneness either. My context is really just an analytic artifice that I come up with to limit my focus enough so I notice something going on in the crashing and splashing all around that sometimes seems about to drown me. I use one manner of thinking for one such artifice, and another for another. And I get really confused when I find that the streams of flow they help me visualize actually converge, forcing me to confront their incompatibilities – only to see them later diverge, just when I thought I had a handle on them. And, I suspect, the same for you. You have multiple logics too, which complicates our efforts to communicate, bringing together yet more factors of potential conflict. But it also heightens the potential delight and surprise of our communion, however passing or lasting that communion may turn out to be.

Multilogics is an unlovely word too – as bad as *assemblages* and *post-human* and *biological economy* – and does not have the familiar ring of the word *systems*, which is seemingly everywhere now. So I don't think it will work well for my dean in justifying my work or that of the Center for Integrated Agricultural Systems. The Center for Integrated Agri-Food Multilogics? I don't think so.

So at our center we keep the word *systems* in our name, at least for now. But we also try to talk in the next breath about context and consequence, which are also familiar words, giving us a great way to take the conversation deeper. And we also talk a lot about dialogue and engagement, which do much the same narrative work as multilogics, without bogging things down in long technical explanations (see Bell 2011 for more on the relationship of dialogue or dialogics to multilogics). I think we might want to use the word *enact* more, though. That one is also familiar sounding and nicely conjures up the activeness of the relational that I have been stressing. Good word. Thanks, Mike Carolan. You too, Philip Lowe.

In the meantime, we should keep experimenting with language that both specifies what we want it to and readily communicates it to others. For we are not what we once thought we could be: singular, universal, transcendent, and value-free. And it is increasingly acceptable to be what we are: plural, local, immanent, and value-engaged. The inescapable politics of the edible is forcing us to recognize the diversity of tongues, what they taste, what they say, and what they sometimes spit and shout. Capitalists and rationalists alike beware, for there is no way around it: Not everyone likes the same food.

References

Bell, M. M. (2008) 'Shifting agrifood systems: a comment', *Geojournal*, vol. 73, no. 1, pp. 83–85.

Bell, M. M., with Abbott, A., Blau, J., Crane, D., Jones, S. H., Khan, S., Leschziner, V., Martin, J. L., McRae, C., Steinberg, M. and Stowe, J. C. (2011) *The Strange Music of Social Life: A Dialogue on Dialogic Sociology*, ed. A. Goetting, Temple University Press, Philadelphia, PA.

Bland, W. L. and Bell, M. M. (2007) 'A holon approach to agroecology', *International Journal of Agricultural Sustainability*, vol. 5, no. 4, pp. 280–294.

Bland, W. L. and Bell, M. M. (2009) 'Beyond systems thinking in agroecology: holons, intentionality, and resonant configurations', in Patrick Bohlen and Gar House (eds), *Sustainable Agroecosystem Management: Integrating Ecology, Economics, and Society*, CRC Press, Boca Raton, FL, pp. 85–94.

Fackler, M. (2015) 'Biracial beauty queen strives for change in mono-ethnic Japan', *New York Times*, www.nytimes.com, accessed 29 May 2015.

Gladstone, R. (2015) 'U.N. reports about 200 million fewer hungry people than in 1990', *New York Times*, www.nytimes.com, accessed 29 May 2015.

Kershner, I. (2015) 'Water revolution in Israel overcomes any threat of drought', *New York Times*, www.nytimes.com, accessed 29 May 2015.

Orne, J. and Bell, M. M. (2015) *An Invitation to Qualitative Fieldwork*, Routledge, New York.

Reuters (2015) 'Cameroon food stocks dwindle as Boko Haram violence disrupts farming', *New York Times*, www.nytimes.com/reuters, accessed 29 May 2015.

14 Geographers at work in disruptive human–biophysical projects
Methodology as ontology in reconstituting nature–society knowledge

Erena Le Heron, Nick Lewis and Richard Le Heron

Introduction

Discussed in Chapter 1, the Biological Economies research project (BE) engaged eight agri-food researchers from four New Zealand universities in a five-year, major public-good-funded project to rethink value creation in New Zealand agri-food economies. The project aimed to make decisive theoretical and political interventions in national agri-food debates impoverished by a hegemonic discourse of export-oriented productivism and the dominance over food imaginaries by a deeply entrenched agri-science industrial complex (Campbell et al. 2009). The team's initial challenge was to identify a conceptual field in which to position the project in relation to these debates, its own established interests in regional development and value chains, and its emerging interests in the agency of the more-than-human. The team sought inspiration from literature that brought theoretical edginess to political and normative positioning, in ways that we saw as necessary to confront the New Zealand agricultural and food research community, and give our intellectual work international saliency. The three Auckland-based team members who author this chapter formalised the challenge into a thought experiment to explore the knowledge politics of innovative research initiatives elsewhere in the world. This chapter reflects on that experiment, which involved identifying what we termed 'disruptive' knowledge production projects and developing an on-going 'dialogue at a distance' with them. This dialogue continues in our reflection here, and allows us to explore the politics of agri-food knowledge.

The chapter has three main parts. Firstly, it outlines what we mean by a disruptive knowledge project and explores the potentiality of such projects to know and do otherwise in situated intellectual, institutional and investment contexts. Secondly, it outlines our thought experiment in bringing into relation a hybrid of disruptive knowledge-making initiatives at various human–biophysical interfaces. Thirdly, the chapter considers a number of BE research encounters to examine the disruptive content of BE itself. Aided by later email correspondence with those whose work we privilege here as disruptive, we focus attention on the different ways in which their projects politicised the production of knowledge. The observation helps us to confirm that, in its own turn to post-structuralist political economy (PSPE) via grounded politics and enactive research, BE has produced an increasingly grounded and enactive politics of knowledge production. This leads us to comment on the generative potential of 'methodology as ontology' in the production of knowledge, particularly in reconstituting knowledges of what Latimer and Miele (2013) label 'natureculture'. Inspired in part by Carolan (2013), our narrative is stubbornly, perhaps 'wildly', auto-ethnographic, and, while it touches down in descriptions of the rooms, moments and encounters of more recognisable research practice, its auto-reflexivity will almost certainly frustrate those bound by established representational knowledge making. Of this we are understanding, but for it we make no excuses, if only because of our confidence that reading the work will produce better representational knowledge, even if it does not shift agri-food scholarship into the realm of disruptive experimentation.

Disruptive human–biophysical projects: a situated experiment

Conversations about naturecultures across the human/physical geography divide were not uncommon in the 2000s, as the discipline sought to rediscover a distinctive vantage point after the social-theoretic turns of the 1990s and as the discovery of the Anthropocene loomed (Harrison et al. 2008). They became the foundation for a number of research initiatives that looked outwards from the discipline and broke with conventional geographic thought and research practice. Led by prominent geographers, these initiatives emanated from the intellectual ferment around nature–society knowledge in the international geographical literature of the 2000s, pushed at multiple frontiers of thought, and prompted our curiosity at a distance as the BE team developed its project. We saw them as unsettling and undisciplined, as 'disruptive projects' that fractured and de-centred existing knowledge and that, in bringing something from the wild, had subversive potential.

In mid-2008, we assembled publications and web-based material from a hybrid selection of these projects, and initiated our experiment with an at-a-distance and voiceless engagement with them. We reviewed the literature, but as projected interventions rather than discrete commentaries; and we did not contact the authors. We selected projects that were theoretically experimental, methodologically disruptive and, like ours, committed to building new knowledge formations in place. In designing the experiment, we built on glimpses of the enactive potential of disruptive research projects in the conception of enactive research, nascent in Law and Urry's (2004) recognition that research and researchers perform work in shaping and making realities through knowledge-building practices, and in the experience of the Building Research Capability in the Social Sciences (BRCSS) experiment in New Zealand (Le Heron, E. et al. 2011). BRCSS, in which Richard and Nick played prominent roles, built a national platform for on-going cross-disciplinary engagements between social scientists, and launched specific projects of knowledge production. It taught us that disruptive projects might lead to new research practices, ways of knowing and forms of expertise as much as new knowledge.

From a long list of 15 or so initiatives we settled on seven, which brought a critical methodological perspective to political and normative projects associated with community and/or enhanced socio-ecological relations. We characterised these initiatives, not all focused explicitly on agri-food, as embodied in the work of particular geographers: Henry Buller, Susanne Freidberg, Julie Guthman, Diana Liverman, Paul Robbins, Neil Ward and Sarah Whatmore. By labelling them 'disruptive projects', we interpreted them as interventions to perform the world differently: trajectories with an ordering but an open directionality and temporality, and a focus not just on possibilities and opening directions, but on enactive experimentation and journeying. Assembling them into a hybrid collection allowed us to pursue a simple benchmarking of the conceptual choices and practical decisions contributing to disruptive qualities (see Lewis et al. 2013). This gave us a living resource available should we 'keep in touch' with this literature, and a base from which to consider trajectories in those projects as new publications emerged.

We launched our experiment in 'voiceless dialogue at a distance' by positioning BE against these disruptive projects in a special session at the Australasian Agrifood Network conference in Sydney in December 2008. In what was a moment of 'coming out' among friends for the project, we identified five fields of knowledge making (or targets for a politics of agri-food knowledge) as the basis for scrutinising the relative emphases of each project: biology; the science–social science interface; policy; performativity; and knowledge production itself. Significantly, these fields were imagineered from what we took at the time to be potential lines of flight for BE, away from the emphasis on the nexus of place and chain as a source of value set out as the core interest of BE in the funding document. They also signalled lines of disruptive departure from conventional research framings in geography, where theoretically informed conversations between social science and science to animate research were sporadic. Few geographers beyond those on our list were working concertedly with the science, technology and society (STS) lens, and the post-human turn had yet to grip geography, as the BE use of the inadequate yet axiomatic label 'biological' to capture this emphasis demonstrates. The turn to practice and performativity was also in its infancy, and geographers even now rarely study knowledge production as a space in which the world gets made.

An emergent experiment: situated possibility and the possibilities of situatedness

In spite of the BE team's deep disquiet over the New Zealand agricultural research community's productivist bent, the team had little sense of where its commitment to building alternative knowledge and introducing new narratives might lead it, beyond initial flirtations with sustainability and diverse economies. However, it did face an urgency to explain BE to the Australasian agri-food and New Zealand geographical communities in such a way as to indicate that alternative biological economic knowledge was possible and should be explored. In Sydney, and at a later conference in Christchurch, we used spider diagrams to disentangle the emphases of the disruptive projects, and arrange them in relation to each other, our impressionistic readings of publications, and web material. The exercise was a form of assemblage practice as well as analysis (see Le Heron, E. et al. 2013), with the spider diagrams representing the five dimensions of knowledge making that we had been exploring as 'lines of flight'. Thinking through them gave us a performative platform for plotting alternative agri-food futures and future directions for BE itself, and weaving them into co-constitutive practices.

Figure 14.1 is a composite diagram of independent figures we used to map the different initiatives. It imposed a temporary ordering that simplified the diverse conceptual spaces occupied by the disruptive projects, and traced BE as an assemblage of emergent energies and priorities. The diagrams prompted demanding questioning from conference audiences about our motives, understandings and ambitions. Two features of this discussion grabbed our attention: the biological was less prominent in the disruptive projects than we had anticipated; and there was little attention to broader shifts in capitalist economies.

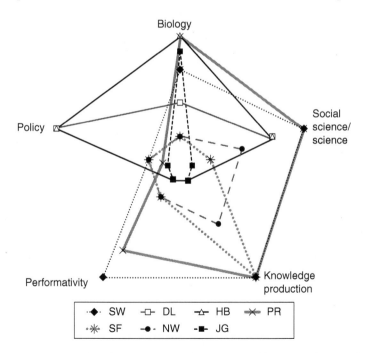

Figure 14.1 A thought experiment with experimental literature: theoretical emphases at the frontiers of biological economies

Note: SW = Sarah Whatmore; DL = Diana Liverman; HB = Henry Buller; PR = Paul Robbins; SF = Susanne Freidberg; NW = Neil Ward; JG = Julie Guthman.

These were, and are, pivotal targets for disruptive thinking in New Zealand. Rather, the projects embodied a more sustained focus on nature–society relations, on the interplay of naturecultures in places where the practice and politics of both knowing and production–consumption are situated and immediate. The exercise gave us intriguing glimpses of how knowledge production issues were being approached in different places, but we were once again alerted to how BE was situated differently, and the significance of this situatedness.

We drew three further conclusions from our analytics. Firstly, 'none of the projects explicitly problematized territoriality or a politics of engagement with mainstream economic actors as part of their emphases' (Lewis et al. 2013: 184). Again a feature of situated knowledge production, the observation was closely related to our second conclusion that BE was located much closer to the politics of agri-food-led national development and the actors involved than the disruptive projects emerging from the discipline internationally. In its relations with its objects of empirical investigation, as well as its expectations and aspirations, BE was anchored more centrally in the agri-food politics of place and the possibilities that knowledge production might engender for doing otherwise. Alongside a politics of potentiality fostered by proximity to actors and events, and its underpinning aspirations and responsibilities, funding of blue skies social science inquiry in New Zealand demands greater engagement with national development priorities. Intriguingly, while we had become accustomed to looking enviously from afar upon the flexibility and openness afforded projects in other settings by these freedoms from the politics of place, we now began to see the political entanglements of our work as theoretically productive. The observation has become pivotal to our work with PSPE thought and practice (see Chapter 1), an intellectual *aide de confort* in the investment and institutional rigidities of the New Zealand context.

Thirdly, distanced from the disruptive projects of others by intellectual and political traditions as well as geography, we were less well positioned to see potentiality in the lines of flight of these projects than we had expected, even if we were able to identify directionality. Ironically, however, the spider diagrams helped us to confront what Whatmore (2002: 4) terms the 'spatial habits of thought' that constrained us. The projects of others highlighted the emergent dimensions of BE more clearly, and helped us to recognise the co-constitutive interplay between the imagination, configuration and practice of our knowledge making and the conduct of science and government (and science as government). Replete with possibility and constraint, we began to recognise in this inescapable situatedness a certain comfort. As Robbins and Moore (2013: 16, original italics) were later to reflect:

> by directly confronting what we *want* as scientists and citizens and acknowledging where these desires put us relative to others in the world, we can begin to sort through what to measure and want to change, what to alter and what to preserve. And in so doing, we can come to terms with our fears.

Disrupting reflections: disruptive directions

As BE developed, the heightened sensitivity to both emergence and disruptive knowing and doing generated by our thought experiment with the disruptive projects of others disrupted its intellectual certainties and challenged its coherence. The project became defined by unanticipated theoretical explorations and research encounters. BE escaped its project boundaries and, in doing so, disrupted the business as usual of knowledge production in New Zealand agriculture. The nexus of chain and place became metrology and assemblage, while we began to rethink both agri-food economy and the production of knowledge about it, as experimentation rather than revealed best practice or choice, from a meaningful basket of alternative narratives (Lewis et al. 2013). The politics of knowing and doing in such open fields are more akin to a preactive and performative playing out of unanticipated encounter than scripted performance. None of this openness was explicitly apparent in the disruptive projects surveyed, but the spirit and practice of disruption, encouraged by the thought experiment with the projects, stimulated what we now recognise as a 'disruptive' agri-food geography.

So what material forms did this disruptive geography and its underlying experimentation begin to take? Early in the BE project, and at the request of a group of small wine enterprises with which Nick had an earlier research relationship, we organised a workshop designed to contribute disruptive ideas in a review of the governance of the peak body of the New Zealand wine industry, a review supported by government and undertaken by PWC (Lewis 2014). Our contribution, understood in early BE terms of the nexus of place and chain, was to assemble an unlikely set of encounters among academics, policy makers, investors and global management consultants, and to stimulate a discussion in unfamiliar terms of the value-adding dimensions of spatial imaginaries and the collective ownership of provenance. Perhaps the greater legacy of the event, however, was to prepare us for a later chance encounter in the form of a remark made to Richard by a senior policy official that what New Zealand needed was a series of 'regional provenance propositions'. The remark focused attention on possibilities to build alignments among actors that we had not fully grasped or made explicit in our wine economy workshop.

What followed was experiments in more up-close, in-voice and multiply entangled dialogue between BE and two other disruptive academic projects. The first, titled 'Performing provenance in contemporary food geographies', was with Peter Jackson's CONANX project at a special session of the Association of American Geographers conference in Seattle in 2011. A British-based exploration of consumer anxieties in relation to the provenance of food (Meah and Watson 2013), CONANX focused on consumption, which is perhaps why it had escaped our attention when we assembled our selection of disruptive projects for the Sydney Agrifood conference. The experiment was later reproduced with Terry Marsden's Cardiff-based 'eco-economy' project, which sought to build knowledge foundations and a political mandate for an ecologically resilient agri-food economy (Marsden 2013). BE met eco-economy at the European Rural Sociology conference in Florence in 2013. These engagements both contributed more than simply intellectual stimulation. The exchange with CONANX provided resources (including confidence and international validation) for the focus on provenance in the first of BE's enactive workshops in Wellington in 2013. Marsden participated in this workshop, which built on his own Chatham House experiments in the British context (Ambler-Edwards et al. 2009).[1] The focus on provenance, especially when sensitised with ideas of eco-economy, meanwhile, has subsequently translated into a platform for on-going engagements with institutional and investment actors, including the Maori trust that we discuss below.

As our experience with BRCSS had taught us (see Le Heron, E. et al. 2011), the 'unprojected' opportunism of our provenance encounters gave us new disruptive possibilities for a grounded politics. At the core of this potentiality lay the recognition born of our thought experiment that the end of research was not really about delineating provenance (a technical exercise) or even identifying the value-creating potential of provenancing (as we named our enactive approach to assembling on-going expertise and knowledge). Rather it was the urgency to develop ideas about the generation of collective ecological and economic rent as a platform for new forms of collective enterprise for regional development. This ambitious target reset our thinking, not just about regional development, but also about biological economies, naturesociety and knowledge production. Much of this rethinking is caught up in the notion of enactive research, which in our account here privileges experimentation, encounter and emergence, and is inescapably onto-genetic in character. Drawing on insights derived from the directions taken by our selection of disruptive projects, we now turn to four disrupting research encounters from BE to illustrate this point.

Disruptive encounters 1: knowing animal, plant and other biota in profusion

Buller (2014: 310) observes from an animal geographies perspective that the 'social' of social science is not a phenomenon, 'a purely human domain' or a 'collection of disciplines'. In echoing Latour (2005: 5), he stresses that the connectivities that constitute the social 'are not always pre-structured by normative orderings/otherings'. New Zealand's contemporary land uses were forged out of a colonial settlement that also 'settled' productive (and therefore preferred) models of biota–technology–fertiliser–human intra-actions via a range of large-scale investments (Brooking and Pawson 2011). Science took on the role of enhancing the productivity of existing production systems, de-legitimating and precluding alternative thinking. This orthodoxy created the absence of alternative farming systems as much as invisibilising their presence (see Chapter 12).

Engaging meaningfully with living biota in BE proved a deep but necessary challenge. The BE team recognised that productivism restricted discussion about productivity to existing activities and their institutionalised knowledge and expertise rather than other approaches such as organics or biological farming (see Campbell 2006; Smith 2010; Rosin 2013). This orthodoxy imposed institutional and cognitive road blocks to alternative thought, as did the situated politics of disconnection between production here (in New Zealand paddocks) and consumption over there (in foreign settings). Two moments of BE highlight the limitations of this frame, and the possibilities of a disruptive politics in response.

Firstly, in a regional parallel to the national provenancing workshop held in Wellington, BE hosted a Hawkes Bay workshop with regional policy actors and investors focused on 'connectivities'. We used the workshop to stage an encounter between orthodox and biological farming (BF), a holistic, soil-health-centred approach to farming prominent in the region, but marginalised and invisibilised in conventional accounts of the regional economy. We invited leading protagonists from both groups and placed them in the same break-out group. While the biological farmers were well versed in advocating the alternative productivity of mutual relations between humans and non-humans, the conventionalists were better versed in cynical dismissal of BF than in arguing the relative merits of productivism. While initially uncomfortable, both sets of actors eventually engaged faithfully with the theme of productive possibilities, and in the spirit of Chatham House, to produce a generative experience.

Biological farmers used scientific evidence to demonstrate the benefits of soil health and maximising its constitutive biota, and to confront conventional farmers who dismissed BF out of hand as non-scientific. They talked of economic, environmental and well-being gains from embracing different frameworks of evaluation. Although they faced repeated push-back from those who refused to step outside the boxes of standard thinking and measures, they were able to demonstrate themselves to be farmers with serious economic and scientific credentials and aspirations. BE cannot claim to have fashioned a 'road to Damascus' moment for non-believers, but the encounters revealed more productive lines of difference than the easy dismissals of an absent other. As science now grapples with how better to conceptualise the vital materiality of plant–human relations with respect to challenges such as gluten intolerance (Atchison et al. 2010), such conversations take on greater significance.

Ironically, the second moment upon which we report is the way in which our work with BF, on the one hand, and experimentation as a modality for biological economy, on the other, has created opportunities for BE in the new funding context of the National Science Challenges (OMSI 2013). The Our Land and Water (OLW) Challenge, under which agricultural science and economy will now be funded, took initial shape around thoroughly orthodox knowledge boxes that excluded researching different production systems and ways of creating value (http://www.msi.govt.nz/update-me/major-projects/national-science-challenges/). With the benefit of our encounters with BF, provenance and other disruptive projects, we have been able to point to the economic and environmental limits of conventional farming practices, and to argue for new research directions to open up the real worlds of land use competition, environmental degradation and shifting global demand. A recent 'gap analysis' of government-funded research relevant to OLW identified interactions among soils, plants, animals, water resources and water knowledge as a pivotal absence. While BE's struggle to secure a position in the organisation of OLW is on-going, our work with BF has given us a position from which to negotiate a role by asking what a commitment to BF could mean for NZ's ecological and economic performance.

Disruptive encounters 2: pursuing possibilities beyond productivism?

As a mentality of growth and productivity, productivism has stifled alternative thinking about agri-food futures in New Zealand. The export orientation of most primary production has channelled thinking into supply chain analysis that projects questions of product saliency, value and desirability uncritically on to distanced and abstracted world markets. Little effort has gone into reimaging production–consumption relations as consumption–production relations in place. Major investors, institutional actors and academic critics alike take for granted a world in which food from nowhere is released into channels to anywhere, missing crucial commercial dynamics as well as production–consumption relations. The growing segmentation of the agri-food economy into food from somewhere as well as nowhere, and into large corporates and small and medium businesses, for example, is rarely addressed.

BE had to work both with and around these knowledge impediments. Its foundational metaphor of the 'place–chain nexus' foregrounded the co-constitutiveness of place and chain in value relations, while the almost routine geographical rethinking of place as a bundle of resourceful relations rather than stable assets disrupted productivist orthodoxy. However, the nexus metaphor failed to capture the complexity, relationality and groundedness of contemporary value relations or to overcome the contradiction between its familiarity and our disruptive intent. Rather, engaging with the disruptive projects of others offered up the intellectual resources of assemblage thinking, initiated our experimentation with enactive research, and opened up our pursuit of possibilities beyond productivism. We are now better resourced to perform disruptive knowledge making in multiple settings.

Susanne Freidberg (2003), one of our disruptive thinkers, suggested some time ago that transcending production and consumption, and entering the spaces 'in and between different parts of the world', offers opportunities to put interests in STS interests, political ecology, and cultural and political economies of agri-food on the same page. The reflection resourced BE's engagement with CONANX and its thinking about the political possibilities of provenancing initiatives. In our own exploration of the wine economy as an open assemblage (Le Heron, E. et al. 2013), we emphasise that value creation can come from anywhere and be appropriated anywhere, but that it is always a product of a relational resourcefulness that has collective dimensions that are necessarily open for co-exploring amongst investors, policy makers and communities. Taking this insight into a national science context re-institutionalised by OLW sets new challenges. While OLW prioritises productivism, export revenues and supply chain enhancement, it has used the emerging literature of creating shared value (Porter and Kramer 2011) to demand that these be aligned with, and validated against, stakeholder and environmental values. As Freidberg (2013: 589) argues in her critique of supply chain thinking, the contemporary governance of capitalism is 'quixotic' and resists reduction to a technical problem. Debates over normative projects such as shared value cannot be resolved by gathering information, while the 'tools of governance' are not only created out of epistemic uncertainty but decided politically. Our own work points to the generative potentiality of engaging with measurers in a politics of possibility as an alternative, but this can only be achieved by getting into the room (see Le Heron, R. 2009).

Disruptive encounters 3: empowering and authorising alternative imagination

In New Zealand, Maori agri-business and land trusts are seen by many commentators (Potaka 2015) as not only a growing component of the agri-food economy but potentially a dominant force. The BE team was approached by a medium-sized Maori trust to outline our ideas about provenancing. This was an opportunity to change the register of our research and engage with agential processes in the making of economy. With it came the challenge of thinking about creating a provenancing framework.

In meetings with trust officials, the BE team sought to elaborate its understandings about provenance practices into a performative engagement with the complicated contingencies of 'making provenance decisions and managing provenance claims and their future contestation in many settings'. In practical terms, the team had to make a case for understanding the concept outside traditional business framings, and co-develop a research-led plan for fostering innovative business competiveness. To guide discussions, we drew a distinction between branding, where the emphasis is on image, and provenance claims, which spring from 'actual connections, relationships and practices in places and in enterprises'. Provenancing, then, was the practice of identifying critical relations between product/enterprise and place, and pursuing and authenticating these qualities and related premiums and social dividends. It may extend from deploying on-farm/in-enterprise production practices to particular effect, to developing connections and relationships on and off the farm, investigating and creating markets, and fostering non-monetary values. In short, and in discussion with the trust, provenancing became defined as 'revealing, representing, practising, elaborating, certifying, and valuing place and connection to place'.

Two disruptive experiences stand out in this effort to empower and authorise new imaginaries. The first is the sensitising question we used to approach the task and convert a conceptual research interest into a business-facing proposition: What in 40 years would a provenance-driven organisation really need to measure, understand and tell stories about? The second experience was the agency-level tensions that challenged the discussions: the ambiguous presence of external (*pakeha*) researchers talking about Maori history in a post-colonial setting, the management and governance protocols that confused lines of authority, and the interplay between provenancing for profitability and provenancing for social and environmental knowledge and good across different planning horizons. Ultimately, while those charged with working with BE recognised through whiteboard sketching exercises dimensions of provenancing that they had previously not comprehended, the CEO concluded that 'The trust is not ready for provenance.'

In their enactive engagements with the politics of flooding, Andrew Donaldson, Stuart Lane, Neil Ward and Sarah Whatmore (Donaldson et al. 2013: 615) found that it is the multiplicities of politics that shape relations and can call into question distributed assumptions. The internal politics of the trust, the relational politics of our own embodied engagements, and the external post-colonial politics of both economic development and knowledge production shaped the possibilities and practice of our research, from its conception all the way through to our representation of it here. It is inseparable from our knowledge and practice of provenancing in those rooms, and these pages. We were unable to make space between existing aspirations and attempts to enact new understandings, even had we desired to do so. As Latimer and Miele (2013: 18–19) observe, researchers are 'never simply engaged in making one world together' but are constantly moving between and altering different worlds with 'questionably compatible demands and different logics'.

Disruptive encounters 4: enacting co-production, co-producing enacting

The set of positions with respect to the politics and practice of knowledge making that we have been describing here (situated, engaged, experimental, enactive, and emergent) set out key dimensions of PSPE (see Chapter 1). In addition, PSPE takes seriously the presence of powerful individuals and organisational actors, and the urgency to engage with them directly in building knowledge, and thus confronting shifting and contingent power relations and our indeterminate knowledge of political economy. As we have alluded to above, the BE team hosted workshops aimed at exploring new and unexpected framings of provenance and connectivity in regional and national settings. Beginning with the national provenance workshop, which involved willing leaders from industry, finance, community, Maori trusts and the academy, the events sketched and debated the nature of connections that would serve provenance. The regional workshops were more situated experiments, covering the idea of connecting to create a platform for regional development in a free trade world, finding value in a region and building a platform for the rural economy. Together, the workshops framed dialogue and deliberation around knowledge propositions that were purpose driven, future oriented and open-ended. They were distinguished by their commitment to make and 'enact' new and disruptive knowledge, by using the affective impulses generated to probe how this new knowing could be crafted into different production–consumption relations.

This forging of frontiers of knowing and doing led to key new understandings of what in-the-room type thought experiments could accomplish. As Gibson-Graham (2008) had taught BE, politics must be about revealing and exploring possibilities that are unseen or latent, possibilities that are uncomfortable knowledge for vested interests, and possibilities that offer contrasting paths for making different futures. The enactive workshop is a novel methodology for making new connections, relations and practices that stimulate and enable such a politics. It disrupts and reframes existing knowledge, and resources participants not just to co-learn and co-produce knowledge, but to become thought leaders. But how should we judge this methodology?

A senior manager from a large state agri-business corporate said of the national workshop: 'Every time I see academics and practitioners get together, good stuff happens; today was no exception. I found it value accretive.' The exercise had succeeded in mobilising an untested knowledge field in 'positive and hopeful' (Liverman 2014) directions. It created an analogue for the 'safe spaces' that Paul Robbins would later suggest to us in an email of 2015 were critical 'for people wanting to break out of bad political, epistemological, and institutional habits' or in the BE case for those prepared to trial our experiment. The strategy of building the workshops around disruptive concepts with a discernible yet uncharted application fostered affective bonding and the building of new relationships among the willing. It yielded new knowledge grounded in co-learning, relations among individuals, and hints of self-interest and transformative potential, such as that of the co-extensive economic and social values of 'spatial imaginaries' in provenancing. Put differently, the workshops were both trust and capability building, creating a resource of new relationships and shared expectations that could potentially enable parties to come together into durable relations in which transactions would occur and various nameable practices might be honoured. But how radical is this? With Gibson-Graham (2008), we suggest that the affective dimensions of the thought experiments resource a disruptive disposition and on-going challenges to dominant knowledge practices.

Conclusions

This chapter has described a journey of disrupting discoveries that has distinguished the life of the BE project, built capability and opened the conceptual horizons of team members and others. Stimulated by thought experiments with disruptive projects, this has been highly affective stuff (Latimer and Miele 2013), and greatly influenced our own personal and group research identities and practices. When in early 2015 we approached the geographers at the core of the disruptive projects with which BE began its journey, and asked them to comment back upon the thought experiment, most warmed to the term 'disruptive human–biophysical project' as a way of talking about the unsettling of fixed categories of knowledge (personal communication, Neil Ward, 17 February 2015). They saw it as an unexpected label that had application to the projects that they had led, especially with regard to destabilising culture–nature boundaries. Paul Robbins (personal communication, 21 February 2015), for example, spoke of the disruptive work of political ecology as seeking to 'up-end approaches to the world that don't acknowledge and engage their own complex politics, contradictions and classed, colonial and patriarchal privileges'. Diana Liverman (personal communication, 10 June 2015) referred us to her latest work, where she calls for opening up new 'positive and hopeful' fields of knowledge (see Liverman 2015). Reflecting back ourselves, the locus and mode of the disruptive engagement were 'putting relations in tension', something that was missing in orthodox research. Our motivation was the conviction that we needed to leave behind the entrapments of existing knowledge framings and develop alternative framings, but we did not recognise on launching the thought experiment that we would be challenging the ontological politics of scholarship. While having earlier characterised the discipline of geography as an exercise of methodology as ontology (Le Heron, R. and Lewis 2011), we had yet to consider the practice of enactive research, to which BE committed itself in its funding document, as quite so deep a challenge to the way in which research projects create socio-ecological worlds.

The strategy adopted in this chapter of following our own following of other geographers' projects reveals that, at this time in natureculture relations, scholars have begun to push the boundaries of their conceptual, institutional and political worlds so as to do and know differently. This is nowhere clearer than in Castree's contribution to *Nature Climate Change* (Castree et al. 2014) and Diana Liverman's latest institutional work with Future Earth. Combining this with reflections on selected research encounters in BE, we show how we have gone from commentators on the politics, ethics and practicalities of business-as-usual agri-food relations and agri-food research to engaging enactively in disrupting and doing them differently. This took us to new connections with geographers and others in sympathetic fields (see Lewis and Rosin 2013), to new initiatives in New Zealand to which we had been blind, to new strategies for conversing with those embedded in the day-to-day worlds of agri-food, and to direct engagements at the political and research funding levels of agri-food.

What do we now know about creating disruptive and new knowledge 'in context'? We read beyond published journal articles into their contexts and political projects. One string to the bow of a wider challenge to productivism is provenancing. As Morgan et al. (2006) suggested in a different way, this de-centres quantity and re-centres quality, territory, power and narrative in value relations. If BF is an example of integrating the theoretical desire to be ethical for non-humans with economic imperatives, then provenancing is a supporting set of practices, the trust an example of its potentiality, and OLW an institutional framework of knowledge making waiting to be grabbed. At the heart of our work in rescripting methodology as ontology in the social enterprise of knowledge making lie the onto-genetic enactive workshops that disrupt normal research power relations and co-produce knowledge for collective futures beyond business as usual. From debates about wine industry governance with PWC directors to those about provenance with the CEO of a major agri-food land investor, they are beautifully disruptive, as they are endlessly repeatable and adaptable to probe different ends and means in many settings. Refusing any kind of comfortable and comforting standard encounter or result, they generate instead a disruptive co-produced imagination which will always challenge the 'is' in naturesociety relations. If, as our experiences and those evident in the disruptive projects that we began with indicate, much making of 'is' and 'should' and 'can be' is co-produced knowledge and action, then different philosophies and modes of politics make differently our agri-food futures.

Note

1 Known for its formal protocols to suspend power relations by invoking conditions of candid engagement because participants accept and trust individually and collectively the 'no attribution' rule, the approach underpinned the set of 'enactive' workshops with agri-food actors that pursued the potentiality of key productive concepts and ultimately distinguished the work of BE.

References

Ambler-Edwards, S., Bailey, K., Kiff, A., Lang, T., Lee, R., Marsden, T., Simons, D. and Tibbs, H. (2009) *Food Futures: Rethinking UK Strategy*, report, Chatham House, London.

Atchison, J., Head, L. and Gates, A. (2010) 'Wheat as food, wheat as industrial substance: comparative geographies of transformation and mobility', *Geoforum*, vol. 41, pp. 236–246.

Brooking, T. and Pawson, E. (2011) *Seeds of Empire: The Environmental Transformation of New Zealand*, I. B. Tauris, London.

Buller, H. (2014) 'Animal geographies I', *Progress in Human Geography*, vol. 38, no. 2, pp. 308–318.

Campbell, H. (2006) 'Consultation, commerce and contemporary agri-food systems: ethical engagement of new systems of governance under reflexive modernity', *Integrated Assessment*, vol. 6, no. 2, pp. 117–136.

Campbell, H., Burton, R., Cooper, M., Henry, M., Le Heron, E., Le Heron, R., Lewis, N., Pawson, E., Perkins, H., Roche, M., Rosin, C. and White, T. (2009) 'Forum: from agricultural science to biological economies?', *New Zealand Journal of Agricultural Research*, vol. 52, no. 9, pp. 1–97.

Carolan, M. (2013) 'The wild side of agrifood studies: on co-experimentation, politics, change, and hope', *Sociologia Ruralis*, vol. 53, no. 4, pp. 413–431.

Castree, N., Adams, W., Barry, J., Brockington, D., Büscher, B., Corbera, E., Demeritt, D., Duffy, R., Felt, U., Neves, K., Newell, P., Pellizzoni, L., Rigby, K., Robbins, P., Robin, L., Rose, D., Ross, A., Schlosberg, D., Sörlin, S., West, P., Whitehead, M. and Wynne, B. (2014) 'Changing the intellectual climate', *Nature Climate Change*, vol. 4, pp. 763–768.

Donaldson, A., Lane, S., Ward, N. and Whatmore, S. (2013) 'Overflowing with issues: following the political trajectories of flooding', *Environment and Planning C*, vol. 31, no. 4, pp. 603–618.

Freidberg, S. (2003) 'Not all sweetness and light: new cultural geographies of food', *Social and Cultural Geography*, vol. 4, no. 1, pp. 3–6.

Freidberg, S. (2013) 'Calculating cost in supply chain capitalism', *Environment and Society*, vol. 42, no. 4, pp. 571–596.

Gibson-Graham, J. K. (2008) 'Diverse economies: performative practices for "other worlds"', *Progress in Human Geography*, vol. 32, pp. 613–632.

Harrison, S., Massey, D. and Richards, K. (2008) 'Conversations across the divide', *Geoforum*, vol. 39, pp. 549–551.

Latimer, J. and Miele, M. (2013) 'Naturecultures? Science, affect and the non-human theory', *Culture and Society*, vol. 30, nos 7–8, pp. 5–31.

Latour, B. (2005) *Reassembling the Social: An Introduction to Actor-Network-Theory*, Oxford University Press, Oxford.

Law, J. and Urry, J. (2004) 'Enacting the social', *Economy and Society*, vol. 33, no. 3, pp. 390–410.

Le Heron, E., Le Heron, R. and Lewis, N. (2011) 'Performing research capability building in New Zealand's social sciences: capacity–capability insights from exploring the work of BRCSS's "Sustainability" theme, 2004–2009', *Environment and Planning A*, vol. 43, no. 6, pp. 1400–1420.

Le Heron, E., Lewis, N. and Le Heron, R. (2013) 'Wine economy as open assemblage: thinking beyond sector and region', *New Zealand Geographer*, vol. 69, no. 3, pp. 221–234.

Le Heron, R. (2009) '"Rooms and moments" in neo-liberalising policy trajectories of metropolitan Auckland, New Zealand: towards constituting progressive spaces through post structural political economy (PSPE)', *Asia Pacific Viewpoint*, vol. 50, no. 2, pp. 135–153.

Le Heron, R. and Lewis, N. (2011) 'New value from asking: "Is geography what geographers do?"', *Geoforum*, vol. 42, no. 1, pp. 1–6.

Lewis, N. (2014) 'Getting savvy and the flawed crisis of over-supply: a conceptual fix for New Zealand wine', in P. Howland (ed.), *Social, Cultural and Economic Impacts of Wine in Zealand*, Routledge, Abingdon.

Lewis, N. and Rosin, C. (2013) 'Emergent (re-)assemblings of biological economies', *New Zealand Geographer*, vol. 69, no. 3, pp. 249–256.

Lewis, N., Le Heron, R., Campbell, C., Henry, M., Le Heron, E., Pawson, E., Perkins, H., Roche, M. and Rosin, C. (2013) 'Assembling biological economies: region shaping initiatives in making and retaining value', *New Zealand Geographer*, vol. 69, no. 3, pp. 180–196.

Liverman, D. (2014) 'How to teach about climate without making your students feel hopeless', *Washington Post*, 20 August, http://www.washingtonpost.com/posteverything/wp/2014/08/20/how-to-teach-about-climate-without-making-your-students-feel-hopeless/.

Liverman, D. (2015) 'Climate change and environmental transformation', in T. Perreault, G. Bridge and J. McCarthy (eds), *Handbook of Political Ecology*, Routledge, London.

Marsden, T. (2013) 'From post-productionism to reflexive governance: contested transitions in securing more sustainable food futures', *Journal of Rural Studies*, vol. 29, pp. 123–134.

Meah, A. and Watson, M. (2013) 'Cooking up consumer anxieties about "provenance" and "ethics": why it sometimes matters where foods come from in domestic provisioning', *Food, Culture and Society*, vol. 16, no. 3, pp. 495–512.

Morgan, K., Murdoch, J. and Marsden, T. (2006) *Worlds of Food: Place, Power and Provenance in the Food Chain*, Oxford University Press, Oxford.

OMSI (Office of the Minister of Science and Innovation) (2013) *Implementing the National Science Challenges*, OMSI, Wellington.

Porter, M. and Kramer, M. (2011) 'The big idea: creating shared value', *Harvard Business Review*, vol. 89, nos 1–2, pp. 62–77.

Potaka, T. (2015) 'Kaupapa Maori as relevant as profit in tribal bodies', *New Zealand Herald*, 30 April.

Robbins, P. and Moore, S. (2013) 'Ecological anxiety disorder: diagnosing the politics of the Anthropocene', *Cultural Geography*, vol. 20, no. 1, pp. 3–19.

Rosin, C. (2013) 'Food security and the justification of productivism in New Zealand', *Journal of Rural Studies*, vol. 29, pp. 50–58.

Smith, G. (2010) 'A convention theory analysis of justifications for biological agricultural practices in New Zealand dairy farming', unpublished M.Sc. thesis, University of Auckland.

Whatmore, S. (2002) *Hybrid Geographies: Natures, Cultures, Spaces*, Routledge, London.

15 Food utopias

Performing emergent scholarship and agri-food futures

Paul V. Stock, Christopher Rosin and Michael Carolan

The premise of the Biological Economies project (as discussed in Chapter 1) asks us to embrace new ways of seeing, doing and practising social science. An important aspect of this more expansive thinking involves the development of novel methodologies with the capacity to supersede existing lines and patterns of inquiry. In this chapter we introduce an emergent methodology informed by our readings of utopian studies and political philosophy that, we believe, offers a fruitful tool for enactive engagement with the social, inclusive of both the human and the non-human. Reflecting our research interests, we have focused on applications of this methodology to the study of agri-food systems and have coined it 'food utopias'.

If we are to take our engagement with the non-human seriously, we must think beyond familiar methodological forms. In a world inhabited by vital non-humans, we cannot but become aware of the multiple sources of agency. Furthermore, our role as researchers in such a world cannot remain that of objective observers, for the products of our observing (our data, analysis and learning) become agents as well. 'Food utopias', thus, reflects our wrestling with the challenges of doing research that acknowledges the agency in our action as well as honouring the agency of others, both human and non-human. Its potential lies in de-essentializing the agency of (particular) humans and focusing on the emergent (and unexpected) nature of the systems they seek to design. In particular, we seek to distinguish food utopias from the more familiar productivist and political economic takes on food.

Our intent is to introduce a means for doing agri-food research differently. We start by briefly tracing our independent ontological journeys (Campbell and Rosin 2011) with regard to agri-food research, during which the concept of utopia emerged as a viable and productive approach to research. In our collaboration, we have identified its potential as an inroad to conversation across entrenched battle lines in debates on the future of feeding the world. Based on our journeys and understandings of utopia as method, we propose three aspects of food utopias that utilize critique, experimentation and process as guiding themes to a critical and enactive scholarship of food. In concluding, we encourage others to engage with food utopias on their own terms, with the aspiration that our experiences will provide some guidance for fellow actors in our pursuit of a better food system.

Why food utopias?

Firstly, we must acknowledge the achievements of critical food systems research by rural geographers and sociologists. An important insight of such analysis is the recognition of society's distanciation from our food and the consequences of its production (Buttel 2006: 219–220). In the conclusion to *Food Systems Failure* (Rosin et al. 2012), we introduced the idea of food utopias as a hopeful response to such distancing. Reflecting on the crisis of high commodity prices, we proposed utopias as a means to pursue an agriculture focused on human flourishing (see Seligman 2012) rather than solely on alleviating scarcity, a process given more explicit formulation in *Food Utopias* (Stock et al. 2015). Subsequently, we have also recognized its potential to engage with and further a post-human social science.

We have each arrived at this ontological convergence following diverse pathways. In order to more accurately represent the performative nature of utopias, in this section we briefly trace our separate paths. In doing so, it is not our intention to suggest that these are the only ways in which to approach and utilize utopias. Rather, we wish to emphasize the potential for the concept to enable dialogue and convergence – a quality we have observed in drawing together diverse interests and viewpoints in conference and workshop settings.

Paul's engagement with utopias has deep roots. When he was a graduate student studying first organic farmers (Stock 2007) and then the history of the Catholic Worker farms (Stock 2010a, 2012, 2014), Ruth Levitas's work became important to help make sense of the fragmentation in critical agri-food studies (Buttel 2001). Levitas's sociology of utopia (or the imaginary reconstitution of society) emphasizes that all sociology (and analyses of any kind for that matter) is comparative. If we offer a critique that something is 'bad' – as in out of the ordinary or normatively wrong – then it must be in comparison to something we deem better or right. Levitas claims that this is utopia – non-existent, yet always there to offer comparisons of how things are against how we claim they should be. This opens up some of the hidden assumptions embedded in our work as social scientists. At the same time, Paul's work as an environmental and rural sociologist expanded to, first, a research position in an interdisciplinary research centre and then a joint appointment with an environmental studies programme. This increasing inter- and transdiciplinarity and collaboration kept pushing to identify language to share ideas of critique, and how to make sense of the process (of experimentation on farms as well as the process of doing research). Thinking with utopia provided a framework and language to engage with scholars doing work similar in spirit, but different in theoretical and practical application.

Eschewing a single theoretical lens has made collaboration in multiple areas possible, exploring: utopias as critique (Rosin et al. 2012; Stock et al. 2015);

autonomy and cooperation (Stock and Forney 2014; Stock et al. 2014); eating insects (this volume, Chapter 11); the idea of good farming and continuity (Forney and Stock 2014; Nelson and Stock 2015); and experimenting with multiple methods (Stock 2010b; Stock and Burton 2011). All of this contributes to questions of what good farming and moral action in relationship to farming and community, both socially and ecologically understood, mean. When people undertake organic, sustainable or local production, is that a moral choice whether they are intentional about their ethical stance or not? The wider project embraces a long-term process by using utopias as an idea and language that help to engage with these normative questions about agriculture and farming and the environment across and beyond disciplines. By no means is the work finished, but it's helped Paul orient a body of work and helps makes sense of what looks confused taken separately.

Chris encountered utopias as an analytical and political framing in his readings of conventions theory (Chiapello 2003), which offered an alternative – more performative – approach to scholarly critique. Their references to the work of Paul Ricoeur on ideology and utopia offered a new perspective on the persistence of agricultural practices with undesirable social and environmental consequences. In the context of organic agriculture, the prevailing argument was that it was difficult (if not impossible) to propose an alternative food system within a capitalist ideology (being subject to a process referred to as conventionalization by Buck et al. 1997). Utopia, seen as a vantage point external to ideology, reinforced the contention that organic and other alternative food projects offered a viable critique, and had the potential to initiate positive change (Rosin and Campbell 2009).

That a multiplicity of utopias could exist was also relevant to work on the global food system and to climate change and food production. In the first instance, it was plausible to argue that a new utopia superseding that of the Green Revolution was required to meet the context of the twenty-first century (Rosin et al. 2012; Rosin 2014). The attraction of a food utopia rooted in the pursuit of increasing production was also apparent in the response of New Zealand meat and dairy farmers to the imperative to mitigate methane emissions and, thereby, the contribution of the sector to climate change (Rosin 2013). These encounters with the societal benefits argued to underlie justifications of productivist agricultural systems demonstrated the power of ideology and the need for utopian critique as well as the potential for a positive utopian politics of food.

Michael enters utopias scholarship through the back door. Unlike some of his collaborators (especially Paul), he has not been particularly influenced by critical utopia thought or really any thought that wears the utopian label. Like his collaborators, however, he is interested in more-than-critical scholarship: scholarship interested in possibilities versus that which focuses on what can't be done, which explains his interest in wanting to be a 'critical optimist' (Carolan 2015) and why he also considers himself a 'disgruntled political economist' (Chapter 16). While it is impossible to trace the beginnings of his (back door) journey to any one event, a clear publication marker for Michael was his 2013 article in *Sociologia Ruralis* titled 'The wild side of agro-food studies: on co-experimentation, politics, change, and hope' (Carolan 2013b). This is his most detailed (and earliest) articulation of what we call experimentation. But Michael was not comfortable with this as an endpoint, as the piece could be taken to suggest an 'anything goes' type of politics, where merely doing something different is the end (political) goal. More recently, he has attempted to move beyond that enlivened micropolitics to one more attuned to consequences, from an anarchic optimism to a critical optimism (see Chapter 16). As he notes elsewhere in his book:

> Yet as a general rule – after all, we need heuristics; without them our scholarship would be paralyzed, dead – we would be well served to follow those scholarly styles that add to the world. Following this rule of thumb: adoption diffusion styles of scholarship would be considered problematic, whereas I am comfortable with those projects outlined in the vignettes. All make a difference. But whereas the adoption and diffusion of innovation scholarship seems to subtract from the world the latter – the hydroponic study, food stamp challenge experiment, and critical, hopeful, and enlivened diffractions – helped in their own ways in making the unthought-of thinkable and the undoable routine.

The goal is, then, to make both the unthought-of thing and the undoable routine. Before we can do difference we have to think difference. How do societies imagine difference, especially wild difference versus the piecemeal sort that tweaks while leaving largely intact the (utopia) status quo? But with that, how can we continue to practise being critical as scholars while embracing – indeed, practising ourselves through our scholarship – a politics of addition. In other words, if we are serious about wanting to do more than just critique for critique's sake then we need to engage with our own utopias as scholars; we need to make them more explicit – remember, they are there regardless of whether we wish to admit to them – which in turn will allow us to contribute to the world/s in a hopeful way.

This brings to mind the metaphor of the Trojan Horse and the solution that it offers. As a gift, it allowed the Greeks to enter Troy's wall following an extended siege involving celebrated victories and painful losses on both sides. We believe global food issues are encircled by similarly impenetrable walls of ideology or discourse. These walls are consistently reinforced by the social belief in the solutions of quantity – what elsewhere we refer to as the utopia of quantity (Stock and Carolan 2012) or productivism (Rosin 2013). These include the promises of the Green Revolution and the Next Green Revolution, and technological solutions from chemical fertilizers and pesticides to genetic modification.

No matter the battering imposed upon these ideological walls by critical political economic analysis and the evidence of power dynamics that underpin inequalities, the focus on quantity remains. Thus these walls establish and reinforce a false sense of security and accomplishment associated with farmers' ability to produce more. Fortunately (or, perhaps, not for those looking for the simple solution), we are not in combat with an irreconcilable foe and need not massacre the inhabitants of the walled beliefs. Rather than a military victory, our Trojan Horse's 'deception' provides openings wherein dialogue and collaboration can occur. We must also acknowledge that the deception is our own: as enactive researchers we look to actively introduce novel and experimental ways of conceptualizing food (its production, provisioning and consumption) and food systems that become entangled with those of other agents. In the same way, we offer food utopias as a highly promising and hopeful way of situating the political project of studying agri-food systems.

In order to better explain food utopias as methodology, we introduce three aspects of utopias that are integral to its enactive nature. While they are addressed sequentially here, none is prior to or more important than the others. Rather, they each contribute to a comprehensive project of enactive research. We begin with critique, as it is a practice familiar to most social scientists. We follow with discussions of experimentation and process. Each aspect further represents an entry point to utopian scholarship taken by us, individually, and informed by a distinct set of literature and experience. We believe that combined, however, they demonstrate the collective potential to re-think food systems (and, more broadly, the social).

Utopias as critique

Here we are informed by Paul Ricoeur's examination of the related concepts of ideology and utopia (Ricoeur 1986). Engaging with Mannheim's distinction between ideology and utopia, Ricoeur begins his analysis by establishing both concepts as foundational to society: 'ideology' is the set of shared beliefs and understandings of how society operates that ensure the functioning and survival of a society; 'utopia' is the ideal set of relationships around which social agreement on a better society can be developed (Ricoeur 1986: 172–180; Mannheim 1998). For the social critic, utopia is a potent and unique methodology that offers an external standpoint from which an ideology's normalized features can be better perceived. Ricoeur argues that any viable critique of ideology and associated power structures necessarily relies on a utopian vision of a better society in order to transcend our own complicity in the ideologies that form the societies we inhabit:

> This is my conviction: the only way to get out of the circularity in which ideologies engulf us is to assume a utopia, declare it, and judge an ideology on this basis. Because the absolute onlooker is impossible, then it is someone within the process itself who takes the responsibility for judgment.
> (Ricoeur 1986: 172)

Some examples of food utopias as critique will help. The most common engagements with organic agriculture address its characteristics as an idealized alternative within a food system that is increasingly governed by industrial logics that threaten both social and environmental well-being. In Ricoeur's terms, while organic agriculture could not develop completely outside of the agricultural ideology that privileged quantity and yield, its proponents articulated organic agriculture as a critique of the ideology while offering a different way of farming (Rosin and Campbell 2009; Stock and Carolan 2012). Critics of organic agriculture note the inescapableness of the ideology of productivism and document that, in practice, the application of an organic label to a product does not necessarily reflect the achievement of a radically different food provisioning system. Too often, officially designated organic food remains the product of practices that degrade the environment and marginalize labour (Guthman 2004). As one among many possible food utopias, organic agriculture provides a basis on which to construct an idealized vision of what a food system could be. Therefore, using Ricoeur's insights, the current state of 'official' and sanctioned organic agriculture is subject to the critical assessment of those occupying the utopian viewpoint. This assessment, rather than eliminating organic practice as a potential alternative, provides the basis for renegotiating (the legitimacy of) the set of 'organic' practices. Even a glance at the local farmers market or grocery store reveals the cracks created by the organic category, as designations 'spray free', 'organic but not certified' or 'used to be organic' illustrate the lack of uniformity of offering critiques of the prevailing ideology of commodity agriculture as well as the neoliberalization of the organic labelling and auditing process (Campbell et al. 2012).

Grasping Ricoeur's conceptualization of utopia as a critical method with which to engage ideology is, however, a double-edged sword. Acknowledging that we are all embedded in current ideologies also raises the issue that we are complicit in them. Ideologies, according to Ricoeur, perpetuate because they facilitate social interaction. Not everyone benefits equally by participating in a society and its structuring ideology, but we accept the conditions of participation because of the benefits of the social coordination achieved through the ideology (Chiapello 2003). The wider food utopias framework sees this critique as valuable, but also recognizes the inherent technological utopianism in which efficiency overshadows all other goals regardless of the social, biophysical and ecological costs of a given technology (Stock 2015).

A food utopias approach, thus, requires us to critically examine our own involvement in the food system, and the extent to which this either perpetuates its failings or enables its modification. In this manner, food utopias as a critical, performative method also leads us toward the potentially transformative. Whereas critique is a necessary element of food utopias as methodology, it is not sufficient for realizing transformation. To that end, we raise the equally necessary element of engaging with experimentation in the process of articulating food utopias to encourage the opportunity for people, communities and food to flourish.

Utopias as experimentation

If we are trapped in ideological ways of living, 'How then do we *do* otherwise?' asks Michael Carolan (2015). As we note in Ricoeur's argument, adopting utopias is the only way to prevent the totalizing effects of ideology. Food utopias, as we envision the concept, is also a method of intervention, a technique to disrupt, even if only for a moment, the stylings of ideology, to introduce the novel and to thereby challenge the taken-for-granted understandings and practices of space. 'Utopias enable us to explore the structural limits of what is thinkable' (Levitas 2013: 120). Utopian studies offers concrete ideas to instantiate other ways of living in the world via communes and intentional communities (Miller 1998; Lockyer and Veteto 2013).

One possibility for utopian action is experimentation (Carolan 2013b). Experimentation has the potential to shake one from the stupor of ideology and allow the enactment, even if only temporary, of spaces of freedom. Experimentation expands what we do; it multiplies and evolves from practice. And, in doing this, it creates openings for knowing the world (and futures) differently (Carolan 2013a).

For food utopias, a sense of experimentation identifies and encourages new ways of food in the world. Rather than 'thinking up' alternatives in the first instance, food utopias – as method of experimentation – recognizes the importance of looking down, to the routines, practices and performances that make thoughts thinkable in the first place. As researchers and actors, we have to read for difference, finding the small, the marginal and the new in food and broadening how we think about it. Importantly, these interventions can take wildly different forms, including such diverse offerings as the Practical Farmers of Iowa (Bell 2004), the Land Institute (Jackson 2011; Head 2015), Slow Food Presidia (Piatti 2015), urban agriculture in social economy Basel (Walliman 2015), utopian communities (Lockyer 2015) and La Via Campesina (Wald 2015).

The worldwide peasant movement La Via Campesina draws on the historical resilience of practices and traditions surrounding peasant agriculture, including an emphasis on individual and communal autonomy (Wittman et al. 2010; Ploeg 2013; Stock et al. 2014). Rather than adopt the typical pursuit of food security promoted by NGOs and governments, which is about quantity of food, the movement seeks to challenge how we think about food labour and gender relations, private property, land reform, and methods of economic exchange. But how does it do this? Certainly it operates in the conventional social movement sense, but it also works to reconfigure relations in a way that brings new modes of seeing, being and believing into existence, which can be of significant effect/affect. Take, for example, the distinctive ritual of seed exchange (Phillips 2013). This practice signifies the centrality of seed not only in the production of food but also in the very production of food utopias itself.

Food utopias as a method of inquiry and collaboration seeks to piece together, envision and practise the diverse, marginal or small experiments in doing food differently that are just, respectful and ecologically sound. In this respect, then, food utopias parallels Urry's (2011) efforts around climate change with 'the purpose . . . of relating and integrating, of binding into a coherent whole the fragmented domains of action and being–becoming' of possible food futures (Adam and Groves 2007: 162).

As with a broader utopian method, food utopias is limited, being 'imperfect, subject to difficulties, inconsistencies, faults, change. And utopia is not a necessary outcome of the present but a possible future, which may or may not be achieved' (Levitas 1990: 198). But a shared recognition that there may be better ways of living in the world together can be the starting point of change. With that, we turn our focus to the importance of process in understanding food utopias.

Food utopias as process

Among many utopists, realizability took hold as the core variable that deemed one utopia worthwhile in comparison to others (Levitas 2013). With any challenges to the status quo, we often obsess over declarations of success and failure (Stock 2014). Following Levitas, we step away from realizability as the primary goal of utopias and emphasize process. Ben Anderson (2006) helpfully points to the hope at the core of Ernst Bloch's (1995) interpretation of utopia – hope for the unfinished nature of reality, its 'not-yet-ness'. Bloch's not-yet helps us see the world as 'a constant state of process . . . whose direction and outcome is not predetermined' (Levitas 1990: 102). Thus, we emphasize the uncertain path, with the idea that food utopias, like humans, are in an unending process of becoming.

In this manner, we have an affinity with Erik Olin Wright's (2004: 37) Real Utopias project in which the 'challenge of envisioning real utopias is to elaborate clear-headed, rigorous, and viable alternatives to existing social institutions that both embody our deepest aspirations for human flourishing and take seriously the problem of practical design.' Where Wright maintains a 'socialist compass', food utopias, at its core, is about creating spaces that allow and encourage multiple envisionings of becoming a more just, open and flourishing world (via food). Our focus on hope, imagination and possibility enables experiments without concern over long-term success. The important thing is to try and keep trying.

Society and our systems of organization can be improved, especially food as it is, without succumbing to an assumption of progress. Technological utopianism, according to Richard Stivers (1999), drawing on the French writer Jacques Ellul (1980), has driven us into systems that privilege profit and efficiency (of all kinds). The more reliant we become on narratives of cheapness (Carolan 2011), while anticipating technological solutions for continued cheapness, the more we avoid doing the necessary work of creating alternatives and building community. It is in the not-yet-ness that we will find hope.

A promising example of process, for both food utopias experimentation and the role of academics, is evident in national and regional food plans. Harriet Friedmann's (2012) enactive and performative work as professor at the University of Toronto engages with emancipatory food relations within extant institutions. She explores how we scale up – not just in terms of quantity, but also to secure similar positive outcomes in different places. Following an extended process to expand options on campus, food activists tackled the connection between food and health by helping to change food provisioning in a local hospital (Friedmann 2007, 2012). Thus, issues of food security (in its broadest and most inclusive sense) in the Toronto area illustrate the ongoing process of change in food systems as the weaving of a web of local producers, unions, retailers, consumers, hospitals, universities and schools (Friedmann 2007).

Despite working without guarantees of success, we can hope that the future, albeit unsettled, is better: that it enables more autonomy, more connectedness, more decentralization and more sharing. But in general we continue to engage with what Carolan (2011) identifies as the ambivalence of our modern food system. He concludes that, particularly around food, ambivalence (that is, literally the holding of two equally weighted, contradictory views simultaneously) does not guarantee any capacity to address those problems regardless of geography, income or choice. So just because we know more about the problems of food does not mean we can always do good food.

Conclusion

Food utopias, as methodology, provides a useful means of engaging with the more-than-human. The three elements of that methodology move social research toward a more open and enactive project, specifically in the context of agri-food systems. Critique, as proposed in this chapter, de-essentializes power or specific social relations (for example class) by acknowledging these as important dynamics among many in an over-determined set of social conventions. Experimentation raises awareness of the innovative and inventive (whether mainstream or marginal), as well as opening space for the pursuit and promotion of alternative ways of doing and becoming. Process completes the utopian methodology, emphasizing the emergent nature of the social. In this emergence, we acknowledge the ever-changing and never fully complete project of flourishing food in which 'failure' is often as valuable as progress. As noted above, none of these elements is novel in the realm of social science. Framed under the umbrella of a food utopia as an objective that exists outside our lived ideologies, however, they move the social researcher toward creative engagement with and participation in better food futures.

By working to create a world (through food, in our case) that is fairer and more just – not just imagining it – we are working with love and grace (Ricoeur 1986; Levitas 2013). Working with grace is to work toward and to enact projects that build a world in which it is easier for people (and food systems) to flourish. 'Utopia in this sense is analogous to a quest for grace which is both existential and relational' (Levitas 2013: xii–xiii). And this is not just in the doing and sharing of food, but also in our role as academics – we are challenging systems of oppression, alienation and ideology.

While we can identify encouraging examples, it remains a daily struggle to create that space of the not-yet-ness – those spaces of hope (Harvey 2000). And, as Sargent (2010: 117) contends, we 'can only build spaces of hope locally. . . . It can only be done by not being conned by the rhetoric and instead building oppositional networks which actually do something.' To help in this struggle, we argue, along the lines of Tim Lang et al. (2009) and Fred Kirschenmann (2011), that what is desperately needed is a new narrative about, and a methodology for, researching and enacting food that can nudge us in the right direction.

The recognition of those personal relationships aids in the discovery and animation of possibilities. And those possibilities, made thinkable with food utopias, then 'shatter a given order; and it is only when it starts shattering order that it is a utopia. A utopia is then always in the process of being realized' (Ricoeur 1986: 273). Thus only in the doing – for activists, practitioners, farmers, policy makers, consumers, academics and the lot – can food utopias become real.

References

Adam, B. and Groves, C. (2007) *Future Matters: Action, Knowledge, Ethics*, vol. 3, Brill, Leiden.
Anderson, B. (2006) '"Transcending without transcendence": utopianism and an ethos of hope', *Antipode*, vol. 38, no. 4, pp. 691–710.
Bell, M. (2004) *Farming for Us All: Practical Agriculture and the Cultivation of Sustainability*, Penn State Press, University Park.
Bloch, E. (1995) *The Principle of Hope*, vol. 3, MIT Press, Cambridge, MA.
Buck, D., Getz, C. and Guthman, J. (1997) 'From farm to table: the organic vegetable commodity chain of Northern California', *Sociologia Ruralis*, vol. 37, pp. 3–20.
Buttel, F. H. (2001) 'Some reflections on late twentieth century agrarian political economy', *Sociologia Ruralis*, vol. 41, pp. 165–181.
Buttel, F. H. (2006) 'Sustaining the unsustainable: agro-food systems and environment in the modern world', in P. Cloke, T. Marsden and P. Mooney (eds), *The Handbook of Rural Studies*, Sage, London, pp. 213–29.
Campbell, H. and Rosin, C. (2011) 'After the "organic industrial complex": an ontological expedition through commercial organic agriculture in New Zealand', *Journal of Rural Studies*, vol. 27, pp. 350–361.
Campbell, H., Rosin, C., Hunt, L. and Fairweather, J. (2012) 'The social practice of sustainable agriculture under audit discipline: initial insights from the ARGOS project in New Zealand', *Journal of Rural Studies*, vol. 28, pp. 129–141.
Carolan, M. (2011) *The Real Cost of Cheap Food*, Routledge, London.

Carolan, M. (2013a) 'Doing and enacting economies of value: thinking through the assemblage', *New Zealand Geographer*, vol. 69, no. 3, pp. 176–179.

Carolan, M. (2013b) 'The wild side of agro-food studies: on co-experimentation, politics, change, and hope', *Sociologia Ruralis*, vol. 53, no. 4, pp. 413–431.

Carolan, M. (2015) 'Re-wilding food systems: visceralities, utopias, pragmatism, and practice', in P. Stock, M. Carolan and C. Rosin (eds), *Food Utopias: Reimagining Citizenship, Ethics and Community*, Routledge, London, pp. 126–138.

Carolan, M. (2015) 'Adventurous food futures: knowing about alternatives is not enough, we need to feel them', *Agriculture and Human Values*.

Chiapello, E. (2003) 'Reconciling the two principal meanings of the notion of ideology: the example of the concept of the "spirit of capitalism"', *European Journal of Social Theory*, vol. 6, no. 2, pp. 155–171.

Ellul, J. (1980) 'The power of technique and the ethics of non-power', in K. Woodward (ed.), *The Myths of Information: Technology and Postindustrial Culture*, Coda Press, Madison, WI, pp. 242–247.

Forney, J. and Stock, P. V. (2014) 'Conversion of family farms and resilience in Southland, New Zealand', *International Journal of Sociology of Agriculture and Food*, vol. 21, no. 1, pp. 7–29.

Friedmann, H. (2007) 'Scaling up: bringing public institutions and food service corporations into the project for a local, sustainable food system in Ontario', *Agriculture and Human Values*, vol. 24, no. 3, pp. 389–398.

Friedmann, H. (2012) 'ASA plenary session: Sustainability 2014', American Sociological Association, http://videoarchive.asanet.org/presentations/2012ondemand_plenary_session_sustainability.html?plist=2012, accessed 10 June 2013.

Guthman, J. (2004) *Agrarian Dreams: The Paradox of Organic Farming in California*, University of California Press, Berkeley.

Harvey, D. (2000) *Spaces of Hope*, Edinburgh University Press, Edinburgh.

Head, J. (2015) 'Sketching a global agro-ecology eutopia: the Land Institute in directional context', in P. Stock, M. Carolan and C. Rosin (eds), *Food Utopias: Reimagining Citizenship, Ethics and Community*, Routledge, London, pp. 143–170.

Jackson, W. (2011) *Consulting the Genius of the Place: An Ecological Approach to a New Agriculture*, Counterpoint Press, Berkeley, CA.

Kirschenmann, F. L. (2011) *Cultivating an Ecological Conscience: Essays from a Farmer Philosopher*, University of Kentucky Press, Lexington.

Lang, T., Barling, D. and Caraher, M. (2009) *Food Policy: Integrating Health, Environment and Society*, Oxford University Press, Oxford.

Levitas, R. (1990) *The Concept of Utopia*, Syracuse University Press, Syracuse, NY.

Levitas, R. (2013) *Utopia as Method: The Imaginary Reconstitution of Society*, Palgrave Macmillan, Houndmills.

Lockyer, J. (2015) '"We should have a culture around food": toward a sustainable food utopia in the Ozark–Ouachita bioregion', in P. Stock, M. Carolan and C. Rosin (eds), *Food Utopias: Reimagining Citizenship, Ethics and Community*, Routledge, London, pp. 57–78.

Lockyer, J. and Veteto, J. R. (2013) *Environmental Anthropology Engaging Ecotopia: Bioregionalism, Permaculture, and Ecovillages*, Berghahn Books, Oxford.

Mannheim, K. (1998) *Ideology and Utopia*, Psychology Press, London.

Miller, T. (1998) *The Quest for Utopia in Twentieth-Century America: 1900–1960*, Syracuse University Press, http://www.environmentalhealthnews.org/ehs/news/2014/aug/wingedwarnings1essay.

Nelson, J. and Stock, P. V. (2015) 'Zombies and peasants: the contradictions of empire', European Society of Rural Sociology, Aberdeen, 18–21 August.

Phillips, C. (2013) *Saving More than Seeds: Practices and Politics of Seed Saving*, Ashgate, Farnham.

Piatti, C. (2015) 'Slow Food Presidia: the nostalgic and the utopian', *Food Utopias: Reimagining Citizenship, Ethics and Community*, Routledge, London, pp. 88–106.

Ploeg, J.D. van der (2013) *Peasants and the Art of Farming: A Chayanovian Manifesto*, Fernwood, Winnipeg.

Ricoeur, P. (1986) *Lectures on Ideology and Utopia*, ed. G. H. Taylor, Columbia University Press, New York.

Rosin, C. (2013) 'Food security and the justification of productivism in New Zealand', *Journal of Rural Studies*, vol. 29, pp. 50–58.

Rosin, C. (2014) 'Engaging the productivist ideology through utopian politics', *Dialogues in Human Geography*, vol. 4, no. 2, pp. 221–224.

Rosin, C. and Campbell, H. (2009) 'Beyond bifurcation: examining the conventions of organic agriculture in New Zealand', *Journal of Rural Studies*, vol. 25, pp. 35–47.

Rosin, C. J., Campbell, H. and Stock, P. V. (2012) *Food Systems Failure: The Global Food Crisis and the Future of Agriculture*, Earthscan, Abingdon.

Sargent, L. T. (2010) *Utopianism: A Very Short Introduction*, Oxford University Press, Oxford.

Seligman, M. E. P. (2012) *Flourish: A Visionary New Understanding of Happiness and Well-Being*, Simon & Schuster, New York.

Stivers, R. (1999) *Technology as Magic: The Triumph of the Irrational*, Continuum, New York.

Stock, P. V. (2007) '"Good farmers" as reflexive producers: an examination of family organic farmers in the US Midwest', *Sociologia Ruralis*, vol. 47, no. 2, pp. 83–102.

Stock, P. V. (2010a) 'Catholic Worker economics: subsistence and resistance strategies of householding', *Bulletin for the Study of Religion*, vol. 40, no. 1, pp. 16–25.

Stock, P. V. (2010b) 'Sociology and the mix tape: a metaphor of creativity', *American Sociologist*, vol. 41, no. 3, pp. 277–291.

Stock, P. V. (2012) 'Consensus social movements and the Catholic Worker', *Politics and Religion*, vol. 5, no. 01, pp. 83–102.

Stock, P. V. (2014) 'The perennial nature of the Catholic Worker farms: a reconsideration of failure', *Rural Sociology*, vol. 79, no. 2, pp. 143–173.

Stock, P. V. (2015) 'Contradictions in hope and care: technological utopianism, Biosphere II and the Catholic Worker farms', in P. Stock, M. Carolan and C. Rosin (eds), *Food Utopias: Reimagining Citizenship, Ethics and Community*, Routledge, London, pp. 171–194.

Stock, P. and Burton, R. J. F. (2011) 'Defining terms for integrated (multi-inter-transdisciplinary) sustainability research', *Sustainability*, vol. 3, no. 8, pp. 1090–1113.

Stock, P. V. and Carolan, M. (2012) 'A utopian perspective on global food security', in C. J. Rosin, P. V. Stock and H. Campbell (eds), *Food Systems Failure: The Global Food Crisis and the Future of Agriculture*, Routledge, London, pp. 114–128.

Stock, P. V. and Forney, J. (2014) 'Farmer autonomy and the farming self', *Journal of Rural Studies*, vol. 36, no. 0, pp. 160–171.

Stock, P. V., Forney, J., Emery, S. B. and Wittman, H. (2014) 'Neoliberal natures on the farm: farmer autonomy and cooperation in comparative perspective', *Journal of Rural Studies*, vol. 36, pp. 411–422.

Stock, P., Carolan, M. and Rosin, C. (eds) (2015) *Food Utopias: Reimagining Citizenship, Ethics and Community*, Routledge, London.

Urry, J. (2011) *Climate Change and Society*, Polity, Cambridge.

Wald, N. (2015) 'Towards utopias of prefigurative politics and food sovereignty: experiences of politicised peasant food production', in P. Stock, M. Carolan and C. Rosin (eds), *Food Utopias: Reimagining Citizenship, Ethics and Community*, Routledge, London, pp. 107–125.

Walliman, I. (2015) 'Urban agriculture as embedded in the social and solidarity economy Basel: developing sustainable communities', in P. Stock, M. Carolan and C. Rosin (eds), *Food Utopias: Reimagining Citizenship, Ethics and Community*, Routledge, London, pp. 79–87.

Wittman, H., Desmarais, A. A. and Wiebe, N. (2010) *Food Sovereignty: Reconnecting Food, Nature and Community*, Fernwood, Winnipeg.

Wright, E. O. (2004) 'Envisioning real utopias', *Renewal* (London), vol. 12, no. 1, pp. 69–75.

16 The very public nature of agri-food scholarship, and its problems and possibilities

Michael Carolan

I have said it before and I will say it again: there is something "wild" about agri-food scholarship (Carolan 2013). Our style of studying the world, like all other fields, operates and circulates, at least in part, through a currency of things – for example, states, representations, objects, and categories. That is to say, we are expected to study phenomena and report on our findings, to talk about our conclusions with stakeholders, decision makers, and other scholars, lecture on them to students, and publish them. We are also all expected (at least, if we wish to keep our jobs!) to engage in stylized forms that presuppose the making of "cuts": of what's relevant and what's not, of subjects (just take a quick glance at any journal article's methods section), and of objects and states – oh so many words, charts, and PowerPoint slides that convey a world far more stable and representable than it actually is. Better than other fields, however, we have learned to live *with* these "things" versus thinking our scholarship exists "because" of them.

Our foremothers and fathers have always done scholarship a bit differently from those more closely tethered to their respective disciplinary narratives. Rural sociology, for instance, arguably our mitochondrial Eve as far as disciplinary ancestry goes (Lowe 2010; Carolan 2012; Le Heron 2013), has long been populated with scholars who resisted the "knowledge for the sake of knowledge" mantra. Those hooligans believed knowledge needed to "do" something to be valid. Perhaps that is why pragmatism has such deep roots in rural sociology (Gilbert 2001; Lowe 2010), a philosophical outlook that is decidedly unphilosophical in the truest Western sense of the term. (Western thought has a rich history expressing its love of disembodied-rational-brain-in-a-vat wisdom). And yet, and yet: should not we be even wilder? As this question might suggest, I want to be clear that we have a choice between being tame and being wild: the choice I am referring to lies in our reflexivity, between grasping the implications of what we do or not. What we do is wild regardless of whether we want to admit it. As an acutely "engaged science" (Lowe 2010: 311), which I take to mean a science that is not afraid to do more than just study the world, agri-food scholarship is uniquely positioned to ask how it makes a difference. Taking Philip Lowe's (2010: 311) point to heart, about how "a social science that does not strive ceaselessly to understand itself is hardly worthy of the name," this chapter seeks to make some sense of how agri-food scholarship does not just study the word but contributes in its making.

My interest is in highlighting some of agri-food studies' "public" engagements. I begin by making observations that few readers, if any, will find controversial, such as my likening agri-food scholarship to what Michael Burawoy (2005) famously advocated in his 2004 American Sociological Association presidential address: public sociology. But that, as I have said, is my starting point. Burawoy's grasp of "public" is terribly narrow. It is too Cartesian – representational. It is too Euclidean – focused on borderlines versus borderlands. In sum, it is too tame for what it really means to "do" scholarship. At the risk of making a terribly unscholarly statement, I hope the discussion that follows makes readers uncomfortable. I believe the risk is worth taking, however, as a key part of my argument is that scholarship is not about knowledge in the classic representational sense. Scholarship – agri-food, definitely, but what I am about to argue applies to all fields – makes worlds by giving us a "feel" for how things ought to be. There is a lot wrapped up in that sentiment: that science is as much about feeling as it is about knowing; that to know is to do and thus to enact, which means the question that ought to interest us is not "if" but "what" realities we are performing (a point I return to later); and that scholars, especially those unafraid to study "societies" in the widest and wildness sense, should not be afraid of nudging audiences out of their comfortable grooves of the mind and body.

Before I start discussing all that, let us begin a little closer to home, in a comfortable space nestled warmly amongst those grooves.

Public agri-food studies: from Burawoy to more-than-Dewey

In 2004, Michael Burawoy gave a notable presidential address to the American Sociological Association, which has since been published, in different iterations, in a variety of outlets around the world. As an agri-food scholar, especially one working at a land-grant university (Colorado State University), I felt an immediate tug from his argument:

> Responding to the growing gap between the sociological ethos and the world we study, the challenge of public sociology is to engage multiple publics in multiple ways. These public sociologies should not be left out in the cold, but brought into the framework of our discipline. In this way we make public sociology a visible and legitimate enterprise, and, thereby, invigorate the discipline as a whole.
>
> (Burawoy 2005: 4)

Burawoy goes on to distinguish across, while acknowledging overlap between, four types of "sociological labor" that lead to four forms of knowledge: professional, critical, policy, and public. Funny, I remember thinking, how poorly this division expresses itself in the fields I travel within. For the most part, agri-food scholarship embodies a curious blend of all four forms of labor – one of the reasons in fact I was originally drawn to it. But really, there is nothing terribly wild about Burawoy's thesis. Actually, its aim is worrisomely tame. He seems to forget that sociological scholarship – "all" of it – is populated by feeling, passionate, affected bodies-in-the-making, as evidenced by his silence about what might be called sociological activism. It is a queer omission given that the discipline is arguably founded on this very style of scholarship. Marx, after all, famously proclaimed, effectively, that the point of inquiry is not to interpret the world but to change it. I especially appreciate agri-food scholars' lack of modernist pretensions in this respect. Those I know are not afraid to admit feeling a need to do more than just study things. There is far too much urgent work that still needs to be done to be contentedly cloistered away behind categories – for example, subjectivity/objectivity, science/non-science, and fact/fiction – that supposedly represent the world but which actually just serve to absolve scholars of responsibility for the assemblages, feelings, and imaginaries they take part in enacting.

And then there is Burawoy's reference to sociological "labor." Interesting word choice, as all of its roots lead back to a decidedly non-epistemological (in the classic representational sense) place, namely, to bodily exertion, which also implies feeling and thus knowing in a more-than-representational way. The word choice is made even more curious given his grasp of what public sociologists do:

> Public sociology . . . strikes up a *dialogic* relation between sociologist and public in which the agenda of each is brought to the *table* in which each adjusts to the other. In public sociology, *discussion* often involves values or goals that are not automatically shared by both sides so that reciprocity, or as Habermas calls it *"communicative action,"* is often hard to sustain. Still, it is the goal of public sociology to develop such a *conversation*.
> (Burawoy 2005: 9, emphasis added)

There we have it. Public sociology according to Burawoy involves striking up a dialogue, at a table no less (quite the idealized image of knowledge exchange), so that values and goals can be shared and, ideally, communicative action achieved. Where is the labor, the "affective materiality," in this image of what public scholars "do"?

John Dewey (1946), the great American philosopher and an early developer of pragmatism, worried about the interests, beliefs, and ideologies of elites becoming "fixed" and assuming a taken-for-granted status within dominant political and social cultures. To combat this he prescribed the technique of "experimentalism," which essentially involves the recruiting of (social) bodies – what he called "publics" – to constantly reflect upon and push back against conventional habits and beliefs. Dewey believed this constituted an important first step in breaking up imposed rules of order that is necessary if meaningful social change is to occur. What these creative coming-togethers look, feel, sound, and taste like however is where I part company with many contemporary pragmatics – a camp I would locate Burawoy squarely in. It is their unreasonable (or more accurately over-reasonable) faith in reason, in good ol' fashioned talk, that I have a problem with (Carolan 2015).

What these communication-centered arguments miss is that we do not come together as mouths, brains (in a vat), and ears but as bodies – as "societies," in the sense in which Whitehead (1967) used the term. Deweyan publics presuppose, in other words, a "material" coming-together, of which talking together is but a small piece. This might appear an innocuous observation, that these coming-togethers involve feelings, vibrant materialities, and bodies of all shapes and sizes (and species). Yet its implications could hardly be more profound. For if most of what we know cannot be reduced to words – if the majority of our knowledge is tacit (Polanyi 1966), or more-than-representational (Carolan 2008a), or embodied (Ingold 2012) – then we have been engaging in a very short-sided form of politics for a very long time. Science, reason, and research, all done with an eye toward a world that is more wonder than words, though each practiced in ways that create dismissiveness toward the more-than-representational – the very stuff of wonderment and wisdom.

Method: from third thing to intra-active "thing"

The world does not conform to the cuts made (and presumed) by the fields of ontology, epistemology, and ethics, but is what Karen Barad (2007: 185) refers to as – get ready to wince (remember what I said about needing to be made uncomfortable) – an ethico-onto-epistemological encounter, "an appreciation of the 'intertwining' of ethics, knowing, and being." Method-as-ontology-as-epistemology-as-ethics: who can forget Foucault's (for example [1978] 2001: 216–217) early performative angle, decades before certain rabble-rousers in the social sciences began playing with the idea – the critique that those pledging to innocently measure attitudes and perceptions through surveys to map the contours of populations were in fact "enacting" bodies and worlds through those very methods?

Method, as conventionally conceived, is the notorious third thing, that which "connects" object and subject, mind and body. The objective scientist reaches across the divide by way of carefully crafted methods to observe/measure what *is*. As ideally conceived, methods are something like a Cartesian hazmat suit, which allows mind (reason) to touch reality and bring it back unadulterated for all to see, while leaving reality itself unblemished.[1] Just to be clear. I have yet to meet a social scientist who actually believes in this idealized image. The practice of inquiry is a whole lot messier than suggested by this caricature. "How" we respond to this messiness is a matter of considerable debate, however.

The more tame position would have you believe these entanglements can be contained through technique. Ethnographers, for instance, occasionally feel compelled to describe steps taken to minimize observer effects, also known as researcher effects or the Hawthorne effect. There may therefore be expectations to hone one's awareness of possible effects (Patton 2002) and, when possible, take steps to mitigate their "distortive nature" (Spano 2006). This technique-talk does have its place. If you came to me and explained you wished to study food cultures in, say, La Paz, Bolivia, by interviewing Wyoming (USA) cattle ranching families I would say, among many other things, that you are going to need to rethink your methodological techniques. My point is that we need to be more open to the productive nature of our methods. Put another way, the aim should not be to make our research more objective but to make it more-than-objective – to make it better attuned to "Things that matter and the mattering of Things."[2]

That is going to take some work, as I detail in a moment. But first I need to move the discussion beyond methods.

Enacting more-than . . .

Quite a lot of ink has been spent in recent years describing how methods help make reality, especially after the publication of Law and Urry's influential piece "Enacting the social" in 2004. Not unlike Foucault's, their point is that social methods "do not simply describe the world as it is, but also enact it" (Law and Urry 2004: 390). And thus, "if social investigation makes worlds, then it can, in some measure, think about the worlds it wants to help make. It gets involved in 'ontological politics'" (Law and Urry 2004: 390). Do not get me wrong; I think there is value in exploring this "methodological creativity" (Lowe 2010: 312), as there is something profoundly political about the enactive potential of our research. This point is nicely described by Campbell and Rosin (2011), when explaining how their research helped to enact certain technologies of audit that in turn gave shape to the very farms and orchards the Agricultural Research Group on Sustainability (ARGOS) team was charged with investigating. Campbell and Rosin describe their team's becoming-with their subject of study as follows:

> Much of the formal dialogue and interaction between industry, sectors and the ARGOS group from the outset of the programme concerned the deployment of a large number of measures of "farm performance." . . . Within a few years of the commencement of monitoring within the ARGOS farms and orchards, multiple industry sectors began to use ARGOS results in reviews and reconfiguration of their audit systems. This was, on the surface, exactly the kind of outcome that the ARGOS group had sought. However, the presence of a large database of ARGOS-derived measures was also reinforcing the particular way in which audit systems more generally were being practiced. . . . While ARGOS was set up to study the introduction of new audit systems, it was, unexpectedly, influencing not only the content and authentification of audit measures,

but the very architecture of the audit process itself. At the same time, the farmers and orchardists themselves used ARGOS results to reinforce their emerging identities as audited subjects.

(Campbell and Rosin 2011: 359)

Research such as this builds on a rich and growing base of literature within agri-food studies on the enactive qualities of "things," from standards (Loconto and Busch 2010; Butler and Roe 2014) to food packaging (Hawkins 2012) and conventional agricultural and economic development practices (Lewis et al. 2013).

My concern is that too much focus on methods risks distracting from all the other ways our scholarship "becomes-with" the world, acting like a smokescreen of sorts, absolving scholars from assemblages they help enact that may not be the result of methodological technique. Method myopia engenders the view that *that* is the only time our scholarship reaches out and touches the world, hence the need for technical protections (the Cartesian hazmat suit), or at least it risks instilling the feeling that it is the only moment during our *doing* of scholarship that we have an ethical responsibility to the lives we touch. As evidenced by past actions in the field, agri-food scholars seem open to accept broader responsibility for what they do.

An example of this lies in the eventual rejection of the adoption–diffusion model of change, causing a pre-eminent rural scholar in the mid-1990s to ask, "What happened to technology adoption–diffusion research?" (Ruttan 1996: 51). Beginning in the late 1940s, rural sociology took a turn toward the social psychological. Buttel and colleagues (1990: 44) describe this period as the "social psychological-behaviorist era of rural sociology," which "would remain unchallenged in rural sociological studies of agriculture until the early to mid-1970s" (p. 46). This era is defined by considerable energies directed toward the adoption–diffusion research tradition. The adoption–diffusion model is primarily concerned with the processes by which a technology is communicated through social channels. It therefore ignores such sociological questions as "Should this technology be adopted in the first place?" and "Who benefits and who loses from its adoption?" The adoption–diffusion model came under increasing scrutiny in the 1970s for promoting – for "enacting" – a top-down, expert-driven model of social change, what Buttel et al. (1990: 46) called a "promotional posture toward technology." Agri-food scholars, in other words, realized that their ethical responsibility to the world did not stop with the construction of methodologically sound survey instruments to evaluate a technology's relative advantage, compatibility, and so on.[3]

What then do we do? I am not proposing anything goes with regard to our research. Similarly, it would be an inappropriate critical response to debate whether or not our scholarship ought to become-with the world – that horse has long been out of the barn, arguably since the Big Bang, if not "before" (Barad 2007). Instead, the debate ought to center on questions of what becomings-with are to be protected, by whom, and with what effects and affects, which of course also implies a collective grappling with those processes that have been abandoned. When grasped through this orientation, the adoption–diffusion model was abandoned not because scholars realized that it made a difference. It was abandoned because of the *type* of difference it made, which, to put it plainly, was to *subtract* from the world rather than to add to it. Note what the model was eventually replaced with, practices like farmer first (Chambers et al. 1989) and citizen science (Wynne 1996) – all participatory, empowering, and "multiplying" practices of knowledge construction and exchange (Carolan 2008b).

With what space remains, I would like to unpack and play with this thinking a bit. I now offer three reflections on projects I have been involved with in recent years. I offer them because they are good to think with.

Vignette 1: indoor hydroponic gardening in Colorado

In November 2000, Colorado (USA) voters passed Amendment 20, which amended the state constitution to allow the medical use of marijuana. Twelve years later, voters returned to the polls to vote on whether recreational marijuana use ought to be legal in the state. Colorado voters passed Amendment 64 in November 2012, making the limited sale, possession, and growing of marijuana for recreational purposes legal for adults 21 and over (it remains illegal in the eyes of the federal government, however). I have been studying for roughly two years how a small but growing group of individuals are drawing upon entanglements-with-hydroponics to grow and thus do food: diverse becomings-with that are giving rise to novel food imaginaries (see also Carolan 2015).

The generative capabilities of my *doings* became apparent very early in the research, starting with the focus group. The four people brought together for the initial focus group did not know one another. Thus, with this simple act, I helped increase the mass of the networks assembled on that cool winter day in early 2013, a research-induced collaboration that proved to be of consequence, as all stayed after the focus group concluded to talk further about their experiences growing food without soil. As one participant later wrote to me in an email: "I want to thank you for introducing me to [Kim]. We've gotten together at least a half dozen times. Exchanged lots of tips. I must admit, never thought I'd get so much out of participating in this research [smiley face]."

This is not a particularly profound finding. After all, one of the reasons we conduct research is to generate and help disseminate knowledge. There is nothing particularly scandalous in admitting this. Yet it can be a bit unnerving for scholars to learn that knowledge exchange does not start only after research stops. Doing research presupposes doing knowledge exchange. To acknowledge this is to acknowledge our active involvement in the altering of networks we claim to be innocently studying.

There are also indications that the research process itself helped amplify an already-emergent ethical assemblage (*agencement*). This is a concept from Deleuze (1988) that speaks to spatialities that have the potential to give rise to ethical forms of action. Think of it as offering a sociological counterweight to conventional understandings of ethics and morality, which, at least in Western thought, view it (and it is always an "it" according to this intellectual tradition) as a top-down affair. Value, conventionally speaking, is some-"thing" we deduce. The ethical assemblage offers a far more wild understanding of the origins of our "oughts." Thus, following Barry (2004: 200), "rather than examine ethics as an abstract set of principles, such an approach would focus on the specificity of the discursive and non-discursive assemblages that are expected to generate ethical forms of conduct."

The research helped give shape to diverse becomings-with that altered how respondents (and their families) felt about the worlds they were helping to make possible. For the sake of brevity I will give just one example. A reason why the "n" of my sample increased from 18 participants to 39 over the course of the study was because the project was exciting to those involved, quite literally, as in: to "excite" – to stir, call forth, to increase response in, to stimulate. I was repeatedly told, or overheard others being enthusiastically told by participants, that this research was, for example, "interesting," "gratifying," and "timely." I also had one person confess that "the study validates something that I've known in my heart for years" and that "it just feels good to know that others out there see what we're doing as important." But I did not need respondents to tell me this to know it. I could see it. Indeed, I could "feel" it. Unlike some other research projects, it was easy to find willing participants. No one denied a request to be interviewed, and everyone who grew food with the help of hydroponics earnestly invited me (typically multiple times) into his or her home. And this excitement extended through me too, which undoubtedly helps explain why I chose to extend the project for as long as I did (how many times have you extended a project because you had a good "feeling" about it?).

In a word, the research became notably "sticky." As I talked with people about, and was given tours of, hydroponic setups, enduring ethical assemblages were taking shape. I watched children develop feelings of pride for what their parents were doing – "Cool; I didn't realize Mom and Dad were doing something worth studying!" I recall one teenager telling me. I felt novel "oughts" being reconfigured within families and communities: a mother showing her young children how to grow vegetables using hydroponics (and the excitement they displayed in being shown this); a husband and wife proudly making salsa in their kitchen using tomatoes grown in a spare bedroom (a very old family recipe, I was told); or a neighborhood potluck where everyone kept wanting to talk about, and then later see, "the setup that grew that kickass salsa" (in the words of a 20-something in attendance).[4] And, of course, I told others about my research – students, various public audiences, and garden enthusiast friends. Some were really interested and excited by this information, to the point of wishing to be placed into contact with people I had interviewed. There was nothing innocent about this research.

Vignette 2: food stamp challenge as co-experimentation

A while back I organized an experiment: participants were recruited, in exchange for a US$50 gift card, to take the so-called food stamp challenge – an exercise that involves purchasing food using only the monetary equivalent of what one would receive if they (or their family) qualified for the Supplemental Nutrition Assistance Program (SNAP), formerly (and colloquially still) called food stamps. The average monthly benefit for one person is around US$135, which means the "challenge" part centers on trying to eat healthily on about US$4.50 a day. Participants were asked to eat this way for two weeks. During that time, I observed and interacted with them as they made purchasing decisions at the store as well as participated in activities at their homes as they (and in some cases their families) prepared food and ate it. At the end, these individuals came together in a focus group setting to talk about their experiences. The initial aim of this research was to better understand how people make food provisioning decisions when financially constrained – for example what heuristics are used, and how are concepts like "nutrition" understood when viewed through the lens of, for example, "cheap"? I quickly discovered, however, that the project did so much more.

For one thing, it gave participants a feeling, a small one but a feeling nevertheless, for what it is like to live, or perhaps more accurately to eat, like a body-on-food-stamps. It reminded me that it is never enough to know difference; we have to feel it, to know it in a more-than-representational way, if we hope to ever start healing those rifts that divide. While interacting with respondents at stores and in their homes and during the final group interview I noticed emerge what Taylor (1992) calls a politics of recognition. This is also why I believe our educational techniques have to become more "public" too, knowing that recognition of another's standpoint has to be experienced, to be somehow felt, to be grasped – reading a book or being lectured on becomings-with (in this case, "becoming-with-food-stamps") is not enough. Of course, one can never know perfectly another's standpoint, in terms of experiences, feelings, and the like. But that is no reason for not trying. And besides, the moment we start chasing the ghost of perfect representations we have lost our way anyway.

The reason for the US$50 gift card was to incentivize participation and involve individuals who might not be otherwise inclined to participate in such a study. This strategy worked in enrolling, for example, Bill (pseudonym), who admitted to me his belief that "people on food stamps are generally lazy and looking for a free-ride." But even this self-proclaimed "pull-yourself-up-by-your-bootstraps conservative" admitted, by the experiment's end, to having "developed a greater understanding for what the working poor are put through."

Arguably because of this research there are a few more people out there who now know (not perfectly but they admit to "recognizing") certain feelings that go along with living on food stamps. As with any good research experiment,

I did not "tell" participants how to think or act. Yet I fully recognize that the project was responsible for instilling within at least some bodies what Massumi (2007: 219) calls "actuatable know-how" – affective ways of knowing that go beyond cognitive recall. Though, be honest, can you name one example from your own scholarship that did not do this?

Vignette 3: critical, hopeful, and enlivened scholarship

Deleuze (1987) argued that the history of philosophy is one of repression, where we are tamed into believing that we cannot think without having read so-and-so's book about Plato, Descartes, and Kant: "A formidable school of intimidation which manufactures specialists in thought – but which also makes those who stay outside conform all the more to this specialism which they despise. An image of thought called philosophy has been formed historically and it effectively stops people from thinking" (p. 13). Like Deleuze, I worry about the worlds that our *style* of scholarship enacts. Yes, methods help make reality. But methods are but one technique of scholarship. Others: theory and the stories that we tell.

I occasionally refer to myself as a disgruntled political economist. On the one hand, I appreciate the analytic value of this approach and others like it. You will miss a lot about food without some grasp of those so-called political economic (analytic) categories – for example the state, markets, and capital – that weigh so heavily in our lives. But equally, and this is why I consider myself "disgruntled," I do not know how you can grasp those political economic "things" without understanding how they are constituted, co-created, and enacted/enacting.

The frameworks we employ to make sense of the word are well tuned for grasping patterns, such as, or perhaps "especially," those more enduring circulations we ascribe to neoliberalism – those assemblages that make it seem like an "it." This comes at a cost, however. One potential hazard involves falling into a kind of structuralist paranoia, whereby we inadvertently reproduce the same dominant order that we are seeking to critique. Or, in performative terms, an obsession with recurrence risks enacting the very stabilities we pride ourselves in being critical of while interfering with the performance of other realities. Disgruntled or not, I believe that we need to be attuned to power and the emergence of enduring-yet-mutable patterns if we ever hope to understand food. Clearly, some relationalities matter, in a structural sort of way, more than others (Carolan and Stuart 2015). Yet not even the weightiest of assemblages (for example neoliberalism) are totalizing. We are surrounded by opportunities to make and enact difference. Conventionality is littered with cracks and weak points: spaces where a social "experiment" can ripple out and become a social "movement."

As an educator and someone who gives the occasional public lecture, I have been witness to just how debilitating these narratives of dominance-power can be. There was that student who told me, "After reading that book I wanted to crawl under a rock and stay there, it made me so depressed." Or another: "Given that we're heading to hell in a hand-basket anyway why bother doing anything? I'm beginning to wonder if it's even worth caring about the future anymore." These are actual statements from individuals after being treated to a dose of scholarly literature – agri-food scholarship, no less. They remind me of our collective obligation to care about the worlds we help enact by way of our written scholarship. Lest we forget, representations may present the world as fixed, but representations too have legs – "feelings" even – and enact multiplicity as they become-with social bodies.

We need to acknowledge, in the worlds of Haraway (2006: 141–142, emphasis added), the risks that come from being "stuck in that relentless complaint about technology and techno-culture and not getting the extraordinary *liveliness* that is also about us." In light of its enactive qualities, we might contemplate the value of critical yet hopeful (and lively too!) scholarship. Too often we confuse criticism, to the point of focusing only on what is bad and wrong, with gritty realism. That is not realism but pessimism (Sharpe 2014). What is real is that there are margins of maneuverability (Massumi 2002: 212) that reside, often unenacted, in every situation – what I like to call difference-power.

But that only gets us halfway there. Hopeful should not be confused with lively. How do we make our scholarship, and especially our representations, livelier? After all, scholars tend to live by the written and spoken word – three words, publish or perish. To further enliven our scholarship, I suggest aiming for "diffractive representations": a style of representation that acknowledges its limits, that is not afraid to feel, and that rejects treatments that seek purity and transcendence (like avoiding the personal pronoun "I") while recognizing the enactive nature of scholarship to bring forth new worlds. (Moving away from geometrical optics, Haraway [1992: 300] draws from physical optics when speaking of diffraction: "Diffraction is a mapping of interference, not of replication, reflection, or reproduction. A diffraction pattern does not map where differences appear, but rather maps where the *effects* of differences appear.") Part of this process involves employing what Deleuze and Guattari (1987: 99) call "atypical expressions" and "agrammaticality." As Massumi (2002: xxii, original emphasis) explains, "The atypical expression pulls language into a direct contact with its own futurity. It forcibly twists it into glints of forms, hints of contents, as-yet functionless functions which, however unmotivated or arbitrary, *could be*." In other words, neologisms, while they might make us uncomfortable and are generally frowned upon in the academic literature, can be good to think (and become) with. And this is especially so when intended to help us think through, and beyond, dominant imaginaries/discursive practices.

More *more-than* publics

The above vignettes, all in their own way, speak to the multiplication of "Things." There is nothing we can do to keep our scholarship from entangling-with the world we study. I do believe, however, we have a duty to be mindful – and bodyful – of the types of worlds we help enact. It is not for me to decide precisely what worlds we ought to make real. That is a decision for societies, in the broad Whiteheadian sense: judgments that need to be "felt" through a coming-together of companion species. Yet as a general rule – after all, we need heuristics; without them our scholarship would be paralyzed, dead – we would be well served to follow those scholarly styles that add to the world. Following this rule of thumb, adoption and diffusion styles of scholarship would be considered problematic, whereas I am comfortable with those projects outlined in the vignettes. All make a difference. But whereas the adoption and diffusion of innovation scholarship seems to subtract from the world the latter – the hydroponic study, food stamp challenge experiment, and critical, hopeful, and enlivened diffractions – helped in their own ways in making the unthought-of thinkable and the undoable routine.

In sum, this chapter is a full-throated endorsement of "public" agri-food scholarship. And I mean that in the fullest sense, which is to say we also need to shake ourselves from the humanist tradition that so many in the social sciences doggedly cling to. That is another uncomfortable conclusion we must face and feel: the moment we stop privileging representationalism the gates to the agora open, allowing for all sorts of interesting more-than-human "collaborations." This is not to deny the suffering of those that I would consider my closest companion species. (To quote Haraway [2008: 99], "I never wanted to be posthuman, or posthumanist, any more than I wanted to be postfeminist. For one thing, there is still urgent work to be done in reference to those who must inhabit the troubled categories of women and human." This explains my preference to use the term "more-than-human," to avoid the implication that we are beyond those troubles we have been grappling with for centuries.) It suggests, rather, that that suffering is a product of us not caring fully for everyone involved (Carolan 2015). Allow me to point to Chapter 12, on biological agriculture (BA) dairying. By "thinking" soil as nothing more than a medium for root growth and nutrient transfer and organizing "practices" around those imaginaries, which include methods allowing soil scientists to find what they are looking for, conventional agriculture essentially "enacted" such a reality on many farms around the world. But this neglect for certain companion species – in particular soil microbes – has made much of the world (save for perhaps petrochemical firms) worse off. Assuming that a more-than-human public harms those in the troubled category of human is to operate from the old politics of subtraction, of zero-sum games and limited goods, when in actuality such collaborations, more often than not, *add* to the world.

Not that we have a choice in any of this. To "do" is to be connected, regardless of whether that doing involves a call center, mail survey, or focus groups; even the seemingly solitary act of writing, as noted in the previous section, is far from an innocent act. We can also deny those more-than-human relationships, but that does not make them any less real – if anything it makes suffering more acute. The publics that matter (and that are "mattering") are not interested in promoting the coming-together of rational actors but in processes that engender more-than-human flourishing.

More-than-human flourishing: an apt place to conclude, as, ultimately, is that not an aim we all share, to experience increased justice, equity, companionship, and wellbeing? To flourish, according to the *Oxford English Dictionary*, means "To be in a vigorous state" (and vigorous: "Endowed with bodily or mental strength or vitality"). The ontology of more-than-human flourishing, like scholarship, is not all transcendent and clean. It is ultimately something we have to feel.

So: what does "your" scholarship feel like?

Notes

1 My use of optic references is intentional. The word "idea" traces back to the Greek verb "to see" as well as to the concept of "outward appearance." "Seeing is believing," "to take it all in with your eyes," and "the truth will reveal itself" are typical optic-oriented phrases for knowledge in English-speaking Western countries (Kearnes 2000; Carolan 2009).
2 The Latourian, via Heidegger, Thing: "much too real to be representations and much too disputed to play the role of stable, obdurate, boring primary qualities, furnishing the universe once and for all" (Latour 2000: 119).
3 I am referencing here the various "characteristics of innovations" studied by adoption–diffusion scholars (see Rogers 2003).
4 I question whether these specific events would have occurred, at least when they did, had the research not taken place, for instance with regard to the impetus leading to the neighborhood.

References

Barad, K. (2007) *Meeting the Universe Halfway: Quantum Physics and the Entanglement of Matter and Meaning*, Duke University Press, Durham, NC.
Barry, A. (2004) 'Ethical capitalism', in W. Larner and W. Walters (eds), *Global Governmentality*, New York: Routledge, pp. 195–211.
Burawoy, M. (2005) 'For public sociology', *American Sociological Association*, vol. 70, pp. 4–28.
Butler, H. and Roe, E. (2014) 'Modifying and commodifying farm animal welfare: the economization of layer chickens', *Journal of Rural Studies*, vol. 33, pp. 141–149.
Buttel, F., Larson, O. and Gillespie, G. (1990) *The Sociology of Agriculture*, Greenwood Press, New York.
Campbell, H. and Rosin, C. (2011) 'After the "organic industrial complex": an ontological expedition through commercial organic agriculture in New Zealand', *Journal of Rural Studies*, vol. 27, pp. 350–361.
Carolan, M. (2008a) 'More-than-representational knowledge/s of the countryside: how we think as bodies', *Sociologia Ruralis*, vol. 48, pp. 408–422.
Carolan, M. (2008b) 'Democratizing knowledge: sustainable and conventional agricultural field days as divergent democratic forms', *Science, Technology and Human Values*, vol. 33, no. 4, pp. 508–528.
Carolan, M. (2009) '"I do therefore there is": enlivening socio-environmental theory', *Environmental Politics*, vol. 18, no. 1, pp. 1–17.

Carolan, M. (2012) *The Sociology of Food and Agriculture*, Routledge, Abingdon.
Carolan, M. (2013) 'The wild side of agro-food studies: on co-experimentation, politics, change, and hope', *Sociologia Ruralis*, vol. 53, no. 4, pp. 413–431.
Carolan, M. (2015) 'Adventurous food futures: knowing about alternatives is not enough, we need to feel them', *Agriculture and Human Values*, online first, DOI 10.1007/s10460-015-9629-4.
Carolan, M. and Stuart, D. (2015) 'Get real: climate change and all that "it" entails', *Sociologia Ruralis*, DOI: 10.1111/soru.12067.
Chambers, R., Pacey, A. and Thrupp, L. (eds) (1989) *Farmer First: Farmer Innovation and Agricultural Research*, Institute of Development Studies, University of Sussex, Brighton.
Deleuze, G. (1987) *Dialogues*, Columbia University Press, New York.
Deleuze, G. (1988) *Spinoza: Practical Philosophy*, City Lights Books, New York.
Deleuze, G. and Guattari, F. (1987) *A Thousand Plateaus*, Minneapolis: University of Minnesota Press.
Dewey, J. (1946) *The Public and Its Problems*, Greenwood Press, New York.
Foucault, M. ([1978] 2001) 'Governmentality', in J. D. Faubion (ed.), *Power: Essential Works of Foucault, 1954–1984*, vol. 3, Penguin, London, pp. 201–222.
Gilbert, J. (2001) 'Agrarian intellectuals in a democratizing state: a collective biography of USDA leaders in the intended New Deal', in C. M. Stock and R. D. Johnston (eds), *The Countryside in the Age of the Modern State: Political Histories of Rural America*, Cornell University Press, Ithaca, NY, pp. 232–244.
Haraway, D. (1992) 'The promises of monsters: a regenerative politics for inappropriated others', in L. Grossberg, C. Nelson and P. Treichler (eds), *Cultural Studies*, Routledge, New York, pp. 295–337.
Haraway, D. (2006) 'When we have never been human, what is to be done?', interview with Donna Haraway, *Theory, Culture and Society*, vol. 23, nos 7–8, pp. 135–158.
Haraway, D. (2008) 'Encounters with companion species', *Configurations*, vol. 14, no. 2, pp. 97–114.
Hawkins, G. (2012) 'The performativity of food packaging: market devices, waste crisis and recycling', *Sociological Review*, vol. 60, no. S2, pp. 66–83.
Ingold, T. (2012) 'Toward an ecology of materials', *Annual Review of Anthropology*, vol. 41, pp. 427–442.
Kearnes, M. (2000) 'Seeing is believing is knowing', *Australian Geographical Studies*, vol. 38, pp. 332–340.
Latour, B. (2000) 'When things strike back – a possible contribution of science studies to the social science', *British Journal of Sociology*, vol. 51, no. 1, pp. 107–123.
Law, J. and Urry, J. (2004) 'Enacting the social', *Economy and Society*, vol. 33, no. 3, pp. 390–410.
Le Heron, R. (2013) 'Rethinking the economic and social history of agriculture and food through the lens of food choice', in Anne Murcott, Warren Belasco and Peter Jackson (eds), *The Handbook of Food Research*, Bloomsbury, New York, pp. 50–68.
Lewis, N., Le Heron, R., Campbell, H., Henry, M., Le Heron, E., Pawson, E., Perkins, H., Roche, M. and Rosin, C. (2013) 'Assembling biological economies: region-shaping initiatives in making and retaining value', *New Zealand Geographer*, vol. 69, no. 3, pp. 180–196.
Loconto, A. and Busch, L. (2010) 'Standards, techno-economic networks, and playing fields: performing the global market economy', *Review of International Political Economy*, vol. 17, no. 3, pp. 507–536.

Lowe, P. (2010) 'Enacting rural sociology: or what are the creativity claims of the engaged sciences?', *Sociologia Ruralis*, vol. 50, no. 4, pp. 311–330.
Massumi, B. (2002) 'Navigating moments', in M. Zournazi (ed.), *Hope: New Philosophies for Change*, Pluto, Sydney, pp. 210–243.
Massumi, B. (2007) 'Potential politics and the primacy of preemption', *Theory and Event*, vol. 10, https://muse.jhu.edu/journals/theory_and_event/v010/10.2massumi.html, accessed 29 October 2014.
Patton, M. (2002) *Qualitative Research and Evaluation Methods*, Sage, Thousand Oaks, CA.
Polanyi, M. (1966) 'The logic of tacit inference', *Philosophy*, vol. 41, no. 155, pp. 1–18.
Rogers, E. (2003) *Diffusion of Innovations*, Simon & Schuster, New York.
Ruttan, V. (1996) 'What happened to technology adoption–diffusion research?', *Sociologia Ruralis*, vol. 36, no. 1, pp. 51–73.
Sharpe, S. (2014) 'Potentiality and impotentiality in J. K. Gibson-Graham', *Rethinking Marxism: A Journal of Economics, Culture and Society*, vol. 26, no. 1, pp. 27–43.
Spano, R. (2006) 'Observer behavior as a potential source of reactivity: describing and quantifying observer effects in a large-scale observational study of police', *Sociological Methods and Research*, vol. 34, no. 4, pp. 521–553.
Taylor, C. (1992) 'The politics of recognition', in A. Gutmann, S. C. Rockefeller, M. Walzer and S. Wolf (eds), *Multiculturalism and the Politics of Recognition*, Princeton University Press, Princeton, NJ, pp. 25–103.
Whitehead, A. N. (1967) *Adventures of Ideas*, Free Press, New York.
Wynne, B. (1996) 'May the sheep safely graze? A reflexive view of the expert–lay knowledge divide', in S. Lash, B. Szerszynski and B. Wynne (eds), *Risk, Environment and Modernity: Towards a New Ecology*, Sage, London, pp. 44–83.

17 Eating bioeconomies

Michael K. Goodman

It's in between lunch and dinner, and I have just finished off a rather large bag of Cheese and Jalapeno Crunchy Snack Mix. I shopped for and purchased these today at Aldi, a local, small-scale discount supermarket desperately expanding its numerous ranges to capture the growing numbers of middle-class shoppers like me looking for bargains. This is not, by any stretch of the imagination, a healthy snack at 27 grams of fat – and I do know this, as I looked at the nutritional information on the label – but they are good and I wolf down the whole bag. In the meantime, I have prepared some dinner for the family that I would be eating later: a spaghetti sauce in the slow cooker full of vegetables and using a minced meat substitute known as Quorn. I have used this 'fake meat' and protein substitute to produce a much healthier meal for myself and the family – as Quorn's annual report puts it, it has '90% less saturated fat' than spaghetti made with beef (Quorn 2015) – and to cut down on the family's carbon footprint by not eating livestock for at least one meal this week. For us it will be a Meatless Wednesday and *not* a Meatless Monday.

But why did I eat this way today? Why did I enter into these rather contradictory engagements with these unhealthy and then more healthy foods over the day? Again, shouldn't I have clearly avoided the snack mix (which turned into my lunch) even if I (mistakenly) thought it might be cancelled out by the healthier dinner? Essentially there is no satisfactory or profound answer to these questions, I think, beyond the fact that what I ate today ended up being *what I ate today*. I ingested the snack mix because I hadn't eaten lunch and it did really look as though it would taste great: I had a visceral, affective response to the 'tasty' colours of the packaging, to the memory of eating this stuff before (but was it sour cream and chive? Ah, no matter!), and I was just plain hungry after making my spaghetti sauce that needed to cook on low for another four hours. I prepared the spaghetti to make sure that I – and the family of course – would get a hot, healthy meal. I thought that cooking and eating this way would lower our carbon 'foodprint' and I had to make sure I had food on the table that we would all enjoy. I was *eating* and acting like an *eater* and not – as many an economist and even food scholar might put it – merely consuming or acting like a consumer. Indeed, what we as humans do *is* eat, in all of its material, meaningful, visceral and (un)conscious contradictions, complexities and complications.

We as food scholars need to recognise, account for (at least partially) and work with this messy complexity in our efforts to understand food–society relationships and the networks they effect, create and inhabit. This is certainly the case with respect to the development of a biological economies approach as put forward in this book and as this invaluable perspective is taken forward. What we need, amongst other things, is more theoretically and empirically rich – but also specific – ways to explore food–society relationalities. For me, this begins with a rhetorical and conceptual shift that moves from those rather narrow, economistic notions of 'consumers' and 'consumption' to the more messy, complex and perhaps theoretically and empirically deeper notions of 'eaters' and 'eating'.

Before I get ahead of myself, however, I want to better position the contents and intentions of this chapter. Overall, in the spirit and context of working with and on a biological economies approach to food and food studies, I offer here a polemic and several short provocations designed as possible interventions to this approach but also to the field of agri-food studies more broadly. My polemic surrounds this desire to shift our rhetoric and conceptualisations from consumer to eater. Three short provocations then follow. The first begins to question the ways that the 'vital materialisms' work by Jane Bennett and others has been applied to food and eating. The second short provocation here is one that looks to bring in the inescapable role of the media in governing the biological economies of food, especially with respect to eating. One look around and, in the Global North at least, the media's obsession with food and telling us how and what to eat – as well as exposés, documentaries and other forms of food media – becomes abundantly clear. In effect, a biological economies approach to food and food politics must have contemporary food cultures, whether that be about the cultures of eating or those with respect to food media, front and centre to its understandings of the social worlds of food and how we might make them less unequal and more 'non-human' in concern. The final provocation is one that encourages the development of more enactive and performative research methods and encounters, specifically through the use of autobiography by food scholars. For too long, we as scholars *and* eaters have been asked to step out of the way in describing the contemporary social life of eating and food, and I want to make a plea here for more and better autobiographies of our own encounters with food as a form of social engagement, experimentation and legitimised methodology in biological economies research. There is value in this approach, perhaps as evidenced in my opening above, not only as one important way to get at the complexities and complications of food itself, but also as a way of 'doing' and 'enacting' more and better food scholarship and food politics.

All of these points in this chapter come in the form of relatively short statements and arguments; they are somewhat reflectively fuzzy, open-ended and partial and will have to be fully enacted upon by others – if, of course, there is enough here and these points are worthy of being acted upon! What links them, however, is a recent notion in the context of better understanding food–society relationships I have begun to work with (Goodman, M. 2015). This is the idea of the 'relational contingencies' of food and eating, which builds on food scholarship tied into what the editors call post-structural political economy in the work of Allison and Jessica Hayes-Conroy, Elspeth Probyn, Emma-Jayne Abbots and Anna Lavis as well as the 'critical fat studies' approach of Julie Guthman, Robyn Longhurst, Rachel Colls and Bethany Evans, whereby eating is a practice relational to/with bodies and foods and essential for this relationality to come into being. Indeed, food is only really 'food' when we, as eating bodies, enter into a relational engagement with it. But, as these critical scholars would have it, the nature of these relationalities is conditioned by and contingent upon a number of factors – taste, feelings, identity, class, culture, access and political economies – as they shift over time, space and place. Thus, the practice of eating is and should be seen in non-determinist but contingent ways when we consider what, how and why we eat. The biological economies approach could, and perhaps should, consider this much more fully, as this lens is used for further theoretical development and/or empirical research. I hope the polemic and accompanying interventions in this chapter might begin to push on the open doors provided by this volume just a little bit more. Indeed, might it be the case that certain critical aspects of bioeconomies don't even really come into being *until* we eat? Eating, as concept, practice and empirical category, is not simply a conceit of post-structuralists or diverse economy types but rather one of the key sites we can work to understand and engage with and in which we can incorporate both food cultures and political economies into a biological economies approach to the 'knowing and growing' (Goodman, D. and DuPuis 2002) of contemporary food networks, assemblages and politics.

Moving from consumer to eater, consumption to eating: a short polemic

Ever since agri-food scholarship emerged out of the multi-coloured haze of Marxism, political economy and the cultural and post-structural turns, food scholars (and others) have been waving the consumptionist flag in earnest. We must consider consumers and consumption as well as the relationships of consumption and production, many argued, demonstrated and theorised, through the numerous lenses of post-structuralism, political ecology, actor–network theory and assemblage work. Consumers are actors in their own right and are worthy – nay, it is required! – of and for conceptual and theoretical consideration as well as empirical exploration as part and parcel of agricultural and food systems. Indeed, this is recognised in the moniker of agri- or agro-'food', and a great deal of valuable work has been done in this regard, from important theoretical and conceptual engagements (for example Goodman, D. and DuPuis 2002) to empirical work (for example Kneafsey et al. 2008), both in geography and across food scholarship more broadly (for example Belasco 2009; Johnston and Baumann 2010; de Solier 2013).

Building on this earlier work, the deployment of the 'foodscape' concept has been used to more fully and formally incorporate food production and consumption within one lens (for example Potter and Westall 2013; MacKendrick 2014). As Josée Johnston and I recently put it in the pages of *Food, Culture and Society*, 'the idea of a foodscape not only attends to the cultural *and* material dimensions of food, but it crucially and at its most powerful highlights the dialectical *relationalities* between and among food culture (values, meanings and representations) and food materiality (physical landscapes, ecologies and political economy)' (Johnston and Goodman 2015: 207, original emphasis). While perhaps a slightly diffuse and unfocused lens,

> a foodscape presents a culturally-mediated lay of the land wherein the material reality of food and people's livelihoods matter – what kind of food is being sold, who controls the food system, who eats well (and who does not), as well as how resources are sustained (or deteriorated) through our food practices and engagements.
> (Johnston and Goodman 2015: 207)

Similarly, the use of 'place' in food scholarship, especially in the work of Ben Coles and his colleagues (for example Coles and Crang 2011; Coles 2014), has been (re)deployed as a way to explore the connected relationalities of food production and consumption. Coles's work has uniquely explored the 'topologies' of place – how production and consumption are culturally, economically and materially linked – in the creation of more 'ethical' food–society relationships.

But, even in this more inclusive work and these more inclusive frameworks, consumption and production have often stood apart as essentialised, albeit relational, categories. Consumption for the most part – the work mentioned above notwithstanding – has been much more of a residual category even in writings signalling the need to consider it theoretically and empirically. And, importantly, the body in all its multi-faceted, affective complexity has remained relatively inert in the more anodyne considerations of consumption and the figure of the consumer in food-related scholarship. This has been most recently pointed out in the two significant and debate-leading volumes produced by Emma-Jayne Abbots, Anna Lavis and colleagues (Abbots and Lavis 2013b; Abbots et al. 2015), which explore these relationalities of foods, bodies and affect in their vast Technicolor hues. Indeed, a great deal of what is proposed here draws on and builds from the ground-breaking theoretical and empirical innovations of Abbots and Lavis's pioneering volumes and their own separate work (for example Abbots 2011, 2013a, 2013b; Lavis 2015b; see also Lavis 2014, 2015a; Abbots 2015a, 2015b; Abbots and Attala 2015). We thus need – both across agri-food scholarship and in thinking about and engaging with the bioeconomies of food – new language forms and conceptual tools that animate eating bodies and consider the complex and contradictory practices of food consumption more fully: tools that build on and further open up theoretical and empirical space that pays homage to these relational contingencies of the human–food and society–food relationships. Here, then, is my polemic: I'd like to see us move away from talking about and considering 'consumption' and 'consumers' to begin to conceptualise, explore and investigate human–food and society–food relationalities through notions of 'eating' and the figure of the 'eater'. Importantly, this shift is both rhetorical and conceptual in nature: the use of these terms is meant to signal new theoretical conventions and considerations, conceptual engagements and lines of inquiry, and at the same time signal a rhetorical shift away from what I would suggest are the less vibrant and more narrow metaphors of food consumption and the food consumer. In short, considering eating and eaters has the capacity to do novel and deeper conceptual and rhetorical work that we as food scholars need in order to honour, do justice to and build on the relationalities of foods, bodies and political ecologies as we continue to explore, critique and examine these human relationships to food through the lens of bioeconomies.

For me, there are four brief reasons for this suggested shift to eating and the eater. First, the uses of eat, eating and eater signal that eating is *different* from any other act or practice of consumption. While many might disagree with this given its essentialising logics, eating is a unique form of consumption. Through the act and practice of eating we incorporate the external world into ourselves, our bodies and our identities. It is always and only an intimate material experience that crosses the boundaries of the inside and outside in ways crucial to our survival and well-being. To eat, eating and being an eater literally and figuratively make us what we are, should be and can become. Furthermore, the use of these terms and concepts signals, from the outset, the conceptual and empirical need to consider the intimate relationalities embedded in and created by the practices of ingestion and metabolisation (Abbots and Lavis 2013a).[1] Similarly, and again from the outset, the concepts of eating articulate the lively relationalities of food to bodies and minds through the practices of ingestion, incorporation and metabolisation. My desire here is that – by taking up the charge of the likes of Abbots and Lavis as well as other critical food scholars mentioned here – through the deployment and use of the terms and concepts of eat, eating and eater we begin to signal the very ontological difference of eating versus other forms of consumption, say of cars, books, clothes and computers. Eating and being an eater mean that – in more post-structural and post-disciplinary parlance – we are doing more-than-consumption and being more-than-consumers. This re-conceptualisation works to both specify open up novel terrain across the practices and forms of our very human – and indeed inseparable social and individual – relationships to the non-human world we so choose or are required to incorporate into our bodies. In short, working through the terms and concepts of eating and the eater is my way of working to add more meaning, meaningful resonance and more meaningful conceptual and empirical purchase to the food–society relationalities that inhabit our everyday practices and experiences.

Second, more fully giving eating and the eater their conceptual and empirical 'due' not only works to situate the relationalities of food, bodies and people at the centre of our analysis but requires we see these relationalities in their 'real world' messiness, complexity and contingency. As I tried to show in my opening, eating, and being an eater (and/or a food preparer for others), is conscious, unconscious, affective, rational, porous, bounded, material, fleshy, fleeting, indistinct, sometimes contradictory and multiple; and at other times it is perfectly sensible and singular. Eating is, as I have suggested, relationally contingent: its practice is fuzzy, partial, unformed, ever-changing, hard to articulate, engaging and fundamentally different across different people, families, regions, cultures and countries. Considerations of the multiplicities and complexities of eating and the eater are about accounting for and getting at the more 'true-to-life' experiences, engagements and practices of our relationships to food.

These more true-to-life considerations of eating sit directly at the centre of a number of key writings by food scholars. For example, the collective of Clive Barnett, Paul Cloke, Nick Clarke, Alice Malpass and Jennifer Pykett, through the twinned lenses of fair trade and organic foods (Clarke et al. 2008; Barnett et al. 2011), have made deep empirical and theoretical interventions on this front. For them – through the (more diffuse) lenses of ethical and politicised consumption – the politics of eating is 'a facet of integrated and dispersed practices' (Barnett et al. 2011: 200) of the 'doings' of responsibility that 'is [much] less an individualistic economic act and more of a means of acting in relation to larger collective projects which . . . innovate new forms of shared responsibility' (p. 201). Not only is this more-than-consumption held together by a whole network of institutions, feelings, economies and cultures, but a great deal of these eating politics are 'not undertaken as "consumers" at all [but rather] embedded in practices where they are being parents, caring partners . . . good friends and so on' (p. 201). Important sociological, albeit spatialised, research here has been diligently pursued by Josée Johnston and her various colleagues (for example Johnston and Szabo 2011; Johnston et al. 2011, 2012). Her work sits directly at the centre of this eating-focused, more-than take on consumers and consumption by critically disturbing both the figure of consumers and their practices through research showing that, as both poor and rich eaters construct notions of 'ethical', 'good' food, accompanied by equally apparent moral quandaries, 'place and privilege are just as important as personal taste and ethics in shaping daily food choices' (Johnston et al. 2012). In Johnston's work, Sayer's (2011) ghostly theoretical imprint of 'lay normativities' (see also Wheeler 2012) takes empirical shape in the context of ethical eating and the multiple foodscapes these practices and those of the figure of the ethical eater render.

Others – mainly feminist geographers – operating in this vein have sought to explore the multiple, complex and indeterminate relationship of food, bodies and eating. Building on the likes of Elspeth Probyn (2000, 2012), Deborah Lupton (1996) and Gill Valentine (1999, 2002),[2] Robyn Longhurst (2011) has, through an innovative and rich autobiographical account, explored the deeply personal, gendered, embodied but also profoundly paradoxical 'real' and reflective experiences of eating (less) in efforts to 'become smaller'. Allison and Jessica Hayes-Conroy (Hayes-Conroy, A. and Hayes-Conroy 2008, 2010, 2013; Hayes-Conroy, A. 2010; Hayes-Conroy, J. and Hayes-Conroy 2010, 2013) have taken to exploring the visceral affects/effects of the relationalities of bodies and food through the practices of eating and the potential for the re-capture of an everyday politics of eating through questions of taste. For them, and similar to Mike Carolan's (2011) work on embodied food politics, because eating *is* indeterminate and malleable, it holds promise as a form of politics in the context of health, access to healthy, nutritious foods, food ethics and alternative food networks. Further, as Emma-Jayne Abbots and Anna Lavis (2013a: 1) eloquently articulate:

> Eating, as a conceptual and a physical act, brings both foods and bodies into view; food does not remain on a supermarket shelf, in the kitchen or on a plate, but is placed in the mouth, chewed, tasted, swallowed and digested. Its solidity is thus broken down and rendered into fragments that both pass through, and become, the eater's body. This is a process that concomitantly establishes and ruptures social relations between bodies, whether those of the food's producers, retailers, microbiological components or even of the original animal sources. Unpacking the encounters between foods and (human and non-human) bodies then, offers a way to take account of the many networks and relations embedded in and performed by eating.

Finally, here, those writing from within the field of 'critical fat studies' (for example Guthman and DuPuis 2006; Colls 2007; Evans et al. 2011; Guthman 2011; Colls and Evans 2014) have worked to situate considerations of eating and eaters at the centre of their analysis designed not just to make 'space for fat bodies' but to question and reverse the 'received wisdom' of the causes and consequences of the 'epistemological violence' that the labels of 'obese' and 'obesity' do to individual and social bodies. Focus is thus directed to more indeterminate, situated and relational pathways of exploring, understanding and conceptualising obesity/fatness that have inter-corporealities, inter-subjectivities and people's lifecourses – *as eaters* – at their centre.

At their most broad, these shifts to eating and eater are meant to fundamentally and more fully socialise and situate the practices of eating and the figure of the eater in the temporal and spatial networks of the co-creation, materialities and affects/effects of human–food relationalities (Abbots and Lavis 2013a). These rhetorical and conceptual moves are designed to shed and indeed bury the accompanying implicit and/or explicit definitional baggage of 'individualistic', 'rational' and 'free chooser/choice' that comes with the continued use of 'consumer' and 'consumption'. Thus, from the outset of our research and theorising, the figure of the 'eater' is one that is always and everywhere embedded in food's multiple socio-material assemblages, while it is the act of eating that co-creates these same multiple, (in)determinate socio-material assemblages. To put it more simply, as we shift to the use of eaters and eating, we might begin to throw off that old and unhelpful baggage embedded in the term 'consumption' and the figure of the consumer. Such a shift will open up new and possibly more dedicated space to explore the powerful and power-filled food–eater–society relationship that forms the rich mosaic of (increasingly unequal) everyday spaces and places of the foodscape.

Third, the uses of eating and eater work to encapsulate and capture both production and consumption within them and consider them as necessarily relational rather than essential categories. Eating is the practice of consuming and ingesting food that has, of course, been produced somewhere by someone through other sets of practices. One cannot eat – at least as a material practice – without stuff that has been produced in some form, shape or another that is primarily designed to allow us to stuff ourselves. Additionally, being an eater is also about the production of one's identity, social reproduction and material reproduction. The conditions of 'being an eater' and of 'practising eating', thus, have at their ontological but also practical core *both* production and consumption as thoroughly non-essentialised and intimately and always relational. In other words, the use of eating and eaters in describing the human–food relationship works to signal that this relationship is only articulated through the inseparable relationalities of production and consumption, which now, according to my polemic, are collapsed and conceptualised through the practices of eating and the figure of the eater. The practice of eating is, everywhere and always, more-than-consumption but also more-than-production.

More can be said here in this context, however. Eating is ultimately a practice of intimate connection. It connects us, as articulated above, to the 'outside' world, to nature, to the environment, to others and to other places of both production and consumption. If, as Alkon (2013) has it, food is the ultimate socio-nature, then eating is the ultimate *relationship* to socio-nature for us humans. Eating connects us to places and spaces; it is the, if not *the*, most intimate practice of geography, and food, once ingested, literally becomes part of us. For Annemarie Mol (2008), eating 'figures' and re-figures subjectivities, agencies and materialities, to which I think we can and should now add the figuring and re-figuring of *geographies*. In important ways, eating and being an eater bring together the geographies of the production and consumption of food into novel conceptual framings designed to provide more analytical and theoretical purchase in more sophisticated, relevant and ontologically insightful ways.

Fourth and finally, in addition to calling for the further and better socialisation of eating in ontological terms, I wish to have these rhetorical and conceptual shifts also do work to 'humanise' the act of eating and those who eat. There is, thus, a normative logic to the use of the language of eating and being an eater; at the same time it contains within this logic the attributes of understanding, empathy and commonality. We all eat, but we all eat in different ways, through different means and through different logics, practices and cultural affects/effects. Eating is complex, slippery, contradictory and irrational and, when we work to understand why certain people eat the things they do, these multiple, competing and paradoxical rationalities need to figure into our scholarly and wider understandings of eating patterns and behaviours in as non-judgemental a fashion as possible. This is critical in our current era of austerity, poor shaming and creation of 'bad' food citizens, as, in the UK in particular, foodbanks have continued to spread and the poor, more and more now, have to choose between eating and other critical 'modern' services like petrol and electricity (Lambie-Mumford 2013; Lambie-Mumford et al. 2014). Eating and eater-centred work can, in my mind at least, work to cut across and disturb these media-generated and sustained debates on good/bad foods and good/bad food citizens as we work for more and better understanding, situatedness and an exploration of the complexities of the everyday decisions marginalised citizens make as they shop, cook and eat. It is my hope that working to understand and study eating and eaters in their messy, unsettling and opaque splendour might begin to stand as a rhetorical and conceptual bulwark to the contemporary revanchist food politics and their growing impact on the biopolitics of the bioeconomies of food.

A short tale of three provocations for bioeconomies

There are three provocations that, I think, follow from the rhetorical and conceptual shifts to eater and eating as suggested above. The first works to engage with and question the 'vital materialisms' of food as presented in Jane Bennett's theorisations of the same (Bennett 2007, 2010) and the ways that this perspective might be slightly tempered through the lens of the eater and the practices of eating.

For Bennett – in building as she does on both previous and contemporary work that has explored the socio-material lives of things from the likes of Latour (1993) and Appadurai (1986) and its application in the specific context of food (for example Murdoch 1997; Goodman, D. 1999; Murdoch et al. 2000; Cook et al. 2004; Probyn 2012) – there is a longing to recover and re-purpose the material agency of food for ontological and empirical as well as affective, moral reasons. Here, modernist and other dualisms get chucked into the dustbin of history to be replaced with agent-like, food(y) things, assemblages and networks that do this vitalist work on foodscapes and bodies. Yet even this is too minimalist and politically inert for Bennett, who wishes to take us into a 'post-relational' ontological era (Braun 2011). For her, 'food is an active inducer–producer of salient, public effects, rather than a passive resource at the disposal of consumers.... [F]ood ... possess[es] an agentic capacity irreducible to (though rarely divorced from) human agency' (Bennett 2007: 145). She formulates this through an analysis of the ways that fat acts to shift bodily moods and affective states as well as the political affects/effects that Slow Food has on the relationalities of eating. Recent findings from the nutritional sciences confirm and further describe the impacts of the eating of fast food on rates of depression (Buchanan 2015) and the ways that sugary drinks contribute to global morbidity rates (Owen 2015). In more scholarly work, critical nutritionists[3] have begun to explore the ways that eating can begin to change our very genetic make-up (Guthman and Mansfield 2012).

This work is clearly exciting and opens up new avenues for how we might theorise about food, its agency and its political affects/effects (for more specifically on this, see Abbots forthcoming). The problem I have, however, is the ways that this vital materialisms perspective has the potential to obfuscate not only human agency – and that of the wider vital materialisms of food's political economies – but also the ways that food is only and ever relational to humans and societies. Foods don't become vital through some sort of 'immaculate conception': they are made and (re)made in particular politicised, material and social ways that are, in the case of industrial food networks, embedded in corporate relations of profit and market expansion. Our bodies and tastes, as Mike Carolan (2011) has it, are thus *tuned* to and for particular foods, with food's vital materialism only realised through the foods that people choose or are able to 'tune in' to through the practices of eating.

Thus, this focus on eating and the eater might work, in a slight way, to correct the ontological 'exuberances' of the vital materialism approach to food not only by centring the relationalities of foods, bodies and affects in our analysis but also by working to uncover the powerful social, spatial and economic relations that get foods into the vital material states of, say, 'healthy', 'unhealthy', 'industrial' and/or 'alternative' in the first place. Most importantly, however, in these times of austerity eating, inequality and nutritional insecurity, analysis of food's ontological agency as presented to us in Bennett's vital materialisms lens should not overtake its practical or biological agency as food. Rather, the lens of eater and eating can and should work to build up the power of a vital materialisms approach *as political critique* by articulating and fundamentally critiquing ways that food's vital materialisms are absent for some (that is, not enough to eat) or are relational in particularly harmful or unhealthy ways in the constructions of the bioeconomies of eating.

The second provocation builds on the first to suggest that if food's vitalities and specific materialisms are crucially brought to vibrant life through ingestion and metabolisation – eating, in other words – serious theoretical and conceptual consideration needs to be given to the cultural and media grammars that articulate what it is appropriate or not to eat and what it means to be a 'good' or 'bad' eater. In this, bioeconomies, and indeed eating and being an eater, are as much vibrantly discursive and 'spectacular' as they are material and materially vibrant. Food's vitalities as media object are a function of its bioeconomy at the same time as these discourses work invariably to create its bioeconomy. Indeed, media are one of the key ways we get to know the biological economy of food and farming as eaters, and one of the ways that the discourses of good and bad foods and good and bad eaters circulate in the public sphere. In short, media surrounding eating and being an eater have infiltrated almost all aspects of our everyday, ordinary food spaces – from television to magazines, books, social media and the internet – such that they form a key area of analysis of what and how we are supposed to perform the biological economies of food.

Specifically, recent writings have stated, much as has been argued here, that food media are an inseparable and embedded component of the foodscape and should be theorised as such (Johnston and Goodman 2015).[4] Other work, hailing from the classical cultural studies approach of critical discourse analysis, has explored the role of celebrity chefs (Hollows and Jones 2010a, 2010b; Bell and Hollows 2011; see also Slocum et al. 2011) and the 'campaigning culinary documentary' (CCD) as intermediaries that impact upon our relations to food. Bell et al.'s (2015) findings are particularly interesting given the nuanced way that CCDs can work to uphold but also critique the neo-liberal approach to healthy eating. Some television programmes work to fully responsibilise eaters in their food choices, while others work to critique and responsibilise both the state and corporations in the context of unhealthy food provisioning. Indeed Jamie Oliver personifies this conflict through his *Jamie's 30 Minute Meals* programme, which worked to responsibilise those (most likely women) watching to make cheap, healthy family meals while his UK and US *School Meals* programmes worked to hold the state responsible for providing healthy meals to school children. Still other work has looked to uncover and analyse audience reactions and 'uses' of food media, intermediaries such as food celebrities, and the biopolitics that these encounters create. For example, Piper (2015; see also Piper 2013) has traced the ways that audiences take celebrity chef ideas, practices and information, interpret all this differently and then work to incorporate this lifestyle advice in ways that make sense to them as eaters. Barnes (2015), in related research, has explored the ways that audiences have, through social media, worked to perform themselves as eaters by publicising their engagements with celebrity chef programmes, but also how audiences have worked to 'talk back' to these same celebrity chefs, also through social media. Overall, analysing food media and their role in the creation of food politics – let alone the role that food media play in constructing eating and what it means to be an eater – is crucial for understanding the shifting and complex food cultures that make up its bioeconomies.

My final provocation is short and it's this: in order for us to get at more enactive and vibrant bioeconomies of food and eating, I'd like to see more autobiography and autoethnography in our work on the bioeconomies of food, eating and food politics. Longhurst (2011) has done this successfully in her fascinating discussion of working to eat differently and lose weight as she developed a critical feminist perspective to understanding an eater's relationship to (less) food. Carolan (2011) begins his ambitious book on *Embodied Food Politics* by exploring the ways he was, as a child, tuned to canned mushrooms. His analysis is then built around the ways our bodies have been tuned to industrially produced foods and how a 're-tuning' might be the basis for an alternative food politics. The Hayes-Conroys have worked to inject a strong autobiographical voice into their work on alternative foods and school food projects as well as their research on social movements more broadly. Allison Hayes-Conroy (2010) in particular has explored the ways she did 'visceral' fieldwork with the Slow Food movement and how this approach allowed her to garner novel and interesting insights that would have been unavailable to her through the use of more conventional methods (see also Longhurst et al. 2009). Ian Cook et al. (2004) has also injected a strong autoethnographic voice into his work, namely through his all-encompassing desire to 'follow the thing' in the shape of a papaya. I've even flirted with autobiography in my own work (Goodman, M. 2014) as a way to explore the multiple and conflicting ethical and moral character of eating and food choice. Clearly, my opening to this chapter, successful or not, was designed to highlight the possibilities of this approach and showcase how it might contain within it academic potential and social relevance.

Further, more and better autoethnography in our work on the bioeconomies of eating food is not merely a conceit of the privileged or a solipsistic exercise that remains in the realms of the personal. Rather it suggests that this shift to eaters and eating is taken seriously, as we too are people who eat and engage with food on a daily basis. As Longhurst (2011: 872) suggests, exploring and critiquing our own embodied geographies as eaters can work, as in her case and in her words, to 'offer an account that positions my paradoxical experiences as central to my critical scholarship on fat bodies'. Autobiography can, in Longhurst's (2011: 875) words, produce powerful writing that can 'combine cultural analysis with stories of the self, resulting in thick description that helps to further understand individuals' and groups' (that is, eaters' in this case) lives'. Insurgent autobiography is key here. This is a form of autoethnography that works to destabilise and question dominant assumptions about eating and being an eater and is well positioned to develop a critical voice to the current state of food politics. In this, enactive and enlivened bioeconomies – something this book calls for – could and indeed might just start with ourselves and our own experiences as eaters.

Acknowledgements

Many thanks to Nick Lewis and Richard Le Heron, but especially Hugh Campbell, for providing me with this space in addition to their editorial and personal support in putting this chapter together. Portions of this chapter build on ideas that did not make the cut from my *Progress in Human Geography* food geographies review (Goodman, M. 2015) and my chapter in my Ashgate volume with Colin Sage (2014) entitled *Food Transgressions* (Goodman, M. 2014). More broadly, though, I have been personally inspired by the diverse and exciting writings and theorisations of a number of amazing scholars exploring what it means to eat and be an eater: Annemarie Mol, Allison and Jessica Hayes-Conroy, Josée Johnston, Mike Carolan, Julie Guthman, Becky Mansfield, Elspeth Probyn, Robyn Longhurst, Rachel Colls, Bethany Evans, David Bell, David Goodman, Colin Sage, Ben Coles, Emma-Jayne Abbots and Anna Lavis. I am greatly in their intellectual debt here (and elsewhere), and our various and (body) multiple engagements, conversations and encounters must to be given their full due!

Notes

1 For more in this vein, see FitzSimmons and Goodman (1998).
2 For more contemporary but equally inspiring work on food and bodies, see the collections of Abbots and Lavis (2013b) and Abbots et al. (2015).
3 Many have been concerned with the vital materialisms in the context of bodily health and well-being for a quite a while now (see Hayes-Conroy, A. and Hayes-Conroy 2013, Hayes-Conroy, J. and Hayes-Conroy 2013 and Mansfield 2008 for more).
4 And while I don't have space to elaborate this here I would argue that food documentaries and investigative reporting are among the key ways we have been able to uncover and learn about Robbins's (2014) 'cries from along the chain of accumulation' and those for food specifically.

References

Abbots, E. (2011) '"It doesn't taste as good from the pet shop": guinea pig consumption and the performance of class and kinship in highland Ecuador and New York City', *Food, Culture and Society*, vol. 14, no. 2, pp. 205–224.
Abbots, E. (2013a) 'The substance of absence: exploring eating and anorexia', in E. Abbots and A. Lavis (eds), *Why We Eat, How We Eat: Contemporary Encounters between Foods and Bodies*, Ashgate, Farnham, pp. 35–52.
Abbots, E. (2013b) 'Negotiating foreign bodies: migration, trust and the risky business of eating in highland Ecuador', in E. Abbots and A. Lavis (eds), *Why We Eat, How We Eat: Contemporary Encounters between Foods and Bodies*, Ashgate, Farnham, pp. 119–138.
Abbots, E. (2015a) 'Caring about careless eating: class politics, governance and the production of otherness in highland Ecuador', in E. Abbots, A. Lavis and L. Attala (eds), *Careful Eating: Bodies, Food and Care*, Ashgate, Farnham, pp. 69–88.
Abbots, E. (2015b) 'The intimacies of industry: consumer interactions with the "stuff" of celebrity chefs', *Food, Culture and Society*, vol. 18, no. 2, pp. 223–244.
Abbots, E. (forthcoming) *The Agency of Eating*, Bloomsbury, London.
Abbots, E. and Attala, L. (2015) 'It's not what you eat but how and that you eat: social media, counter-discourses and disciplined ingestion among amateur competitive eaters', *Geoforum*, DOI: 10.1016/j.geoforum.2014.11.004.
Abbots, E. and Lavis, A. (2013a) 'Introduction: contours of eating: mapping the terrain of body/food encounters', in E. Abbots and A. Lavis (eds), *Why We Eat, How We Eat: Contemporary Encounters between Foods and Bodies*, Ashgate, Farnham, pp. 1–12.
Abbots, E. and Lavis, A. (eds) (2013b) *Why We Eat, How We Eat: Contemporary Encounters between Foods and Bodies*, Ashgate, Farnham.
Abbots, E., Lavis, A. and Attala, L. (eds) (2015) *Careful Eating: Bodies, Food and Care*, Ashgate, Farnham.
Alkon, A. (2013) 'The socio-nature of local organic food', *Antipode*, vol. 45, no. 3, pp. 663–680.
Appadurai, A. (ed.) (1986) *The Social Life of Things*, Cambridge University Press, Cambridge.
Barnes, C. (2015) 'Mediating good food and moments of possibility with Jamie Oliver: problematising celebrity chefs as talking labels', *Geoforum*, doi:10.1016/j.geoforum.2014.09.004.

Barnett, C., Cloke, P., Clarke, N. and Malpass, A. (2011) *Globalizing Responsibility: The Political Rationalities of Ethical Consumption*, Blackwell, London.

Belasco, W. (2009) *Food: The Key Concepts*, Berg, London.

Bell, D. and Hollows, J. (2011) 'From *River Cottage* to *Chicken Run*: Hugh Fearnley-Whittingstall and the class politics of ethical consumption', *Celebrity Studies*, vol. 2, no. 2, pp. 178–191.

Bell, D., Hollows, J. and Jones, S. (2015) 'Campaigning culinary documentaries and the responsibilization of food crises', *Geoforum*, DOI:10.1016/j.geoforum.2015.03.014.

Bennett, J. (2007) 'Edible matter', *New Left Review*, vol. 45, pp. 133–145.

Bennett, J. (2010) *Vibrant Matter: A Political Ecology of Things*, Duke University Press, London.

Braun, B. (2011) 'Book review forum: *Vibrant Matter: A Political Ecology of Things*', *Dialogues in Human Geography*, vol. 1, no. 3, pp. 390–405.

Buchanan, R. (2015) 'Fast food can make you depressed and unable to control your emotions, new study suggests', *The Independent*, http://www.independent.co.uk/life-style/health-and-families/fast-food-can-make-you-depressed-and-unable-to-control-your-emotions-new-study-suggests-10339017.html.

Carolan, M. (2011) *Embodied Food Politics*, Ashgate, Aldershot.

Clarke, N., Cloke, P., Barnett, C. and Malpass, A. (2008) 'The spaces and ethics of organic food', *Journal of Rural Studies*, vol. 24, pp. 219–230.

Coles, B. (2014) 'Making the market place: a topography of Borough Market, London', *Cultural Geographies*, vol. 21, pp. 515–523.

Coles, B. and Crang, P. (2011) 'Placing alternative consumption: commodity fetishism in Borough Fine Foods Market, London', in T. Lewis and E. Potter (eds), *Ethical Consumption: A Critical Introduction*, Routledge, London, pp. 87–102.

Colls, R. (2007) 'Materialising bodily matter: intra-action and the embodiment of "fat"', *Geoforum*, vol. 38, pp. 353–365.

Colls, R. and Evans, B. (2014) 'Making space for fat bodies? A critical account of "the obesogenic environment"', *Progress in Human Geography*, vol. 38, no. 6, pp. 733–753.

Cook, I. et al. (2004) 'Follow the thing: papaya', *Antipode*, vol. 36, pp. 642–664.

de Solier, I. (2013) *Food and the Self: Consumption, Production and Material Culture*, Bloomsbury, London.

Evans, B., Colls, R. and Horschelmann, K. (2011) '"Change4Life for your kids": embodied collectives and public health pedagogy', *Sport, Education and Society*, vol. 16, no. 3, pp. 323–341.

FitzSimmons, M. and Goodman, D. (1998) 'Incorporating nature: environmental narratives and the reproduction of food', in B. Braun and N. Castree (eds), *Remaking Reality: Nature at the Millennium*, Routledge, London.

Goodman, D. (1999) 'Agro-food studies in the "age of ecology": nature, corporeality, biopolitics', *Sociologia Ruralis*, vol. 39, pp. 17–38.

Goodman, D. and DuPuis, M. (2002) 'Knowing and growing food: beyond the production–consumption debate in the sociology of agriculture', *Sociologia Ruralis*, vol. 42, vol. 1, pp. 6–23.

Goodman, M. (2014) 'Eating powerful transgressions: (re)assessing the spaces and ethics of organic food in the UK', in M. Goodman and C. Sage (eds), *Food Transgressions: Making Sense of Contemporary Food Politics*, Ashgate, Aldershot, pp. 109–130.

Goodman, M. (2015) 'Food geographies I: relational foodscapes and the busy-ness of being more-than-food', *Progress in Human Geography*, DOI: 10.1177/0309132515570192.

Guthman, J. (2011) *Weighing In: Obesity, Food Justice and the Limits of Capitalism*, University of California Press, Berkeley.

Guthman, J. and DuPuis, E. M. (2006) 'Embodying neoliberalism: economy, culture and the politics of fat', *Environment and Planning D: Society and Space*, vol. 24, pp. 427–448.

Guthman, J. and Mansfield, B. (2012) 'The implications of environmental epigenetics: a new direction for geographic inquiry on health, space and nature–society relations', *Progress in Human Geography*, vol. 3, no. 4, pp. 486–504.

Hayes-Conroy, A. (2010) 'Feeling Slow Food: visceral fieldwork and empathetic research relations in the alternative food movement', *Geoforum*, vol. 41, pp. 734–742.

Hayes-Conroy, A. and Hayes-Conroy, J. (2008) 'Taking back taste: feminism, food and visceral politics', *Gender, Place and Culture*, vol. 15, no. 5, pp. 461–473.

Hayes-Conroy, A. and Hayes-Conroy, J. (2010) 'Visceral difference: variations in feeling (slow) food', *Environment and Planning A*, vol. 42, pp. 2956–2971.

Hayes-Conroy, A. and Hayes-Conroy, J. (eds) (2013) *Doing Nutrition Differently: Critical Approaches to Diet and Dietary Intervention*, Ashgate, Farnham.

Hayes-Conroy, J. and Hayes-Conroy, A. (2010) 'Visceral geographies: mattering, relating and defying', *Geography Compass*, vol. 4, no. 9, pp. 1273–1282.

Hayes-Conroy, J. and Hayes-Conroy, A. (2013) 'Veggies and visceralities: a political ecology of food and feeling', *Emotion, Space and Society*, vol. 6, pp. 81–90.

Hollows, J. and Jones, S. (2010a) '"At least he's doing something": moral entrepreneurship and individual responsibility in Jamie's Ministry of Food', *European Journal of Cultural Studies*, vol. 13, no. 3, pp. 307–322.

Hollows, J. and Jones, S. (2010b) 'Please don't try this at home: Heston Blumenthal, cookery TV and the culinary field', *Food, Culture and Society*, vol. 13, no. 4, pp. 521–537.

Johnston, J. and Baumann, S. (2010) *Foodies: Democracy and Distinction in the Gourmet Foodscape*, Routledge, London.

Johnston, J. and Goodman, M. (2015) 'Spectacular foodscapes: food celebrities and the politics of lifestyle mediation in an age of inequality', *Food, Culture and Society*, vol. 18, no. 2, pp. 205–222.

Johnston, J. and Szabo, M. (2011) 'Reflexivity and the whole foods market consumer: the lived experience of shopping for change', *Agriculture and Human Values*, vol. 28, no. 3, pp. 303–319.

Johnston, J., Szabo, M. and Rodney, A. (2011) 'Good food, good people: understanding the cultural repertoire of ethical eating', *Journal of Consumer Culture*, vol. 11, no. 3, pp. 293–318.

Johnston, J., Rodney, A. and Szabo, M. (2012) 'Place, ethics, and everyday eating: a tale of two neighbourhoods', *Sociology*, vol. 46, no. 6, pp. 1091–1108.

Kneafsey, M., Holloway, L., Cox, R., Dowler, E., Venn, L. and Tuomainen, H. (2008) *Reconnecting Consumers, Producers and Food: Exploring Alternatives*, Berg, Oxford.

Lambie-Mumford, H. (2013) '"Every town should have one": emergency food banking in the UK', *Journal of Social Policy*, vol. 42, no. 1, pp. 73–89.

Lambie-Mumford, H., Crossley, D., Jensen, E., Verbeke, M. and Dowler, E. (2014) 'Household food security in the UK: a review of food aid, final report', Defra, https://www.gov.uk/government/uploads/system/uploads/attachment_data/file/283071/household-food-security-uk-140219.pdf.

Latour, B. (1993) *We Have Never Been Modern*, Harvester Wheatsheaf, Brighton.

Lavis, A. (2014) 'Engrossing encounters: materialities and metaphors of fat in the lived experiences of individuals with anorexia', in C. Forth and A. Leitch (eds), *Fat: Culture and Materiality*, Bloomsbury, London.

Lavis, A. (2015a) 'Careful starving: reflections on (not) eating, caring and anorexia', in E. Abbots, A. Lavis and L. Attala (eds), *Careful Eating: Bodies, Food and Care*, Ashgate, Farnham.

Lavis, A. (2015b) 'Food porn, pro-anorexia and the viscerality of virtual affect: exploring eating in cyberspace', *Geoforum*, DOI: 10.1016/j.geoforum.2015.05.014.

Longhurst, R. (2011) 'Becoming smaller: autobiographical spaces of weight loss', *Antipode*, vol. 44, no. 3, pp. 871–888.

Longhurst, R., Johnston, L. and Ho, E. (2009) 'A visceral approach: cooking "at home" with migrant women in Hamilton, New Zealand', *Transactions of the Institute of British Geographers*, vol. 34, pp. 333–345.

Lupton, D. (1996) *Food, the Body and the Self*, Sage, London.

MacKendrick, N. (2014) 'Foodscapes', *Contexts*, vol. 13, pp. 16–18.

Mansfield, B. (2008) 'Health as a nature–society question', *Environment and Planning A*, vol. 40, no. 5, pp. 1015–1019.

Mol, A. (2008) 'I eat an apple: on theorising subjectives', *Subjectivity*, vol. 22, pp. 28–37.

Murdoch, J. (1997) 'Towards a geography of heterogeneous associations', *Progress in Human Geography*, vol. 21, no. 3, pp. 321–337.

Murdoch, J., Marsden, T. and Banks, J. (2000) 'Quality, nature, and embeddedness: some theoretical considerations in the context of the food sector', *Economic Geography*, vol. 76, no. 2, pp. 107–125.

Owen, J. (2015) 'Sugary drinks are killing 184,000 adults around the world every year, says study', *The Independent*, http://www.independent.co.uk/life-style/health-and-families/health-news/sugary-drinks-are-killing-184000-adults-around-the-world-every-year-says-study-10353449.html.

Piper, N. (2013) 'Audiencing Jamie Oliver: embarrassment, voyeurism and reflexive positioning', *Geoforum*, vol. 45, pp. 346–355.

Piper, N. (2015) 'Jamie Oliver and cultural intermediation', *Food, Culture and Society*, vol. 18, no. 2, pp. 245–264.

Potter, L. and Westall, C. (2013) 'Neoliberal Britain's austerity foodscape: home economics, veg patch capitalism and culinary temporality', *New Formations*, vols 80–81, pp. 155–178.

Probyn, E. (2000) *Carnal Appetites: Food, Sex, Identities*, Routledge, London.

Probyn, E. (2012) 'Eating roo: of things that become food', *New Formations*, vol. 74, pp. 33–45.

Quorn (2015) 'Sustainable development report', http://www.quorn.co.uk/sustainability/.

Robbins, P. (2014) 'Cries along the chain of accumulation', *Geoforum*, vol. 54, pp. 233–235.

Sayer, A. (2011) *Why Things Matter to People: Social Sciences, Values and Ethical Life*, Cambridge University Press, Cambridge.

Slocum, R., Shannon, J., Cadieux, K. and Beckman, M. (2011) '"Properly, with love, from scratch": Jamie Oliver's food revolution', *Radical History Review*, vol. 110, pp. 178–191.

Valentine, G. (1999) 'A corporeal geography of consumption', *Environment and Planning D: Society and Space*, vol. 17, pp. 329–351.

Valentine, G. (2002) 'In-corporations: food, bodies and organizations', *Body and Society*, vol. 8, no. 2, pp. 1–20.

Wheeler, K. (2012) *Fair Trade and the Citizen-Consumer*, Palgrave Macmillan, Basingstoke.

18 Conclusion

Biological economies as an academic and political project

Hugh Campbell, Richard Le Heron, Nick Lewis and Michael Carolan

The intention of this book has been to provide a site where scholars from many parts of the world might bring together a cluster of ideas around the intellectual project of biological economies. At the start of this gathering process (as outlined in Chapter 1), a series of projects, teams, conference sessions and other discussions had repeatedly come around to one (or more) of three new theoretical and methodological insights as being important to our understanding of economic worlds of food, farming, and rural change: the more-than-human, post-structural political economy (PSPE), and the new politics of enactive research strategies. As time passed, however, and these discussions became even more animated, the idea of biological economies emerged as something that is more than just a meeting place for scholars interested in one of these three sites of new thinking. Rather, it became something that promised to generate insight through the combination of these three new areas of discussion into one wide-ranging and (hopefully) productive conversation.

This book is the result of that wider conversation. It doesn't represent the totality of scholars of agri-food worlds who might be interested in the more-than-human, PSPE or enactive research strategies, but it has brought together enough of us to make it a site where the generative potential of combining all three new trajectories can be experienced. We wish to reflect on how useful this 'collective' impulse in its multiple forms has been in two (linked) ways.

First, we do so by examining the key themes, ideas and critiques that link many, if not all, of the chapters in ways that mark them as different or disruptive of taken-for-granted ideas in our framing and production of academic knowledge about agri-food worlds. We want to know whether our speculative assembling and experimenting through these three areas of insight actually do useful work across a whole body of work. In this sense, we are interested in the potential of biological economies as an academic project – a place where linked ideas come to be placed together, reworked and reassembled into new ways of changing the world – which brings us to the second point of examination.

We want to examine biological economies in a second kind of way: as a political project. In Chapter 13, Michael M. Bell challenges all the scholars gathering in this space to give urgent and particular attention to the politics and values being generated, resisted, transformed and enacted in this kind of discussion. His challenge is that all epistemological projects are also political projects, a point endorsed by Michael Carolan (Chapter 16), who insists that they are and should at the same time be moral projects. Even the most sterile empirical agricultural science was nevertheless highly politically consequential through its expressed disavowal of any political or values influences. We don't want to make the same omission, and a number of chapters in this collection directly promote the overt recognition of the politics and values (and processes and practices which enable or suppress these) inherent in our work. These ambitions take us into new interpretive territory where we are able to discuss the book as more than the sum of its parts.

The key themes in the book

1 Post-structural political economy

This book contains a lot of work that has been directly or indirectly influenced by authors like J. K. Gibson-Graham (1996, 2006) who began to question the categorical and essentialist causality attributed to the classic political economy account of capitalism, in which they were trained, and by a new generation of younger academics, whose background is often informed by natureculture ideas and the more-than-human. PSPE is both a critique and an opportunity: breaking existing categories of political economy-influenced analysis open in order to find smaller economies, other networks of actors, the communities of value creation, and a diminished interest in State and (capitalist) Economy in favour of governance, governmentality, spaces, processes and flows. Many of the chapters in this collection are influenced by such critique, its politics of knowledge making, and the re-formatting of knowledge that this implies. They reach for PSPE, whether in name or simply inspiration, to contextualize richer empirical accounts of situated development, but do not slip into totalizing narratives.

To use some examples, David Evans (Chapter 2) deconstructs the idea of the food consumer as a category for explaining a whole set of practices and replaces it with a more relational set of multiple practices and partners in order to situate and understand household food practices. His primary aim is to remove those categories that obscure other relations (like the production-centric approach of much agri-food work) or a simple notion of 'consumption' and open up space to see more relational realms of practice. Gareth Enticott (Chapter 3) examines the small democracies of knowledge built up between farmers, animals, vets and scientific testing regimes that reached workable understandings of TB and its incidence (and thus prevention) that contrasted with interpretations that opted to privilege big actors like the State or big governance projects like neoliberalism. Janka Linke (Chapter 4) introduces the world of caterpillar fungus harvesting in Tibet to supply the needs of traditional medicine markets (and expensive food additives) in urban China. At one level, her chapter is a traditional juxtaposition of small-scale peasant herders undertaking an arduous (but lucrative) task crawling through alpine pastures in Tibet to collect the fungus, while urban-based corporate biopharmaceutical businesses strive to substitute the natural fungus with industrial alternatives. However, inside this story is a series of smaller stories as to why only one corporate actor has been successful, and the unusual strategies and actors enrolled in that success, while the nomadic herders continue to maintain their own complex community economy. Jérémie Forney (Chapter 5) engages one of the big structuring categories of political economy (and political activism) by demonstrating the inadequacy of the industrial/corporate versus cooperative/local binary to understand the economic and cultural dynamics of new cheese varieties in Switzerland. He avoids the binary structural trap by examining simultaneously two cheese ontologies, one realizing the world of neoliberalized market relations, while the other realizes cooperative relations between small-scale economic actors, growing environments, local cultures and the cheeses themselves. Angga Dwiartama and his co-authors (Chapter 6) question the usefulness of traditional Green Revolution-inspired development models to truly explain worlds of rice in Indonesia. Matthew Henry and Michael Roche (Chapter 7) provide a historically grounded exposition of colonial economies of meat. It is orthodox in every way, until they radically reframe the trade, from that which concerned farms and abattoirs in New Zealand, carcasses, ships, and marketplaces in Britain, into that which also concerns economies of taste for meat. They thoroughly disrupt the usual categories for economically understanding the colonial meat trade and use this disruption as a launching point for a completely new way of understanding the 'stabilization' of economic worlds of meat.

All of these chapters have the opportunity to mobilize standard categories of political economy – State, capitalism, Empire/colony, labour, regions, industries, sectors, markets, supply chains, neoliberalism – but chose to make these, if mentioned at all, minor actors in their narrative: choosing rather to pull aside the big categories and reveal the many small economies and complex networks that explain what lies outside the formally explained economy, or which are actually constitutive of those economic relations that we often describe using the shorthand of 'categories'. Their contributions reveal much about how the absence of bigger-picture overviews allows new connections, relations and practices to be pushed into view around things like TB, rice, cheese, the taste of meat, household food practices, and the curious fungus that grows inside caterpillars in alpine pastures in Tibet.

2 The more-than-human

If Gibson-Graham represent one set of key shared influences, even more influential in the work across this whole volume are the legacies of Bruno Latour (2005), John Law and his actor–network theory (ANT) colleagues (Mol 1999; Law 2002; Law and Urry 2004; Lien and Law 2011) and Jane Bennett (2009).

Collectively, these scholars talk about worlds in which this shift from categories to relations cannot be restricted to economic worlds alone, and point to how the insights derived from a focus on things in the chapters of this book extend to the significance of their 'thinginess' itself and the 'mattering' of their matter. On a broader canvas, human actors are de-centred and the non-human or, more recently, more-than-human contributors to the assembling of economic, environmental and social worlds are revealed. The more-than-human epistemological project has obvious relevance to an academic project that so explicitly names itself as *biological* economies.

This is borne out in the almost total engagement of chapters with more-than-human assembling. Janka Linke's (Chapter 4) Tibetan caterpillar fungus attributes considerable agency to both the caterpillars and their fungal invader in shaping much larger worlds of economic action. Jérémie Forney's (Chapter 5) Swiss cheeses have an essential cheesy-ness that anchors particular cheese ontologies, and Gareth Enticott's (Chapter 3) vets are vets with bodies, and the technologies of testing interact with human (and animal) bodies to create a workable regime of disease control. Henry and Roche's (Chapter 7) meat is 'meat as tasted and eaten'. Its economies are aligned with (changing and manipulated) regimes of embodied human taste. Along the same lines Angga Dwiartama and colleagues (Chapter 6) tell a story of village worlds of rice in Indonesia in which one particular rice variety sits as the key agent, along with small 'finger knives', climates, geographies and other local economic actors, to situate rice at the heart of life in rural Indonesia. Harvey C. Perkins and Eric Pawson (Chapter 10) unfold a global-scale economic assemblage which revolves around the fineness of a particular kind of wool (and the package of measures that standardize and order economic activity around merino wool). Roseanna M. Spiers and Nick Lewis (Chapter 8) introduce a vibrant network of actors including bees, beekeepers, plants and hives to show how the potentials of the bee–honey network are shaped by the actions of non-human species and material objects.

This broadening and deepening of the more-than-human disrupts the usual economic narrative of how value is created, how economic actors come together, how institutions form around economic activity, and how economic activity is regulated and controlled by introducing other non-human actors like caterpillars, rice and cheese, and the introduction of human bodies into the mix: vets' bodies, or human taste buds. The unlikely objects and the relationalities of qualities that distinguish them offer new foundations for the scripting of fresh metaphors and accompanying narratives.

It is important, however, to take an even bigger step towards the de-centring of economic networks by introducing not only other familiar food actors like rice and cheese, but also the other vital materials that Jane Bennett suggests are undervalued in our explanations. For example, Matthew Henry and Michael Roche (Chapter 7) point to the world of standards and measures (metrologies) that allow tastes to be stabilized, Perkins and Pawson (Chapter 10) do the same for the measurement and stabilization of fine wool,

Dwiartama and colleagues (Chapter 6) have a little 'finger knife' in the skilled hands of an Indonesian peasant as the vital other to particular kinds of rice, while Spiers and Lewis (Chapter 8) encounter and contemplate the design of the Langstroth beehive.

This kind of vital materiality also influences a number of other chapters. Katharine Legun (Chapter 9) re-narrates the development of a celebrated variety of apple through an analysis focused on the quality of 'redness'. It is a distinctly different way to understand the actors and assemblages that constitute industrial production regimes. Michael K. Goodman (Chapter 17) examines the aesthetics of food packaging, the colours, shapes and images that are relationally bound to the act of eating junk food. David Evans (Chapter 2) brings us the vital materiality of waste: a category of matter, of ex-food, that disrupts and remakes worlds of consumption. Once revealed in these terms, food waste becomes vital material made visible, where in both the world of consumption and that of academic narrative it was previously rendered invisible.

3 Experimentation and the enactive: bringing the economic and methodological to politics and values

Established categories of political economy tend to tie down or occlude either moral or political positions or both a priori and are largely empty of actual agents. In moving away from such categories, and by adding in a range of other actors and materials that both enhance and render somewhat more messy the economic networks and assemblages that constitute economic worlds, we then are confronted by questions of the politics and moral grounds of research. This is not only a logical extension of the deconstruction of previous stable categories that underpinned orthodox (and left-leaning) political critique; it also comes from the epistemological project of post-structuralism more generally. We can't pretend to hide behind detached worlds of observation, commentary and critique. Neither can we rely on the old categories to help explain this world.

Both the PSPE initiative and the turn to more-than-human agency charge our thinking to consider what it means to couple the many into macro-accounts of economic and ecological context. As we have argued elsewhere (Lewis et al. 2013), a powerful opening up comes from knowing so much more of situated agency. The situatedness methodology flows into epistemological re-crafting and ontological questioning. Asking about for whom and to whom we are speaking, why we believe we have entitlement to make such connections and representations, and how we undertake these activities become matters that compel rethinking around the political and moral. Esbjörn-Hargens (2010) provides a valuable insight into these relations by emphasizing the co-constitutiveness of the three big questions in research: who is asking (epistemology), how (methodology) and about what (ontology). To these, we add some additional big 'W's (see Lewis and Rosin 2013): 'why and for whom' (politics and morality) and 'where and when' (situatedness). Although not explicitly including the more-than-human, this enhanced Esbjörn-Hargens framing encourages us to assemble a number of interdependent threads: a recognition of the otherwise, in the spirit of J. K. Gibson-Graham; an imperative to the moral politics of research a la Carolan by foregrounding the question of 'for whom'; and a further imperative to practise a moral economy by delving into the immediate by 'de-distancing' and highlighting moral sentiments as in Jackson et al.'s (2009) conceptions of 'consumer anxiety'.

This call to be multiply situated is a disposition that encourages us, as we suggested in Chapter 1, to confront what it might mean to think and act morally in the Anthropocene. We will return to the Anthropocene later in this discussion. Significantly our engagement with Esbjörn-Hargens has taught us to see that there are two idealized routes by which politics and moral matters are entwined – the idea that politics springs from moral positions, and the idea that moral positions emerge from politics. The former suggests a production of political knowledge guided, and possibly depoliticized, by a priori positions. The latter exposes the ways in which the moral is often deployed to justify business as usual: either the business of critique distanced by clumpy categories or by dispassionate micro-analytics; or the business of reproducing the status quo by policy. The two offer starkly different experimental and enactive mentalities, something that Noel Castree and colleagues have argued about in their *Nature Climate Change* paper (2014) calling for a change in the intellectual climate. Understood more openly as co-constitutive, however, the two thrusts direct us to sketch out our value positions, in terms of the details of their transformative potentialities, and what that actually means for whom and so on. They point instead to emergent potentiality, which is not the same thing as a politically compromised morality.

We realize that to speak of moral and political questions in one breath is a great leap into the unknown for many of those who regard themselves as agri-fooders. Teasing apart moral and political moves in political projects of knowledge making in this way made us very nervous. We may have accepted and adopted increasingly nuanced political strategies, but, as Gibson-Graham (2006) forewarn, to veer into the apparent maws of moral issues is discomforting for scholars. However, we now recognize that the institutional configuration of knowledge and politics in any context invites efforts to make space for other agency on agri-food agendas. The interplay of the moral and the political is always present in making knowledge about directions for the future; knowledge making around investment and consumption is agentic (economies are moral economies), and strategies to reveal the nature and effects of means are political (economy is political). These distinctions and their situated interconnections force us to answer, with situated others, why we are engaging in enactive research, what makes our academic experimentation worth performing, and what sensed futures we are committing ourselves to.

To explain this kind of thematic transition, Chapter 12 by Le Heron and collaborators on an alternative soils movement provides illustrative material.

Recognizing the hegemonic or monolithic presence of the industrial chemical farming complex in the heart of many agricultural regimes, how do alternatives form? This is usually answered through questions of scale (local versus global) or institution (for example corporate versus cooperative). In the biological agriculture movement, these authors find an assemblage of actors centred around a reframing of the semiotics and science of soils. The embodied experiences of farmers and cows, global policy discussions, the development of new assays and measures, the position of charismatic scientists, and the all-important actions of soils themselves as living entities assemble a counter-project to industrial chemical farming. Where this analysis goes beyond the prior themes of PSPE and/or introducing the more-than-human qualities of something like soil is that these authors interrogate the role of the researchers (including themselves) and other scientists as actors in the political worlds of knowledge production around soils. A similar narrative can be found in Rosanna M. Spiers and Nick Lewis's (Chapter 8) account about the expertise of bees, their experimental adjustment to hives, and human apprehension of these qualities and features. Here the researchers see their activities and the material objects of their research as participating in the opening up of possible futures. They point to seemingly inert objects like charts and tables in which they connected the networks and multiple causalities of biological agriculture as doing potentially important work in influencing the trajectory of alternative economies. In this, they recognize the call by Philip Lowe (2010) (and Law and Urry 2004) for researchers to be more aware of the enactive powers of research to unmake and make the categories by which actors understand and represent their worlds.

A similar spirit infuses Stock et al.'s (Chapter 11) consideration of insect eating (entomophagy) or, more precisely, the specific dynamics of a political project to enact more possibilities for entomophagy by a group of students in London. In this narrative, not only do the authors see themselves as giving recognition (and thus political oxygen) to an interesting new start-up, but the politics of insect eating are clearly situated within the idea of economic *experimentation* and are enveloped in deeply moral attitudes and morally inflected perceptions.

Once we recognize the spaces that sit outside mainstream economies – be they biological agriculture, harvesting caterpillar fungus, or new ontologies of cheese – we also have to recognize that the traditional explanations and categories of how change comes to economic worlds need much reworking. In a world where the more-than-human are key actors, where metrologies re-order economic networks and economic processes flow and assemble outside the mainstream, where human bodies, household consumption practices, and wild ecologies of species like bees and apples hold the potential to disrupt and cohere, the idea of experimentation suggests a different way to understand how economic worlds are stabilized and destabilized.

Many of the chapters are interrogating and, at times, enabling economic experimentation. New cheeses, eating insects, building beehives, re-tuning human taste buds: these all speak to new forms of experimentation, with new connections, networks and potentials. This leads to a further insight on the need not only to recognize where experimentation is happening but also to evolve our methodological approaches to match experimental economic worlds. As an example, Chapter 11 studies one start-up project in London that runs a variety of publicity events to introduce people to eating insects, but actually has no commercial products on the market. It is an exercise in re-designing options and opening possibilities for future action around food security. The political and experimental qualities of the group – ENTO – mean that researchers must engage and evaluate (and enact) based not only on what is, and its often undeclared moral economy, but also on what might be and what it is hoped will be, views that spring from explicit and implicit moral underpinnings. The methodological ask then combines new moral explorations and the politics of experimentation based on the clarification of horizons and possibilities that might give content to differing horizons. This is no straightforward question of writing a case study.

There are a cluster of chapters that start to map out how far down this path we should go. One of the most interesting things about reflecting on this collection is how many different chapters reached the watershed of intertwined moral and political directions, but arrived down multiple different theoretical, epistemological and methodological pathways. Michael M. Bell (Chapter 13) put it most bluntly: politics is in your face every time you eat! Michael Carolan (Chapter 16) elaborates Burawoy's call for 'public sociology' by calling for all-out engagement and enactment by agri-food scholars. Michael K. Goodman (Chapter 17) argues for a political reorientation around a world of eaters. We pitch beyond this when we suggest that the manner in which politics and moral economies are conceptualized will have to be faced in the Anthropocene.

Some took other pathways. Chapter 12 on soils is a subtle and complex account of how alternative agriculture might flourish, but it is also unashamedly moral and political: it is about how alternatives form and contest the problematic mainstream, and how a bit of methodological experimentation might help enact that alternative. In a similar way, the eating of insects (Chapter 11) is explicitly engaged as a political and value proposition. It is a potential solution to global food insecurity. It is therefore a utopian project we want to encourage.

Two chapters make this kind of more morally grounded politics the centre of their narrative and challenge. Le Heron et al. (Chapter 14) embroil themselves in the intellectual emergence and experimental methodologies (and thus moral positions and politics) of doing a particular kind of intellectual project, biological economies, in New Zealand. They provide vignettes of attempts to link the framing of value propositions or moral positions to debate over means at the level of practices. The variety of their disruptive experiments in thought encourages them to prioritize wherever possible an open assembling approach that puts aside, in whatever form the experimentation might take, existing categories. Instead they contend that the strategy of situated assembling of a selection of myriad possible contextual narratives is a first methodological step in framing up possible pathways to different futures. Rosin et al. (Chapter 15), in a similar strategy, invoke the utopias project in current scholarship to assert strongly that scholars should not only study utopian thinking but enact utopian projects. Utopias do not sit outside daily practice. They help make explicit the political and value or moral propositions that set desirable goals, define dystopian futures to be avoided, and encourage methodological experimentation to step outside stifling ontological frameworks, and into the rethinking of possible worlds. The application of this can be clearly seen in the relevance of utopian thinking and doing in the context of the ENTO experiment in London (Chapter 11).

What we want to go on to talk about is that all these chapters also cohere around a political and epistemological project that Carolan (Chapter 16) advocates in arguing for a bit of wildness in agri-food studies. This is a call to recognize the embodied quality of being an eater as well as a scholar. It is also a call to recognize that agri-food worlds are wild, they are vital, they are material, and they are thus encountered at both a visceral and an intellectual level by scholars. In the world of wild agri-food studies, predictable categories are going to be much less useful than a bit of experimentation. But it also wilds up the separation of knowledge production from political and value propositions (as demonstrated by so many of the chapters in this collection). This ushers in the second key question in this concluding chapter: what is biological economies as a political project?

Biological economies as a political project

There is something more needed than just a recognition that all our work, our scholarly practices, and the worlds with which we engage are saturated in more or less visible political claims, and moral values and valuations. When groups of scholars come into dialogue, when conversations start, when projects assemble and when relationships cohere between researchers and other participants in economic worlds, we are potentially creating something greater than just a space where politics and values get transacted and enacted. We have the potential effect of being a political project, what Larner et al. (2007) define as an alignment of agencies, relations and strategic narratives. For example, even if the empirical dissection of neoliberalism reveals a myriad of small practices and projects that might struggle to be seen as a coherent entity, there is a more coherent political project of neoliberalization. When the new rural sociology and new rural geography took shape in the 1980s around a set of novel theoretical insights into the relationship between capitalism and agriculture, this was both a theoretical project and a political project. The new science initiatives around GMOs that sought to dramatically reframe the style of science, the valuation of kinds of scientific 'product', and the structure of institutions, and (in a utopian sense) to change the set of possibilities of the future of the planet can be best understood as a political project. To use the insights of convention theory, there was a set of justifications and identification of desired 'goods' and undesirable 'bads' that created coherence around myriad component practices, processes and knowledge claims in each of these projects.

So can we understand biological economies as a (somewhat smaller) political project?

First, the main political progenitor of many of the theoretical ideas that act as the precursor to the ideas being discussed here is structural political economy. As a political project it was defined as anti-capitalist, anti-different kinds of national development, anti-corporate, anti-big, anti-neoliberal, and pro-collective, pro-socially embedded, pro-local and (maybe) pro-environment. This formed the sea in which many of us learned politically and intellectually to swim. The insights of PSPE, ANT and other 'post' approaches to the structural traditions of political economy have been the source of considerable political angst and fear that such transitions have blunted the political critique of earlier approaches (as demonstrated by the hugely significant debate over the content and consequences of David Goodman and Michael Watts's collection *Globalising Food* in 1997 as well as the polarizing effect of Gibson-Graham's *The End of Capitalism (As We Knew It)* (1996)). All the chapters in this volume, and the collection of shared themes and approaches listed above, mark the work of biological economies as being very different to the political economy project that gave birth to much of its early scholarship.

We've already itemized the various ways in which scholarly theorizing, epistemic approaches and framing mark biological economies as different to structural political economy. So how does it constitute a distinctive political project that differs, for example, from political ecology, which has also challenged the explanatory and political capabilities of political economy as a platform for enacting change in response to the parlous state of the capitalist world, and built a political and moral project on rendering more explicit the environmental dynamics and consequences of capitalist development? We see four formative lines of difference that make biological economies something other than an alternative project to put the environment back into discussions of economy and inequality: an emphasis on difference power to complement the critique of dominance power and foster new political imagination; a radical de-centring of economy; a recognition of the increasing ontological, epistemological and methodological instability of 'the environment'; and an openness of ontological stance founded on the constitutive centrality of experimentation in thought and practice. These lines of difference help us to give content to what we claim is a distinctive, albeit far from formalized, political project of biological economies:

1 Biological economies pays close attention to 'difference power' as well as dominance power (Carolan 2013), and in so doing transcends a narrow (and narrowing) analytical and political focus on relations of sameness (globalization, corporatization, commoditization, neoliberalization and financialization) where dominance power can be claimed to be operating. Biological economies works on the idea that sameness has its epistemological (and thus political and moral) limits and dominance power has political limits. This leads to different questions, including: What happens outside

the world of seemingly unchanging yet changing sameness? What happens at the interface of sameness and difference as these properties emerge? And in what ways are they co-constitutive? Working with these questions, it makes good political sense to focus not only on the mainstream, but also on the alternative – on sites of experimentation, and on other assemblages and acts of assembling. In the biological economies world, these sites carry promise and may change the possibilities and potentials for future actions. They are not lesser sites, or acts of courage or foolishness waiting to be squashed by greater powers.

2   Attentiveness to the more-than-human radically de-centres the causality and explanation of how economic worlds are assembled and a reframing of new kinds of knowing, doing and being. The collected chapters emphasize the ways in which this epistemic shift enlivens the micro-politics of the worlds in which we work. Michael K. Goodman (Chapter 17), for example, performs the ontological shift that discards the category of 'food consumer' and replaces it with the multiple relationalities that constitute the ontological position of 'eaters'. By discarding these epistemic categories, he performs an ontological flattening but highlights instead the multiple politics within the multiple relationalities. An ontologically flattened world is not a politically neutral world – it is a world that is there for the making. This has important consequences for how we are politically and morally positioned and how we position ourselves to become politically and morally enactive. Melanie DuPuis's latest book – *Dangerous Digestion* – performs the similar remarkable feat of turning upside down the world of economic production and reframing it as a world of eaters: from human consumers right back to gut bacteria that convert our food via eating it themselves, through to macro-economies of 'meta biome' (DuPuis 2015). This re-conception is strikingly post-anthropogenic. While she gives much attention to the force of disruptive innovation in food, her re-reassembling of humans as mostly not human (particular our poundage of alimentary bacteria), or at least profoundly dependent on and affected by unseen biota, raises countless fresh starting points in the reframing of agri-food research, and efforts to design new kinds of social experiments and enact other futures from these.

3   The environment is becoming more unstable as an epistemic and ontological object. The insights of resilience theory in ecology have reinterpreted ecological causality through a consideration of the inherent instability (panarchy) of ecological systems, thus overturning the comfortable prior assumptions that previously assumed that environments were the stable (or acted/impacted upon) substrate of economic worlds. Resilience theory in this mode is arguably post-structuralist ecology. It emphasizes shock, surprise, discontinuity and multiple pathways to outcomes in direct contrast to the dominant ecological paradigms of systems, functions, stability and equilibrium: that is, 'bounce somewhere' rather than the 'bounce back' imagined by systems thinking. More recently, resilience theorizing in the social sciences

is confronting resilience in multiple ways, including the consideration of socio-ecologies, indigenous knowledges and adaptive management and recognition of shock and surprise. In this genre the emphasis is on the preparedness of differing framings or ontologies of resilience for the unpredictabilities of both the social and the ecological domains. In this sense, the epistemological turn towards the vitality of materials and non-human actors is very important, as is the need to complement, if not turn from, the 'big impacts' narratives of political ecology (not that these aren't important or threatening) towards the multiple, small, contingent spaces where eco-social assemblages create multiple potential reservoirs, buffers, potentials and resources.

4   The openness of thought and ontological stance that distinguish biological economies as a political project are only made possible by disrupting established categories of thought. The focus on experimentation outlined in Part 1 of this volume highlights the generative effects of unfamiliar connections, relations, agency and commitments, all of which are practised but heretofore unknown. They must be stitched together and imagined into existence and significance by an open category making that establishes 'principles of pertinence' (see Peck 2015) 'in train' rather than ex ante or ex post. This imagining cannot but help engage (intra-sect) with existing categories. Here, authors in Part 2 of the book offer some guidance to confronting the very difficult challenges to making and enacting knowledge posed by the co-constitutiveness of ontology, methodology, politics, morality and epistemology. Dealing with them, and thereby finding ways to identify principles of pertinence that offer temporary and contingent closures to the required openness of thought and practice and thus a politics that transcends the particular, is one of the frontiers ahead for agri-food research. A disposition towards experimentation as a way in which the co-constitutiveness of visibilizing, knowing, doing and enacting can be grasped, represented and enacted into new worlds promises to take us some way forward.

The politics of the Anthropocene

In Chapter 1 we said that the political intent of this book is to enable a politics and ethics of food that might guide and intervene in a world perched across a set of food precipices. These precipices are articulated, in their collective force, through the idea of the Anthropocene, and it is to this that we now turn to examine the explicitly political character of the biological economies project. In Chapter 1 we positioned the Anthropocene by arguing:

> In this volume, the authors do not make this association ritually or presume a stable, singular meaning for the Anthropocene. Rather, as reference to a new geological time-scale in which humankind is the most significant force in shaping earth and environmental processes and into which we have been propelled by resource-hungry global social processes, it is a defining context for agri-food futures. The Anthropocene is a discourse

that aligns multiple more than human crises looming at local and global scales, and ties them to myriad localised causes and effects.

In this we take the Anthropocene as the defining intervention that allows us to consider a coherent global macro-political project (following Crist 2013; Castree et al. 2014).

We approach the Anthropocene as a place-marker for an era characterized by social and environmental uncertainties. Unquestionably it topples assumptions we have made about living within an external environment. As a nascent category it is the nature of how it is working in different contexts that attracts our attention. Foremost, its arrival a decade ago, with the planetary boundaries idea, fractured the science–politics political settlement of the twentieth century, in which both political economy and political ecology were nursed and flourished. It has forced, in the words of Ursula Le Guin (2014), new kinds of noticing, describing and imagining. Our book's message has many similarities. Indeed, the book rests on noticing more, describing and explaining differently from novel experimentation in knowing anew, afresh and ahead, and taking heed of the challenge that to do something requires engaging differently.

Our preliminary conclusions about the insights from researching and conversing in the conceptual zone of PSPE, the more-than-human and the enactive encourage a receptivity to taking on new responsibilities in thought, and in commitments in place. This is an Anthropocene mentality, though it may be arrived at by other routes, and attract other political projects at different scales. A menu in the spirit of Le Guin and others may be enacted in the name of the Anthropocene, but it is the desire to frame new practices in places and sites that has to be the main reason for engaging. This we see as the means to opening agri-food research as a site where all the big issues can be legitimately and productively conversed about. Moreover, the critique of the Anthropocene is demolishing the cherished notion of anthropocentric supremacy embodied in the figure of the intentional, controlling individual. It demonstrates instead that we are bound up in other organisms, that it is impossible to exist as an individual, and that humans are enacted in their ignorance by other biota and the vitalities of human–non-human intra-actions as well as our own impoverished understandings and foolhardy actions.

We have an initial list of why knowledge making in agri-food is likely to be nurtured by lines of engagement with the burgeoning Anthropocene literature. First, it provides a macro-framework that is deliberately broad and unbounded. The idea of the Anthropocene is not to define what is inside and outside the boundary created by a categorical definition. It is to define a set of colliding forces of global-scale economy, society and ecology that compels us to think of global-scale crises. Second, it allows us to move into the same terrain as structural political economy (and engage with many of the same actors) without the historical baggage and elision that are introduced the moment we use macro-frameworks, for example of capitalism, state, region, neoliberalism, industrialization or globalization. Third, it is a dramatic embedding of both human and planetary concerns in the one nexus. The Anthropocene locates multiple crises that are implicitly indivisible into realms of human and non-human causality. Fourth, it opens up the opportunity to ask difficult, global-scale questions in compelling but non-deterministic ways, and in ways that require a moral politics. The Anthropocene directs attention to grand global challenges such as Wendy Larner's (2011) five 'C' crises (credit-crunch, climate change, China, crusades and cyborgism), as well as the pandemics and other disturbances that loom in emergent assemblages of livestock, industry, pathogens, antibiotics, and the localized vital materialities considered in this volume. And fifth, it adds a new significance to thinking about all these questions together, and thus builds a new platform for mobilizing and revitalizing the discourses of sustainability and resilience. That is, these questions presuppose the generation of new knowledge as well as a new politics and ethics; and these must be assembled with the vital and more-than-human materialities with which humans must now engage differently.

The urgencies, scalar complexities and more-than-human materialities of politics and moral economy cannot be stilled. The three themes of this book urge and inform a necessary politics of the Anthropocene that opens up and aligns new politics and moral dispositions with new knowledge made in different ways. An abstract category itself, the Anthropocene was brought into existence to simplify the nature of urgencies and uncertainties. It is too abstract to be a transition tool, but it does demand the political projects at multiple scales, projects such as biological economies, which might bring about a transformative knowing and doing.

Our final comment is about the book project itself as a political and moral project born in and of the Anthropocene. The book is made up of provocations that are proactive and experimental, moral and political, utopian and wild, risky and uncertain, and global in intent and practice, but highly situated in their constitutive inspirations. It is disruptive but constructive. In all these ways it is explicitly of and for our times. However, perhaps most constructively disruptive and urgently immediate of all, it is an intergenerational assemblage that was unthinkable and undoable without a new generation of scholars. The new-generation impetus and creativity and intergenerational conversations constitute a utopian and affective global project of scholarship, a project that is radically open to experiments in thought and action and embraces the vital materialities of both ideas and things. There is something promising and revitalizing in the doing of agri-food scholarship in this way, something to be grasped and encouraged to grow, and something that demonstrates how we should, indeed must, make knowledge in and for the Anthropocene. It is in co-producing knowledge across all manner of boundaries, including the generations, that we might make knowledge that is at once political, moral, affective, and attentive to the more-than-human and to shifting investment trajectories in many different ways and at multiple scales, and all at the same time.

References

Bennett, J. (2009) *Vibrant Matter: A Political Ecology of Things*, Duke University Press, Durham, NC.
Carolan, M. (2013) 'Putting the "alter" in alternative food futures', *New Zealand Sociology*, vol. 28, no. 4, pp. 145–150.
Castree, N., Adams, W., Barry, J., Brockington, D., Büscher, B., Corbera, E., Demeritt, D., Duffy, R., Felt, U., Neves, K., Newell, P., Pellizzoni, L., Rigby, K., Robbins, P., Robin, L., Rose, D., Ross, A., Schlosberg, D., Sörlin, S., West, P., Whitehead, M. and Wynne, B. (2014) 'Changing the intellectual climate', *Nature Climate Change*, vol. 4, pp. 763–768.
Crist, E. (2013) 'On the poverty of our nomenclature', *Environmental Humanities*, vol. 3, pp. 129–147.
DuPuis, M. (2015) *Dangerous Digestion: The Politics of American Dietary Advice*, University of California Press, Berkeley.
Esbjörn-Hargens, S. (2010) 'An ontology of climate change', *Journal of Integral Theory and Practice*, vol. 5, no. 1, pp. 143–174.
Gibson-Graham, J. K. (1996) *The End of Capitalism (As We Knew It): A Feminist Critique of Political Economy, with a New Introduction*, University of Minnesota Press, Minneapolis.
Gibson-Graham, J. K. (2006) *A Postcapitalist Politics*, University of Minnesota Press, Minneapolis.
Goodman, D. and Watts, M. (1997) *Globalising Food: Agrarian Questions and Global Restructuring*, Psychology Press, London.
Jackson, P., Ward, N. and Russell, P. (2009) 'Moral economies of food and geographies of responsibility', *Transactions of the Institute of British Geographers*, vol. 34, no. 1, pp. 12–24.
Larner, W. (2011) 'C-change? Geographies of crisis', *Dialogues in Human Geography*, vol. 1, no. 3, pp. 319–335.
Larner, W., Le Heron, R. and Lewis, N. (2007) 'Co-constituting "after neoliberalism": political projects and globalizing governmentalities in Aotearoa/New Zealand', in K. England and K. Ward (eds), *Neoliberalization: States, Networks, People*, Blackwell, Oxford, pp. 223–247.
Latour, B. (2005) *Reassembling the Social: An Introduction to Actor-Network-Theory*, Oxford University Press, Oxford.
Law, J. (2002) 'Objects and spaces', *Theory, Culture and Society*, vol. 19, nos 5–6, pp. 91–105.
Law, J. and Urry, J. (2004) 'Enacting the social', *Economy and Society*, vol. 33, no. 3, pp. 390–410.
Le Guin, U. (2014) Keynote address at Arts of Living on a Damaged Planet conference, Santa Cruz, CA, May.
Lewis, N. and Rosin, C. (2013) 'Emergent (re-)assemblings of biological economies', *New Zealand Geographer*, vol. 69, no. 3, pp. 249–256.
Lewis, N., Le Heron, R., Campbell, C., Henry, M., Le Heron, E., Pawson, E., Perkins, H., Roche, M. and Rosin, C. (2013) 'Assembling biological economies: region-shaping initiatives in making and retaining value', *New Zealand Geographer*, vol. 69, no. 3, pp. 180–196.
Lien, M. E. and Law, J. (2011) '"Emergent aliens": on salmon, nature and their enactment', *Ethnos*, vol. 76, no. 1, pp. 65–87.
Lowe, P. (2010) 'Enacting rural sociology: or what are the creativity claims?', *Sociologia Ruralis*, vol. 50, no. 4, pp. 311–330.
Mol, A. (1999) 'Ontological politics: a word and some questions', *Sociological Review*, vol. 47, no. S1, pp. 74–89.
Peck, J. (2015) 'Cities beyond compare?', *Regional Studies*, vol. 49, no. 1, pp. 160–182.

Index

accreditation schemes 154
Acres journal 173
Actor–Network Theory (ANT) 3, 10, 26, 34, 71
aesthetics, political aesthetics, aesthetics becoming 127–129, 138
agency 11, 24, 26, 51, 61, 70–71, 82–3, 87, 98, 112, 121, 123, 153, 183–184, 196, 212, 248–249, 260–261; actors 6, 11, 31, 51–54, 67–69, 70–71, 75–76, 82, 96, 109–110, 154; agentic intervention 13; agentic questions 10; relations of agency 11
alternative agriculture 174–176
animal breeding 147
animal disease 373–379, 44, 47
Anthropocene 2, 4, 124, 267
apples 127–138, 262
assemblage, assemblying 2–7, 26, 65–66, 82–83, 86, 92, 96, 106, 110, 191–193
Australasian Agri-food Research Network (AFRN) 4, 13, 264
autobiography 241, 250
auto-ethnographic methodology 197, 240

Bees; *Apis melifera* 109–112, 114–124, 259
Bennett, Jane 241, 248, 258
bio-economy 6, 19, 65
biological agriculture/farming 76, 170–171, 173, 176, 184, 186, 203
biopolitical intervention 109, 121
biosecurity 18, 37–39, 47–48, 49
biotechnology 52, 56, 65
borderlands 37–39, 45, 49, 226

Bovine Tuberculosis 44, 49
Buller, Henry 198–199, 202

Carolan, Michael 1, 7–8, 97, 212, 218, 225, 256, 263
Castree, Noel 261, 264
caterpillar fungus, *Ophiocordyceps sinensis* 51–64, 64–66, 257
China 53–55, 60, 62, 64–66
colonial meat trade 97, 101, 258
commodification 65, 156
competition 61, 68–69, 74–75, 103–104, 106, 108, 127–137, 151, 204
CONANX (consumer anxiety) project 9, 35, 201–202, 204
co-operativism (cooperatives) 69–70, 138, 175
consumer desires 97, 154
consumption 9–10, 13, 19, 23–36, 52–53, 59 65, 70, 83, 88, 140, 144, 156 166, 176, 200–204, 216, 241–247, 252, 257
contextual thinking 171, 174, 176, 263
Convention Theory (CT); multiple worths of farming systems 171, 179, 186, 211, 264
cultural artefact 83, 85, 90–92

Deleuze, Gilles and Guattari, Felix 3, 11, 17, 109, 125, 231, 238
democracy 125, 139, 254
design 5, 9, 62, 68, 117, 142, 147, 151–152, 156, 158–160, 165–166, 183, 212, 219, 242, 263, 266
dialogue 3, 35, 167, 195–196, 198, 201, 223, 227, 229, 238, 253, 264
disgust 158–161, 163, 166, 168

disruptive knowledge politics, disrupting reflection, disruptive knowledge 16, 196, 201, 204
DuPuis, Melanie 9, 266

eating 23, 26, 95, 98, 102–104, 129, 134, 157–167, 240–251, 252–255
eco-economy 6, 201–202
edibility: *see* taste
embodiment, embodying merino 180, 145, 151
enactive knowledge, enactive practices, enactive research 2, 3, 6, 10–11, 13–15, 23–4, 68–72, 77–79, 109–110, 122–124, 197–198, 202, 241, 250–251
economic stabilisation 266
encounter 109–123, 162, 179–180, 197, 201–209, 214, 228, 241, 246
entomophagy 159–164, 169
epidemiology 38–39, 43, 45–49
everyday practices 244
experimentation 63, 102–103, 157–158, 160–161, 165–167, 183, 197–198, 201, 212–213, 217–218, 260–262; emergent experiments 198; thought experiments 207
expertise 3, 6, 14, 41, 46–47, 174, 186, 198, 202, 220, 262

farm management 96, 100, 103, 183; farming practices 184, 203
fashion garments 152, 154
fashionable bodies 151–152
fibre production 152–154
finger knife (Indonesia) 260
food: localism 67, 77, 79; media 241, 250; politics 250–252; regimes 5, 10; safety 31, 52, 55, 60–66, 164, 167; scares 53, 56; security 78, 84, 159, 163–167, 172, 219–220, 263; utopias 157, 167; waste 13, 24, 27–28, 29, 34, 260; ways 160, 166, 212–224
freezers/fridges (refrigeration) 29, 97
Freidberg, Susanne 30, 97, 198–199, 204–205
freshness 24, 30–34

Gibson, Kathie 5–6, 9; *see also* Gibson-Graham, J-K
Gibson-Graham, J-K 4, 7, 10–12, 23, 68, 72, 77, 123–124, 158, 207, 257–258, 261, 265, 270

grade, grades, grading, graded 55, 98, 99, 102–105, 132–133; standards 37–38, 40, 55, 61, 71, 77, 130, 132–138, 145, 230, 259
Goodman, David 10, 12, 251, 265
Green Revolution 84, 87, 214
Guthman, Julie 198–199

High Yielding Varieties (HYVs) 84, 87
home economics 190–191
honey bee 109–112, 116, 122–124
human–non-human relationalities 13, 241; food–society relationalities 244, 246; *see also* more-than-human
hybridity 8

Indonesia 82–89, 92–93
industrial-chemical farming 170–172, 262
insects 157–165, 167–169, 182, 214, 262–263
intellectual projects 5–6, 256, 264
intermediation 150, 154
International Year of Soil 2015 170–171, 171, 202
investment-institutional trajectories 4, 8, 13, 171, 173, 176, 196, 200, 202, 204

Jackson, Peter 9, 34, 201
Java 84, 88, 91

knowledge: categories 10; making 1–16, 48, 52–53, 58, 61–62, 72, 75, 78, 97, 112, 117, 122, 146, 162, 170–172, 174–184, 196–209, 225–228, 231, 256–257, 261–262, 264, 267–268; platform 2, 9, 16; politics 179, 197, 261; production/co-production 2, 6, 7, 117, 122, 183, 197–202, 231, 262, 264; *see also* enactive knowledge

lamb 100–108
Langstroth hive 109–124
Larner, Wendy 269
Latour, Bruno 258
Law, John 258
Levitas, Ruth 213, 218–219
livelihoods 51, 62, 84, 154, 243
Liverman, Diana 198–9, 208
Lowe, Philip 13, 195, 225, 262

market assemblage 51–52; market making 11, 53; marketization 52, 61
markets 32–33, 52–53, 61, 69, 88, 98–99, 102, 104–105, 107, 127, 129, 143, 147, 157–158, 174, 205, 257–258
Marsden, Terry 6, 201
materialism 24, 241, 249, 252; material-semiotic 109, 113, 117–119, 121, 123; materiality/materialities 29, 91, 96, 109–110, 117, 124, 204, 260; materials 37–8, 105, 138, 146, 238
merino, merino brokers 100–101, 141–156
meta-modernism 137
metaphor 5–6, 10, 15–16, 122
methodology as ontology 24
methods 42, 45, 48, 53, 59, 69–72, 135, 144, 147, 214, 228–230
metrics 129; metrology 145, 154, 179, 201
modes of ordering 37–38, 40, 48
Mol, Annemarie 22, 247
moral economy 2, 9, 261, 263
more-than-consumption 244
more-than-human 24, 53, 96, 110, 121, 157–158, 159, 183, 196, 220, 236–238, 256–262, 266, 268–269; non-human actors/agency 14, 51–52, 70–17, 259, 267; post-human 33, 83, 92, 109–111, 118, 121–124
multilogics 194–195
multiplicity 15, 71, 82–83, 85

nature culture 197, 200; nature-culture knowledge 208, 210, 258; nature-society 196–197, 200, 209
neoliberalism 5, 11, 75, 234, 264
New Zealand 1, 5–7, 12–13, 39, 44, 47, 95, 99–105, 117–118, 141–156, 170–174, 196–205
New Zealand Merino Company 141–142, 144, 147–150
New Zealand South Island High Country 142, 150
New Zealand wool clip 141
nexus of place and chain 198, 201
normative projects 172, 198, 205
novel foods 157, 167

Olin Wright, Eric 219
ontology/ontologies 24, 72–80, 123, 184, 196–197, 208, 260; ontological 85, 110–111, 171–172, 178, 185, 266–267; ontological flattening 6, 266; ontological politics 110, 118, 121–122, 266; ontological politics of scholarship 191, 208; politics of ontology 184
other-than-economic values 141, 154

performative research 14, 241; performativity 24, 29, 199
political aesthetics 128; see also aesthetics, aesthetic becoming
political ecology 34, 107, 124, 167, 208, 210, 265, 270
political economy 6, 10–12, 129, 158, 176, 257–258, 260, 265, 268
political project/s 14–15, 257, 269
possibilities of situatedness 198
post-capitalist politics 6
post-structuralism 11–12
public sociology 226–227
post-structural political economy (PSPE) 1, 10, 23, 170, 185–186, 191, 197, 242, 256–257; post-structuralist 10
provenance 9, 62, 68, 74, 158–154, 201–202; provenance – place of origin 10; provenance – product attributes 148; provenancing 202–208

qualification trials 31
qualities 24, 30–34, 55–6, 59, 66, 88, 95, 98–99, 144, 148–152, 184–185, 213; quality 5, 12, 24, 31, 34

Red Delicious apple 127–128, 132–133, 136
regulation 39, 44, 77, 104
representational knowledge 197
resilience 266–267, 269
rice 82–94, 258
Ricoeur, Paul 214, 216
Robbins, Paul 198–200, 207–208

Science, Technology and Society (also Studies) (STS) 9, 109
sensory histories 106
situated experiments 206
situatedness 4, 13–14, 122, 198, 200, 260; possibilities of situatedness 198
social change 228, 230
soil: aggregate formation 173; biota 202–203; conceptions 170; invisibilities

72; metaphors and narratives 171; practice transitions 190–192; topsoil 173, 181; soil resourcefulness 183, 185
standardisation 98, 102
supermarket 27, 30, 68, 74, 76, 127–128, 130, 133, 160, 240, 246
superorganism 110–111, 116, 120,
supply chain 136, 158, 166, 174, 185, 204–205
Switzerland 67–69, 72, 258

taste 96–98, 101, 105–106, 161, 167; taste and grades 104–105; political taste 190; edibility 95–108, 129, 131, 158, 159–162, 164, 166, 167, 182, 228, 249, 258
TB testing 40–41, 44–46
territoriality 200
Tibetan Plateau 51–52, 57
theories of Practice 25–26, 33–34

Traditional Varieties (TV) 87
transformative potential 1, 71, 74, 77, 207

utopias 157, 167, 212–224, 263–264

valuation, value, valuing 1, 5, 13, 18, 31–33, 48, 52–54, 58, 60–64, 68, 76, 79, 101–102, 105, 127–130, 141–156, 178, 183, 196, 198, 201–208
veterinary profession 42
vital materiality, materialism 23–24, 110, 123, 203, 241, 249, 260, 282

Ward, Neil 198–199, 206, 208
Warde, Alan 25
Whatmore, Sarah 9–10, 12, 198–199, 206
wool: coarse 142; fine 142, 154–155, 259; strong 155